PRAISE FOR FAWAZ A. GERGES'S *OBAMA AND THE MIDDLE EAST*

"With characteristic and skillful gusto, Fawaz Gerges goes straight to the heart of the matter. Arguing that a supposedly transformational president has been anything but when it comes to US foreign policy in the Middle East, he lays out an ambitious strategy for navigating a region in tectonic flux. Essential reading for policymakers, pundits, and all students of the contemporary Middle East."

—*Peter Mandaville, author of* Global Political Islam *and director of the Ali Vural Ak Center for Islamic Studies, George Mason University*

"As Fawaz Gerges describes in lucid and deeply informed prose, Obama has lost a historic opportunity to redefine the American political culture—and he has in fact managed to drag it even deeper into a habitual politics of brute force and vulgar violence. Fawaz Gerges' timely and tempered book is too late for Obama but vastly informative and deeply encouraging for the rest of us still committed to a better and more responsible world."

—*Hamid Dabashi, Columbia University*

"Fawaz Gerges is one of the foremost scholars of Middle East politics. Here he delivers a cogent analysis of Barack Obama's foreign policy toward the Middle East. Gerges's verdict is harsh: Obama has neither prioritized the region nor taken the necessary risks required to alter a flawed foreign policy. This is simply the best analysis of the Obama administration's foreign policy toward the region."

—*Samer Shehata, Center for Contemporary Arab Studies, Georgetown University*

W9-BUI-247

OBAMA

AND THE

MIDDLE EAST

THE END OF AMERICA'S MOMENT?

FAWAZ A. GERGES

palgrave
macmillan

First published in hardcover in 2012 by PALGRAVE MACMILLAN® in the US—
a division of St. Martin's Press LLC, 175 Fifth Avenue, New York, NY 10010.

Where this book is distributed in the UK, Europe and the rest of the world, this is by
Palgrave Macmillan, a division of Macmillan Publishers Limited, registered in England,
company number 785998, of Houndmills, Basingstoke, Hampshire RG21 6XS.

Palgrave Macmillan is the global academic imprint of the above companies and has
companies and representatives throughout the world.

Palgrave® and Macmillan® are registered trademarks in the United States, the United
Kingdom, Europe and other countries.

ISBN: 978-1-137-27839-5

Library of Congress Cataloging-in-Publication Data

Gerges, Fawaz A., 1958–
    Obama and the Middle East / Fawaz Gerges.
      p. cm.
    Includes bibliographical references.
    ISBN 978-0-230-11381-7
    1. United States—Foreign relations—Middle East. 2. Middle East—Foreign relations—
United States. 3. Obama, Barack—Political and social views. 4. United States—Foreign
relations—2009– 5. United States—Foreign relations—2001–2009. I. Title.
DS63.2.U5G45   2011
327.73056—dc23
                                                                        2011019900

A catalogue record of the book is available from the British Library.

Design by Letra Libre Inc.

First PALGRAVE MACMILLAN paperback edition: July 2013

10 9 8 7 6 5 4 3 2 1

Printed in the United States of America.

CONTENTS

To my son and daughter, Bassam and Annie,
two fiercely independent minds

ACKNOWLEDGMENTS

I could not have written this book without the critical feedback and insights of many colleagues and friends. There is not enough space to list them all by name and to thank them for their valuable contributions. In particular, I am appreciative for the opportunity to brainstorm with several brilliant doctoral graduates from Oxford University and the London School of Economics. I want to thank Dr. Daniel Zoughbie, who read most of the chapters and provided constructive criticisms. His knowledge of the George W. Bush administration and the Middle East on which he focused his DPhil. at Oxford is unmatched by any young scholar that I know. My thanks go to Dr. Jessica Ashour (whom I also had the pleasure of examining for her DPhil at Oxford), who critiqued several chapters and helped strengthen my arguments. I am appreciative of Andrew Bowen, my research assistant at LSE, who was present at the early stages of researching the book and who contributed immensely to its completion. Andrew edited and synthesized several chapters and organized the footnotes. Dr. Jasmine Gani of LSE took precious time from writing her thesis to read and help improve the first chapter. Hadi Makarem, my research assistant at LSE, researched the chapter on Pivotal States.

Of the many senior scholars whose feedback helped improve the book, I owe special thanks to Professor Avi Shlaim of Oxford University, Professor William Quandt of the University of Virginia, Professor Mohammed Ayoob of Michigan State University, Professor Farid Senzai of Santa Clara University, and Professor Nader Hashemi of the University of Denver.

I want to thank the team at the LSE's Middle East Centre, particularly Dania Akkad and Robert Lowe, for facilitating my research. I am appreciative of my postgraduate students at LSE for challenging me to think harder about many of the ideas advanced in the book.

More importantly, the book belongs to my family, particularly Nora, my sounding board and harshest critic, and my young sweethearts, Laith and Hannah. I often forget that the years spent on researching and writing a book exact a heavy toll, especially in regards to precious time lost. The book is dedicated to my eldest son and daughter, Bassam and Annie, two fiercely independent minds. For example, Bassam is a long-time Obama supporter and a student of history and politics at King's, and he has pushed back at what he views as an underestimation of the bitter inheritance of the Bush years. I hope not. Far from overlooking that inheritance and context, I stress in *Obama and the Middle East* the role of systemic factors in the making of US foreign policy.

Fawaz A. Gerges
London
February 5, 2012

THE END OF AMERICA'S MOMENT?

The Middle East today is undergoing a revolutionary transformation along lines similar to those of the popular-nationalist revolutions of the 1950s that swept the Arab world, from Egypt to Iraq. The important difference between then and now is that the new social uprisings are bottom-up, as opposed to top-down, driven by politics, economics, and the desire for dignity: millions of ordinary Arabs are seeking freedom and a better quality of life. The *mukhabarat,* or state controlled by the secret police, is no longer omnipotent. The psychological fear factor separating public opinion from the ruling elites has been eroded. People across the Arab world feel empowered and even emboldened, whereas autocratic rulers are trembling in fear. They face an uncertain future. The Arab authoritarianism that stabilized and protected US interests for a half century is beginning to seem not so stable. Neither are American power and influence as stable and durable as they used to be. A powerful current of revolutionary social change is eroding the very foundations of America's friends and foes alike. Although the character of the new Middle East remains unknown, one thing is clear. It will never be the same again.

As the forty-fourth president of the United States, Barack Obama inherited a declining American economy, an overextended military, and a bitter legacy in the Middle East. Rising new powers, the so-called BRIC countries—Brazil, Russia, India, and China—have started to challenge America's global preeminence, leading some analysts to speak of a "post-American world."[1] For example, China holds more than a trillion dollars in US debt and is positioned to pounce upon economic territory previously dominated by the United States. Prior to the Iraq debacle, analysts like Fareed Zakaria argued that the post-September 11 world was marked by unipolarity: "American dominance is not simply military. The US economy is as large as the next three—Japan, Germany and Britain—put together."[2] Five years after the declaration of the war on terror, Zakaria reached a very different diagnosis: "We are moving into a post-American world, one defined and directed from many places and by many people."[3] The international system is undergoing a fundamental transformation. A new inceptive multipolar order is replacing the unipolar system of the post–Cold War era. America's dominance is coming to an end, while emerging geostrategic and geoeconomic players accumulate more power at its expense. This redistribution of global power is limiting America's ability to lead and maintain the balance of forces in its favor. Since his inauguration, Barack Obama has faced a turbulent world in which US global leadership is challenged by foes and allies alike, and America's commitments abroad have extended far beyond its vital interests. In this new world, the grand ideals of the Obama presidential campaign and the president's early days in office promised a new era of hope, of a sharp break with the bleak past. But the reality of Obama's Middle East policy carried more continuity than change.

For more than a half century, the United States has fought to preserve its preeminence in the Middle East and to prevent revolutionary challenges that could threaten its national interests. Early on, as a strategic and penetrated theater, the Middle East became embroiled in the US-Soviet Cold War, a rivalry that distorted and froze local politics. The effect of the East-West rivalry was to retard democratic development in the region in two distinct ways: through a strengthening of the executive authority of Middle East rulers at the expense of other branches of government and the citizenry and their rights, and by creating conditions adverse to democracy.[4]

By exploiting the Cold War, regional strongmen and autocrats—from Gamal Abdel Nasser of Egypt to the shah of Iran—maximized their bargaining power and consolidated their authority. For many of the Middle Eastern rulers, democracy was alien, a subversive Western idea that did not fit either the sensibilities or the social conditions of their people and societies; democracy threatened to weaken their absolute control and prevent them from making their countries in their own image.

Nasser was the first revolutionary, populist Arab leader to dismiss liberal democracy as a luxury that his people could not afford. He stressed that the West and its local agents would subvert and hijack democracy to undo the progressive reforms he had implemented after the 1952 Egyptian revolution.[5] His successors Anwar Sadat and Hosni Mubarak, though ideologically different from Nasser, argued likewise that Egyptians were not culturally equipped to determine their future. "You don't understand the Egyptian culture and what would happen if I step down now," Mubarak told Western audiences at the height of the Egyptian revolution in February 2011.[6] Throughout his thirty-year rule, Mubarak played on these Western fears that the promotion of democracy in the Arab world would empower extremists and terrorists. His right-hand man, Vice President Omar Suleiman, echoed the sentiment, stating that Egypt was not ready for democracy because democracy would unleash the forces of religious fundamentalism and bring the Muslim Brotherhood to power, implying that the Brotherhood is extremist of the Al Qaeda variety.[7]

Libyan leader Muammar Qaddafi, who prided himself on following in Nasser's footsteps, dismissed his people's quest for "democracy" and "freedom" as misguided. Libyans were ignorant and manipulated by the colonial West, wrote Qaddafi, because they did not realize that democracy "was a cut throat system, where the biggest dog eats the rest."[8]

When asked in a 2005 interview if the Saudi kingdom would ever become a democracy, King Abdullah retorted, "I believe it is now a democracy."[9] But, ironically, as the Arab region faced an unprecedented wave of democratic revolts, Saudi Arabia's senior cleric, Grand Mufti Sheikh Abdul-Aziz Al al-Sheikh, issued a statement that unequivocally forbade protests in the kingdom. "The correct way in sharia [Islamic law] of realising common interest is by advising, which is what the Prophet Mohammad established. Reform and advice should not be via demonstrations and ways that provoke strife and division, this is what the religious scholars of this country in the past and now have forbidden and warned against."[10]

The interests of the superpowers and local rulers coincided and reinforced the existing autocratic order. In congressional testimony, former US secretary of defense and CIA chief James Schlesinger asked "whether we seriously desire to prescribe democracy as the proper form of government for other societies. Perhaps this issue is most clearly posed in the Islamic world. Do we seriously want to change the institutions of Saudi Arabia? The brief answer is no: over the years we have sought to preserve those institutions, sometimes in preference to more democratic forces coursing throughout the region."[11] Thus, political authoritarianism became deeply entrenched, and it turned the Arab Middle East into an institutional wasteland. The *mukhabarat* and security apparatus almost devoured state and civil society.

After the Cold War ended, the democratic winds that swept across Eastern Europe and Latin America did not reach the Arab lands. America, the surviving superpower, did not rethink its assumptions about the Middle East, home to more than two-thirds of the world's oil reserves and to the Arab-Israeli conflict. US policymakers fully supported Middle Eastern dictators as guardians of stability and the status quo. There existed an implicit, unstated belief among Washington officials that Islam and Muslims were incompatible with democracy; that Arabs and Muslims if allowed to vote would make the wrong choices; that democratic forces, untried and unknown, would not be as pliant and accommodating to American interests in the region as were autocrats; and that the existing system was durable because authoritarian rulers had the will and the coercive means to suppress dissent. The role of agency and human will was absent from their calculations. The former American ambassador to the United Nations, Jeane Kirkpatrick, delivered a famous quip on Arabs and democracy: "The Arab world is the only part of the world where I've been shaken in my conviction that if you let the people decide, they will make fundamentally rational decisions."[12]

This convergence of views among regional rulers and US foreign policy officials on the need for an internal authoritarian political structure shielded the Arab Middle East from the winds of democratic change in the 1990s. There had been, in the late 1980s and early 1990s, a brief opening in the Arab world after the International Monetary Fund and the World Bank implemented structural adjustment policies; they led to social protests and elections. But these led, of course, to brutal crackdowns,[13] and once again, of all regions in the international system, the Middle East, excepting only Turkey, was the odd man out. Religiously based activists or Islamists presented the only credible challenge to the authoritarian order, and they were crushed by the state security apparatus and driven underground. The militant Islamist challenge reinforced the apprehensions of the US foreign policy establishment about the potential alternative to pro-Western authoritarian rulers. The latter used and abused the Islamist threat as a ploy, a scare tactic, in order to avoid being pressured by their superpower patron to open up their closed political systems. "Either us or the extremists," Middle Eastern dictators warned US officials. Viewing the region in bipolar terms—deadlocked between secular autocratic rulers and religious fundamentalists—American foreign policy risked nothing on the rising social forces demanding change. Policymakers found it convenient and profitable to support their local clients. Under both Democratic and Republican administrations, during and after the Cold War, this policy prevailed.

During the administration of George W. Bush things changed. Instead of using September 11 as a catalyst to endear America to the people of the region and to renew American leadership, Bush and the neoconservatives monstrously miscalculated: they tried their hand at imperialism, and they did so with the intention of transplanting America's version of democracy and free-market capitalism to the region.

After the cataclysm, the Bush administration based much of its Middle Eastern policy on the premise that the best way to protect American interests in the long run was through the active and coercive promotion of democracy. America's interests and values, Bush argued, were one and the same. Instead of providing space and room for indigenous forces to organize and develop alternatives to autocrats, he and his agents said they wanted to export Jeffersonian democracy to Iraq, which would be a staging ground for the democratic transformation of the region as a whole. But, in reality, they encouraged the development of a sectarian model along Iranian lines. In November 2003, addressing the US Chamber of Commerce in celebration of the twentieth anniversary of the National Endowment for Democracy, Bush frankly acknowledged America's responsibility for backing dictatorships in the Middle East: his aim, he stated, was to break with a half century of realpolitik:

> Sixty years of Western nations excusing and accommodating the lack of freedom in the Middle East did nothing to make us safe—because in the long run, stability cannot be purchased at the expense of liberty. As long as the Middle East remains a place where freedom does not flourish, it will remain a place of stagnation, resentment, and violence ready for export. And with the spread of weapons that can bring catastrophic harm to our country and to our friends, it would be reckless to accept the status quo.[14]

In their decision to invade and occupy Iraq, Bush, together with his neoconservative mentors, acted unilaterally, against the wishes of America's European allies, except for Britain's Tony Blair. They dismissed as wishful thinking France's warning about the existence of an international system with multiple centers of power. By undermining the sources of American power and grossly miscalculating the forms of Middle Eastern society, Bush, through his wars, consolidated the transition from unipolarity to multipolarity in international relations and awakened the ambitions of other regional and international powers. The Bush presidency unwittingly and unconsciously played a key role in facilitating the emergence of an inceptive multipolar world and, simultaneously, in making a laughingstock of the notion of imposing top-down democracy on Iraq.

Bush's new vision became known as the Freedom Agenda, but its principles were based on an old idea—that America could remake the Middle East in its image, and that it could do so through force.[15] Bush mistakenly linked the invasion of Iraq with the promotion of democracy in Arab and Muslim countries and allowed sheer incompetence to derail post-conflict planning. As importantly, his agenda conjured up bitter historical analogies to past "civilizing" missions carried out by European colonialists. Although initially unsettled and unnerved by Bush's call for democratic reforms, pro-Western Arab autocrats swiftly recovered their footing as the United States got bogged down in Iraq's killing fields. The Freedom Agenda was buried in the shifting sands of that war-torn country. More than one dictator breathed a sigh of relief that his life tenure was secure. And after the 2006 Palestinian elections in which Hamas gained a parliamentary majority, the Bush administration lost enthusiasm for promoting democracy in the region.

By the time Bush left the White House, relations between the United States and Muslim countries had reached the lowest point in the sixty years of engagement in the area. War, not diplomacy, was the mark of Bush's strategy for promoting democracy. There was first the invasion of Afghanistan and the overthrow of the Taliban; then more than 150,000 American troops battled in Iraq, the heart of Arabia, and struggled to subdue a fierce insurgency that killed nearly 5,000 and injured more than 30,000.

The toll among Iraqis was staggering, with reports of the number of civilians killed ranging from a low of 100,000 to a high of one million.[16] The prolonged and devastating war precipitated a profound humanitarian and social crisis. It displaced a few million Iraqis, who fled their homes and neighborhoods for fear of communal slaughter. Additional millions escaped to neighboring states and, as refugees, experienced degradation, humiliation, and misery. Besides dealing death and destruction, the US-led invasion ruined the country's economy and destroyed the only institutions through which it could be governed.

Beyond exacting this human toll, the US action militarized an important segment of the Arab and Muslim public and turned opinion against the imperial Western power. Calls for armed resistance resounded through Muslim lands. For a brief moment, Osama bin Laden's message of transnational jihad was heard by enraged young men who accepted the claim that the West was waging a crusade against their religion and identity. Anti-American sentiments spread like wildfire across most political factions, including among ordinary Muslims. If it were not for the difficulty of travel and the pressure exerted on Arab regimes by the United States to insulate their borders, tens of thousands of young Muslims would have journeyed to Iraq to fight the new "crusaders"; volunteers would have exceeded those of the Afghan jihad against the Soviet invasion of Afghanistan two decades earlier. Nonetheless, despite the difficulty, many made the perilous journey to Iraq to fight the Americans and perished there.

By the end of the Bush presidency, the attitudes of many Muslims toward American foreign policy had hardened into open hostility. A 2007 poll showed that an average of 79 percent of respondents in Egypt, Morocco, Pakistan, and Indonesia agreed that the United States had sought to "weaken and divide the Islamic world"; a similar percentage believed that America wanted "control over the oil resources of the Middle East." An average of 64 percent contended that Washington wanted to spread Christianity in Muslim lands. Three-fourths of the respondents in the four countries supported the goal of getting American troops and bases out of the region.[17]

In addition to the cost to America in blood, treasure, and moral standing, Bush's wars disrupted the fragile balance of power in the greater Middle East, which was based on rivalries among authoritarian regimes like Iran and Iraq, and shattered the confidence and trust that pivotal regional actors, particularly Turkey, Pakistan, and Egypt, had in the United States. Since then, America's regional allies and foes alike have pursued independent, assertive policies that challenge key aspects of US strategy in the area. Ironically, the wars aimed at resurrecting American hegemony initiated the decline of the nation's influence in the Middle East and beyond and fed the increased assertiveness of regional powers, notably Turkey and Iran. Outgoing Secretary of Defense Robert Gates had the 9/11 wars in mind when he bluntly warned that: "Any future defense secretary who advises the president to again send a big American land army into Asia or into the Middle East or Africa should 'have his head examined,' as General MacArthur so delicately put it."[18]

When Barack Obama assumed the office of president, he promised to bring change at home and abroad. But he inherited a bitter legacy in the Middle East, one that implicated America in dealings with dirty dictators who oppressed and tortured citizens; one that associated America with words like "torture" and "crusade"; and one that would prove incredibly dangerous for a politically divided America facing precipitous economic decline. Obama distanced himself from his predecessor's faith-based agenda and stressed that he would not preach to other nations or impose American values. In his address in Cairo in June 2009, Obama spoke of a "new beginning" for the United States and the Middle East: "I know there has been controversy about the promotion of democracy in recent years, and much of this controversy is connected to the war in Iraq. So let me be clear: No system of government can or should be imposed upon one nation by any other."[19] That was consistent with Obama's position as a presidential candidate contending against his chief opponent, Hillary Clinton. He slyly argued that the Bush years were in some ways a continuation of the Bill Clinton years, and that the United States needed to return to the philosophy of an earlier era, a philosophy driven by a realistic assessment of the sobering facts on the ground and US interests in the region. The proselytizing for democracy and the haste to bomb other countries in the name of humanitarian aid, Obama said in a speech in 2006, had "stretched our military to the breaking point and distracted us from the growing threats of a dangerous world."[20]

Obama emphasized that, in his administration, foreign policy in the Middle East and elsewhere would be driven by the national interest and would focus on attaining stability as opposed to the Bush administration's ideology of proselytizing for democracy and the liberal deployment of force in international affairs. Instead, Obama stressed in an address to the Turkish parliament in April 2009, "we seek broader engagement based on mutual interest and mutual respect. We will listen carefully, we will bridge misunderstandings, and we will seek common ground. We will be respectful, even when we do not agree."[21]

In this, Obama came closer to the dominant realist approach of American foreign policy toward the region, an approach that aimed at retaining the status quo through backing pro-Western Arab rulers and eschewing moral imperatives, such as the promotion of the rule of law and human rights. Prior to his 2009 trip to Cairo, he was asked whether he considered Mubarak an authoritarian leader. He responded directly, "No, I tend not to use labels for folks. I haven't met him. I've spoken to him on the phone. He has been a stalwart ally in many respects, to the United States. He has sustained peace with Israel, which is a very difficult thing to do in that region."[22] Indeed, long before he won the presidency, Obama identified himself with traditional foreign policy realists, like President George Herbert Walker Bush.

As a new president, Obama faced economic collapse at home, wars in Iraq and Afghanistan, serious regional threats from Pakistan and Iran, global terrorism, and the ascendance of China and India—all together offering a "vivid" sense of American decline.[23] Obama conceded that the United States was lagging behind in competition with rising global competitors. He warned that powers like India, China, Brazil, and South Korea posed fierce economic competition to the United States by focusing on educated workers, research and technology, and quality infrastructure; the country was not keeping up. The end of the Cold War had marked the beginning of a period in which America went unchallenged worldwide. This era, however, was coming to a close, and the nation had to accept that it was in the midst of a global struggle with rising eastern powers. Indeed, by 2011 a majority of Americans felt that their country had lost its edge to rising powers in the East. A Time Magazine/Abt SRBI poll conducted in October 2011 found that 71 percent of Americans believed that the nation's position in the world had been on the decline in the past few years. And an NBC News/Wall Street Journal survey conducted in November 2011 found that most Americans believed that they were not simply going through tough times as a nation but were at "the start of a longer-term decline where the U.S. is no longer the leading country in the world."[24]

Obama, along with his newly assembled realist advisers, believed he could steer the ship of state safely to the old harbor, repair the damage done by the previous captain, and begin to carry US troops away from Middle East quagmires. Though the war in Afghanistan had been underfunded, mismanaged, and undersupplied by the Bush administration, Obama knew a complete loss would have catastrophic political effects. While many Middle East regimes were clearly in trouble, and while Iran was pursuing a nuclear development program, Obama's primary foreign policy priorities lay elsewhere—chiefly in the South Asian arena, where Pakistan, a heavily armed nuclear power, was fighting a proxy war with India in Afghanistan at the expense of American interests. Obama had told senior members of the administration that Osama bin Laden was to be tracked down; and they were following leads that directed them inside of Pakistan, where the Taliban was being sheltered from US forces.

Foreign policy priorities clearly were being slowly directed away from the Middle East. Obama's outreach to Muslims—coupled with a short military surge in Afghanistan dictated by domestic political and military pressure—was in large part designed to rebuild America's damaged reputation there, reestablish its standing in the world, and degrade and defeat the Taliban and Al Qaeda, respectively. The eventual withdrawal of US forces from Afghanistan and Iraq would allow the administration to turn its attention to far more pressing economic problems at home and to other international matters, such as China's unchecked influence in the Asia-Pacific region.[25] As Benjamin Rhodes, one of the president's national security aides said, "The project of the first two years has been to effectively deal with the legacy issues that we inherited, particularly the Iraq war, the Afghan war, and the war against Al Qaeda, while rebalancing our resources and our posture in the world." He went further: "If you were to boil it all down to a bumper sticker, it's 'Wind down these two wars, reestablish American standing and leadership in the world, and focus on a broader set of priorities, from Asia and the global economy to a nuclear-nonproliferation regime.'"[26]

Another aide, Kurt Campbell, the assistant secretary of state for East Asian and Pacific affairs, put it a bit more bluntly: "We've been on a little bit of a Middle East detour over the course of the last ten years. And our future will be dominated utterly and fundamentally by developments in Asia and the Pacific region."[27]

From the outset of his administration, Obama has asked Americans to look at the Pacific Ocean beyond concerns about Chinese dominance or US job losses and see a diverse region that can be a growing market for American goods and services, yield stronger foreign policy alliances, and help respond to global challenges, such as climate change. Obama calls himself "America's first Pacific president" and presses Americans to think more about Asia—and, in some ways, to think more like Asians do. For example, he highlighted his administration's turn toward the Pacific by hosting the Asia-Pacific Economic Cooperation Summit in Hawaii in November 2011 and visited Indonesia as the first president to participate in the East Asia Summit. In speeches in the United States, China, Japan, South Korea, India, Singapore, and Indonesia, Obama has said his Asia focus is driven by today's economic and demographic trends. Indeed, the global redistribution of economic power is shifting toward the Pacific Ocean region. For example, in the next decade, three of the world's five largest economies will be China, Japan, and India. Political rivalries and struggles might also shift to Asia as these rising states seek to spread their influence and power. Thus, if the United States is to remain the central global power, it will need to be a Pacific power. Accordingly, the Obama administration has launched a series of political, economic, and military efforts that signalled its new engagement in the region and its desire to limit Chinese influence and claims on the South China Sea. In a speech to the Australian parliament, Obama stated that "The United States is a Pacific power, and we are here to stay." His goal is to to reverse the country's decline and allow America to compete effectively against the new rising geostrategic and geoeconomic powers.[28]

Thus, contrary to the public perceptions, Obama's lofty rhetoric about a new start in relations between the United States and Muslim countries did not signify that the region ranked high on his foreign policy agenda. When Israeli-Palestinian peace talks proved much costlier than Obama and his advisers had foreseen, the president first allowed his vice president to be humiliated by the Israeli prime minister and then awkwardly disengaged from the peace process, thereby undermining his own credibility and doing consequent damage to America's prestige and influence. So while Obama has invested some political effort on Mideast diplomacy, he has shown himself unwilling to do more to achieve a breakthrough. That decision speaks volumes about the administration's foreign policy priorities. as well as the decline of American power and influence in the region.

More than anything, the Arab revolts that broke out in Tunisia, Egypt, and elsewhere along the Mediterranean littoral in early 2011 have clearly revealed the inability of the Obama administration to shape the future of the region. Obama and the American foreign policy establishment were caught off guard. Suddenly, the map of the region's coordinates and signposts became as irrelevant as the dusty old maps of the Soviet Union in the US National Archives. Long-serving dictators such as Mubarak of Egypt and Zine El Abidine Ben Ali of Tunisia, guardians of stability and the status quo, fell like ripe fruit. Qaddafi of Libya is history. Others, such as Ali Abdullah Saleh of Yemen and Bashar al-Assad of Syria, are struggling to survive. King Hamad bin Isa al-Khalifa of Bahrain has survived, but only by the use of significant force. In the short and long run, the odds are against Middle East autocrats: they promised heaven to their citizens and delivered dust, misery, and oppression. The rallying cry of protesters—dignity, freedom, and jobs—will not soon be subdued.

Clearly, however, the challenges facing Obama and America in the Middle East are much more complex and run deeper than the changes arising from the Arab popular uprisings of 2011. The wars in Afghanistan and Iraq—along with the worldwide hunt for Al Qaeda, and special operations and drone attacks in Pakistan—have diminished America's power and influence in the Middle East and the international system. So far, the cost of waging a global war on terror has been exorbitant; it soon will top five trillion US dollars in direct and indirect costs and exceed the adjusted cost of World War II. Even with Bin Laden out of the picture, there is no clear end in sight, despite Obama's declared intention in June 2011 to begin withdrawing American troops from Afghanistan.[29] Though the president's highest priority seems to accord with the popular will of the American people, any attempt to draw down forces too rapidly from Afghanistan will be met with great opposition from the military establishment and from seasoned policymakers like former Secretary of Defense Robert Gates, who disclosed to Hamid Karzai, "We're not ever leaving [Afghanistan]." Although Gates is now retired, and had warned against future wars, he speaks for a powerful constituency within the national security establishment that opposes terminating the Afghan mission. Obama had already been accelerating the end of the NATO war in Afghanistan, without terminating the military mission.[30]

The relative decline in US influence in the Middle East must be contextualized. As mentioned previously, there has been a global redistribution of power away from a unipolar world dominated by the United States to an evolving multipolar world with multiple geoeconomic and geopolitical powers. The United States is no longer the supreme power that it was at the end of the Cold War. There now exist many geoeconomic and geopolitical powers such as China, India, and Brazil, that compete with one another for space and resources and actively encroach on America's traditional spheres of influence. In the Middle East, Turkey and Iran have already positioned themselves as pivotal players; they have their own foreign policy agendas and interests that compete and clash with those of the United States. Amid the revolutionary turmoil sweeping the region, these two, and potentially Egypt as well, are likely to fill the void left by the United States.

For the first time in more than a half century, the center of gravity has shifted back to the Middle East and away from the great powers. As popular democratic uprisings play themselves out on Arab streets, the shift in the international relations of the region will become more pronounced and consolidated. Constrained by public opinion and identity politics—key factors in the new Middle East—local governments will be expected by their citizens to act independently and challenge attempts by the great powers to impose their will and agendas. The United States cannot expect its clients in the region to be as pliant as before. The new paradigm in the region will prove as important as the shift from the Cold War to the post-Cold War era.

Today America's position in the region resembles that of Great Britain at the end of World War II, before its sharp decline in the 1950s. We are witnessing the beginning of the end of America's moment in the Middle East. Illegal and unjust wars have not only been costly in lives and money but have also undermined the moral foundation of American power and authority. Although China, Russia, and some European powers may be waiting to grab America's spoils in the Middle East, as the United States did with Great Britain in the mid-1950s, awakened regional powers will actively attempt to fill any vacuum of power and authority in their neighborhood. The United States faces a dramatically altered regional environment in which local actors feel empowered. For the most part, people in the region will determine the political arrangements under which they live. The US will not exercise much influence over the transition process and will have to accept the consequences. In other words, in a multipolar world America neither calls the shots as before nor dominates the regional scene in the way it did after the Cold War ended. America's ability to act unilaterally and hegemonically, unconstrained by the local context, has come to an end.

The coming to power of the Islamists is a case in point. As the Arab awakenings unfolded, the United States, along with other Western powers, feared that

Islamists would hijack the revolutions like their Iranian counterparts did in the 1980s. In particular, US officials viewed the Muslim Brotherhood, the most powerful religiously based organization, as a bitter foe and especially as a threat to Israel, which signed the Camp David peace treaty with Egypt in 1979, ending the state of war between the two neighbours. Since the September 11, 2001, attacks, fear of Islamism in general, not just of Al Qaeda, has taken hold of the Western imagination.

The US and its European allies accepted this binary model of the Middle East, in which religious fundamentalists were seen as the only alternative to pro-Western dictators and shunned engagement with Islamists. There existed an implicit assumption among Western officials that there was no third way, no public opinion, only an "Arab street"—code for the notion that Muslims, if allowed to vote, would make the wrong choices, that democratic forces, untried and unknown, would not be as pliant and accommodating to US interests in the region as the autocrats.

Secretary of State Hillary Clinton acknowledged as much in a 7 November 2011 speech about Washington's response to the Arab uprisings that toppled several US clients. "For years, dictators told their people they had to accept the autocrats they knew to avoid the extremists they feared," she told an audience at a National Democratic Institute event that included the former secretary of state Madeleine Albright. "Too often, we accepted that narrative ourselves."

As Islamists won a majority of seats in the new parliaments in Tunisia, Morocco, and Egypt (and most likely in Libya soon), the Obama administration reversed two decades of mistrust and hostility toward mainstream Islamists and acknowledged the new political reality in the region. It had little choice. In a marked historic shift of US foreign policy, Clinton said that the US would work with the ascendant Islamist parties in Tunisia and Egypt if they played by the rules of the political game. The administration's overtures included high-level meetings between Senator John Kerry, chairman of the influential Foreign Relations Committee, US Ambassador to Egypt Anne W. Patterson, and top leaders of the Brotherhood's political party—Freedom and Justice. "The United States needs to deal with the new reality," Mr. Kerry said. "And it needs to step up its game."[31]

It would be "totally impractical" not to engage with the Brotherhood "because of U.S. security and regional interests in Egypt," a senior administration official involved in shaping the new policy told the *New York Times,* speaking on the condition of anonymity to discuss diplomatic affairs. "There doesn't seem to me to be any other way to do it, except to engage with the party that won the election," the official said, adding, "They've been very specific about conveying a moderate message—on regional security and domestic issues, and economic issues, as well."[32]

The lack of resources is one of several factors that inhibits America's role and limits its ability to shape developments in the Middle East. Another is Obama's "rebalancing" of US foreign policy priorities toward the Pacific Ocean arena and keeping a distance from the region's cataclysms. Obama has not accompanied his rhetorical embrace of the Arab popular uprisings with a set of concrete initiatives that assist transitioning Arab societies in developing their broken economies. As noted, he is preoccupied by the economic crisis at home and US relative decline via China, India, and other rising geostrategic and geopolitical powers. Finally, an awakened public opinion in the Middle East imposes significant constraints on the ability of great powers to dictate terms to local governments. The following chapters will show that America's allies and foes, including Iraq, Egypt, Saudi Arabia, Turkey, Israel, and Iran, now defy the United States and pursue assertive policies that mostly cater to public opinion and constituencies at home. The United States is no longer seen as omnipotent and invincible.

In the wake of the Arab awakenings, a former US official lamented the loss of influence:

> Our policies, opposed from one end of this region to the other, are unlikely to change. Our capacity to succeed at war and peacemaking—the real measure of respect and admiration (Libya notwithstanding)—has diminished along with our street cred. We can't solve the Palestinian issue, can't stop Iran from getting the bomb, can't find a way to achieve victories in Iraq and Afghanistan, and we are still caught up in the devil's bargain with Saudi Arabia and Bahrain.[33]

A qualification is in order. The end of America's moment in the Middle East does not mean that the United States will disengage from the region and cease to exercise influence there. The United States is fully engaged in the oil-producing Gulf arena, a strategic theater necessary for the well-being of the world economy, and has built the largest concentration of military bases there outside the homeland. But the United

States is frequently challenged and forced to retreat in the face of stiff opposition from the Israelis, Iranians, and Saudis. Like other declining hegemons in the past, the United States will have to come to terms with the limits of its power. The writing is already on the wall. As one former US official noted, "the conundrum for America today: stuck in a region (with fewer friends) we can't fix or walk away from."[34]

It is worth providing context to the Obama approach to the Middle East. The Cold War legacy has defined the US foreign policy debate and style.

From its birth in 1947 to the end of the Cold War in 1989, the Truman Doctrine profoundly shaped the way US policymakers looked at the Middle East. The doctrine initially committed the United States to containing Soviet influence in Europe and maintaining stability worldwide; as a globalist prism, however, this single, all-encompassing East-West rivalry subsumed internal challenges in developing states, including those of the Middle East. Every issue and crisis, whatever the country, was rated on the basis of its relevance and importance to the struggle against Communism. In this way the Middle East became important for all the wrong reasons.[35]

In what was largely a one-sided debate, American regionalists—most of them being ambassadors in the field and professional Middle East specialists in the State Department—contrariwise, insisted that local concerns had their own substance and had to be dealt with in their own terms. The regionalist argument, a minority view within official US foreign policymaking, does not subordinate indigenous aspirations and national grievances to "power vacuums" and external causes. Historically, in the 1960s, the Kennedy administration adopted something of a regionalist approach to the Middle East and tried to use soft power to induce Third World leaders to respect US security interests. Yet despite the presence of regionalists in the State Department, he could not escape the shadow of the Cold War in his dealings with the Egyptians and Israel. Nor could President Jimmy Carter in the late 1970s, who, at least at the beginning of his tenure, partially subscribed to the regionalist perspective.[36]

Nevertheless, with these exceptions, most American post-World War II presidents viewed the region and its people in a merely instrumentalist light, an extension of the global rivalry with the Soviet Union, as well as a strategic reserve of inexpensive oil to power the world economy. Although diplomats in the field urged their superiors in Washington to listen closely to the aspirations of indigenous people, particularly their quest for independence, development, and dignity, and to turn away from the falsifications of the global view, their warnings were mostly ignored. From the late 1940s until the late 1980s, the globalists or the Cold Warriors held a near monopoly on the American foreign policy toward the Middle East.

The end of the Cold War did not bring about a congruent long-term shift in that policy. The United States did not rethink its assumptions about the conduct of international relations; neither did it attempt to revise and change the conceptual guidelines that had informed policy. While the United States did fully embrace the transition to pluralism in Eastern Europe and did not oppose the replacement of Latin America's military dictators with elected democrats, it preserved its ties to Middle Eastern autocrats and refrained from taking risks, such as showing support for democratic voices there. In the eyes of policymakers, the region's importance lay in preserving Western access to two-thirds of the world's known petroleum reserves, the longstanding commitment to the security and well-being of Israel, and the stability of America's traditional Arab allies, particularly Saudi Arabia, the Gulf sheikdoms, and Egypt. Business as usual was Washington's game in the Middle East. The only change was that the collapse of the Soviet Union had removed the last constraint on the United States' hold on the global balance of power; it could act unilaterally and aggressively to preserve the unipolar international system. American foreign policy sought to demarcate limits to any internal and external challenge to the status quo and its dominance. As the hegemon, the United States found itself pitted against powerful indigenous forces and non-state actors who aimed to overthrow the existing order and to bring about revolutionary change.[37]

The second and very much related doctrinal Cold War debate among policymakers concerned the Arab-Israeli conflict—the contenders being the Israel-first school versus those who advocated an evenhanded diplomatist approach. After the June 1967 Arab-Israeli war, the Israel-first school dominated American foreign policy. Israel's swift victory over Soviet-supplied Arab armies helped transform the US-Israeli relationship, hitherto an unequal association, into a strategic partnership. The special relationship between America and Israel rests on the assumptions of cultural affinity, common values, and shared strategic interests. After the Six-Day War, however, the Cold Warriors focused on Israel's utility as a deterrent force against Soviet regional allies, and as an affordable luxury that the United States could deploy against its regional foes.[38]

Henry Kissinger, who served as national security adviser to President Richard Nixon and then as secretary of state to Nixon and Gerald Ford, laid out the foundation of this viewpoint in his memoirs. He drew on the Jordanian civil war of 1970 ("Black September")—in which armed Palestinian fighters unsuccessfully challenged the Jordanian monarchy's power—as a case of proxy confrontation between the superpowers, with Israel playing a vital role in frustrating a Soviet-inspired plot to unseat King Hussein, a pro-American ally. At the heart of Kissinger's false globalist reasoning was the notion that all parties in the Middle East were clients of one or the other of the two superpowers, regardless of the innermost wishes of their leaders or the inherent virtues of their positions. Seen in this globalist light, every local crisis was a test of strength between the superpowers, including the June 1967 war, the 1969–1970 War of Attrition between Egypt and Israel, the September 1970 Jordanian crisis, and the October 1973 Arab-Israeli war. In this all-encompassing East-West struggle, Kissinger portrayed Israel as America's regional policeman against the Soviet Union and its clients; therefore, the United States should empower the Jewish state and weaken its enemies because, in his opinion, the partnership was key to combating Soviet influence and maintaining regional stability.[39]

According to Kissinger, the idea of an evenhanded approach in the Arab-Israeli conflict was preposterous and misguided because the overriding goal of American strategy must be to defend its own clients and wean away those of the Soviets. Kissinger complained frequently and scornfully of the naïve optimism of those State Department officials who, in his opinion, deluded themselves into believing that conditions in the Middle East after 1967 were damaging to America and that the United States should actively mediate between Egypt and Israel and press the latter to withdraw from occupied Arab territories. In contrast, Kissinger, the Cold Warrior, said he favored doing as little as possible and shoring up America's own clients, particularly Israel, and leaving Nasser and his allies to stew in their own juice. In fact, Kissinger boasts that he undercut a major diplomatic initiative called the Rogers Plan, outlined by Secretary of State William P. Rogers in 1969, to nudge the warring factions to accept a peace settlement:

> My aim was to produce a stalemate until Moscow urged compromise or until, even better, some moderate Arab regime decided that the route to progress was through Washington.[40]

Although Nixon authorized the State Department to pursue peace initiatives to resolve the Arab-Israeli conflict, he sided with Kissinger when he opposed efforts by US officials to break the deadlock between Israel and its Arab neighbors. The net result was a policy of confusion, which played directly into Kissinger's hand. "By the end of 1971, the divisions within our government, the State Department's single-minded pursuit of unattainable goals—and the Soviet Union's lack of imagination—had produced the stalemate for which I had striven by design." And a few months later: "My strategy had not changed. Until some Arab state showed a willingness to separate from the Soviets, or the Soviets were prepared to disassociate from the maximum Arab program, we had no reason to modify our policy."[41] In fact, the Soviet Union never associated itself with the maximalist program of its radical Arab allies on Israel and accepted UN Resolution 242.[42]

Kissinger's globalist reasoning shaped American Mideast policy for years after that, for preserving the territorial status quo was more important than reaching an Arab-Israeli peace settlement. There existed a correlation between globalists and the Israel-first school, which viewed Israel's superiority over all its Arab neighbors as the key to stability and eventual peace on Israel's terms. The idea that Israel should only make peace from a position of strength and superiority has gained wide currency in US policy circles, especially among globalists and Cold Warriors like Kissinger and Israel's domestic friends; it has become accepted wisdom in much of Washington that pressuring the Jewish state to withdraw from occupied territories or to stop settlement construction on Palestinian lands will not serve the cause of peace and will most likely embolden Israel's and America's enemies.

The Israel-first school did not win simply on the merits of its arguments. Domestic politics played a significant role in advancing its cause. Ironically, Israel's supporters in the United States, many of whom do not ideologically belong to the globalist camp, actively promoted the narrative that Israel is a Western fortress in the heart of Arabia, a force for stability in a dangerous neighborhood, while also stressing the cultural ties and common values between America and the new pioneering state.[43] The arguments in favor of the Israel-first school have even survived the end of the Cold War and the disappearance of the Red menace. With the Soviet Union no longer a factor in global politics, Israel's role now is to combat Islamist extremism and protect the existing pro-US regional order against radical, revisionist powers like Iran, Syria, Hezbollah, and Hamas. In a 1992 article in the Israeli newspaper *Yediot*

Ahronot, retired Israeli general Shlomo Gazit, former head of military intelligence and West Bank administrator, forthrightly spelled out Israel's contribution to US foreign policy in the Middle East. "[After the Cold War] Israel's main task has not changed at all, and it remains of crucial importance," Gazit wrote. "Its location at the center of the Arab Muslim Middle East predestines Israel to be a devoted guardian of the existing regimes: to prevent or halt the processes of radicalization and to block the expansion of fundamentalist religious zealotry."[44] Almost two decades later, in September 2011, Israeli prime minister Netanyahu made the rounds of America's Sunday morning television talk shows and stressed the new common threat of Islamism facing Israel and the United States. When asked about threats facing Israel after the Palestinian bid for statehood in the United Nations, Netanyahu said he is responsible for the "fate of the one and only Jewish state," and he seeks to "erect the wall against insatiable crocodile of Islamism, before it devours us for breakfast."[45]

In the post–Cold War system, Israel's function has not changed much—only the character of foes and nemeses. For example, after 9/11, Israeli leaders and their American supporters portrayed Israel's war with the Palestinians as an extension of the US global war on terror. The late Palestinian leader Yasser Arafat and the Islamist organization Hamas, though ideological and political rivals, were seen as versions of Bin Laden and Al Qaeda, respectively. George W. Bush and his neoconservative advisers, a contemporary incarnation of the Cold Warriors, believed the Israeli assertion that terrorism, not its occupation of Palestinian lands, was the primary cause of conflict in the area. Although the more evenhanded members of the State Department cautioned Bush against viewing the Israeli-Palestinian conflict in this way and called for restarting the stalled peace talks, the influential neoconservatives defeated attempts by their realist counterparts to achieve a diplomatic breakthrough that would force Israel to accept a peace agreement. In a manner reminiscent of Kissinger, the neoconservatives produced a stalemate that suited their purposes, which were to force the Palestinians to either accept peace on Israel's terms or be excluded from the peace process altogether.

In contrast to the globalists and the Israel-first school, regionalists called for an evenhanded approach to the Palestinian issue and a concerted effort to resolve it. The regionalists, far from belittling the threat of the Soviet Union or the balance of power during the Cold War, argued that global priorities do not necessarily preclude attentiveness to the substance of local issues.[46] The regionalist school was represented by George Ball, former undersecretary of state and ambassador to the United Nations during the Kennedy and Johnson administrations. Ball counseled cooperation with the Soviets to resolve festering regional conflicts in sensitive parts of the world, such as the Arab-Israeli conflict, instead of waging proxy wars, as Kissinger had advocated. Evenhanded regionalists like Ball, who was no apologist for Soviet policies and by no means a parochial regional specialist, contested Kissinger's globalist reasoning regarding the superpowers' ability to "ice" local conflicts and questioned the degree of influence that they exercised over their clients: Because issues were left unresolved, time and again in the 1960s, 1970s, and 1980s the outbreak of Arab-Israeli hostilities threatened to draw the superpowers into an escalating confrontation as each sought to protect its clients. As Ball noted:

> The most serious danger faced by the two nations is that they may be propelled into a confrontation neither desired by their involvement in the affairs of third countries. So, rather than drawing up rules to govern our affairs with one another, we should use the leverage of détente to persuade the Soviet leaders to work with us is in resolving local conflicts where we are not supporting opposite sides. . . . [47]

During the Cold War and after, the case of the regionalists has rested on five well-delineated arguments: (1) peace is possible only by joint action with the Soviets and the international community at large; (2) diplomacy of small remedial steps practiced by the United States during the Kissinger era cannot lead to any decisive results; (3) Israel's continued insistence on holding on to occupied Arab territories is a recipe for renewed warfare; (4) left to themselves, the parties cannot be expected to make any progress toward real solutions; (5) a comprehensive Arab-Israeli peace serves American national interests, particularly regional stability and continued access to the Gulf's huge petroleum reserves. Unlike the Israel-first school, this approach calls on the United States to jointly work with other global powers to broker a comprehensive Arab-Israeli settlement, as opposed to acting unilaterally and giving Israel a veto over it.[48]

Three lessons emerge out of these doctrinal debates. To begin with, the Cold War shaped the conceptual lenses through which American officials viewed the Middle East. Four decades of a fierce East-West struggle left deep marks on foreign policy style and imagination. With the nation mobilized against what was described as an existential Communist threat, the globalists gained the upper hand: their simplistic "either us or them" logic resonated with the elite and with a public frightened by the specter of a Soviet conquest of the world and the demise of the American way of life. The Cold War legacy colored the way many Americans felt toward the Middle East and reinforced images of good friends and evil foes, images that have survived the collapse of the Soviet Union.

The globalists and the Israel-first school have reinvented their narrative and adjusted it to the post–Cold War environment, with considerable success. Now more than ever, the US foreign policy establishment views the region through Israeli eyes and equates the threat of "militant Islam" to that of Communism. The September 11 attacks allowed the neoconservatives to convince millions of Americans that they face a clear and immediate danger as perilous as Soviet Communism, and the United States must go on a global odyssey to rescue Western civilization from this menace. The new ideologues invested Al Qaeda, an offspring of the Cold War and a security nuisance rooted primarily in local grievances and foreign policy as well, with civilizational and transformational meanings. Bush and the neoconservatives borrowed ideological terms and references from the Cold War era to drive home the message about the need to confront the new "evildoers" of the Bin Laden and Zawahiri type. The legacy of the Cold War survived in the crusade against the "axis of evil," just as it had operated in yesterday's "military crusade again the evil empire."[49]

During the Cold War, the United States had a modest military deployment in the Middle East that was meant to defend its national interests against Soviet aggression. Afterward, the Pentagon built a formidable long-term military presence throughout the Persian Gulf, including Kuwait, Qatar, Bahrain, the United Arab Emirates, Oman, and Saudi Arabia. Today these forces constitute the largest commitment of American forces outside its own borders.

Second, despite the reasonableness of the regionalist school, it has not gained traction among American policymakers, particularly those in Congress. With very few exceptions, regionalists have been unable to assume direction of American foreign policy. Far from it. Instead, they have become marginalized and ghettoized. Within the foreign policy establishment their very deep knowledge of the Middle East, its cultures and languages, is dismissed as a liability imperiling the national interest. These "Arabists"—a derisive term often used in official circles—are criticized as being too close to their area of study to be trusted to provide detached analyses of the region and its problems. So goes the received wisdom in Washington. In fact, the Israel-first school and its supporters launched a concerted campaign to delegitimize regionalists or Arabists and raise questions about their suitability to participate in policymaking.[50] Israel's advocates have succeeded in pushing regionalists and Arabists out of official positions to the extent that they do not play a significant role in the making of US Mideast policy.[51] Their success may even have surpassed their imagination.

In fact, even during the Cold War era regionalists had a greater say in the foreign policy debate than now, a testament to the transformation of policy and the consolidation of the monopoly of the globalist and Israel-first school. Today in US policy circles it is a rarity to find regionalists of the intellectual and policy caliber and personality of Dean Rusk, George Ball, Adlai Stevenson, Chester Bowles, J. William Fulbright, William P. Rogers, George McGovern, Cyrus Vance, and Jimmy Carter (at the outset of his administration). The Israel-first school has predominated in both Republican and Democratic administrations, including those of Bill Clinton, George W. Bush, and Barack Obama. The likes of Ball and Rusk have been replaced by officials such as Martin Indyk,[52] Elliott Abrams,[53] Dennis Ross,[54] John Bolton,[55] Aaron Friedberg,[56] John Hannah,[57] Richard Perle,[58] Paul Wolfowitz,[59] Douglas Feith,[60] David Wurmser,[61] Matthew Levitt.[62] Obama, a liberal-minded president and no Cold Warrior, added Clinton's appointees to his foreign policy staff; the list favored the Israeli-first school and realists and did not include regionalists and Arabists. Though current and former members of the Obama team—Joe Biden, Jim Jones, Mike Mullen, Denis McDonough, George Mitchell, and especially the president himself—seemed to be more favorably disposed to an evenhanded approach, time and again, the Israel-first agenda has prevailed. For example, shortly into Obama's presidency, Dennis Ross, former head of the influential pro-Israel Washington Institute for Near East Policy (WINEP), was conspicuously moved to the National Security Council as a senior director, where his Israel-first agenda was given a more prominent platform. He announced on November 27, 2011, that he would return to WINEP in December 2011. The advisers with whom presidents surround themselves influence their thinking on international relations, as well as reveal their political preferences. Obama's team is distinguished by the absence of specialists on the Middle East, a flaw that distorts US policy toward the region.

Finally, the regionalist school lacks a supportive political constituency, and in America politicians appeal and respond to constituencies that deliver money and votes.[63] Domestic politics imposes serious constraints on the president's ability to pursue the national interest broadly and rationally defined. There exists no public foreign policy debate to debunk deeply held stereotypes and narratives about the area and its cultures and peoples. Of all the regions in the world, the Middle East elicits exceptionally reductionist views anchored more in ideology and perceptions than reality. Americans' general ignorance of the region and their stereotypical opinions take a toll on farsighted diplomats and politicians alike. As scholar Malcolm Kerr notes, this suggests "a fundamental intellectual and political problem that besets the ability of well-intentioned American presidential administrations to pursue a more positive and effective role in the Middle East."[64]

As this book will argue, the success of the globalists and the Israel-first school lies in shaping public opinion in the United States about the Middle East and in restricting the general parameters of the foreign policy debate. Their success has crippled Obama. There is an agreed set of assumptions and prescriptions to which officials faithfully subscribe. There is no challenging of the foundation of a strategy that, time and again, has led to policy failure. Even when there is a limited measure of ideological discontinuity in foreign policy, as in the case of the George W. Bush administration, failure persists.

On their own, neither the Israel lobby nor special interest groups explain the rigidity and shortsightedness of American policies. As far as the Middle East is concerned, the political system is dysfunctional and broken. Domestic politics, broadly defined, coupled with the failure of the foreign policy elite to educate the public about the internal dynamics of the region, are the driving forces. For example, a president such as Obama will think twice before uttering a single syllable that falls outside the scope of accepted discourse in any debate on foreign policy in the Middle East. Even when he restates principles that were upheld by past Republican presidents like George W. Bush, he is criticized. Presidents persuade themselves—if their savvy advisers do not do so—that they should not wander into domestic minefields; it is a fear that paralyzes ambitious politicians who will seek reelection. Most choose safety and inaction over vision and daring. Now presidential policy in the Middle East, more than in any other region, is hampered by institutional and bureaucratic politics, as well as domestic politics; they are a deadly, toxic mix.[65]

There is an inherent flaw in the system that rewards conformity and groupthink and penalizes diversity of thought and open debate.

As can be seen, Obama inherited a long, bitter, and baleful legacy in the Middle East, a legacy that encompasses the Bush era and goes back to the Cold War, whose patterns are clearly evident today. He also inherited a weak economy, one that fetters his hand and imposes severe limits on his stated wish to refashion America's engagement with the Middle East. In order to overcome the bitter legacy between America and Middle Eastern peoples and societies, Obama must show leadership and challenge the political culture of conformity and orthodoxy. He must educate the American public about the region and take on deeply entrenched special interests that have powerful political constituencies. He will need to invest considerable political capital in building a constituency for peace and change at home and to reallocate the enormous resources of military programs to peace programs. And just as important, Obama will have to have the political will, resolve, and stamina to pursue such a transformational strategy.

After more than three years of miasma in the White House, the fog has lifted, and there is clarity to Obama's foreign policy record. There is no longer any ambiguity about where he stands on the important challenges facing the United States, particularly in the Middle East. It is time to evaluate Obama's stance. This book will attempt to answer several critical questions: To what extent is Obama's foreign policy transformational or centrist-realist? Does Obama, despite his uplifting rhetoric, represent continuity rather than change? Has he challenged the basic premises on which US Mideast policy is based—the Israel-first school, America's relations with oil-producing regimes, and the war on terror? How high does the Middle East stand on Obama's foreign policy agenda? What does his response to the Arab popular uprisings in early 2011 say about American influence and engagement in the region? What does the Obama presidency reveal about American foreign policy toward the Middle East and the potential for continuing failure? What is it about the broken American political system that so often makes the practice fall short of the rhetoric? What can be done to close the gap between rhetoric and reality in US foreign policy, or, rather, to repair the dysfunctional political system in order to overcome the legacy of bitter relations between America and Middle Eastern societies?

CHAPTER 1

AMERICA'S ENCOUNTER WITH THE MIDDLE EAST

A Bitter Legacy

A LOVE AFFAIR GONE SOUR

Until the end of World War II the United States did not actively participate in Middle Eastern politics. It limited its engagement to educational and missionary activities and commercial investment in the region's oil sector. On the whole, American foreign policy had been isolationist from the birth of the Republic. Then, at the end of World War I, it supported limited self-determination for colonized people, including Arabs aspiring to self-governance and independence. In his Fourteen Points, detailed in a speech to a joint session of Congress in January 1918, President Woodrow Wilson expressed sympathy for Arab sovereignty: "The other nationalities which are now under Turkish rule should be assured an undoubted security of life and an absolutely unmolested opportunity of autonomous development."[1]

To support this position, Wilson sent a delegation (after the peace conference had ended) headed by Dr. Henry King, president of Oberlin College, and Charles Crane, a Chicago businessman and Arabist, to the Middle East to survey Arab opinion. Ultimately, the King-Crane Commission had no impact—its report was not published until 1922 after the European mandates providing for direct colonial rule by Britain and France had already been in place. The commission's recommendations were unpopular with France and Britain, who felt their interests were being challenged, and they withdrew from participating in the commission; the report was also viewed with skepticism by the American public and politicians.

The commission stated in its report that the delegates had initially been very favorably disposed toward the Zionist cause. But having gauged the views of those living in Palestine and Syria, they noted that the overwhelming majority of inhabitants were opposed to a Zionist homeland that envisaged the displacement of the Arabs. Moreover, they noted the following:

> With the best possible intentions, it may be doubted whether the Jews could possibly seem to either Christians or Moslems proper guardians of the holy places, or custodians of the Holy Land as a whole. The reason is this: The places which are most sacred to Christians—those having to do with Jesus—and which are also sacred to Moslems, are not only not sacred to Jews, but abhorrent to them. It is simply impossible, under those circumstances, for Moslems and Christians to feel satisfied to have these places in Jewish hands, or under the custody of Jews. There are still other places about which Moslems must have the same feeling. In fact, from this point of view, the Moslems, just because the sacred places of all three religions are sacred to them have made very naturally much more satisfactory custodians of the holy places than the Jews could be. It must be believed that the precise meaning, in this respect, of the complete Jewish occupation of Palestine has not been fully sensed by those who urge the extreme Zionist program. For it would intensify, with a certainty like fate, the anti-Jewish feeling both in Palestine and in all other portions of the world which look to Palestine as "the Holy Land." In view of all these considerations, and with a deep sense of sympathy for the Jewish cause, the Commissioners feel bound to recommend that only a greatly reduced Zionist program be attempted by the Peace Conference, and even that, only very gradually initiated. This would have to mean that Jewish immigration should be definitely limited, and that the project for making Palestine distinctly a Jewish commonwealth should be given up.[2]

The King-Crane Commission's only stated goal was to outline the wishes of the Arab people, who clearly expressed their desire for autonomy from imperial domination (Turkish or otherwise). The commission did make some clear recommendations regarding their own (and Arab) preferences for an American mandate. However, this was in contradiction to America's official policy of nonintervention and overt reluctance to intrude in European spheres of influence. In fact, the US government was acutely aware that Britain and France were not satisfied with the goals of the commission, and so in recognition of the need to keep the Europeans on their side, the Americans concluded—contrary to the recommendations of the report—that Syria should be mandated to France and Mesopotamia to Britain owing to the "international need of preserving friendly relations between France and Great Britain."[3] Moreover, Congress ruled in favor of a Zionist settlement, also dismissing the report's recommendations.[4]

Nevertheless, Britain and France split up the territory of the defeated Ottoman Empire between themselves and arbitrarily determined the borders, as well as the political organization, of the modern Middle Eastern state system—the nation-state. Although the United States did not actively oppose its European allies' control of the former Arab territories of the Ottoman Empire, it refrained from direct rule over the region's inhabitants.

Through the King-Crane Commission America gained a moral leadership that was recognized in the region. Its physical distance, detached policy, and apparent lack of political designs endeared it to most Arabs and Muslims and set it apart, in their eyes, from its domineering European allies. On balance, America was seen as a neutral island in a sea of European colonial reach. The Middle Eastern encounter with America and its citizens was mostly cultural and apolitical, and its mainly positive character nourished a romantic feeling about the newly rising Western power. Arab immigration to America reinforced a nascent love for a promised land shaped by personal stories and tales of riches made and dreams come true.

In 1924, Princeton historian Philip Hitti, an Arabist, wrote in *Al-Hilal* of his conception of America:

> You will feel as though you arrived in a country whose inhabitants are giants among men. . . . You will then realize that you are not among a people like others, but rather among a people superior in their qualities, distinguished in their vitality, and unique in their abundance of energy. The matchless skyscrapers, the quick pace of life, the ability

to focus on one's own work, are none other than manifestations of the dynamism of a nation that is full of youth and pulsating with tremendous energy.[5]

A generation later, before the dust settled after World War II, US diplomats in the field urged their superiors in Washington to listen closely to Arab aspirations, particularly their quest for independence and unity, and to avoid viewing the region in a merely instrumentalist light. In a 1945 conference between US ministers to the Middle East and a new president, Harry Truman, George Wadsworth, the minister to Syria and Lebanon, conveyed Arab sentiments toward the United States based on his experience and residency in the area:

> [T]he United States can play a leading role. Our moral leadership is recognized today. The governments to which we are accredited want most of all to know whether we are going to implement that leadership, whether we are going to follow through after our victory or leave the field, as we did at the end of the war, to others.[6]

Wadsworth, speaking on behalf of US ministers in Egypt, Saudi Arabia, and Palestine, warned the new president, who lacked experience in foreign affairs, that if the United States failed to recognize vital Arab interests, these countries would align themselves with Communist Russia and would "be lost to our civilization."

The warnings of Wadsworth and other diplomats were ignored. Washington's globalist lens reflected the field's regionalist perspective. The Truman administration, and later Eisenhower's, sacrificed indigenous aspirations for independence and urgently needed social and political development and reconstruction on the altar of a narrow, shortsighted outlook meant to deter the Soviet Union and safeguard access to Saudi and Iraqi petroleum. Ironically, by neglecting the local context and viewing the region in this way, Truman and Eisenhower gradually sowed doubt and suspicion about American intentions among leaders and people in the region. Rather than persuading the Arab governments to join with the West, the United States motivated many of them to turn to the Soviet camp for assistance. Middle Easterners' love for America quickly turned sour as leaders in the region saw the inconsistency between American rhetoric and American policy. The region's infatuation with America—which lasted from the beginning of the twentieth century until the end of World War II—had raised unrealistic expectations and set the stage for subsequent mistrust, disillusionment, and rejection because it was based more on nostalgia and opposition to colonial Britain and France than on an understanding of US foreign policy.

There was no single event or specific policy that transformed America's relationship with the Middle East from potential friend to bitter foe. The deterioration into mistrust and antipathy was incremental, a product of an accumulation over a half century of both camps' policies, encounters, and miscalculations. The most egregious of these policy mishaps, in the eyes of people in the region, were US support for the establishment of the State of Israel, the 1953 coup against the popularly elected Mohammad Mossaddegh in Iran, the shift to strong support for Israel after the Six-Day War in 1967, the oil embargo of 1973, the Iranian revolution of 1979 and the subsequent hostage crisis, and America's military intervention in the Gulf in 1991 that resulted in the permanent stationing of troops in Saudi Arabia, the birthplace of Islam.

The eminent Oxford historian Albert Hourani perceptively noted the crux: "Nevertheless the attitude which the Arabs will take up towards the West is not entirely a matter for the Arabs themselves; it depends very largely upon the attitude which the West takes up towards them."[7]

THE PALESTINE TRAGEDY

The events that defeated Palestine and culminated in the establishment of the State of Israel in 1948 were the beginning of the end of the Middle East's love affair with America. To the dismay of Arabs and Muslims, Truman actively lobbied the United Nations to vote for the partition of historic Palestine into two states, one Jewish and the other Arab. Despite serious reservations on the part of the State Department, the military, and the Central Intelligence Agency (CIA) about supporting Jewish statehood in Palestine, Truman insisted on exercising control of American policy toward Palestine and ordered the US delegation at the United Nations to support the partition. What Truman did not foresee was the human suffering and Palestinian disenfranchisement that resulted from the partition.

Ever since, the Palestine tragedy has haunted America's relationship with the Arabs and with many Muslims. For them, the division of historic Palestine was a "pivot" away from the positive century-and-a-half-long relationship between the United States and the Arab world. Palestinian scholar Ussama Makdisi put it bluntly: "At a moment when the rest of the world was entering the age of decolonization, the Palestinians were made stateless. More than any other single factor, the presence of Israel has altered the course of U.S.-Arab relations."[8]

Truman repeatedly expressed annoyance at efforts by career diplomats to encroach on the presidential powers: "I wanted to make it plain that the President of the United States, and not the second or third echelon in the State Department, is responsible for making foreign policy, and, furthermore, that no one in any department can sabotage the President's policy."[9]

Initially, Truman was merely interested in relieving the misery and plight of displaced Jews by urging their admission to British-controlled Palestine, and he rejected "a political structure imposed on the Near East that would result in conflict," i.e., partitioning Palestine into two states. He was aware that antagonizing the Arabs would tilt them toward the Soviet Union and open the gates of the region to Communist penetration. Yet Truman ultimately changed his mind, disregarded the warnings of most of his advisers, and was among the first to recognize the establishment of Israel in 1948.

According to officials who observed the decision-making process of that era, domestic politics—along with the discovery of extermination camps in Germany, and relentless pressure by Zionist groups—was the driver behind Truman's change of heart. Whatever the motives for Truman's decision, that act—viewed by Arab opinion makers as an example of America's duplicity and manipulation—marked the end of America's innocence in their eyes; the "shining city on a hill" was merely another new colonial power, willing to trample their rights to advance the electoral interests of its leaders at home.

Palestine represented a rupture between America and Muslims, particularly Arabs, who could not reconcile US leaders' early rhetorical support for Arab unity and independence and their betrayal of the colonized and indigenous Palestinian population. While liberal Arabs admired Western rationalism and science, they saw in Western support for Zionism a "bigotry" for which they could not account.[10]

In the late 1940s, Sayyid Qutb, then a mainstream public intellectual who subsequently became the master ideologue of revolutionary Islam, published an article,

"The American Conscience and the Palestine Question," in *Al-Risala* magazine. In it he railed against America's "treachery" and "duplicity":

> We finally discovered the U.S. conscience that had captured the hearts of many people in the East, who considered it to be different from the British conscience and the French conscience and those of the rest of Europe. . . . Many had been deceived by the American conscience because they had less contact with America than with Britain, France, and Holland. But America's role in Palestine exposed the deceptiveness of the American conscience that gambles away the future of other people and their human rights to purchase a token of votes in the presidential elections. . . . This is America exposed for all to see. This is Truman revealing the truth about the American conscience, which is the same as every Western conscience—unscrupulous, and only fools trust it.[11]

Qutb bemoaned Muslims' love affair with America, which was, in his opinion, based more on ignorance and infatuation than on a moral bond. He called on fellow Muslims to lift the veil and take a hard look at the real America that had pierced their hearts, and challenged them to prepare for the coming struggle in Palestine:

> If you want to be saved from the jaws of the Western beast, there exists only one way out . . . : begin the jihad and ignore any traitor who tries to trick you into trusting the Western conscience. All Arabs, all Muslims, need to stand up to defend Palestine. It is the struggle between the rising East and barbaric West—between God's laws and the laws of the jungle.[12]

Qutb was not alone in turning against the new Western superpower. Truman's support for the partition of Palestine had a transformative impact on the Arab elite and public opinion alike and poisoned their attitudes toward the United States. More than any other issue, the loss of Palestine, coupled with the tragedy of Palestinian refugees, radicalized large segments of Muslim opinion and left a "deep-seated chagrin" at America's support of Israel and caused "almost everyone [to be] suspicious of our professed intentions," according to a senior US diplomat stationed in Syria who spoke to opinion makers.[13] On this score there exist no differences between nationalists and religiously based activists (Islamists), secularists, and leftists;

all blame America—which they had initially admired for its anti-colonial stance—for tipping the balance in favor of the Jewish state. For Qutb and his liberal-leaning generation, the old progressive America was dead, replaced by a menacing, immoral superpower.[14] Before and after the partition in 1948, US diplomats in the region cautioned their superiors in Washington that Israel would become an aggravating, independent factor in relations between the United States and Arab peoples and societies: the Arabs' "universal resentment against an Israel" would produce a "corollary resentment against [the] US as [the] power primarily responsible for Israel's existence."[15]

In his seminal work, *The Arab Awakening*, George Antonius reflected on the loss of Palestine: "To place the brunt of burden upon Arab Palestine is a miserable evasion of the duty that lies upon the whole of the civilized world. It is also morally outrageous. No code of morals can justify the persecution of one people in attempt to relieve the persecution of another."[16] Even pro-Western Arab politicians, who were disposed to establish close relations with Washington, confided to their American counterparts that "cooperation with US in political or economic sphere will be plagued by criticism and opposition because of the US connection with Palestine tragedy."[17] In particular, the loss of Palestine transformed the views of America among young nationalist army officers such as Gamal Abdel Nasser of Egypt and Hafiz al-Assad of Syria. They had looked to the new rising Western power as a potential friend. But from this moment, as Assad confided to an interviewer, "the contest with Zionism became the major theme [of my life]."[18] Assad's political development and socialization mirrored that of his generation throughout the Arab world.

In spite of the critical Arab response to Truman's action, the US recognition and legitimation of the Jewish state, on its own, did not determine the nature of American-Israeli relations or Arab-American relations. America's de jure recognition of Israel did not entail any material commitment to the newborn Jewish state. It was not till the 1950s and 1960s that Israel emerged as an independent variable, a significant factor, in American foreign policy.

The polarization of America's relations with the Middle East occurred during the Cold War, a struggle that deepened and widened the rift between the new superpower and the people of the region.

THE COLD WAR INHERITANCE

At the end of World War II, the US foreign policy establishment made a strategic decision to fully engage in the international system. The nation's policymakers aimed at projecting unprecedented American economic and military power to construct a new international liberal economic order and global security architecture. A consensus existed among these officials that petroleum resources, particularly the unparalleled resources in the Middle East, were a prerequisite in the postwar reconstruction of Europe and Japan and in the power struggle against the Soviet Union. Therefore, from the outset, the economic and strategic value of the Mediterranean and the Middle East shaped American foreign policy.[19] Arguably, the Cold War began in the Middle East, not in Europe, which points to the strategic and economic importance of the area in the post-WWII era.

The Soviets' refusal to withdraw their troops from Iranian territories in Azerbaijan in 1946 was the first major postwar crisis of the US-Soviet alliance and is viewed as the spark that ignited the Cold War. Although there is no record of Truman's explicitly threatening the use of nuclear weapons, Joseph Stalin was well aware of American capabilities. The memory of the nuclear attacks on Hiroshima and Nagasaki, only a few months earlier, was no doubt fresh in his mind.[20]

Thereafter, the United States sought to establish a position of dominance in the Middle East and to deter the Soviet Union and exclude it from participation in regional diplomacy. Beginning with Truman, American strategy aimed at encircling the Soviet Union by building a string of Western defense pacts with local allies such as Turkey, Iran, Iraq, and Pakistan.

Throughout the Cold War, the struggle against Soviet Communism was a constant in US calculations and topped all other priorities, including local aspirations for reformist government and institution building and a sustained financial effort aimed at social and economic reconstruction. The Truman administration dispensed with Roosevelt's rhetoric of idealism and sympathy for Middle Eastern countries in their struggle to retain their independence and achieve "complete liberty" and unveiled a new and aggressive posture for America's role in the world.[21]

Disregarding the costs, the Truman Doctrine committed the United States to containing Soviet influence and maintaining the status quo. George Kennan's 1946

Long Telegram introduced the concept of "containment"; the Truman Doctrine put it into effect. The doctrine subsumed internal challenges in developing states under this single, all-encompassing East-West rivalry. Equally important, the doctrine became the cornerstone of America's active global interventionist role in the international system, including the Middle East, and it has shaped America's role in the world until the present, two decades after the collapse of the Soviet Union.[22]

Instead of viewing the region from the inside out, American officials looked at it from the outside in, through a globalist prism. Every issue, crisis, and country was rated by its relevance and importance to the struggle against worldwide Communism and by its ability to guarantee America's access to material and strategic resources, especially petroleum.

American presidents, with the exception of John F. Kennedy and, to a lesser extent, Jimmy Carter, regarded the Middle East as a key battleground in the Cold War. The Soviets treated regional actors similarly. As a consequence, the East-West struggle retarded democratic development in the region.[23]

The US leaders feared that radical governments and leftist movements would strengthen Soviet influence in the Middle East and endanger Western vital interests. In practice this meant that American foreign policy aimed more at preserving the status quo than spreading liberal democratic values. With rare exceptions, US officials fiercely and violently opposed indigenous populist movements and regimes, such as radical secular nationalism, socialism, and local Communist parties that aimed at modernizing and reconstituting the old order along progressive lines and took active steps to undermine them and block their progress. In the eyes of the people of the region, the US stand was fundamentally contradictory and hypocritical: while America claimed to be the leader of the free world, it allied itself with autocrats who facilitated its penetration of their countries. America's drive for hegemony "profoundly undermined whatever limited possibility there might have been of establishing any kind of democratic governance in a range of Middle Eastern countries."[24]

The goal of US strategy was to preserve the stability of pro-Western conservative or reactionary regimes, particularly those that produced oil, and to obstruct potential threats to their survival. Thus American policy became deeply embroiled in the region's labyrinthine internal affairs.

As early as 1949, the United States intervened in Syria's fractious politics. It helped General Husni al-Za'im overthrow the regime of Shukri al-Quwatli because the Soviet Union had shown an interest in the country. Although American officials portrayed al-Za'im as a "Banana Republic dictator type"—that is, no democrat—they saw him as a pliant dictator who had pledged to work with the West against Communism, to sign an armistice with Israel, and to improve relations with pro-American Turkey. Al-Za'im delivered on his pledges by steering Syria into the Western orbit. Unfortunately for the Truman administration, he was assassinated less than five months later; his death was followed by two more military coups, and Syria plunged into social and political upheaval.[25]

Far from learning any useful lessons from the Syrian fiasco, the United States intervened regularly in the internal affairs of other Middle Eastern states, seeking to prop up pro-Western dictators and block "leftist" and populist movements from making political inroads within their societies. More and more people in the region began to view America in a mistrustful light similar to that in which they viewed Britain and France. The irony is that policymakers in Washington were aware of the rising tensions and polarization in America's relations with the Arab peoples. In the early 1950s US diplomats in the field cautioned their superiors that anti-American sentiment in the region was spreading. One diplomatic cable by a senior diplomat was blunt:

> It is hard for many Americans, unless they have recently visited certain parts of this area, to realize how general and how deep-seated is the distrust, and in some cases hatred, for the British and the French because of their past or present colonial policies and activities. The United States is increasingly being put in the same imperialist category.[26]

These warnings were not taken seriously in Washington. There existed a disconnect, a divide between the regionalist perspective and the globalist school, between diplomats in the field and Cold Warriors. On balance, American foreign policy toward the Middle East was an extension of the East-West battle, one that intensified in the 1950s and 1960s and caused considerable harm to America's moral leadership and standing in the region.

THE CIA COUP AGAINST MOHAMMED MOSSADEGH

Iran became a major battleground in the Cold War in the Middle East in 1953. There the CIA, together with the British Secret Intelligence Service (SIS), carried out a successful clandestine operation that facilitated a coup and the removal of a constitutional government led by Premier Mohammed Mossadegh. The nationalization of the Iranian oil industry in 1951—a hard blow to the Anglo-Iranian Oil Company (AIOC), holder of a large concession—triggered a diplomatic crisis with Britain that almost starved the Iranian economy. A power struggle unfolded between Mossadegh and the shah, Mohammed Reza Pahlavi, a pro-Western monarch who feared the British and opposed confrontation with them over the oil concession agreement.

Mossadegh repeatedly called on the United States to assist his financially strapped country and relieve the political and economic pressure exerted by Britain. Both the outgoing Truman administration and the incoming Eisenhower administration flatly refused to do so.[27] But as Britain tightened the naval siege of Iran and choked its oil-dependent economy, documents show that initially the Truman administration made an effort to mediate between Mossadegh and the British. US officials grew exasperated with the British rule-or-ruin policy and thought that their ally was suffering from an old-fashioned imperial complex.[28]

Nevertheless, after Mossadegh refused to compromise, Truman agreed to a proposal by Prime Minister Winston Churchill for a joint US-British approach to neutralize him and restore the shah's authority. The United States decided to synchronize strategy with Britain lest "Iran disappear behind the Iron Curtain and the whole military and political situation in the Middle East change adversely."[29]

What tipped the scales in Washington was the East-West rivalry and the fear of weakening the newly established North Atlantic Alliance (now known commonly as NATO). American officials did not want Mossadegh, an unreliable radical nationalist, to set a dangerous precedent through nationalization of petroleum resources in the region; that would have threatened the dominant interests of American oil companies everywhere, in both the Middle East and the world economy. The overthrow of Mossadegh and preservation of the status quo was mandatory. But the implementation of that policy was left to the Eisenhower administration, which came into office in January 1953. Unlike his predecessor,

Eisenhower did not invest much time in trying to broker an agreement between Iran and Britain.[30]

John Foster Dulles regarded the internal power struggle between Mossadegh and the shah as part of the historic Soviet drive to control oil-rich Iran: "If they could control Iran, they would control the Persian Gulf," Dulles told those assembled. "This has been their dream, their chief ambition, ever since the days of Peter the Great."[31]

Echoing Dulles, Kermit Roosevelt, the CIA official in charge of the Middle East, called the Soviet threat to Iran "genuine, dangerous and imminent," stressing that "time seems to favor the Russians and their unwitting ally, Dr. Mossadegh."[32]

"So this is how we get rid of that madman Mossadegh," the US secretary of state said after perusing the written version of the CIA-SIS clandestine plan at a meeting to discuss the fate of the Iranian premier.[33] Taking charge of the operation code-named Ajax at an estimated cost of $100,000 to $200,000, Roosevelt secretly journeyed to Iran and coordinated internal efforts that brought about Mossadegh's downfall on 19 August 1953. Three days later, the shah left his temporary exile in Rome and returned in triumph to Tehran.[34] Mossadegh was captured and sentenced to three years in prison. An oil agreement was swiftly signed between Iran and an international consortium of Western oil companies that conformed to the prevailing pattern in the Middle East of fifty-fifty profit sharing.[35]

In his memoirs, President Eisenhower wrote that he conferred daily with his top advisers on the Iranian crisis and read the reports of the US representatives (CIA) who worked actively with the shah's supporters. "Throughout this crisis, the United States government had done everything it possibly could to back up the Shah," Eisenhower acknowledged.[36] Indeed, the United States helped restore the shah's rule and subsequently backed him both politically and financially, replacing Britain as his great power patron until his downfall in 1979.[37]

The removal of Mossadegh initiated a pattern of US secret and open actions against indigenous radical nationalist leaders who challenged the status quo at home and aimed at pursuing an independent foreign policy. Mossadegh was not even militantly radical. He was, in fact, a firm believer in international law. Despite his uncompromising stance on the Anglo-Iranian Oil Company, he repeatedly appealed to presidents Truman and Eisenhower for US assistance. He tried to reassure them of his desire to have close relations with the Western power.[38] Yet, American policymakers viewed him as a potential threat to Western interests in the region and a "madman" who would offer Iran to the Soviets on a silver platter.

In a reflection of elite American public opinion at the time, a *New York Times* editorial celebrated the ouster of Mossadegh:

> Underdeveloped countries with rich resources now have an object lesson in the heavy cost that must be paid by one of their number which goes berserk with fanatical nationalism. It is perhaps too much to hope that Iran's experience will prevent the rise of Mossadeghs in other countries, but the experience may at least strengthen the hands of the more reasonable and far-seeing leaders.[39]

Although the role of the CIA and the SIS was critical in the ouster of Mossadegh, the coup could not have happened without the support of elements of the imperial court, the clergy, the army, and the bazaar. Nevertheless, the CIA's appetite for intervention in the internal affairs of newly decolonized states, including those in the Middle East, expanded considerably. One of the lessons learned in Washington was that the CIA was an effective tool of American foreign policy, useful for co-opting friends and coercing foes—a state of mind that gained momentum in decision making. The Eisenhower administration empowered and unleashed the CIA worldwide with serious long-term repercussions for American primary interests.

US policymakers did not consider the lasting harm that their clandestine intervention would inflict on Iran and on America's moral leadership in the region. The ouster of Mossadegh by America and Britain turned him into a nationalist icon, a symbol of resistance to foreign domination and exploitation, a unifying figure for the religiously based opposition and the secular opposition alike, and an example of injustice, a concept that resonates powerfully in Shiite Iran.

American officials also overlooked how Iranian opinion would view their intimate association with the shah, especially (as his regime matured) his repressive policies and widespread violation of human rights. Iranians viewed America as an accomplice of their tormentor, as providing him with pivotal political and military support and bolstering his rule. Anti-American sentiment took hold of the Iranian imagination. It is little wonder that Ayatollah Khomeini, the clerical leader of the Iranian revolution in the late 1970s, made defiance and resistance to America the hallmark, the raison d'être, of his Islamic revolution, a revolution that put an end to the rule of the Pahlavi dynasty, Washington's enforcer in the Gulf.

The ouster of Mossadegh transcended Iran and reverberated through the Middle East.[40] The message was loud and clear: as a superpower, the United States would actively oppose indigenous populist leaders and movements that challenged the status quo. It offered local actors a stark choice between good and evil: they could join either the leader of the free world or the Soviet-led Communist camp.

Similar to the Mossadegh case, but less successful for the Americans, was the attempted coup against the pro-Soviet Syrian regime in 1957. The coup ultimately failed, but the fact that it was attempted emphasizes the point that, driven by its Cold War strategy, the United States had continued its aggressive interventionist policy after the overthrow of Mossadegh, neglecting the negative repercussions on its standing in the world.[41]

AMERICA CONFRONTS RADICAL ARAB NATIONALISM

America's rocky relations with Egyptian strongman Gamal Abdel Nasser, a populist Arab nationalist, exemplify the bitter legacy of the Cold War and its endurance. Ironically, before they carried out their coup against the British-supported old regime in July 1952, Nasser and his junta of young army officers apparently informed only the US embassy in Cairo of their impending scheme. The conspirators, calling themselves Free Officers, were no doubt motivated by a desire to obtain American support in case Britain deployed the thousands of troops it had stationed in Egypt to smother their "blessed movement" at birth.

Nasser, together with most of his comrades, was socially, politically, and psychologically disposed toward America. They believed that Washington could provide aid, investment, and support in pressuring Britain to withdraw from Egypt. They were also convinced that the United States opposed imperialism and supported the right of newly independent states to self-determination. Immediately after seizing power, Nasser and other Free Officers spent many evenings socializing with American diplomats in the US Embassy in Cairo, hoping to strengthen their bargaining position vis-à-vis Britain. Egypt's new rulers sought US backing and requested arms for defense and financial assistance.[42]

The intimacy of US-Egyptian relations at this time was demonstrated by the Americans' helping to organize and train Egyptian intelligence services.[43] According to US documents, at this stage, from 1952 to 1954, Nasser and his comrades stressed to American officials that they wanted to establish a close relationship with the new superpower and expressed their opposition to Communism. Confidential undertakings by the Free Officers to American diplomats prompted the US ambassador to Cairo, Jefferson Caffery, to conclude that the political philosophy of Egypt's military rulers was "anti-communist and relatively pro-Western."[44]

Ambassador Caffery was correct. The dominant view among the young army officers was that the Soviet bloc had nothing concrete to offer Egypt. Nasser and others were ideologically suspicious of Communism because they feared it would polarize the Egyptian working class.[45]

The Soviets saw the coup as part of a pattern in the decolonized world—from South America to the Middle East—in which the United States would use reactionary elements within the new states to tighten its grip. Initially, Joseph Stalin and his successor, Nikita Khrushchev, were hostile to the coup, believing that it was "just another one of those military take-overs which [they also] had become accustomed to in South America."[46] They saw it as either a product of Anglo-American rivalry or a covert US plot to abort a genuine populist revolution.[47] It is no wonder that the leading Soviet analyst on Egypt, L. N. Vatolina, characterized Nasser and the army officers as "madly reactionary, terrorist, anti-democratic, demagogic."[48]

Not only did the Russian media attack the July 1954 Anglo-Egyptian Agreement as contrary to Egyptian national interests, as well as to those of Arab states, but they also persisted in labeling Nasser, the head of the revolution, a "fascist" lackey of the West, and accusing him of treason and urging the Egyptian masses to revolt.[49]

Egypt, the most populous Arab country and the region's capital of cultural production, was ripe for a strategic alliance with the United States. Nevertheless, American foreign policy proved to be its own worst enemy in Egypt and the greater Middle East by overlooking the perspective of the regionalist school of diplomacy in favor of the Cold War lens. This dominant narrative in US foreign policy neglected the hopes, aspirations, and fears of the young leaders of the decolonized states and their anti-imperialist stance. There was little appreciation in Washington of how the European colonial legacy colored the attitudes of the rising new elite in the Middle East. US officials ignored internal and local priorities and thereby turned potential allies into bitter foes.

Nasser and the young army officers are a case in point. The United States might have strengthened economic and technical ties with the new Egyptian leaders and helped them achieve real independence and modernization. Neutrality and non-alignment were gaining momentum among developing states in the mid-1950s, but Eisenhower and Dulles were hostile to the whole idea. As the president put it, how could one be neutral between right and wrong, good and evil, decency and indecency? Nasser and his comrades were bluntly told that American military and financial assistance to Egypt was conditional on the country's taking sides in the Cold War struggle, joining Western defense pacts, and achieving a rapprochement with Israel.

Although receptive to America initially, Nasser and his comrades rejected Washington's and London's repeated requests to align their policy with the West. In a meeting with Dulles, Nasser said that Egyptians and Arabs generally regarded colonial Britain, France, and now Israel, rather than the Soviet Union, as enemies. He stressed that pressing social and economic concerns, not international Communism, were the real threat to peace and stability in the region. Washington's emphasis should therefore be placed on socioeconomic development rather than on the construction of regional military pacts, Nasser pleaded.

The top priority of the new army officers was to free their country from foreign occupation and modernize their backward society. Nasser, who emerged as the strongman of the Egyptian revolution, told the Revolutionary Council (the executive ruling junta), that he was not going to replace one Western master, Britain, with another—the United States.

Eisenhower and Dulles, as Cold Warriors, did not accept Nasser's nationalist-populist narrative, even though top US diplomats in the region urged their superiors in Washington to listen closely, for Nasser had become a symbol of pan-Arab nationalism. The challenges and difficulties facing America in the Middle East, wrote the US ambassador in Egypt, were not "primarily due to an ideological clash between our brand of democracy and Communism"; rather, the drivers motivating nationalist leaders like Nasser were anticolonialism and economic hardship and the quest for development and modernization.[50]

In contrast, as records of official deliberations in Washington show, the Eisenhower administration diagnosed the problem as Nasser's "disregarding the interests of Western Europe and the United States in the Middle East region."[51] Eisenhower and Dulles viewed Nasser as an unruly troublemaker who challenged the United

States and provided the Soviet Union with a foothold in the area by purchasing arms from Moscow, thus breaking the West's monopoly on weapons sales to Middle Eastern countries. American policymakers feared a "major catastrophe"—particularly the loss of the region's oil resources, which were (and are) vital to Western security—unless Nasser was effectively countered and cut to size.[52]

Moreover, Eisenhower viewed as a hostile act Nasser's 1956 decision to recognize Communist China, a decision that was motivated mainly by Nasser's fear of Russia's reneging on its pledge to sell arms to Egypt. Dulles told the Egyptian ambassador to Washington, Ahmed Hussein, that the United States believed that "Nasser had made a bargain with the Devil with the hope of developing his own power and establishing an empire stretching from the Persian Gulf to the Atlantic Ocean."[53]

The Eisenhower administration overrode warnings by the US ambassador in Cairo and intelligence assessments alike, and decided to retaliate against Nasser. It would severely punish him by withdrawing the US offer to finance the Aswan Dam, a developmental project of political significance to Egypt. Dulles believed that if the Egyptian leader could not build the dam, it would mean "the end of Nasser."[54] Nasser swiftly retaliated against Washington's rebuke by nationalizing the Suez Canal Company on 26 July 1956; he portrayed the US decision as an act of war against the revolution and an extension of Western colonialism to thwart Egyptian independence.[55]

Nasser's action formally marked the end of Britain's moment in the Middle East and the deepening of Soviet influence there. Thus the origins of the Suez Crisis lay in Washington's confrontation with radical Arab nationalism, a populist, anti-colonial movement deeply suspicious of the great powers. Although Eisenhower played a key role in forcing Britain, France, and Israel to withdraw their troops after invading Egypt in October, the US role in triggering the world crisis was neither forgotten nor forgiven. For people in the region and beyond, America had inherited its European allies' hegemonic mandate in the region, even though it utilized different tactics to impose its political will.

THE EISENHOWER DOCTRINE

Far from bringing a rapprochement between the United States and rising pan-Arab nationalist forces, the aftermath of the Suez War increased mistrust and suspicion. Fearing "power vacuums" in the Middle East after the withdrawal of British, French, and Israeli troops from Egypt, Eisenhower and Dulles assumed the global responsibilities of their European partners in the Middle East and institutionalized the power shift. Building on the Truman Doctrine, Eisenhower told a joint session of Congress in January 1957 that the Middle East was important to US security and warned of the threat that international Communism posed to pro-Western governments in the area. He proposed a resolution that would authorize him to deploy American armed forces and defend local allies under attack by any Communist-controlled state.[56]

The new Eisenhower Doctrine deepened Washington's involvement in the Middle East and embroiled it further in the region's internal affairs. Ever since, the United States has been a Middle East power. Eisenhower and his advisers saw the dirty hand of international Communism behind troubling developments with Nasser, and regarded him as a Soviet tool. The consensus was that Nasser had to be isolated and weakened. "We regard Nasser as an evil influence," said Eisenhower. Dulles even regretted that the British had withdrawn their troops from the Suez before ousting Nasser.[57]

In addition to suspending the modest US program of technical and commodity aid to Egypt, Eisenhower encouraged Saudi Arabia to assume greater leadership in the Arab world and to "build up King Saud as a figure with sufficient prestige to offset Nasser." Washington's goal was to drive a wedge between Egypt and Saudi Arabia, the two pivotal Arab states; US officials viewed this as essential to weakening Nasser's regional leadership.[58]

The result was that inter-Arab quarrels became fully entangled in the Cold War in what came to be known as the Arab cold war.[59] For example, in the late 1950s an internal power struggle in Lebanon was swiftly internationalized: the United States intervened militarily in the tiny pro-Western country to stem the tide of radical Arab nationalism that had already destroyed the Iraqi monarchy and almost overwhelmed Jordan. America's growing involvement in the internal affairs of Middle Eastern states increased peoples' suspicion and hostility; the United States was accused of fueling tensions and rivalries among indigenous states in an effort to divide and control. That attitude still resonates widely in the region.

Eisenhower's idea of building Saudi Arabia into a regional counterweight to Egypt subsequently evolved into deploying Islam and its powerful symbols to counterbalance Nasser's relatively secular pan-Arab nationalism. As pro-Western conservative monarchies and regimes, including Iraq, Jordan, and Lebanon, fell or teetered on the brink of collapse one after another in the late 1950s, Eisenhower was taken with the idea of an Islamic pact under King Saud's leadership as a viable alternative to Nasser's secular radical Arabism.[60]

As Eisenhower put it, King Saud "professed anti-Communism and he enjoyed, on religious grounds, a high standing among all Arab nations." Why not, he asked, construct an alliance, headed by Saud, of Islamic-based states and groups that possessed sufficient religious prestige and legitimacy to challenge the dominant ideology of secular Arab nationalism?[61] This thinking, guided by Cold War logic, marked the beginning of an implicit alliance between America and religiously oriented states and movements, or political Islamists, which climaxed in Washington's sponsoring and financing of the Afghan jihad in the 1980s.

THE KENNEDY AND JOHNSON YEARS

In its twilight hours, however, the Eisenhower administration signaled its willingness to coexist with pan-Arab nationalism and recognized its neutralist character. The Kennedy administration, going further, made a clear distinction between Communism and indigenous populist movements and deployed foreign aid as a weapon to influence the conduct of leaders like Nasser. Unlike his predecessor, Kennedy adopted a regionalist approach—looking at the region from the inside out—and hoped to use soft power to induce Third World leaders to respect US security interests.[62]

Although Kennedy was as determined as Truman and Eisenhower to wage the Cold War, he did not view the developing world, including the Middle East, through a globalist blinder. Kennedy's nuanced approach took into consideration the local context and did not lump it into the East-West struggle. He wanted to demonstrate the New Frontiersman's commitment and willingness to assist developing states.[63]

Kennedy also increased funding for the Israeli military—true, this was not so much a result of Cold War reasoning as it was adherence to a loyalty to Israel inherited from previous administrations and a response to the pro-Israel sentiment in Congress. Thus, in this sense, Kennedy's policy could arguably be seen as no less problematic in terms of the Arab-Israeli conflict.[64]

Unfortunately, Kennedy's presidency was short-lived, and so was his complex foreign policy. Lyndon Johnson's ascent to power brought about a marked shift in policy toward the Middle East—away from cooperation and reconciliation and toward confrontation. There existed no single factor or variable that accounts for this qualitative change.

Arab-Israeli tensions intensified in the 1960s, and Israel emerged as one of the fundamental challenges in US relations with the Arab states. Johnson's sympathy with Israel inflamed Arab-American relations and poisoned public attitudes. Arab nationalists led by Nasser criticized the biased US approach to the Arab-Israeli conflict and specifically accused Johnson of duplicity and antagonism toward their cause. Similarly, the revolutionary pan-nationalist Ba'th Party stated that the Palestine problem was the most divisive issue between the Arab people and the West.[65]

Moreover, Nasser's regional ambitions, particularly his military intervention in Yemen and his support for the rebels in the Congo in the 1960s, led to a direct confrontation with the United States. The Johnson administration pressured Nasser and threatened to withhold much-needed economic aid to Egypt in order to force him to change his conduct.[66] This effort, in counteraction, increased Nasser's economic and military dependence on the Soviet Union.

Personal animosity between Johnson and Nasser, by now the undisputed leader of pan-Arab nationalism, aggravated policy differences between the United States and the rising social forces in the region. Nasser had an instinctive dislike of Johnson, whom he suspected of being a strong supporter of Israel and a "wheeler-dealer" with a Cold War mentality. Likewise, Johnson was unsympathetic to radical pan-Arab nationalism and suspected Nasser of entertaining imperial designs to dominate the region, using Soviet support.[67]

Kennedy's early–1960s tolerance toward populist-nationalist movements, such as pan-Arab nationalism, contrasted sharply with Johnson's views, which resembled those of Truman and Eisenhower. To Johnson, a unified Arab foreign policy under Nasser's leadership would create a colossus of oil geopolitics, a development detrimental to American vital interests: "The U.S. interest requires that America and its allies have a dependable and steady access to Near East oil independent of the vicissitudes of international politics."[68]

From the onset of the Cold War to the twenty-first century, the United States has opposed pan-nationalist schemes and movements that aim at developing a unified Arab foreign policy. There exists no mystery about this stance: Arab unity of the Nasser and Saddam varieties would threaten America's access to oil as well as imperil the security of Israel and pro-Western conservative Arab regimes. Large Arab and Muslim constituencies know this and have turned against American foreign policy for its visible hostility to their cause, which is empowerment, self-determination, and a better life. The US predicament in the Middle East lies more with the indigenous peoples than with their governments.

Once again, US diplomats in the region dissented from their Washington superiors and expressed their concerns about Johnson's insensitivity to indigenous issues and his leaning toward Israel; they argued that Johnson's public statements convinced the peoples of the region that "enlightened Kennedy policies have given way to Truman-like pro-Israeli policies." Pleading for utmost restraint, the ambassadors questioned whether the president understood the erosion of US influence in the area and the likelihood of a backlash against American interests there.[69]

Like Truman and Eisenhower, Johnson ignored his diplomats' counsel and tightened the screws on his Middle East nemesis. He deployed aid as a two-pronged political weapon—to deter Nasser and bring him to heel and to strengthen the material basis of conservative Arab rulers.[70]

The stage was set for a fierce confrontation between the United States and Nasser, a collision that climaxed in the June 1967 Arab-Israeli War, also known as the Six-Day War. Within a week, Israel crushed the Arab armies, including that of Egypt, "the most powerful army in the Middle East," a defeat that left a lasting scar on the Arab imagination and widened the rift between America and Muslim opinion in general.

Initially, Nasser was ambivalent about blaming the United States, but when told of Israel's crushing defeat of his troops, he changed his mind and issued a public statement with King Hussein of Jordan charging that US carrier-based fighter jets had participated in attacks on Egypt. As Arab arms lay smoldering on the battlefield, Nasser accused the United States of giving Israel a green light to attack the Arabs and of taking sides in the war as well. Six Arab states—Egypt, Syria, Iraq, Yemen, Algeria, and Sudan—broke diplomatic relations with the United States.

Although the break was based on a false charge, it reflected Arab conviction, largely true, that Johnson's support of the Jewish state had played a key role in

Israel's swift victory over the Arab armies.[71] America's hostility to the Arab cause became an article of faith uniting differing social and political groups in the area. Even Islamists who rejoiced at the humiliation of their nationalist nemesis, Nasser, believed in America's guilt and intrinsic hostility to Muslims.

The humiliating defeat of popular Arab nationalist forces, together with a second massive exodus of Palestinians from the West Bank, newly occupied by the Israelis, fed the flood of anti-American sentiment in Muslim societies. The war left a deep imprint on the Arab psyche, and its aftermath led to the radicalization and militarization of Muslim public opinion and to a rupture in America's relations with the region and with other Third World countries.

Washington's decision to allow Israel to keep Arab territories it occupied during the 1967 war ensured that the American victory over the leader of secular Arab nationalism would create its own terrible dynamic. As one scholar noted, "Nasser may have fallen, and with him the dreams of a generation, but pax-Americana helped usher in an age of defiant religiosity, resistance, and cynicism. . . ."[72]

American foreign policy toward the Middle East in the early twenty-first century remains in the shadow of the June 1967 war and the decisions made immediately afterward. Unlike Eisenhower, who pressed Israel for swift withdrawal from Egyptian territory in 1956, Johnson supported Israel's occupation of Arab territories pending Arab willingness to make peace.[73]

Comparing and contrasting the US conduct in the two wars, Israeli foreign minister Abba Eban noted that Johnson fully backed his country's stance: the United States was "giving us support such as we have never known before."[74] Johnson concurred with the official Israeli assessment and disagreed with the State Department's description of the American position as "neutral in thought, word, and deed." "Neutral" is the wrong word, said Johnson.[75]

Whereas Eisenhower had rejected the use of conquered territory as a lever in international bargaining, Johnson hoped to use it to force the Arabs to recognize Israel. The dominant view expressed by the National Security Council and shared by Johnson is that Soviet policy in the region lay in "ruins," and that Nasser's fate was sealed. Johnson's post-1967 strategy was to consciously seize the new opportunity afforded by the humiliating defeat of the pro-Soviet Arabs and redraw the geostrategic map of the Middle East in favor of pro-American regional allies, particularly Israel, Turkey, and Iran. According to Johnson and his senior advisers, the advantages of American active engagement in the Arab-Israeli theater outweighed the inherent costs.[76]

For Johnson and his senior advisers, Israel's striking military performance was a welcome diversion from America's prolonged, costly, and futile war in Vietnam. In their eyes, Israel's effective military performance turned it into a regional strategic asset. The origins of the "special relationship" between the United States and Israel can be traced to Johnson, a president who was disposed to the Jewish state by temperament and "domestic political calculation."[77]

In this respect, the Johnson presidency represented a watershed. American assistance to Israel quadrupled during the Johnson and Nixon eras. Regardless of their political orientation, US presidents accepted Israel's plea for greater security and territorial expansion and committed the United States to maintaining Israel's military superiority over all of its Arab neighbors.[78]

THE 1970S

The logic behind the new shift in US policy lay in viewing Israel as a key to regional stability and a counterweight to the radical leftists and nationalist and Islamist indigenous forces that dominated the region after June 1967. For example, President Richard Nixon and his chief foreign policy adviser, Henry Kissinger, convinced themselves that Israel would thwart Soviet designs in Egypt and elsewhere as it allegedly did during the Soviet-inspired Syrian invasion of Jordan in September 1970. Although the Soviet Union had little to do with the internal crisis in Jordan and the subsequent Syrian response, Nixon and Kissinger viewed the crisis through the Cold War lens and overemphasized the Soviet role.

Israel's cooperation with the United Sates and King Hussein of Jordan during that crisis consolidated its image in Washington as a bastion of deterrence and stability in a highly dangerous region. The result of these misperceptions, lamented William Quandt, the dean of US diplomatic history on the Middle East, was an American policy that was too narrowly focused on Israel and the Soviet Union and on preserving the military balance of power in favor of Israel at the expense of a comprehensive peace settlement.[79] In his memoirs, as noted earlier, Kissinger acknowledged his direct role in undermining the State Department's diplomatic efforts to facilitate a peace settlement between Israel and its Arab neighbors. As a

Cold Warrior, Kissinger said that preserving the territorial status quo was more important than Arab-Israeli peace because the US-Israeli strategic relationship was key to combating Soviet influence and maintaining regional stability.[80] While Nixon and Kissinger provided unprecedented aid to Israel, they paid hardly any attention to the mounting frustrations in Egypt, Syria, and among the Palestinians and to the continued growing restiveness and activism of the Arabs, who had begun to recognize the potential power they possessed, particularly their petroleum resources. Even when Egyptian President Anwar Sadat precipitately expelled more than ten Soviet military advisers in July 1972, Nixon and Kissinger didn't feel a need to intensify their efforts to promote a peace settlement. For the two realist policymakers, US Mideast strategy was a success as long as the region remained comparatively calm, and Soviet influence seemed to be declining. Theirs was a short-sighted and unenlightened stance.[81]

It would take another devastating Arab-Israeli war, the Yom Kippur War of October 1973, together with an Arab oil embargo, to shatter several basic assumptions that were central to US foreign policy: stability in the Middle East was not ensured by Israeli military predominance, and Israeli strength alone would not lead to a political settlement, as Johnson had hoped it would after the Six-Day War.[82]

The Yom Kippur War shattered the strategic and diplomatic deadlock existing on the Arab-Israeli front. Moreover, the war in October 1973 escalated into a severe international crisis that pitted the two superpowers against one another and almost brought them to the brink of a nuclear confrontation. The Yom Kippur War was a rude awakening to Nixon and Kissinger, who had mistakenly believed that Soviet influence in the Middle East had reached its limit and that Israel, as a strategic asset, had thwarted Russian designs in the region.[83]

Before the dust settled on the Arab-Israeli battlefield, Nixon and Kissinger began to revise their previously held assumptions and to devote much more attention to the Middle East. One of the important lessons learned by the US leadership was that the region was highly volatile and dangerous and could disintegrate, with serious consequences for America's global and regional vital interests. The October war thus produced an important shift in how American policy approached the Middle East. At the heart of this shift in US policy lay a conscious effort to improve relations with the major Arab states, especially Egypt, and to actively mediate peace talks between the Jewish state and its Arab neighbors.[84]

As a result of this activation of US diplomacy, the cease-fires and then disengagement agreements were concluded between the belligerents, with Israel still holding most of the Arab territories captured in 1967. These accords eventually paved the way for the Camp David Accords between Egypt and Israel in 1978.

Nixon and Kissinger pledged to play an "honest broker" role between the Arabs and the Israelis and to strive for a comprehensive political settlement. To the Arabs, however, Kissinger's step-by-step diplomacy was aimed at buying time and reducing pressure on Israel and the United States. In their eyes, the Nixon legacy is remembered more for stemming the Arab military momentum in the first days of the October war—through a massive airlift of American arms to Israel—than for subsequently brokering the cease-fires and disengagement agreements at the expense of the Palestinians.

Arabs vividly remember that in addition to a full-scale airlift of military equipment to Israel, Nixon asked Congress to appropriate $2.2 billion in emergency aid to Israel, including $1.5 billion in outright grants. This decision triggered a collective Arab response: a total oil embargo of the United States as a "principal hostile country."[85]

Through these endeavors, Israel became the single largest recipient of US foreign aid. Whereas in 1972 total American aid to Israel amounted to $350 million, by 1974 it reached more than $2.6 billion, and from the mid-1970s it hovered around $2 billion annually. Since the 1980s, American aid to Israel has risen to more than $3 billion a year, 70 percent of which goes for military supplies.[86]

The massive increase in aid to Israel after the October war shows the strengthening of strategic ties between the United States and Israel and the emergence of a special relationship between the two countries. While from the late 1940s until the end of the 1960s, Israel was an important factor in US foreign policy in the Middle East, other issues, such as the East-West struggle and inter-Arab rivalries, predominated. The United States kept a healthy distance from Arab-Israeli disputes and armed skirmishes, frequently criticized both camps for escalation, and used developmental schemes to get Israel and its Arab neighbors to substitute cooperation for confrontation.

After the Six-Day War, Israel colored Arab and Muslim perceptions of American foreign policy above all else. Israel has become the most divisive wedge between the Christian West, especially America, and the world of Islam. Although various US presidents have professed to follow an "evenhanded" or "balanced" policy toward the Arab-Israeli conflict, their message has mostly gone unheeded by people in the region.

Far from being seen as an "honest broker," the United States is regarded as an active participant in the conflict, taking sides against the Arab cause. Arab opinion and Muslim opinion in general hold the United States responsible for empowering Israel and maintaining its military superiority over all its Arab neighbors. A widely held belief among ordinary people is that, were it not for American matériel and political support, Israel would not have occupied Arab territories and expanded the construction of Jewish settlements on Palestinian land.

One of the consequences of the internationalization of the Arab-Israeli conflict is that America has become deeply embroiled in its quagmire. There is a causal link between Washington's strong ties with Israel and increasing Muslim societal hostility toward the United States. On the whole, Arabs transferred their antagonism toward Israel to America and imposed the present on the past, viewing their relationship with the superpower through the Palestine-Israel lens. The history, however, is much more complex than that.

Throughout the 1950s and early 1960s, the Arab-Israeli conflict was not a focus of US policy. True, various presidents, including Eisenhower, Kennedy, and, initially, Johnson, attempted to broker peace talks between Arabs and Israelis and offered technical and financial rewards as inducements. But they never invested any considerable political capital in achieving an Arab-Israeli peace, nor did they treat the Jewish state as a strategic ally.

For Arabs, however, the American-Israeli special relationship originated with the founding of the Jewish state. Similar backward reasoning and historical revisionism have occurred within the dominant American foreign policy elite; it, too, paints the US-Israeli relationship as having always been "special" and "strategic." For five decades the US public has been fed a steady diet of the strong ties that bind America to Israel, culturally and politically, and have been told that there exists no daylight between the two countries. The special relationship has become an article of faith hardly challenged in influential US policy circles. In this contest over American foreign policy, the Israel-first school has gained the upper hand.

These two narratives reinforce one another and deepen misunderstanding and resentment. For Arabs, America partnered with their ruling tormentors at home and their chief foreign foe—Israel. In war and peace, many Arabs suspect America of conspiring against the Arab cause. The Camp David Accords are a case in point. Although to many it seems that, in this case, President Jimmy Carter did act as a mediator and invested considerable political capital in an effort to broker a peace treaty between Egypt and Israel, there is another point of view. Deploying the power of the presidency, Carter effectively twisted the arms of President Anwar Sadat and Prime Minister Menachim Begin and got them to reach a settlement. Yet Carter's strategy, as a reputable US scholar pointed out, was essentially a continuation of Kissinger's step-by-step diplomacy and American unilateralism; it overlooked the centrality of the Palestine question. Thus, without apparently intending it, Carter and his advisers wound up with a policy stance in the Middle East that rests on the foundations laid down by Henry Kissinger—everything, including a comprehensive peace settlement and recognition of Palestinian nationalism, was subordinated to gaining advantage over the Soviet Union.[87]

The dominant Arab narrative today views Carter's role as an unmitigated disaster. Camp David formalized Egypt's exit from the Arab state system by putting an end to the state of war between the most populous Arab country and the Jewish state. The accords neutralized Egypt militarily and crowned Israel as the dominant regional superpower. After the ouster of President Mubarak in 2011, Egyptians publicly questioned the utility of the accords. Egypt had been the centripedal Arab power, and its exit from the system left its affiliated states off balance, in a state of disequilibrium, and fueled centrifugal tendencies and internal turmoil. Lebanon's civil war of 1975–1990, an internal struggle, would not have occurred, it is argued, if Egypt had retained its role as a balancer in Arab politics; in its absence, Lebanon became a battleground for warring Arab regimes and Cold War rivalries.

ISRAEL'S INVASION OF LEBANON

Similarly, a consensus exists in Arab circles that Israel would not have invaded Lebanon in 1982 if Egypt had not been neutralized by the Camp David peace deal. With the most powerful Arab country gone missing, Israel felt emboldened to invade its neighbor and occupy its capital, Beirut. For Arabs, what was even worse, the United States gave Israel a green light to attack Lebanon and expel the Palestine Liberation Organization (PLO) from the country. Israel's invasion left another deep scar on the Arab imagination and increased Muslim suspicion and resentment of the United States.[88]

In his provocative book, *Beware of Small States*, the veteran British journalist David Hirst notes that Israel's "imperial hubris" coincided with the advent of the Reagan administration, which, as Begin acknowledged, was more favorable to Israel than any previous administration. It included many luminaries of the so-called neoconservative movement, who viewed international relations through the lens of the titanic struggle against "the evil empire"—the Soviet Union. For the neoconservatives, now achieving real political influence for the first time, American and Israeli interests were one and the same. The PLO was an enemy of peace, a Soviet proxy, which, as then–Israeli Defense Minister Ariel Sharon put it, was "converting [Lebanon] into the world centre for terrorism operated by the Soviet Union."[89]

It is no wonder then, says Hirst, that before Begin and Sharon sent their 90,000-man army (six and a half divisions, plus one in reserve, with some 1,300 tanks and 1,500 armored personnel carriers) to Lebanon, they got a green light from US Secretary of State Alexander Haig. As Haig's assistant secretary for the Middle East, Nicholas Veliotes, later put it, he spoke to Sharon in such a way that, "however [he] intended it," a man like Sharon could only see it "as a hunting licence."[90]

Indeed, Israel's "war of choice" in Lebanon killed 20,000 people, overwhelmingly civilians. Israel laid siege to an Arab capital, drove Yasser Arafat and the PLO leadership out of the country, destroyed the guerrilla state-within-the-state, and presided over the Lebanese forces' massacre of Sabra and Shatila, a genocidal slaughter of 3,000 Palestinian civilians in September 1982.[91]

Israel's war in Lebanon created a new Shiite enemy, from whose ranks has arisen a grass-roots resistance movement, Hezbollah, more formidable than the PLO it had largely defeated. Hezbollah was a creation of Israeli hubris. "Had the enemy not taken this step," said Hassan Nasrallah, the leader of Hezbollah, many years later, "I don't know whether something called Hezbollah would have been born. I doubt it."[92] Ehud Barak, the Israeli defense chief, agrees. He told *Newsweek* on July 18, 2006: "When we entered Lebanon . . . there was no Hezbollah. We were accepted with perfumed rice and flowers by the Shia in the south. It was our presence there that created Hezbollah."[93]

The Israeli invasion and occupation of Lebanon fueled terrorism against American interests and citizens and signaled the beginning of a stormy phase in relations between the United States and the region's people and the translation of anti-American sentiment into violent deeds. Shadowy Islamist factions in Lebanon and elsewhere carried out attacks against US targets, and the war and its aftermath radicalized a new generation of Muslims who blamed America for Israel's actions.

Osama bin Laden claimed that Israel's invasion of Lebanon turned him violently against America:

> The events that affected my soul in a direct way started in 1982 when America permitted the Israelis to invade Lebanon and the American Sixth Fleet helped them in that. This bombardment began and many were killed and injured and others were terrorised and displaced.
>
> I couldn't forget those moving scenes, blood and severed limbs, women and children sprawled everywhere. Houses destroyed along with their occupants and high rises demolished over their residents, rockets raining down on our home without mercy. . . .
>
> And the whole world saw and heard but it didn't respond. . . .
>
> And as I looked at those demolished towers in Lebanon, it entered my mind that we should punish the oppressor in kind and that we should destroy towers in America in order that they taste some of what we tasted and so that they be deterred from killing our women and children. . . .[94]

THE REVOLUTION: IRAN TURNS ISLAMIC

Israel's misadventure in Lebanon followed the 1979 Iranian revolution and a subsequent Shiite revival that swept the region. The loss of the shah, a pivotal US ally, and the accession to power of Ayatollah Khomeini—a charismatic, revolutionary cleric and a fierce nationalist who opposed the great powers' preponderant influence in Iran, particularly that of America—shocked the Carter administration and may be seen as its greatest setback.

Since the removal of Mossadegh, the United States had built its relations with Iran almost exclusively through the person of the shah. In 1972, Nixon told the shah that he could purchase any conventional weapons he wanted and anointed him the policeman of the Gulf, though a "twin pillars" policy under Nixon emphasized the roles of Iran and Saudi Arabia as guardians of regional stability. Coming to power in 1969, facing a weak international economic environment, challenges in Vietnam, and the Soviet Union as a formidable rival, Nixon decided to scale back the open-ended commitment that previous presidential doctrines entailed and rely on regional allies to act as bulwarks against Soviet influence and involvement in their respective regions.[95] It is no wonder then that "the fall of the Shah," noted former National Security Adviser Zbigniew Brzezinski, "was disastrous strategically for the United States and politically for Carter himself."[96]

Far from exploring opportunities for reconciliation with the new ruling clergy in Tehran, the United States backed away from the untried Islamists and dealt with the Western-educated moderates who were nominally in charge of the provisional government.[97] In fact, after the shah's departure, US policymakers spearheaded by Brzezinski encouraged the Iranian army to carry out a coup in the event that Khomeini decided to return home from his exile in Paris. As Carter stated: "The threat of a military coup is the best way to prevent Khomeini from sliding to power."[98]

Carter had only contempt for Khomeini's "irrational" statements and actions, as well as for the "street mobs" who whipped anti-American feelings to a fever pitch. "We are dealing with crazy people in Iran," wrote Hamilton Jordan, Carter's chief of staff.[99]

At the heart of America's misreading of the Iranian upheaval, notes Gary Sick, then National Security Council staff member for Iran and chief assistant to Brzezinski, lay a deep cultural clash and blinder—Carter's Western-secular worldview versus Khomeini's Islamic-theocratic vision. According to Sick, although Carter and Khomeini were both deeply religious men, their faiths had almost nothing in common:

> Khomeini was the archetype of the medieval prophet emerging from the desert with a fiery vision of absolute truth. His goal was a harsh and vengeful deity—full of fury, demanding the eye and tooth of retribution for human transgression of divine law. . . . He was a man riven with hate—hatred for the shah, hatred for Carter and America, hatred for those who dared oppose his vision.[100]

In their explanations of the US-Iranian crisis, Sick and other US officials like Warren Christopher, deputy secretary of state, and Harold Saunders, assistant secretary of state for Near East Affairs, stress the unbridgeable chasm between two different cultural systems, as reflected in the very different personalities of Carter and Khomeini. American officials found Khomeini's call for the establishment of an Islamic state to be "absurd," as it ran counter to the entire modern history of the Western secularizing revolutions. The US foreign policy elite were thus unprepared to deal with the unthinkable—the emergence of a cleric-dominated Islamic republic in Iran.[101]

"We are all prisoners of our own cultural assumptions," Sick concludes.[102]

According to Sick, Carter administration officials' profound cultural blinder was "so persistent that it interfered fundamentally with the normal processes of observation and analysis on which all of us instinctively depend."[103] Even after Khomeini set up an Islamic state, the judgment of Carter administration officials was impaired by an intrinsic cultural conviction: the "exotic extremes" of the Khomeini regime were bound to destroy it because of its "wildly irrational" character and its flouting of all the normal rules of accepted political behavior.[104]

For US policymakers, the hostage crisis, which lasted for more than fourteen months, was more than a test of political wills between the United States and Iran; it was a clash of two differing value systems. The crisis riveted and preoccupied the attention of Carter and the US public as few events ever have. As the hostage crisis dragged on, anti-Muslim feelings spread across the American heartland.

Americans felt angry at the humiliation inflicted on their nation and its diplomats by Khomeini, who in an infamous speech in November 1979 proclaimed: "Americans are the Great Satan, the wounded snake."[105] Never before had a Muslim leader used the pulpit to denounce America as the epicenter of evil. In the American imagination, revolutionary Islam came to be associated with terrorism and the promotion of subversive activities.

American and Muslim attitudes toward one another hardened. The Iranian revolution and the subsequent hostage crisis poured fuel on a smoldering fire. Carter administration officials were concerned about the security implications of the Islamic revolution and the potential effect of a spillover into neighboring Gulf states.

For example, in November 1979, the echoes of the Islamic revolution were felt in Saudi Arabia. A group of militant Islamists or jihadis seized the Grand Mosque in Mecca, Islam's holiest shrine, and threatened the authority of the monarchy. That act sent shock waves through the Islamic world and the US foreign policy establishment. Subsequently, American diplomats were attacked and embassies in Pakistan, Kuwait, Libya, and Afghanistan were attacked and burned.

Fearing that an anti-American wave was sweeping the entire Muslim arena, Secretary of State Cyrus Vance ordered the evacuation of all nonessential American personnel from sensitive posts in the region. He and others feared that US interests would be targeted.[106] Brzezinski was also alarmed: "The resurgence of fundamentalist Islam throughout the region, culminating in the fall of the Shah and the convulsions of Khomeini's Iran, created a continuing danger to our interests in a region on which the well-being of the West as a whole very much depends."[107]

Carter and his senior advisers decided to take steps to punish Khomeini and "unseat" him as well. Carter noted bluntly: "I want to punish them as soon as our people have been released; really hit them. They must know they can't fool around with us."[108] Carter said he wanted to "get our people out of Iran and [then] break relations. Fuck 'em."[109]

The challenge facing Carter and his foreign policy team was how to defeat Khomeini and thereby prove the bankruptcy of an Islamist revolution but to do so without driving Iran into the arms of the Soviets or causing its disintegration.[110] In spite of the rupture in US-Iranian relations and the hostage crisis, American decision makers still assigned a higher priority to the global rivalry with the Soviet Union and viewed Khomeini's revolutionary Islam through the lens of the Cold War.

Although alarmed by the convulsions of Khomeini's Iran and the danger to American vital interests in the Gulf, American officials were reminded by the 1979 Soviet invasion of Afghanistan that the struggle against the Communist camp dwarfed their recent feud with the mullahs in Iran.[111] As Carter noted, the Russian invasion "could pose the most serious threat to the peace since the Second World War."[112]

It is no wonder then that the United States actively supported the Afghan mujahideen and turned a blind eye to—without actually encouraging—the recruitment and flow of foreign fighters and jihadis into that war-torn country. For the Carter and Reagan administrations, the struggle against the "evil empire" took precedence over everything else, including the possibility that revolutionary Islamism and jihadism could spill over the Afghan border and destabilize neighboring Muslim countries like Pakistan, Saudi Arabia, Egypt, and Turkey.

Therefore, when Russian troops marched into the Afghan minefield, US officials, who had been caught napping, swiftly seized the opportunity to mobilize

Islamic resistance and tap into the anticommunist sentiments of the now-dominant "fundamentalist clergy" in Iran and elsewhere.[113]

Containing Soviet Communism, said Brzezinski, dictated an avoidance of anything that could split Islamic opposition to the Russians, especially an American-Iranian military confrontation: "It now seemed to me more important to forge an anti-Soviet Islamic coalition," Brzezinski stressed.[114]

As in the 1950s and 1960s, the United States hoped to deploy religion and political Islam as a counterweight to radical, secular nativist forces, and their atheist ally—the Soviet Union. The Carter and Reagan administrations recognized the new possibilities for cooperation with Islamist activists and hoped to harness their religious and ideological fervor against Soviet expansionism. Obsessed with the struggle against godless Communism, they were naturally inclined to flirt with and align their country with the warriors of God in the Muslim world. They paid hardly any attention to the potential militarization of Muslim politics and the rise of a new generation of young militants who could wreck the existing order. Nothing distracted the Americans from the engrossing game that great powers play.[115]

Since the late 1940s, the American foreign policy establishment had gotten socialized into an anticommunist mind-set. For the Carter and Reagan foreign policy teams, Islamist resurgence was a temporary distraction from the Cold War, and Khomeini and his revolutionary disciples were more of a security irritant than a strategic threat to US interests.

American foreign policy still revolved around the containment and rollback of Soviet Communism and remained wedded to supporting conservative religious elements against populist and socialist local movements and leaders. In a way, the war resulting from the Soviet invasion of Afghanistan represented a continuity, not a discontinuity, in post–World War II US Mideast policy.

Carter and Reagan officials viewed the fielding of a mujahideen army in Afghanistan, including foreign veterans, as an extension of their war-in-proxy against the Soviet Union. After September 11, 2001, commentators went to great lengths to ferret out clues to Bin Laden's hostility to and hatred of the United States and the West in general. Several points need to be made clear.

To begin with, the United States, along with its allies, was in the same trenches as the mujahideen battling the Soviet Union. There was little daylight between America and the holy warriors in Afghanistan.

Next, most of the accounts of Bin Laden's Al Qaeda tend to impose the present on the past or read the past through the distorted lens of September 11 and its bloody aftermath—the war on terror. During the Afghan war of the 1980s, Bin Laden was the main point man between the Saudi security services and their Pakistani counterparts; he was an integral part of the American chain of support for the Afghan mujahideen. According to his close confidantes, Bin Laden often met with Pakistani military intelligence officers, particularly General Mahmoud Ahmad, and coordinated tactics and strategy with them. He was in direct contact with the office of Prince Turki al-Faisal, head of Saudi intelligence, and frequently requested and received instructions from him.[116]

Although there was little love lost between the United States and the mujahideen, the Soviet invasion of Afghanistan, which coincided with the Islamist revolution in Shiite Iran, brought the Sunni-based mujahideen and America closer. Sayyid Imam al-Sharif Fadl (alias "Abd al-Qadir Ibn Abd al-Aziz" and also known as "Dr. Fadl"), who worked closely with Bin Laden in Afghanistan, acknowledges that the interests of the jihadist movement and America coincided and converged in Afghanistan and benefited both camps. Both suspended their misgivings against one another and focused on the common goal, battling the greater Communist menace.

However, US officials gave little thought to what would happen after the Afghan struggle ended: What was to be done with tens of thousands of hardened, radicalized, and skilled fighters baptized into a culture of martyrdom and emboldened by victory over a rival superpower. How could these warriors be demobilized and reintegrated into their societies as law-abiding citizens? Could the jihad genie be put back into the bottle? American officials hoped that the mujahideen and allied foreign fighters could be contained and kept under control by local rulers once the Afghan conflict was over.

When the Soviet army retreated in defeat from Afghanistan in 1989 and the Soviet empire collapsed soon afterward, inherent tensions between an emboldened mujahideen movement and the surviving superpower quickly reasserted themselves. The United States lost interest in the war-torn country and distanced itself from its former mujahideen allies. The latter accused the United States of stabbing them in the back once the Soviet Union collapsed. The Americans reportedly hunted down former foreign fighters in Afghanistan worldwide and handed them over to the intelligence and security services of its Middle Eastern allies.[117]

America's tactical partnership with the mujahideen did not survive the Afghan jihad or the end of the Cold War. Yesterday's friends became bitter enemies. America's new foes (Afghan foreign fighters) spearheaded armed resistance to it and brought war to its shores; they were creatures of the Cold War. And through these bitter heirs the East-West struggle reached the American homeland.

THE END OF THE COLD WAR

Although the end of the Cold War ushered in America's moment in the Middle East, that did not bring about a shift in US foreign policy. Far from it. The United States did not rethink its assumptions about the conduct of international relations, including the Middle East. While the superpowers had exercised restraint during the Cold War, the collapse of the Soviet Union left the United States the dominant hegemon in world politics. American foreign policy was no longer constrained by the global balance of power, and the United States acted unilaterally and aggressively to preserve the new unipolar international system.

Once again, the Middle East was a battleground. There the United States sought to oppose any challenge to the status quo and its hegemony. Saddam Hussein's invasion and occupation of Kuwait in 1990 provided the US foreign policy establishment with an opportunity to restructure the regional balance of power and build a new world order in its own image. The administration of George H. W. Bush deployed a half million troops to Saudi Arabia to expel Iraqi soldiers from Kuwait and to consolidate American control of the oil fields by establishing permanent military bases in the Saudi kingdom.

The 1990–1991 Gulf War was another turning point in relations between the United States and the region. The presence of thousands of US troops in the heart of Arabia and the sight of thousands of Iraqi soldiers (many of whom were conscripts) burned alive in their trucks on the killing fields on the Kuwait-Iraq highway while fleeing Kuwait became a symbol of arrogance and injustice etched in the Arab and Muslim imagination. Instead of valuing American intervention in the Gulf as an effort to free a small Arab country occupied by an aggressive neighbor, Arabs, and Muslims in general, viewed it as an extension of the colonial West's effort to dominate the region and humiliate its people.

Hostility toward America skyrocketed across the Muslim world. The rise of Osama bin Laden's Al Qaeda can be traced to the Gulf War and its aftermath, particularly the stationing of American troops in Saudi Arabia, Islam's birthplace and Bin Laden's home. Bin Laden did not express strong anti-US views until after the 1990–1991 Gulf War. When he returned to Saudi Arabia from Afghanistan in 1989, he was welcomed like a hero and was on good terms with the royal family. He continued to wage an anti-Marxist crusade, targeting the socialist government of South Yemen for ouster. Between 1989 and 1990, there was no marked change in his conduct or worldview. Some analysts note that Bin Laden encouraged a boycott of US products because of America's support for Israel.[118] But this example hardly characterizes Bin Laden as a belligerent anti-American voice or disproves the hypothesis that before 1991 he was at war with Communist Russia, not capitalist America.

Bin Laden viewed American actions in the Gulf War and afterward, however, as part of a US conspiracy to establish military bases and dominate Muslim lands and siphon away their oil resources. He also resented Saudi rulers for disregarding his proposal to mobilize a mujahideen force to confront the army of Saddam Hussein and, instead, relying on the Americans to defend their regime. What comes across in Bin Laden's speeches is his strong objection to US sanctions against Iraq and their effect on civilians.

America's stationing of its troops in Saudi Arabia after the Gulf War ended was a key factor in Bin Laden's revolt against his former masters, the royal family and its superpower patron. In his first declaration of jihad in 1996, Bin Laden called on Muslims to wage defensive war against the Americans for their continued military presence in the Kingdom of Saudi Arabia: "[T]he greatest disaster to befall Muslims since the death of the Prophet Mohammed—is the occupation of Saudi Arabia, which is the cornerstone of the Islamic world, place of revelation, source of the Prophetic mission. . . ."[119]

To appeal to a wider Muslim audience, Bin Laden zeroed in on America's military "footprint" in the Persian Gulf, not just in Saudi Arabia: "The presence of the USA crusader military forces on land, sea and air of the states of the Islamic Gulf is the greatest danger threatening the largest oil reserve in the world. The existence of these forces in the area will provoke the people of these countries because they view foreign presence as aggression against their religion, feelings, and prides; that pushes them to take up armed struggle against the invaders occupying the land."[120]

For millions of Arabs and Muslims, the United States has become more of a Middle Eastern actor than a foreign power, for it sustains the autocratic regional order and imposes its dictate by force. US-led sanctions against Iraq—some of the most stringent sanctions in modern history—cost tens of thousands of innocent lives, if not many more, and intensified anti-American sentiments throughout the Muslim world and beyond. The sanctions and their consequences brought home the severity and inhumanity of the US response, as well as the weakness and impotence of the Arab state system. Non-state actors, such as Hezbollah, Hamas, and the nascent Al Qaeda, tried to fill the power vacuum left by the Arab states and spearheaded resistance to the United States.

By the late 1990s the internal repression by the US-backed authoritarian regimes tightened considerably and triggered widespread opposition and resistance, mostly underground. By 2000 there was also disillusionment with the failures of the Arab-Israeli peace process, and the breakout of the second Palestinian intifada became an additional factor in the backdrop of resentment and opposition to American foreign policy just prior to September 11.

On balance, people in the region transferred their opposition and hatred of oppressive local rulers at home to American foreign policy; rightly or wrongly, they held the United States accountable for their predicament. That bitter inheritance provided the context of the September 11, 2001, attacks on New York and Washington, fueled extremist ideologies like Al Qaeda, and allowed Osama bin Laden and his cohort to spread their poisonous message near and far. In other words, the bitter legacy of the Gulf War is key to understanding the rise of Al Qaeda and the September 11 attacks and their aftermath.

The difference from American views of the same event was stark. According to the official dominant narrative, US foreign policy has been successful, on the whole, by ensuring a half century of stability and access to petroleum in the Gulf: although wars occurred during the Cold War, they did not endanger American vital interests. The dominant foreign-policy narrative rejects linkage between the Gulf War legacy and 9/11, noting that US foreign policy has only failed when it strayed from realism, as with Bush's wars in Afghanistan and Iraq.

Bin Laden, along with like-minded associates, tried to exploit and capitalize on widespread anti-American sentiment to build a power base. His litany of grievances against American foreign policy was embedded in the bitter inheritance of the Gulf War. Although the overwhelming majority of Muslims opposed Bin Laden's terrorist tactics, many were favorably disposed toward his anti-US rhetoric and his listing of grievances against the West. After September 11, many Western analysts mistakenly confused Muslims' empathy with Al Qaeda's rhetoric with support for terrorism.

There existed little appreciation in Western foreign policy circles of the heavy burden of history and the depth of resentment of the United States in the region. US officials dismissed all dissonance as either extremism or intrinsic hostility to the American way of life. Instead of deactivating the political minefields with Muslims and restoring trust, President George W. Bush and the neoconservatives decided to engineer social change in the Middle East in their own image. Bush's global war on terror, particularly the invasion and occupation of Iraq, put the United States in a direct confrontation with Muslim societies. The neoconservative program caused a river of tears and blood and destroyed the treasures of a civilization; and it cost America its moral leadership worldwide and further embittered people in the region. For Muslim public opinion, the Bush years represented the lowest point in relations with the United States.

Aware of America's bitter inheritance in the Muslim world, particularly Bush's negative achievement, presidential candidate Barack Obama stressed that he would reach out and open a new chapter in relations with Muslims. In an essay titled "Renewing American Leadership," published in *Foreign Affairs* in 2007, Obama, then a senator, called for the withdrawal of foreign troops from Iraq and political engagement with the people of the region. In the future, he said, a new course had to be set, starting with abandonment of Bush's Freedom Agenda, which provided the underpinnings of the war on terror: "In the Islamic world and beyond, combating the terrorists' prophets of fear will require more than lectures on democracy. We need to deepen our knowledge of the circumstances and beliefs that underpin extremism."[121]

In order to fully confront and understand the challenges facing the United States in the Middle East, Obama advocated a new diplomatic posture:

Throughout the Middle East, we must harness American power to reinvigorate American diplomacy. Tough-minded diplomacy, backed by the whole range of instruments of American power—political, economic, and military—could bring success even when dealing with long-standing adversaries such as Iran and Syria. Our policy of issuing threats and relying on intermediaries to curb Iran's nuclear program, sponsorship of terrorism, and regional aggression is failing.[122]

Barack Obama, the first African American president, was inaugurated on a cold winter day in January 2009. He promised to distance the United States from the neoconservative and increasingly muscular unilateral foreign policy legacy of George W. Bush. He also pledged a new era of multilateral engagement in a globally interconnected world, one that reflected and represented America's values and in which power is exercised in a just and responsible manner.

For Obama, America faced serious challenges in the greater Middle East in terms of pressing military and political commitments, its loss of moral standing and relative power decline, the rise of regional powers, and the need to refurbish America's damaged public image. He began his engagement in the Middle East with his inaugural address, followed by a timely outreach interview with Al-Arabiya (an Arabic satellite television network) the same month, then an important speech in Ankara, Turkey, in April, and finally his historic address in June to Muslims in Cairo, Egypt, the most populous Arab state and the intellectual and cultural capital of the region.

In each of these engagements, Obama borrowed a page from his diverse life story with family members of the Muslim faith. The Obama foreign policy team felt that outreach to Muslims was a strategic asset in the war on terror and in capturing hearts and minds as well. The goal was to dispel perceptions widely held in the Muslim world that the United States was either at war with Islam or was trying to weaken and dominate their countries. Analysts mistook Obama's outreach to Muslims with a desire to remain engaged in the greater Middle East. Far from it. Obama's actions, together with statements by his advisers, clearly show that the real goal was and is to realign America's international relations and shift the focus to Asia and the Pacific Ocean, where the stakes are high. Designed to rebuild US standing and prestige in the world and limit the damage to national interests, Obama's outreach strategy reflected less of a sustained commitment and engagement in the region and more of an effort to cut further losses and perform damage control. The United States no longer possesses the political will and resources to shape developments in that part of the world. The Obama presidency represents a moment of reckoning for American foreign policy, a moment pregnant with risks and opportunities.

The election of Obama, with his soaring rhetoric, background, and charisma, raised high expectations at home and abroad that he might bring about a real change in American domestic politics and foreign policy. A transformational president, many had hoped! From the Arab-Israeli conflict to Iran to America's relations with authoritarian Arab rulers, a sense of cautious optimism spread across the region, an expectation of a new chapter in the tumultuous relationship between the United States and the greater Middle East. There also existed a widespread implicit feeling that a man with the name Barack Hussein Obama—"Blessed Hussein is with us"—would understand the region better than his predecessors, was likely to treat Muslim societies as partners instead of subordinates, and would rectify previous mistakes and misuses of American power.

In the war-torn Middle East, the change in the Oval Office was welcomed with a sigh of relief, though many withheld judgment on the new president and waited to see whether US military ambitions would subside, whether Obama would help establish a Palestinian state, and whether he would quickly withdraw American troops from Muslim lands. Answers to these questions depended on Obama's ability and willingness to challenge the dominant narrative within the foreign policy debate and the American political system as a whole, a costly and risky undertaking for an ambitious, pragmatic president and a politician as well.

Through 2012 in the Obama administration, the pragmatist trumps the idealist, the record shows. The president, who governs by consensus, has shown no desire to alter the dominant foreign policy narrative on the Middle East and to steer the American ship on a dramatically different course. Institutional continuity is the hallmark of the first Obama administration, even though the rhetoric gives the impression of a rupture in the dominant narrative. There is no disconnect between Obama's ideas and thoughts on foreign policy in general and his actual policies. A close reading of his writings, speeches, and interviews reveals a leader who subscribes to the main tenets of the foreign policy tradition, particularly political realism and American leadership. The only way to understand and make sense of the international relations of the Obama administration is to examine his words and policies and the advisers with whom he has surrounded himself.

In particular, Obama's responses to the popular uprisings and revolutions that have swept the Middle East since early 2011 offer a glimpse into the foreign policy mind-set of the president and the relative weight and influence of the United States in the Middle East. There is a window of opportunity for the United States to restore trust with embattled societies in the region and to reverse its declining role there. Obama's response to the popular uprisings is and will continue to be a significant indicator, a barometer, of his Mideast strategy. Will he seize the moment and chart a new beginning with the people of the Middle East and structurally reorient American foreign policy? Will Obama take risks on people's aspirations for open and representative government? Will he fight to obtain the large resources that will allow him to make structural investment in institution building and the economy of transitioning states? More than any rousing words, his actions will speak volumes about the new directions in American foreign policy.

CHAPTER 2

THE BUSH DOCTRINE

Social Engineering

Presidential doctrines have been used to articulate America's foreign policy and worldview since the presidency of James Monroe. The doctrines, though few, have provided strategic guidelines for the nation and established its role in world politics. After World War II, they grew in number. The Cold War rivalry with the Soviet Union gave rise in 1947 to the Truman Doctrine and in 1957 the Eisenhower Doctrine; both sought, in their individual ways, to curtail the spread of Communism and simultaneously to expand America's global reach and influence. A decade later, the Nixon Doctrine proposed a "twin pillars" policy that offered military and economic assistance to Iran and Saudi Arabia as the administration shifted its focus to Southeast Asia and, specifically, to Vietnam. In the post–Cold War era, presidential doctrines encapsulated new strategies to meet the challenges of an unfamiliar, unipolar world. From the onset of the Cold War and after, the greater Middle East has been a strategic theater. There, time and again, American presidents have felt the need to draw a doctrinal line in the sand.

As the Twin Towers fell on September 11, 2001, George W. Bush conceived an ambitious doctrine, a marriage of Wilsonian liberal ideals and a hawkish, muscular neoconservatism, and it guided American strategy during his years in the White House. The Bush Doctrine supplied the ideological foundation for the "global war on terrorism," particularly the worldwide hunt for Al Qaeda through the invasion of Afghanistan and the war in Iraq. At heart the doctrine contained the idea of preventive war, a position vastly at variance with the conduct of American foreign policy in the twentieth century, and proposed the liberal use of force to effect social and political change abroad. Urged to action by an anxious, justice-seeking public and supported by a "Don't Tread on Me" tradition of responding with force in kind, Bush charted a foreign policy course designed to eliminate threats stemming from state or non-state actors that challenged America's preeminent and hegemonic role in the international system. The Bush Doctrine targeted the Middle East, where frustration with and opposition to US foreign policy had been rampant since the onset of the Cold War.

Bush's predecessors had sought to structure a post–Cold War order that paid lip service to multilateralism and collective security while being strongly oriented toward American leadership. Bush relied instead on the unilateral expression of overwhelming force to protect the American homeland and consolidate US dominance worldwide. The Bush Doctrine sought to accomplish something else that was far more ambitious and risky—that is, to engineer social and political change in the Middle East by force. To eliminate transnational terrorists like Osama bin Laden and Ayman al-Zawahiri, the president's neoconservative advisers called for toppling the tyrants who supported them. (The use of this term in the Iraqi context implied that Iraqi President Saddam Hussein backed Al Qaeda and had a hand in the 9/11 attacks on the United States.) They argued against making distinctions between terrorists and their authoritarian protectors. As Bush noted, "[T]he best hope for peace in our world is the expansion of freedom in all the world."[1] Therefore, the full force of the most powerful nation would be deployed to institute a new "balance of power that favors freedom."[2]

According to Bush and his neoconservatives allies, the world had changed in a single morning, and the Bush Doctrine presented certainty and confidence amid the chaos of September 11. However, because it was based on unrealistic ideological assumptions, which were completely opposed by the more regionally focused members of the State Department, Bush's revolutionary response would fail dismally to achieve its grand objectives. In an important misstep, he fell into Al Qaeda's trap, which was not simply to kill thousands of Americans through an assault on monuments to its power, but also to entice the sole superpower into an endless war that would exact a heavy toll in blood and treasure.

Before September 11, hawkish members of the Bush foreign policy team had viewed Iraq, not Al Qaeda, as a preeminent challenge to American national security. A 1998 open letter from the Project for a New American Century, a neoconservative policy initiative, bore the signatures of many future Bush administration officials, including Donald Rumsfeld and Paul Wolfowitz. The letter warned that Saddam presented "a threat in the Middle East more serious than any we have known since the end of the Cold War."[3] Though Al Qaeda had successfully targeted Americans abroad in the late 1990s, and the White House's counterterrorism chief had sent a "Bin Laden memorandum" to Condoleezza Rice, the president's national security adviser, on January 25, 2001, warning of expected attacks, the administration was caught napping when the group's operatives attacked three sites on US soil and killed more Americans in a few hours than the Soviet Union had killed during the entire Cold War.[4] The traumatic events—recorded and replayed over and over again—put the Bush administration under enormous and immediate pressure to respond forcefully and confront heightened threats from transnational non-state actors. His hawkish advisors argued that forceful action could, as a collateral effect, consolidate US hegemony in the greater Middle East.[5] The tragedy of September 11 was thereby transformed from a moment of shock and pain to a moment of political opportunity.[6]

Bush viewed his father's realism and President Bill Clinton's liberalism as ineffective in dealing with the threats of non-state actors; therefore, on a theoretical level he sought out a transformative strategy as a solution, attempting to blend "realist instincts" with traditional American "idealism."[7] At the empirical level, Bush ignored the "regionalist" view of Middle East experts like Flyntt Leverett, who left the White House early on, and instead appointed to advisory posts Cold Warriors like Elliott Abrams, who brought a fierce Israel-first agenda to the interpretation and analysis of Middle East affairs. To defeat a new kind of enemy, undeterred by the threat of prosecution and unrestricted by the practical humanitarian constraints that bind nation-states, the United States would go on the offensive and wage all-out war against real and imagined foes.[8]

But the Bush administration did not speak with one voice, and as it planned for the battles abroad, it also planned for the battles of the Beltway.[9] In response to the 9/11 attacks, traditional realists argued that "police action" against terrorist organizations should be taken while strategic relationships with friendly, dictatorial regimes should be improved. Realists also argued that hostile regimes like Iran and Syria should be engaged in order to keep lines of communication open and prevent dangerous misunderstandings. Neoconservatives countered that America should not compromise on abstract values and "appease terror" by negotiating with despots, because that would reward bad behavior.[10] Like the Cold Warriors, neoconservatives now had an extant "evil empire" to contend with, and the country had to be put on a proper war footing. In their view, the events of September 11 were an affirmation that the United States had not wielded its power with sufficient force after the collapse of the Soviet Union; America had become vulnerable to such attacks because it had failed to make full use of its unrivaled unipolar status.[11] A new transformational strategy calling for the full use of American power was needed, neoconservatives asserted.

Given a choice between the realpolitik of his father's administration and the militant idealism expounded by the neoconservatives, Bush tried to do both. On the one hand, he sought to break with traditional realist theories of international politics, finding their moral agnosticism out of touch with American values, and their slow, patient implementation ill-suited to post-9/11 urgency. On the other hand, at the end of his presidency after encountering the difficult practical reality of implementing his lofty ideals, especially in Iraq, Bush inevitably adopted a realist approach toward the Middle East. The grave inconsistencies inherent in a policy that attempted to combine realism and idealism were not, at the outset of his foreign policy odyssey, clear to him. The devastating impact of a miscalibrated ideological compass would soon become apparent to the whole world.[12]

In attempting to marry realism and idealism, Bush branded his foreign policy. His Freedom Agenda, he believed, would reinforce fragile democracies, support democratic dissidents in countries suffering from oppressive rule, and promote human rights.[13] In Bush's words, the strategy "was idealistic in that freedom is a universal gift from Almighty God. It was realistic because freedom is the most practical way to protect our country in the long run. As I said in my second Inaugural Address, 'America's vital interests and our deepest beliefs are now one.'"[14]

FORGING THE STRATEGY

In the follow-on to September 11, Paul Wolfowitz, the deputy secretary of defense and a staunch Israel-first neoconservative, led the effort to construct the administration's strategic response. The National Security Strategy (NSS) of 2002, one of the core documents that articulates Bush's strategic thinking, includes the central ideas of his doctrine and affirms that the United States, a "benevolent hegemon," must use its unprecedented power to defend and promote liberal democracies worldwide; America could no longer turn a blind eye to oppressive and authoritarian regimes that fostered extremist ideologies, because weak states were now as threatening as strong states. The NSS called for the establishment of a new balance of power in the international system that favored democracy and freedom over oppression and tyranny: In addition to rogue states, transnational non-state terrorist actors that were determined to destroy the American way of life also posed an imminent threat. An unholy alliance between these two enemies might allow them to obtain weapons of mass destruction and, for the first time in history, directly imperil US national security, the NSS warned.[15]

The National Security Strategy proposed that the United States take a new, holistic approach that would confront the rising threats by structurally deploying its diplomatic, economic, and political assets in order to encourage authoritarian regimes to adopt liberal democratic values. Moreover, it would have the United States consider regime change as a last resort if these countries refused to liberalize. The underlying logic of the NSS was that by transforming the structure of Middle Eastern—mostly Muslim—societies, the United States would eradicate the root causes of extremism. Accordingly, the NSS stated that the United States had to aggressively hunt down and destroy non-state terrorist actors by using all the means at its disposal; at all costs, a terrorist actor could not and must not be allowed to acquire weapons of mass destruction.

Finally, the Bush Doctrine called for the United States to confront—diplomatically and militarily—hostile states that develop WMDs and support terrorism. If necessary, the United States had to be prepared to initiate unilateral, preventive military action to halt rising threats and deter new ones. The basic premise informing the National Security Strategy was that the United States was facing a new global war on terror and could not afford to repeat the mistakes of the 1990s, when terrorism was treated as a law enforcement rather than an international security issue.[16]

EXPANDING THE WAR ON TERROR

The first American war of the twenty-first century would have many battlefields; it would be an offensive war having no boundaries. Bush's war on terror would be waged against enemies of the United States, and in keeping with his Freedom Agenda, it would replace tyrants and terrorists with freedom and democracy. Although in the first stage the Bush administration attacked Al Qaeda and the Taliban in Afghanistan, hawkish members of his administration always had their sights fixed on Iraq and other uncooperative regimes. The administration also linked the invasion and occupation of Iraq to the Arab-Israeli conflict; Iraq, Palestine, and democracy formed a core "package," according to Condoleeza Rice.[17] Like the Cold War Warriors before them, the Israel-first neoconservatives lost sight of local context and internal dynamics and displayed a curious inability to view the Middle East through anything but Israeli-made glasses.[18]

Shortly after September 11, they presented Palestine and Iraq as the first substantial targets of the new global war on terror. They argued that America had been hit by the same terrorism that Israelis had been confronting for years. The United States should not distinguish between Osama bin Laden and Yasser Arafat, the Palestinian leader, because they were part of the "same evil."[19] What was needed, Bush stated in a Rose Garden speech on 24 June 2002, was an entirely new, democratically elected leadership in Palestine, not peace talks, to replace the corrupt tyranny of the Arafat regime. Neoconservatives asserted further that terror against Israel and America was organically linked to state sponsors, such as Syria, Iran, and Iraq, and they went a step further by reducing the Palestinian national struggle to terrorism. In short, Israel's fight against Palestinian terrorism came to be viewed as an extension of the US war on terror.

Particularly striking, notes one Israeli scholar, was the ideological convergence between some of the leading neoconservatives, such as Paul Wolfowitz, Douglas Feith, and Richard Perle, and the hardliners in Ariel Sharon's inner circle. From the very beginning of his administration, Bush adopted a hands-off approach to the Israeli-Palestinian conflict, thus automatically favoring Israel. As the Israeli scholar noted: "If Bush Senior was the most even-handed of American Presidents with the possible exception of Jimmy Carter, Bush Junior surprisingly turned out to be the most pro-Israeli President in American history. He is more partial to Israel than Harry S Truman, Lyndon Johnson, Ronald Reagan, and even Bill Clinton, who was once described by an Israeli newspaper as the last Zionist."[20]

For neoconservatives in particular, the longevity of Arafat's and Saddam's brutal dictatorships, among others, signaled a failure of American resolve. They contended that if the United States invaded Iraq and toppled Saddam, after failing to remove him in the 1991 Gulf War, the country could fully redeem itself and would set a precedent in world politics: rogue leaders like Arafat, Assad, and Khamenei who oppressed their people, sought WMDs, and threatened US security would know they would no longer be tolerated.[21] The assumption was that there would be a domino effect, generating momentum and possibly even military action against Iran, Syria, and other enemies of the United States. Once Saddam was brought down, other foes of the United States would fall like ripe fruit.

Paul Wolfowitz and Douglas Feith, both of the Defense Department, with the support of Vice President Dick Cheney and Secretary of Defense Donald Rumsfeld, urged the president to invade Iraq, which, in their opinion, had had a hand in the September 11 attacks.[22] In his memoir *Against All Enemies,* Richard A. Clarke, the White House counterterrorism czar, recalls that during a meeting of the National Security Council at the White House on the morning of September 12, Wolfowitz repeatedly called for striking Iraq instead of Al Qaeda. His focus on Iraq, notes Clarke, surprised Bush, who, at that moment, believed Al Qaeda to be the most pressing threat to the country.

Wolfowitz's desire for a transformative war was shared by Rumsfeld, his boss, who had mentored Cheney.[23] On September 11, moments after he escaped the flaming Pentagon, Rumsfeld reportedly said that the United States had to wipe the slate clean in the Middle East and construct a new order there. He considered Iraq, a pivotal country that lay in the heart of Arabia and that sponsored terrorism, the ideal place to begin the transformation in the region. In contrast to many who regarded Afghanistan as a "war of necessity," he looked at it as a low-value target, a broken country on the edge of the Muslim world that did not offer the United States many opportunities for social reengineering.[24] On the opposite side was Secretary of State Colin Powell, a realist who listened more closely to his regional specialists. He reminded the president that the United States would not have broad international support for an invasion of Iraq; instead, he advocated attacking the Taliban regime for harboring Al Qaeda in Afghanistan.[25] Though Powell was wary of Saddam, he wanted to delay war and engage the United Nations and the international community in order to exhaust all other options.[26] Bush's influential chief of staff, Andrew Card, also stressed that Iraq should not be the first target.[27]

To the disappointment of the proponents of an invasion of Iraq, Bush initially rejected their push for war. The war on terror, he stated, would be not one battle, but many battles, with no fixed ending date. Iraq needed to be tackled, but he believed that all of the diplomatic options had not yet been exhausted and that at that stage going to war would be premature: "I don't want a photo-op war. . . . The American people want a big bang. I have to convince them that this is a war that will be fought with many steps."[28]

However, with the successes of the US invasion of Afghanistan, Bush reconsidered attacking Iraq. Reinforced by the swift collapse of the Taliban, the neoconservatives lobbied hard for an expansion of the war on terror and an invasion of Iraq. They mistakenly thought that American troops could go in with lean numbers and a light footprint, transfer power to Ahmad Chalabi, the exiled head of the Iraqi National Congress, allow democracy to flourish, and leave quickly.

When 9/11 hit, Bush recalled, "we had to take a fresh look at every threat in the world. There were state sponsors of terror. There were sworn enemies of America. There were hostile governments that threatened their neighbors. There were nations that violated international demands. There were dictators who repressed their people. And there were regimes that pursued WMD." For Bush, "Iraq combined all these threats."[29]

At the Pentagon the neoconservatives set up a special intelligence unit under the guidance of Douglas Feith that sought to challenge the intelligence community's considered view that Saddam was not linked to Al Qaeda. Though the director of Central Intelligence, George Tenet, opposed neoconservative speculations and resented the unprecedented interference of unskilled political appointees in the complex process of intelligence analysis, he contributed to the confusion by informing the president that the United States had a "slam dunk" case against Saddam. Tenet subsequently produced a flawed national intelligence estimate for the US Congress and claimed that Saddam was seeking to develop nuclear weapons. Nothing could have been farther from the truth said Joseph Wilson, former US ambassador to Gabon, who had investigated the matter. Wilson argued in a prominent *New York Times* op-ed piece that the evidence that Saddam had been pursuing the development of WMDs was deeply flawed at best. Tenet's pieces of evidence were eventually discredited by the CIA as forgeries; as was proven of the document that claimed Saddam was seeking to obtain uranium from Niger, and other pieces were based on accounts provided by fabricators, like the infamous "Curveball," who admitted that his testimony about mobile weapons labs was a complete fantasy.[30] (For his truth telling, Wilson was targeted for destruction by the neoconservatives in what became known as the Valerie Plame affair.)

Given the stakes and the administration's pursuit of an idealist-realist foreign policy strategy, the containment of Iraq via UN sanctions and no-fly zones no longer sufficed for Bush and the hawkish members of his national security team. Neoconservatives, in particular, loathed the policy of containment as a relic of the Cold War and a testament to the unwillingness of the United States to use its full power unilaterally: In the post-September 11 era in which the United States was threatened by new, elusive transnational non-state actors, the policy of containment was blasphemous. Containment's emphasis on roping Saddam into his own borders created, in the neoconservative worldview, a domestic safe zone within which the Iraqi dictator was free to terrorize his people, develop the technology for WMDs, and train ranks of suicide operatives for battle against Israel and the West. The very survival of Saddam emboldened America's enemies and encouraged them to defy its leadership. Rumsfeld in particular saw the policy as a dismal failure, and Bush considered Iraq's attempts to test the no-fly zone as a "low-grade war against the United States."[31] If the United States had the power to completely remove a threat on its own, it would not have to seek merely to contain small states that endanger its vital interests and the stability of its regional allies.[32]

Specifically, Bush and his neoconservative advisers had four key objections to the containment policy. First, Saddam had become increasingly hostile to the United States after the Gulf War ended in 1991. Acting as if the painful sanctions imposed on Iraq after the war had no real bearing on his regime, Saddam used his position to spread an anti-Israel, anti-US platform. He also viewed the Gulf War as a victory for Iraq, which he called the mother of all battles, and never renounced his claim to Kuwait. Second, the sanctions were becoming increasingly unpopular with the international community because they had devastating humanitarian effects on the Iraqi people. Pressure was mounting on the United Nations to cut the sanctions. Countries like France and Russia were undermining the sanctions regime by concluding illegal trade agreements with the Saddam regime, an embarrassment to the Bush administration, which questioned the resolve of the United Nations and the international community to enforce their own measures. Third, according to a controversial interpretation of the intelligence by Bush neoconservative advisers, Saddam had operational links to Al Qaeda, supported terrorism against Israel, and provided extremist groups shelter in Iraq. Finally, the Bush foreign policy team believed that Saddam was seeking nuclear, chemical, and biological weapons capabilities, some of which he had already used against both Iran and his own population, and would one day use against either the United States or its regional allies. Neocons also asserted that there was a strong possibility that the Iraqi regime would share WMDs with terrorist groups such as Al Qaeda if their use advanced its erratic goals in the region.[33]

Acknowledging the transformational shift that 9/11 had on his thinking about national security, Bush wrote: "I had just witnessed the damage inflicted by nineteen fanatics armed with box cutters. I could only imagine the destruction possible if an enemy dictator passed WMD to terrorists."[34] Similarly, Condoleezza Rice famously remarked that the administration "did not want the smoking gun to be a mushroom cloud."[35] According to administration officials, with threats of terrorist attacks flowing into the Oval Office daily (and disrupting the daily operations of the White House)—many of them involving chemical, biological, or nuclear weapons—the nightmare scenario seemed like a real possibility. Bush said he believed that the stakes were too high to trust Saddam's word against the weight of the evidence—evidence which later turned out to be mistaken—and the consensus of the world.[36] "The lesson of 9/11 was that if the United States waited for a danger to fully materialize, we would have waited too long," wrote Bush. "I reached a decision: We would confront the threat from Iraq, one way or another."[37]

Recognizing that the United States would face a hostile international reception if it did not at least go through the diplomatic motions necessary to confer legitimacy on military action, Bush pursued diplomacy through the United Nations, while planning for war simultaneously. He described his two-pronged approach as "coercive diplomacy."[38] On November 21, 2001, Bush drew Rumsfeld aside and asked him to draft tentative plans to invade Iraq. As American efforts at the United Nations failed to bring tangible progress or change Husein's behavior, war planning drowned out voices of those within the administration who believed that diplomacy was the only feasible path. Failing to gain any significant allies other than Britain, and factoring in the decreasing likelihood that the United Nations would back military action, the Bush national security team increasingly focused on planning for a unilateral, preventive war.[39]

Colin Powell, the lead dissenting voice in the administration, was concerned about the unforeseen consequences of a unilateral war. In a private meeting with Bush on 13 January 2003, he stressed that this was not going to be "a walk in the woods." He impressed on Bush the danger of taking ownership of Iraq because "If you break it, you own it. . . . You are going to be the proud owner of 25 million people. You will own all their hopes, aspirations, and problems. You'll own it all." Disagreeing with the unilateral enthusiasm of the administration, Powell put it bluntly: "If you think it's going to be a matter of picking up the phone and blowing a whistle and it blows—no, you need allies, you need access, you need what-not. You need to understand not just a military timeline but other things that are going to be facing you."[40]

Powell's warnings failed to impress. Bush had already made up his mind to go to war with or without a broad international coalition of support as he convinced himself that diplomacy had not brought significant results and that Iraq had become an increasing threat. Accordingly, Bush informed George Tenet that the country would wait no longer. He told his secretary of state: "Time to put your war uniform on."[41] The moment for diplomacy had come and gone.

THE DEMOCRATIC EXPERIMENT IN THE MIDDLE EAST

One cannot understand Bush's decision to invade Iraq purely in terms of US national security interests; rather, it was his ideological convictions—the Freedom Agenda—that blinded him to the pitfalls in Iraq. Seven years after the US-led invasion and occupation of Iraq, Bush conceded, "I understood why people might disagree on the threat Saddam Hussein posed to the United States. But I didn't see how anyone could deny that liberating Iraq advanced the cause of human rights."[42] In his 2002 State of the Union Address, Bush described Iraq as a member of an "axis of evil." Solemnly, he linked the security threat posed by the Iraqi state with a moral judgment on the Saddam regime.[43] Security interests and ideals had become inseparable in Bush's worldview.

Neoconservatives ignored the great differences between the Axis Powers of World War II—industrialized nations that were bombed into submission with conventional weapons and nuclear bombs—and Saddam's fractured nation and argued that Iraq could be transformed into a vibrant democracy if it experienced the power of freedom, just like postwar Germany and Japan.[44] More importantly, if the United States succeeded in planting the seeds of Jeffersonian democracy in the Iraqi desert, Bush believed it could be a staging ground for the democratic transformation of the Middle East as a whole; he would go down in history as a great statesman and peacemaker.[45]

"The transformation would have an impact beyond Iraq's borders," Bush wrote.

> The Middle East was the center of a global ideological struggle. On one side were decent people who wanted to live in dignity and peace. On the other were extremists who sought to impose their radical views through violence and intimidation. They exploited conditions of hopelessness and repression to recruit and spread their ideology. The best way to protect our countries in the long run was to counter their dark vision with a more compelling alternative. The alternative was freedom. People who choose their leader at the ballot box would be less likely to turn to violence.[46]

One of the most vocal supporters of the war in Iraq was Vice President Dick Cheney, a nationalist-realist who maintained a close relationship and affinity with the neoconservative movement.[47] Bush relied heavily on Cheney, a former defense secretary who had years of foreign policy experience that Bush lacked, to conceptualize, package, and sell the expansion of the global war on terror to the American public.[48] Of all the administration officials, Cheney said he had no doubts that Iraq posed a significant threat to the homeland, and that, after September 11, the United States could not remain ambivalent about it. After the initial success of the invasion of Afghanistan, Cheney became a vocal advocate of war against Iraq.[49]

In a 2002 speech to the Veterans of Foreign Wars, Cheney laid out the rationale and logic behind the urgent need for regime change in Iraq:

When the gravest of threats are eliminated, the freedom-loving peoples of the region will have a chance to promote the values that can bring lasting peace. As for the reaction of the Arab "street," the Middle East expert Professor Fouad Ajami predicts that after liberation, the streets in Basra and Baghdad are "sure to erupt in joy in the same way the throngs in Kabul greeted the Americans." Extremists in the region would have to rethink their strategy of Jihad. Moderates throughout the region would take heart.[50]

Cheney shared with Bush the idea of Iraq's becoming a spark for democratic change and transformation in the Middle East. He considered war in Iraq a contest that would shape the course of history. For the vice president, if the long-term outcome in Iraq was good, short-term consequences did not matter. Believing in the moral responsibilities of leaders, Cheney concurred with historian Victor Davis Hanson, who argued that countries and their leaders are "accomplices to evil through inaction." Therefore, the moral imperative of the United States, as a world leader, was to take action in Iraq, which was much more important than any unforeseen and unintended consequences of war.[51]

The spread of liberal capitalist values through the use of American military force transformed the US security mission into a "crusade" in the Muslim Middle East, as Bush called it in a speech immediately after 9/11. Blinded by seductively simplistic ideological slogans and lacking experience in international affairs, he had embraced the neoconservative agenda; he plunged headfirst into a social engineering project that failed to take into consideration the region's complex social and political realities. His dichotomous, black-and-white worldview, coupled with a natural inertia, kept him from seeking out and engaging counterinformation, and thereby compromised his decision making. On the eve of war, Bush saw only a bright future for the United States and the new Iraq. Not unlike the Cold War era, the globalist blinders dominated the foreign-policy debate after September 11 with devastating repercussions for the region and American foreign policy alike. The only difference is that throughout the Cold War, the globalists, on balance, exercised restraint and avoided actions that risked a military confrontation with the Soviet Union. In contrast, the neocons, having no superpower to oppose them, threw caution to the wind and played empire. They dismissed the local context as inconsequential. They believed that US actions would create new social realities;

which they did by deepening and widening the bitter divide between America and the world of Islam.

FAILURE

The US invasion and occupation of Iraq did not go as Bush and his foreign policy team had so confidently predicted.[52] Initially, with the swift fall of the Saddam regime, neoconservatives boasted that they had won a grand, decisive victory; the Iraqis would welcome their liberators and support America's benevolent mission to reconstruct the Iraqi state and society. The Bush administration savored the opportunity to show the European states that opposed the war, such as France, Germany, and Russia, the success and effectiveness of America's preventive war.

The neoconservative foreign policy elite were abuzz with excitement, convinced that freedom and democracy were on the march in the Muslim world. And as Colin Powell suggested, the Iraq war's greatest proponents viewed it in "Israeli-Palestinian terms": with Iraq swiftly subdued, other long-time holdouts against peace with Israel—such as Iran, Syria, and the radical Palestinian Authority—would soon be transformed into peaceful democratic states that would recognize Israel as a Jewish state.[53] Neocons viewed the 2004 death of Chairman Yasser Arafat, long seen as a roadblock to peace, as an opportunity for the reemergence of a more moderate PLO that would eschew terrorism—the core obstacle to peace. The grand expectation was that, in a few years, the thorns in America's side, namely the Arab-Israeli conflict and Saddam's volatile leadership in Iraq, would be withdrawn once and for all.

Pro-Western Arab authoritarian regimes in Egypt, Saudi Arabia, and elsewhere began to take steps to show the United States that they were committed to "democratic change." Token signs of this change were promised and, in some cases, executed, including the first multiple-candidate presidential election in Egypt's history. President Hosni Mubarak had decided that uncontested elections, in which he won an absolute majority, would no longer be sufficient to shield him from pressure by democracy advocates in Washington.

Soon the realities on the ground in Iraq confounded Bush and the neoconservatives, for they had not drawn up extensive plans for postwar reconstruction. The vice president's office recommended that L. Paul Bremmer, an old friend of Cheney's chief of staff, Scooter Libby, be named the administrator of Iraq. Disregarding the advice of military commanders, Bremmer ran his own show in the war-torn country and failed miserably. Before the US invasion, the Bush administration had not produced a realistic blueprint or roadmap for a postwar Iraq and mistakenly assumed that a transition to democracy would be smooth and swift. Indeed, when Powell recommended to the Defense Department that some of the State Department's best specialists on Iraqi domestic political and social infrastructure assist with postwar planning, Rumsfeld promptly declined the offer because he doubted their support for the war.[54] Acting like a tightly knit clan, the neocons mistrusted realists, particularly those in the State Department and the traditional intelligence community, and monopolized the Iraq portfolio to the detriment of postwar reconstruction and American foreign policy.

Relying on the advice of civilian neocons at the Pentagon who cited the recovery of Germany from its Nazi past as a model, Bremmer dismantled Iraq's leading institutions—the civil service, state ministries, judicial system, and the Ba'ath Party—thereby leaving the bleeding country without the secular national institutions that had provided historical continuity and legitimacy. Bremmer's greatest blunder was to disband the military, making enemies of hundreds of thousands of angry, now unemployed, armed men, many of whom subsequently joined the resistance to the US occupation force.

To fill the vacuum of power with legitimate authority, the United States turned to the country's various established and organized religious sects to construct a new government. The largest sect was the Shi'a, who comprise 60 percent of the population, and who had been suppressed by the Sunni-based Ba'athist regime for decades. Neoconservatives like David Wurmser predicted that the Iraq Shiite community would turn against the Shiite theocracy in Iran, suggesting that a pro-US Iraq would be a counterweight to the Islamic Republic in Tehran. This was wishful thinking, one of the "fairy tales" that the globalists have been spinning about the Middle East since the onset of the Cold War.

Wurmser was dead wrong. In post-Saddam Iraq, Iran's stock and influence rose considerably. As the Shi'a quickly asserted themselves as the rightful leaders and natural owners of the new Iraq, a role to which the United States did not object, Iran positioned itself as a coreligionist ally and strategic partner. The Islamic Republic was one of the main beneficiaries of the toppling of the Sunni-based regime in Baghdad and has built strong ties and links to Iraq's new rulers. It would not be an exaggeration to say that Iran yields more influence in Iraq than the United States, a testament to the unintended consequences that neocons had dismissed as irrelevant. With US troops out of Iraq, Iran's influence is bound to deepen and increase.

Moreover, by empowering political groups and parties that based their legitimacy on religious identity rather than on national identity, the United States indirectly contributed to the strengthening and consolidation of sectarianism in Iraq. The roots of the failure of this religiously focused strategy go back to US policies in the first days and weeks after the invasion. Instead of making Iraq ripe for democracy, the United States helped to establish a sectarian-based political system like that of nearby Lebanon, where religious sect and ethnicity trump other loyalties, including that of the state. In their effort to empower the majority Shi'a and weaken Saddam's Sunni constituency, the postinvasion US strategy allocated power and resources along communal lines. The American occupying authority unwittingly entrenched and institutionalized sectarianism rather than strengthening progressive, liberal forces. The Bush administration was blinded by its desire to turn post-Saddam Iraq into a democratic model for its Arab and Muslim neighbors, and its desire to ensure that all sects were included in the political process led to a destructive intertwining of religious identity with politics at the most basic level.

Intercommunal conflict was further magnified by a lack of domestic security, which was partially a result of the US decision to dissolve the national army and the subsequent reliance on poorly trained and poorly equipped new police and army units. The security impasse and power vacuum allowed Al Qaeda and other insurgent and resistance groups to multiply, feed on, and exacerbate the tensions within the nascent Iraqi state. The result was a tenfold increase in Iraqi civilian casualties and American casualties as well.[55]

Finally, when the abuse of Iraqi prisoners by American soldiers at Abu Ghraib Prison became public, and images of tortured Iraqi prisoners spread across the Arab world, the credibility of the American mission in Iraq was tarnished further. Abu Ghraib exposed the schizophrenia of Bush's realist-idealist foreign policy agenda, which tried—and failed—to blend a purely interest-based ideology with one that was purely moral-based. The sickening hypocrisy of Abu Ghraib was its grotesque result. Strategically, the US-led invasion and occupation of Iraq created more enemies and more terrorists, a shattering blowback; it was a boon to Al Qaeda, elevating a dangerous but inconsequential insurgency into a geostrategic threat and turning them into global actors. From 2003 until 2006, Bin Laden's defiant message fell on receptive ears, particularly among politically radicalized religious activists outraged by what they saw as the occupation of Muslim territories. From London to Algiers and Islamabad to Sana'a, young Muslim men tried to journey to Iraq to fight alongside members of Tanzim al-Qaeda fi Bilad al-Rafi dayn (Al Qaeda in the Land of the Two Rivers), a group that embraces Bin Laden's ideology but maintains its independence.

I have met many young men—Libyans, Tunisians, Syrians, Palestinians, Jordanians, Lebanese, Saudis, Yemenis, Algerians, Moroccans, Pakistanis—who relayed stories of their failed efforts to travel to Iraq and join the "martyrs" brigade. America was waging a "crusade" against Islam and Muslims, and Al Qaeda was a vanguard of Islamic resistance. None of them accepted the premise that the invasion and occupation of Iraq had anything to do with September 11. The consensus was that it was a pretext to occupy Arab territories, siphon their oil resources, and humiliate their people.

As fierce battles raged in Iraq, Bush and his neoconservative advisers faced the reality that their vision was dissolving in Iraq, and that their public support was eroding at home. The terms "civil war," "quagmire," and "Vietnam" filled the airwaves and sapped public support for Bush's Disneyland vision for the Middle East. Hamas's 2006 electoral victory in Palestine and the steady rise of hardliners in Iran further muted America's thirst for democracy in the region.

Perhaps more important than the diminished support of the American public was the war's failure to create the cascade of democracy transformation that had been one of the administration's announced objectives. Authoritarian Arab rulers no longer feared Bush's promotion of democracy as a threat to their rule. An emboldened Iran breathed easier without the twin-pronged threat of a hostile Iraq on one border and a Taliban-led Afghanistan on another. Further discrediting and undermining the Bush Doctrine was Guantánamo Bay. The CIA's "secret prisons" and "extraordinary rendition" were widely seen as symbolic of the duplicity and double standards of US foreign policy. US actions supplied Middle East autocrats with powerful ammunition that they used in a subtle public relations campaign to belittle Bush and the Freedom Agenda and postpone the inevitable opening up of their closed political systems.

Although the Bush administration represented a bit of discontinuity in US foreign policy in terms of rhetoric and action, the end result was the same—a continuity of failure. There existed no natural harmony between Bush's theory and practice, between the Freedom Agenda and its militaristic tendencies. Blinded by ideology, the neocons lost sight of the regional realities and internal social conditions that are supersensitive to Western military and political intervention. The European colonial moment is still very much alive in the memory of Middle Easterners. In this sense, the neocons did more harm than good to the cause of promoting freedom and democracy in the region.

By the midterm congressional elections in 2006, Bush—who lost his legislative majority and asked for the resignation of Secretary of Defense Rumsfeld—had all but given up his grand pipe dream of democracy in the Middle East. The Bush Doctrine had failed utterly, and in 2007 his policies took a sharp, notable turn back toward realism's tested orthodoxy: the president sought to distance himself from the neocons' toxic and catastrophic legacy.

THE LONE BELIEVER

Bush found a belated salvation in the so-called surge, the ramped-up increase of American troops in 2007 in Iraq that provided more security to Baghdad and Al Anbar Province. Hoping that a reassessment of his strategy after the 2006 midterm elections would bring tangible security gains in Iraq and rescue his presidential legacy, Bush replaced the old military leadership with a new one, which included a new secretary of defense, Robert Gates, a realist-pragmatist, and a new military commander, General David Petraeus. The surge, which combined political co-option of the Sunni Arab community, a larger troop presence, intensified counterinsurgency raids, and sheer luck, brought a measurable level of stability to Iraq. A new strongman, Nouri al-Maliki, forged a relatively stable sectarian-dominated alliance and consolidated his authority by controlling the security apparatus. Maliki symbolizes Bush's legacy of a transformed Middle East—more authoritarian and sectarian-based than democratic and inclusive.[56]

With the installation of Maliki as prime minister, the Bush Doctrine was buried in Iraq's shifting sands. Despite the deceptive calm in Iraq today, policymakers in Washington have kept their distance from the monumental hubris of Bush's preventive security doctrine. While the collapse of the Twin Towers may have re-cast security thinking within the US foreign-policy debate, the failures of the neo-cons' war in Iraq brought back a level of realism-pragmatism. The Freedom Agenda was scaled down as the Bush administration faced other large issues at home and abroad: With a great financial crisis impending and its strategic military forces over-extended, the United States could not afford either the financial or the political costs of hyperaggressively promoting democracy.

As the Bush Doctrine lay defunct on the battlefields of Iraq, the neoconserva-tive movement faced a moment of reckoning. Instead of acknowledging that the theory was fatally flawed, neocons turned on Bush and asserted that his specific policies in Iraq had caused the unravelling of the state there. Preventive interven-tion and the expansion of human freedom would have worked, neoconservatives argued, if Bush had implemented the right postwar policies, including meticulous planning for a postinvasion Iraq. While the policymaking establishment distanced itself from neoconservatism, the movement moved on to its next social engineer-ing project—Iran.[57] As the person brought in to control the damage, Robert Gates cryptically suggested that he prevented the administration from "doing some really dumb things," which no doubt included the neoconservative push for military ac-tion against Iran and the vice president's suggestion that Syria be bombed by the United States.[58]

Despite Iraq's continuing fragility, Bush, now in retirement, remains convinced that his doctrine will stand the test of time. He maintains that invading Iraq—as opposed to inaction, which would have been immoral—was the right strategy. "For all the difficulties that followed," Bush writes in his memoirs, "America is safer without a homicidal dictator pursuing WMD and supporting terror at the heart of the Middle East. The region is more hopeful with a young democracy setting an example for others to follow. And the Iraqi people are better off with a government that answers to them instead of torturing and murdering them."[59]

Unfortunately for Bush and the region, his decision to link the Iraq invasion with the cause of universal human freedom ultimately discredited the underlying premise of his Freedom Agenda.[60] The cause of freedom was lost in the sound and fury of war. In fact, the operationalization of the Freedom Agenda caused great levels of human suffering, and it fomented social unrest and turmoil in the greater Middle East. The chaos and bloodshed of Iraq and the haunting images of Abu

Ghraib radically soured Arab and Muslim opinion against US policies in the region. Bush's wars triggered a strategic blowback and further undermined American national security. The administration of Bush and his neocons, more than any other, deepened the mistrust and animosity between America and Muslim peoples and societies.

The Iraq case illuminates the pitfalls of decision making driven by ideology and globalist blinders that neglect the regional view informed by the beliefs and aspirations of millions of people. During the Cold War era, the globalists viewed the Middle East through the East-West struggle; after September 11 the neocons looked at the region through the lens of global terrorism. In both cases, the regionalist perspective was lost in the fog of an ideological struggle. The neocons went much farther than the Cold Warriors by waging a hot war on multiple fronts under the aegis of an ambitious Freedom Agenda that was meant to transform the Middle East. Ideologically and operationally, Bush and his neoconservative allies broke with the consensus in the US foreign-policy debate and sought to unilaterally restructure the international system along new lines. They miscalculated monstrously and weakened the US position in the Middle East irreparably. The reverberations of the neoconservatives' adventure transcend Iraq and the region. They have unwittingly laid the foundation of an inceptive multipolar world, a far-cry denouement from what Cheney, Rumsfeld, Wolfowitz, and their companions had envisioned.

CHAPTER 3

THE OBAMA "ANTIDOCTRINAL DOCTRINE"?

After the eight tumultuous years of the George W. Bush administration left the United States on the verge of financial ruin, Barack Obama sought to chart a new course in American foreign policy. In his presidential campaign he starkly contrasted his policy—envisioning realism, pragmatism, and restraint—with his predecessor's. A new, more enlightened America would return to the world stage.

Obama, in office, seized on the desire of the United States and the world to see America move away from militant unilateralism. They had hoped for a return to the traditional multilateralism in international affairs that had steered the nation calmly and safely through the first decade after the end of the Cold War. The Obama Doctrine was, he said, "not going to be as doctrinaire as the Bush Doctrine, because the world is complicated."[1]

Unlike his predecessor, who refused to "negotiate with evil," Obama styled his foreign policy leadership along the lines of the charismatic John F. Kennedy and the centrist Republican George H. W. Bush. Obama pledged to engage with America's foes politically: "I will meet not just with our friends, but with our enemies, because I remember what Kennedy said, that we should never negotiate out of fear, but we should never fear to negotiate."[2] Now more than ever, he said, diplomacy and engagement were critical to rebuilding "our alliances, repairing our relationships around the world, and actually making us more safe in the long term."[3]

Obama argued that the Bush administration, by relying on hypermilitarism and shunning direct contacts with adversaries, had done considerable damage to

America's vital national interests and moral standing in the world. By punishing rogue states like Iraq, while at the same time displaying questionable adherence to the norms of international law, Bush and his vice president reinforced a widely held belief that the United States believed it stood above international norms and practices.[4]

In his inaugural address President Obama made clear that his approach to international affairs was distinctly different from his predecessor's. His relied not on abstract moral values, or brute military strength, but on real relationships and shared interests with other nations: "Recall that earlier generations faced down fascism and communism not just with missiles and tanks, but with sturdy alliances and enduring convictions. They understood that our power alone cannot protect us, nor does it entitle us to do as we please."[5] Obama understood the country's hunger to restore balance in domestic and international politics. After the experience of Bush's costly war on terror, the shock of a global financial crisis, and the growing problem of the massive and growing federal debt, the America people longed for normalcy, military de-escalation, and above all a refocusing of efforts on the basic issues of the home front rather than on the behavior of dictators in distant lands. Bush's unilateralist, go-it-alone worldview and legacy had harmed the country's standing in the world, and the majority of Americans recognized that the cost of the Bush Doctrine was too high to sustain.

But as early as 2006, then senator Obama had stressed that he was a realist, not an idealist. He favored a strategy in international affairs "based on a realistic assessment of the sobering facts on the ground and our interests in the region." He argued, "This kind of realism has been missing since the very conception of [the Iraq] war, and it is what led me to publicly oppose it in 2002."[6] Common security interests, partnerships, and multilateralism in international relations became the principles of his foreign policy. Obama believed that these principles would allow America to extract itself from the quagmires of September 11 and move its attention toward the challenge of a rising Asia and away from seemingly peripheral nation building in the Muslim world. Obama's stirring speeches sounded idealist and raised high expectations at home and abroad, but his worldview has been consistently to favor the realist approach of American foreign policymakers.[7]

The disconnect between the transformative nature of Obama's rhetoric and his centrist policies disappointed critics on the left and right who looked for ideological clarity and purity. He certainly shifted his approach significantly away from Bush's ideology of proselytizing for democracy and the liberal deployment of force in world politics, but he has not pursued a transformational foreign policy, and he has refrained from challenging the predominant narrative in Washington. In fact, it appears that Washington has changed Obama far more than he has changed Washington.

Disappointment with Obama, and with his failures at the time, led his critics to question whether he had a grand strategy or a coherent foreign policy: while he has excelled at giving rousing speeches and distancing himself from Bush, Obama in office has not offered his own foreign policy vision, a doctrine that will guide America through turbulent international waters. One conservative critic, Niall Ferguson, accused the president of presenting one foreign policy in his speeches and another in his actions.[8] Other conservatives lament that the Obama approach to foreign affairs is fundamentally reactive and defeatist, with the result being that the country is often caught off guard by developments in distant lands. Liberal disappointment, though different from the Republican critique, attacks Obama's unwillingness to put an end to Bush's wars and scars, including closing the military prison at Guantánamo Bay, Cuba, and swiftly bringing the troops home. Historian Robert Kagan declared that the president had overturned half a century of national security doctrines by accepting that America's decline, economically and militarily, was inevitable.[9] Even the sympathetic Zbigniew Brzezinski, Carter's national security adviser, noted the mismatch between the rhetoric and reality of the Obama administration.[10]

White House aides counter by saying that the critiques of left and right overlook that the president is an anti-ideological politician interested only in what works. As television commentator Fareed Zakaria noted, Obama realizes that the post–Cold War world is complex and requires specific approaches tailored to each situation. He understands the idealism-realism debate in Washington, and as former White House chief of staff Rahm Emanuel noted, he comes down on the side of realpolitik.[11] Obama is a "consequentialist," another aide told Ryan Lizza of the *New Yorker*.[12] White House officials dismiss questions about theory or about the elusive quest for an Obama Doctrine as irrelevant because he recognizes differences and nuances among countries and approaches every threat or crisis case by case. They argue that, unlike his predecessor, Obama stresses bureaucratic efficiency, modesty, and humility over ideology and assertion of America's power and affirmation of its exceptionalism. He does not consider his own foreign policy a doctrine and is not averse to revisiting previous decisions that he has made if political conditions and events on the ground change, and if he believes that a shift serves national interests.[13] "When you start applying blanket policies on the complexities of the current world situation, you're going to get yourself into trouble," Obama said in an interview with NBC television news.[14]

Obama's realist foreign policy, though more likely to be cautious and incremental in its evolution than transformational, does not preclude transformational outcomes, such as Arab-Israeli peace. Theoretically, Obama could leverage his policy to match the transformational aspirations of his rhetoric, but only if he were willing to fully engage with the region and work hard at home to achieve such an outcome. This policy-rhetoric divide is not reflective of strategic dissonance, but of an inability to correct the dysfunctional American political system and move his foreign policy from purely preserving the status quo to actually achieving new and tangible outcomes. While Obama has used hard and soft power to undo some of the damage caused by his predecessor, he has not tapped into the presidency's extraordinary power to bring about change and stir hope, nor has he fully engaged the current extraordinary events in the Middle East.

Nowhere else is the gap between Obama's rhetoric and his actions so evident, and nowhere were the hopes so high for him to break away from America's traditional foreign policies. Hampered by entrenched special interests and by Bush's legacy, Obama has been unable to translate his promises into firm policies, thereby opening himself to the charge that his foreign policy approach is muddled and much like his predecessors'. The result? Most of the goodwill that accrued in the Muslim world during the early months of Obama's presidency has been spent, and what remains is a conviction that the United States is weak, financially and militarily, and politically crippled by a dysfunctional political system.

The popular uprisings in the nations fringing the Mediterranean Sea in early 2011 lacked an anti-Western focus. That gave Obama an opportunity to build trust with the peoples of the region and restore America's standing. To understand his response, it is important to supply some context to his stance on the promotion of democracy and nation building in general in the greater Middle East. During Obama's first two years in office, he distanced the United States from earlier democracy-building efforts in the region.[15] President Bush's approach had been to lead with ideology. (For example, Bush tapped his trusted and ideologically aligned staffer Karen Hughes to be his undersecretary of state in public diplomacy, tasked with improving America's image and promoting democracy—with a focus on the Middle East—and gave her nearly $900 million to do so. She resigned two years later to widespread jeers. According to one critic, "Let's say some Muslim leader wanted to improve Americans' image of Islam. It's doubtful that he would send as his emissary a woman in a black chador who had spent no time in the United States, possessed no knowledge of our history or movies or pop music, and spoke no English."[16]) Obama would not preach to other nations. In his historic speech in Cairo in 2009, he said,

> I know there has been controversy about the promotion of democracy in recent years, and much of this controversy is connected to the war in Iraq. . . . So let me be clear: no system of government can or should be imposed upon one nation by any other. That does not lessen my commitment, however, to governments that reflect the will of the people. Each nation gives life to this principle in its own way, grounded in the traditions of its own people. America does not presume to know what is best for everyone, just as we would not presume to pick the outcome of a peaceful election.[17]

NEW ADMINISTRATION, OLD FACES

Change, a dominant theme of Obama's presidential campaign, enveloped Washington in the first six months after his inauguration. Obama, who embodied youth, intellect, and charisma, stood in sharp contrast to George Bush and especially to a largely discredited Dick Cheney. At his inauguration, a youthful and rigorous Obama stood on the Capitol portico, confident and determined to break with the failed policies of the Bush administration. Although the Obama White House appointed progressive academics and public intellectuals from Ivy League schools and think tanks like the Center for American Progress to many administration posts, the new president put the traditional foreign policy elite of the Democratic Party, particularly from the Clinton administration, in charge of America's international relations. These men and women, such as Hillary Clinton, Leon Panetta, and Richard Holbrooke, viewed the Bush administration's years as a misuse of American power, and they longed to return the country to the prosperity and pragmatism of the Clinton era. Notably, Obama asked Robert Gates, Bush's centrist Republican secretary of defense, to stay on and serve in his administration. To further boost his credentials with the military, he appointed retired Marine General James Jones, Bush's former security coordinator for Israeli-Palestinian affairs, as his national security adviser.[18] Though old Washington hands, these individuals approached the Middle East, and specifically the Israeli-Palestinian conflict, with much more of an evenhanded, rather than Israel-first approach.

Obama asked his opponent in the race to be the Democratic nominee for president, Hillary Clinton, to serve as his secretary of state. Although he disagreed with her support of the US invasion of Iraq in 2003, Obama concurred with her steadfast determination to pursue a pragmatic foreign policy that responsibly exercises American power. In addition to championing women's rights, which Obama favored, she was disciplined and loyal, and he knew that she would stand by him. As expected, she filled the State Department with officials who had first worked with her husband, such as Martin Indyk, George Mitchell, and Dennis Ross. In a way, the Obama foreign policy team was almost a carbon copy of that of Bill Clinton, a centrist president well known for his internationalist approach to world affairs.[19]

Obama did include some new and lesser known faces, like Samantha Power, a Harvard professor and human rights scholar, who made headlines on the campaign trail by criticizing Clinton, and close aides like Denis McDonough at the National Security Council. But former Clinton appointees like Dennis Ross (who left the White House in 2011) steadily gained power. After being criticized for staffing his team with Clinton's appointees, Obama retorted: "Understand where the vision for change comes from, first and foremost," he said. "It comes from me. That's my job, to provide a vision in terms of where we are going and to make sure then that my team is implementing [that vision]."[20]

Although Obama had not provided a foreign policy vision so far, he introduced a decision-making process that ended the days of orthodox groupthink that had characterized the Bush administration.[21]

Obama's foreign policy and national security team, while not always in accord, did not manifest the irreconcilable differences that characterized the Bush administration. The president had had greater exposure to other cultures than Bush.

Shaped by life experiences that had carried him from Hawaii to Indonesia, and from Harvard Law School to Chicago's South Side, he could empathize with diverse domestic and international constituencies. Although he exercised good judgment in the Illinois Senate in opposing the Iraq war from its inception and served on the Foreign Relations Committee, he neither had the foreign policy experience of senior colleagues, such as John Kerry, Joseph Biden, or Hillary Clinton, nor showed a serious interest in influencing American foreign policy while serving in the Senate. He reportedly read a few popular international affairs books—Fareed Zakaria's *Post-American World* and Thomas L. Friedman's *The World Is Flat*—but never fully developed his own vision or a grand synthesis for American foreign policy. Domestic affairs, not international affairs, caused him to become an activist on the South Side of Chicago and engaged him as a student at Harvard Law.[22]

Before running for the presidency, Obama entertained a liberal interventionist position after reading Samantha Power's Pulitzer Prize–winning book on genocide, *A Problem from Hell*, and, as noted, he even invited her to become a foreign policy fellow on his Senate staff. But as a presidential candidate, he embraced a realist-centrist approach in foreign policy. Obama summarized his view in Pennsylvania in 2007: "The truth is that my foreign policy is actually a return to the traditional bipartisan realistic policy of George Bush's father, of John F. Kennedy, of, in some ways, Ronald Reagan." While on the campaign trail in New Hampshire in 2007, Obama stressed his disillusionment with liberal interventionism: "Well, look, if that's the criteria by which we are making decisions on the deployment of U.S. forces, then by that argument you would have three hundred thousand troops in the Congo right now, where millions have been slaughtered as a consequence of ethnic strife, which we haven't done." He continued, "We would be deploying unilaterally and occupying the Sudan, which we haven't done." Liberal critics lamented that Obama "seems likely to preside over a restoration of the bipartisan consensus that has governed foreign policy during the Cold War and the 1990s, updated for a post-9/11 world."[23]

Obama is fully aware of the fundamental difference between realism and idealism in the making of American foreign policy and has placed himself squarely on the side of realism, though his rhetoric is loaded with idealist references. As Obama noted in his Nobel acceptance speech in 2009: "Within America, there has long been a tension between those who describe themselves as realists or idealists—a tension that suggests a stark choice between the narrow pursuit of interests or an endless campaign to impose our values around the world." But Obama claimed to have rejected this choice: "No matter how callously defined, neither America's interests—nor the world's—are served by the denial of human aspirations."[24]

THE NATIONAL SECURITY STRATEGY OF 2010

While Obama has never declared a doctrine bearing his name, he has used his National Security Strategy (NSS), as did Bush, to articulate a foreign policy. His National Security Strategy of 2010, reflecting his links and ties with the traditional, centrist currents in American foreign policy, was, in essence, the death knell for the Bush Doctrine. That NSS places a firm emphasis on the endurance of realism in guiding America's international relations.[25]

Thus, Obama follows the path of the George H. W. Bush administration, placing more emphasis on power politics and national interests and less on human rights and the rule of law.[26] In this sense, the 2010 National Security Strategy calls for a rebalancing of America's global commitments, away from the distractions of wars in Iraq and Afghanistan to its more pressing twenty-first-century challenges in Asia and around the Pacific.[27] For the Obama administration, the Middle East was not a foreign policy priority but a region from which the United States should gradually disengage, especially militarily.

In the opening of the 2010 NSS, Obama notes that the strategy

is, therefore, focused on renewing American leadership so that we can more effectively advance our interests in the 21st century. We will do so by building upon the sources of our strength at home, while shaping an international order that can meet the challenges of our time. This strategy recognizes the fundamental connection between our national security, our national competitiveness, resilience, and moral example. And it reaffirms America's commitment to pursue our interests through an international system in which all nations have certain rights and responsibilities. This will allow America to leverage our engagement abroad on behalf of a world in which individuals enjoy more freedom and opportunity, and nations have incentives to act responsibly, while facing consequences when they do not.[28]

Therefore, Obama believes that America is at its strongest when it is economically vibrant and has durable alliances with other states to confront common challenges. He concedes that the United States finds itself in a more dynamic and challenging multipolar international system where it is hard to preserve vital American interests; nevertheless, the country's global leadership—as opposed to its preemptive military capabilities—is the most effective means to ensure progress at home and abroad.[29]

In the NSS, Obama uses key words and phrases to distinguish his administration's break with his predecessor. "I will not preach to other nations" is a catchphrase that Obama uses frequently, implying that national security interests—rather than, for example, the scrutiny of human rights and the rule of law in other countries—are the real drivers of foreign policy.[30]

Eight years after Bush unveiled his ambitious 2002 NSS, Obama adeptly recognized that the world feels cynical about America preaching democracy. In NSS 2010, Obama modestly states that the best way to promote American values is through the power of example: "We promote our values above all by living them at home." Instead of defining what American values are, Obama suggests subtly that American values are ones that all people share and that these common values are what all of humanity seeks.[31] Instead of defining "universal values" as democracy, Obama breaks from Bush's active promotion of democracy and no longer positions the United States at the forefront of value promotion. While he believes deeply in the universality of American values, by leaving them undefined, he can balance them more finely with national interests.

Recognizing that the home front cannot be ignored in any National Security Strategy, Obama aims to bring balance to the government's domestic and foreign policy commitments. Obama devotes a significant section of his NSS to strengthening America at home. The Bush administration, he contends, overcommitted America internationally to the detriment of the home front. He repeatedly emphasizes that, in order to be competitive abroad, the United States must focus more on domestic policies that will ensure that America is strong, vibrant, and innovative, and that the financial and human costs of its foreign commitments do not overburden the government's responsibilities at home. He also underscores the importance of addressing home-grown radicalization and acknowledges that the United States cannot focus only on the threat from the outside. [32]

RESETTING RELATIONSHIPS: THE CAIRO SPEECH

As Obama embarked on his first year as president, he had to contend with the damage the Bush administration had done to the country's relationship with Muslims globally. That relationship had reached a low point largely because neoconservatives, convinced of the backwardness of Muslim societies, had gained the upper hand over Bush's foreign policy team. Instead of drawing distinctions among the many faces of political Islam, they chose a reductionist approach and lumped all Islamists together. They saw mainstream and militant Islamists only through the prism of Al Qaeda. These terrorism experts and ideologues served Bin Laden's agenda by portraying all forms of Islamic fundamentalism, ranging from Hamas to the Muslim Brotherhood, as equivalent to jihadism, a violent, fringe ideology dedicated to random destruction, global subjugation, and the expulsion of Western influences from Muslim societies.[33]

Bush built on this consensus of uninformed pundits and neoconservative ideologues. He called on Americans to be prepared for a global war on terror, the "inescapable calling of our generation."[34] The United States, he proclaimed, had been thrust into a struggle between good and evil. In making these claims, he echoed Reagan's charge, two decades earlier, against the evil empire that was the Soviet Union. He also revived memories of the Truman Doctrine, proclaimed fifty-five years earlier, which envisioned two clashing global systems, one founded on freedom and the other on hatred and persecution.[35] In this way he deployed the images and symbols of the Cold War in the war on terror, a war driven by different motives and impulses.

This war, Bush said, would eradicate the threat of radical Islamist terrorism and target rogue states that sponsored or gave safe harbor to terrorists. With sweeping, ideological language, Bush and Cheney's "crusade" set the stage for the American-led invasion and occupation of Iraq.[36]

The expansion of the war on terror beyond Afghanistan alienated Muslims and provided ideological motivation for Al Qaeda and global jihadis to continue committing acts of violence.[37] They portrayed their worldwide fight against the United States as a defense of the Muslim *ummah* (global community). And so, in the eyes of many Muslims, the war on terror is a war against their religion; to them it seems designed to subjugate their countries and their faith. Few believe the neoconservative's narrative on the promotion of democracy and liberty in the Middle East; instead, they view America's intervention abroad as a pretense to perpetuate its dominance.[38]

Deeply aware of the effects that Bush's wars had had on America's interests and prestige in the Middle East and the Muslim world at large, Obama sought in Cairo to mend the damage and to begin again. Guided by a belief that his pragmatic leadership could transform America's role in the world, Obama spoke out in the graveyard of his predecessor's ambitions and dreams. Successive American presidents had visited the Middle East to speak but not to listen. Obama recognized that this fault, which had debilitated America's image in the region, was not sustainable. Now he sought to use the power of the presidency to cut America's losses and begin bringing the troops home from Iraq and Afghanistan.

Throughout his presidential campaign and his first six months in office, Obama reiterated his commitment to reaching out to Muslims and altering their negative perceptions of the United States. Time and again, the new president stressed that "the United States is not, and will never be, at war with Islam."[39] In his speech to the Turkish parliament in April 2009, Obama asserted that Americans would no longer view Muslims through the prism of terrorism, saying the country would "seek broader engagement based on mutual interest and mutual respect."[40] Obama even offered to engage Iran, which had long been shunned by the Bush administration. His outreach to the Muslim community seemed to pay off: Many Muslims were filled with hope and the expectation that Obama would chart a new course of action, a different foreign policy from that of his predecessors, toward their community.

Hopes were highest in June 2009 when Obama spoke to a tightly packed audience at Cairo University. Symbolically "resetting" US relations with the Muslim world, he eloquently addressed critical challenges and offered a new way to manage them. The speech sent a clear message:

> I've come here to Cairo to seek a new beginning between the United States and Muslims around the world, one based on mutual interest and mutual respect, and one based upon the truth that America and Islam are not exclusive, and need not be in competition. Instead, they overlap, and share common principles—principles of justice and progress; tolerance and the dignity of all human beings.[41]

Obama sought to reframe and shift the debate to the potential for cooperation and partnership between the United States and the Middle East. He raised expectations that concrete action would follow that would speak louder than any words he spoke to his Cairo audience.

In his speech, Obama not only made a break with the Bush administration's confused rhetoric on the Israeli-Palestinian conflict, but also distinguished himself from many earlier presidents by referencing the Quran and speaking frankly about the suffering of the Palestinian people in their pursuit of a homeland:

> For more than 60 years they've endured the pain of dislocation. Many wait in refugee camps in the West Bank, Gaza, and neighboring lands for a life of peace and security that they have never been able to lead. They endure the daily humiliations—large and small—that come with occupation. So let there be no doubt: the situation for the Palestinian people is intolerable. And America will not turn our backs on the legitimate Palestinian aspiration for dignity, opportunity, and a state of their own.[42]

And again, only Obama has so closely and organically linked the establishment of a Palestinian state to America's strategic interests. He described a Palestinian state as one that would be "in Israel's interest, Palestine's interest, America's interest, and the world's interest," adding, "that is why I intend to personally pursue this outcome with all the patience that the task requires."[43] Although Obama did not flesh out the specifics of his vision of a two-state solution, he made it very clear that the United States would not accept the legitimacy of continued Israeli settlements in occupied Palestinian territories. "Israelis must acknowledge that just as Israel's right to exist cannot be denied," he said, "neither can Palestine's."[44] These powerful, symbolic words delivered by the president of the world's most powerful country—and Israel's most significant patron—had the potential to resonate for years to come—if followed by action.

(Action did not follow. Obama's rhetorical stance on the Palestinian-Israeli conflict was politically costly at home. The pro-Israel lobby, which has significant influence in US politics, and which includes a broad spectrum of elements in the Congress, the foreign policy community, and special interest groups, attacked Obama for going too far in pressuring the right-wing government led by Benjamin Netanyahu.[45] Voices in the United States pounced on the president's words and denounced his Cairo speech as "a renunciation of America's strategic alliance with Israel." Writing in the *Washington Post,* Charles Krauthammer said, "the Obama strategy [is] not just dishonorable but self-defeating."[46])

To appeal to Muslims, he wove threads of his own life story into a new narrative:

> I am a Christian, but my father came from a Kenyan family that includes generations of Muslims. As a boy, I spent several years in Indonesia and heard the call of the *azaan* [call to prayer] at the break of dawn and the fall of dusk. As a young man, I worked in Chicago communities where many found dignity and peace in their Muslim faith.[47]

He said he knew Islam from the inside out and that personal and direct knowledge informed his conviction that partnership between America and the world of Islam must be based on what Islam is, not on what it isn't. In a genuine gesture, Obama pledged to educate Americans about the real Islam as opposed to the dominant, negative stereotypes that proliferated after September 11, 2001.[48] To further humanize America in the eyes of Muslims, Obama told of Islam being a part of America's story: the seven million Muslims living in the United States, he argued, have enriched the country.

Obama did not mention the words "terrorism" or "war on terror" during his speech. This was a conscious effort to disconnect the global war on terror from the fight against Al Qaeda, an important symbolic departure from the previous administration. The Obama foreign policy team believed that the Bush administration had gone astray by basing its relationship with Muslims entirely on fighting terrorism and winning an ideological war on the battlefield. Obama now spoke of "extremism" as a common feature of many societies. He addressed the causes that fuel and sustain extremism rather than treating it as an inherent characteristic of Islam.

Although Obama did not apologize for America's mistakes, he was critically reflective. He compared and contrasted the wars in Afghanistan and Iraq and said that the United States invaded Afghanistan out of necessity because Al Qaeda, sheltered by the Taliban, had killed 3,000 people on September 11. But Iraq, he argued, "was a war of choice that provoked strong differences in my country and around the world," implicitly reminding his audience that Obama himself had opposed the Iraq war.[49] He made further concessions in his speech, referring to the abuse and torture that the Bush administration had sanctioned: "I have unequivocally prohibited the use of torture by the United States, and I have ordered the prison at Guantánamo Bay closed by early next year." He pledged to defend his countrymen while being respectful of the sovereignty of nations and the rule of law and working in "partnership" with Muslim communities.[50] His statement on torture, just shy of an apology, showed that he was not afraid to speak truth about critical aspects of US foreign policy to an international audience in a faraway land, knowing full well that his political rivals at home would use his words against him.

Obama's new discourse of engagement, coexistence, and reconciliation between Muslims in the East and Christians in the West was a major point of departure from the Bush administration. Initially, in his first six months in office, Obama shifted the narrative away from confrontation to a heated debate about the possibility of a new American foreign policy. In his Cairo address, Obama brought a new tone of humility by emphasizing engagement and partnership with Arabs and Muslims, thus raising expectations that his administration would bring a new direction to US foreign policy in the Middle East.

THE FINER PRINT: STABILITY OF AMERICAN INTERESTS

While Obama has certainly projected a new posture toward the Middle East through his words, he has, at the same time, recognized that America's core national interests—security of energy resources, stability of traditional allies—must be preserved. Important here are domestic politics that are a massive impediment as he seeks to resolve regional disputes, especially the Israel-Palestine conflict. The challenge Obama faces is to equilibrate past action and future conduct: while he can explicitly acknowledge the past failures of US foreign policies in the region and call for a new beginning, he, like his predecessors, has applied similar conceptual tools and frameworks in order to preserve American primary interests.

When the 2010 National Security Strategy discussed above moves from the overarching goals of reestablished priorities and a stronger homefront to more specifics, the idealistic tone subtly shifts. Obama stresses that relations with regional states will be based on mutual interests and respect, but he views America's interests in the area largely in terms of hard material interests, including "broad cooperation on a wide range of issues with our close friend, Israel, and an unshakable commitment to its security; the achievement of the Palestinian people's legitimate aspirations for statehood, opportunity, and the realization of their extraordinary potential; the unity and security of Iraq and the fostering of its democracy and reintegration into the region; the transformation of Iranian policy away from its pursuit of nuclear weapons, support for terrorism, and threats against its neighbors; non-proliferation; and counterterrorism cooperation, access to energy, and integration of the region into global markets."[51]

Obama's strategy pays lip service to issues beyond hard interests: "It [this engagement] should extend beyond near-term threats by appealing to peoples' aspirations for justice, education, and opportunity and by pursuing a positive and sustainable vision of U.S. partnership with the region. Furthermore, our relationship with our Israeli and Arab friends and partners in the region extends beyond our commitment to its security and includes the continued ties we share in areas such as trade, exchanges, and cooperation on a broad range of issues."[52]

Before the outbreak of the popular uprisings in the Arab world in spring 2011, Obama pursued a subtle and noninterventionist approach toward promoting democracy in the region.[53] He was crystal clear: "America will not impose any system of government on another country, but our long-term security and prosperity depends on our steady support for universal values, which sets us apart from our enemies, adversarial governments, and many potential competitors for influence. We will do so through a variety of means—by speaking out for universal rights, supporting fragile democracies and civil society, and supporting the dignity that comes with development."[54]

Although Obama voiced his preference for open governments because they reflect the will of the people—an implicit criticism of Mubarak and other Arab autocrats—he said hardly a word about the widespread violation and abuse of citizens' rights. Until the fall of Tunisian president Zine El Abidine Ben Ali in early 2011, Obama and his advisers preferred to bolster local autocrats and refrain from saying or doing anything in public that weakened them. During its first two years in office, the Obama administration did not take risks on oppositional forces; its hard-core material interests could not be sacrificed on the altar of human rights and the rule of law. The Obama foreign policy team, led by Secretary of State Clinton, pursued a quiet, gradual, low-risk approach toward the promotion of human rights. Obama officials said they preferred to privately relay their misgivings to regional allies, a contested method that has proved ineffective in nudging Middle Eastern autocrats to respect the human rights of their citizens. In the State Department's annual reports on human rights violations in the Middle East, and in their speeches, officials did mention the need for opening up closed political systems, but the reality is that the foreign policy team did not push Middle Eastern dictators to reform.

Though it is well known that autocratic Arab rulers suppress political dissent and stifle personal initiative and innovation, Obama came into office cautious about appearing overly interventionist or, worse, reckless. Though autocratic regimes' prolonged repressive and failed policies have broken Arab societies and produced chronic poverty, pervasive corruption, and the rise of extremism, the status quo was better than yet another massive failure, reckoned the Obama foreign policy team. Before the onset of the Arab popular uprisings, the consensus in Washington was that there was no credible oppositional alternative to the authoritarian political order in the Middle East. Islamic-based groups and movements like the Muslim Brotherhood, Hamas, and Hezbollah are viewed with suspicion and considered a threat to US national interests. These groups are not believed to be real democrats in the style of one man, one vote, once. Pro-Western local autocratic rulers were seen as the lesser of two evils—pliant, durable, and predictable.[55]

Thus, it is no wonder that the Obama administration quietly embraced pro-American autocratic rulers like Mubarak, whose help the United States needed in tackling thorny strategic challenges, including terrorism, nuclear proliferation, energy security, and the Arab-Israeli conflict. The social uprisings of 2011 that toppled stalwart allies, who were thought to be immune to domestic dissent, came as a surprise. The US foreign policy establishment had not seriously considered or envisioned a post-autocratic Middle East; it had dismissed past warnings about popular dissent as a domestic problem that the region's security services could contain. A "too big to fail" mind-set kept Obama and his predecessors from seriously studying the thin foundations on which the region's leaders had built their rule.[56]

This historic blindness follows from faulty concepts and premises about the structure of Middle Eastern societies and politics. There has been too much attention given to high and elite politics and too little to social movements and public opinion. The "Arab street"—a derisive term so often used by the foreign policy community and even by the best Western journalists—is in great part a myth that has prevented US policymakers from examining or even acknowledging the existence of civil society politics, for it was portrayed as anti-American and violently irrational. The Arab street became synonymous with oppositional, alternative politics. Since the onset of the Cold War, fear of the masses of the Arab street has colored the attitudes of American policymakers. In her farewell speech at the State Department, Anne-Marie Slaughter, Clinton's director of policy planning, diagnosed the problem. She argued that in the twenty-first century America needed to attend to societies as well as states, but such work was undermined by a gender divide at the heart of Obama's foreign policy team:

> Unfortunately, the people who focus on those two worlds here in Washington are still often very different people. The world of states is still the world of high politics, hard power, realpolitik, and, largely, men. The world of societies is still too often the world of low politics, soft power, human rights, democracy, and development, and, largely, women. One of the best parts of my two years here has been the opportunity to work with so many amazing and talented women—truly extraordinary people. But Washington still has a ways to go before their voices are fully heard and respected.[57]

After the outbreak of the social uprisings, Obama White House aides revealed that the president had been aware of discontent in the region and that the status quo was not viable. They say that in August 2010 Obama sent a five-page memo to his top advisers called "Political Reform in the Middle East and North Africa" in which he urged them to challenge the traditional idea that stability in the region always served America's vital interests. Obama reportedly wanted to weigh the risks of both "continued support for increasingly unpopular and repressive regimes" and a "strong push by the United States for reform."[58] According to a White House official, the review requested by Obama concluded that the conventional wisdom in policy circles was wrong, just as the Tunisian protest movement gathered momentum: "All roads led to political reform."[59] Suddenly Obama was confronted with the very fraught idea of the Bush years—the promotion of democracy—that he had studiously kept at a distance. Once again developments internal to the Middle East imposed themselves on Obama's foreign policy agenda and altered his priorities. Presidential administrations are always punctuated with regional crises that force changes in American policy. The Obama presidency proves the rule, not the exception.

Indeed, the 2011 Arab uprisings completely shook the foundations of realism in official Washington circles—in the White House, the State Department, and the intelligence community. The revolts forced Obama to reconsider his engagement with the region. They created an opportunity for him to alter the old premises of American foreign policy, and possibly to chart a new course. Obama equivocated: he wanted to position the United States on the right side of history—with the protesters—and sustain its traditional allies, particularly in the oil-producing Gulf states.

At first he tried to have it both ways, but developments on the ground forced his hand. He had to abandon two loyal friends in Egypt and Tunisia, Mubarak and Ben Ali, who could not be rescued. Throughout the heated debate among his advisers, Obama's overriding concern was effective managment of the crisis and smooth political transition. In fact, Obama and his advisers were mainly concerned about keeping the power structure in place in Egypt and postponing a constitutional and institutional crisis that could not be managed, and whose outcome could not be predicted. Obama and his secretary of state feared that, like other revolutions, the Egyptian revolution could be hijacked by antidemocratic Islamist forces, a fear deeply ingrained in the American imagination since the Iranian revolution of 1979. They sought to have the transition managed by the Egyptian military, an institution with close ties to the US Defense Department. (It has received tens of billions of dollars in American assistance since the late 1970s.) But unlike his secretaries of state and defense, Obama took risks on the protesters and went much further than advisers wished him to do. He even displeased America's close allies—the Israelis and Saudis—who lobbied the administration hard with warnings against humiliating Mubarak. As the Egyptian crisis climaxed in the first week of February, Obama made up his mind and implicitly called for a changing of the guard. Obama got it right. Mubarak was doomed. Obama finally cut America's losses and distanced his administration from a dying ally, a decision driven more by a realist assessment of national interests than an idealist desire to promote democracy. Democracy was an afterthought.

But as chapter 5 will show, by the time Obama made his decision, the outcome had been determined. Whatever Obama said, the Egyptian revolution was unstoppable. The Tunisian and Egyptian revolutions revealed the limits of US power and influence. Power now is in the hands of indigenous social forces that are inward-looking and not weighed down by any complexities about relations with the West, including the United States. The millions of marching protesters who had their sights fixed on bringing about real change at home cared not at all about what Obama and other Western leaders had to say. They wanted to take ownership of their revolutions and be free. In fact, the Obama foreign policy team could hardly keep up with the quickly unfolding internal developments and had to constantly adjust and tune their message. The United States had never been in such an awkward position: it was unable to influence the course of events in the Middle East. That was a testament to an altered regional environment and to hegemonic decline.

The popular uprisings in the Arab nations have starkly exposed the beginning of the end of America's moment there. While Obama officials debated what to say and to do, protesters seized the moment. The awakened peoples and pivotal economic and geostrategic regional states have moved the center of public affairs back to themselves. This power shift has been growing for more than a decade and will most likely expand as political transition in the Middle East progresses in the next ten years.

As far as the Middle East is concerned, the decline in America's influence is most noticeable on the societal and psychological levels. In this regard, Bush's legacy has been poisonous because his actions undermined the moral foundation of the idea of America as a benevolent, rational power that eschews aggression and torture. Far from imparting liberal capitalist ideas to the region's peoples, Bush's actions estranged many from America. Bush got it wrong in the Middle East. At considerable cost to the United States and the region, the neoconservatives' attempt to force democracy on others failed dismally and weakened the United States ideologically, economically, and militarily. The Tahrir generation—Arab protesters—proved to be much more effective in overthrowing their dictators than Bush's armor and Bin Laden's terrorism.

PLAYING REGIONAL CHESS IN 2011

It could be convincingly argued that, regardless of Obama's stance, the Arab revolts, particularly in Tunisia and Egypt, would have reached their climax with more or less similar results. Although Obama's management of the crisis was a factor in persuading the Egyptian military to nudge Mubarak out, it was not decisive. The

United States did not shape developments either in Tunisia or Egypt and found itself watching the Tahrir generation do its work. Even after the ouster of Ben Ali and Mubarak, Obama's celebrated speech at the State Department in May 2011, in which he fully embraced the nascent order in the two countries, reinforced the sense of waning power and influence. Obama's stirring rhetoric about the prospects of political transformation in the Middle East was not matched with firm initiatives. He offered nothing like the Marshall Plan to help repair broken Middle Eastern institutions and economies, only paltry sums in aid, a fact that attests to Obama's foreign policy priorities and America's hard-pressed economy. While the Washington foreign policy establishment celebrated the speech as a watershed, Egyptians and Middle Easterners shrugged it off as too little too late. It neither elicited much public interest nor raised high expectations in the region. America has been brought down to earth in the Middle East, a measure of the changing regional and international balance of forces. Bush, not Obama, is responsible for accelerating the end of America's moment in the region, though Obama has been unable to stop the decline.

The Arab uprisings in 2011 forced Obama to revisit American foreign policy toward the region and recalibrate his stance on the promotion of democracy. Torn between pragmatism and idealism, Obama's position reflects his foreign policy team's diversity of views and uncertainty over the meanings and effects of the uprisings, as well as his awareness of the limits of America's power and relative decline. Despite the new reassessment, Obama did not discard the two dominant prisms—oil and Israel—through which America views the region. The president reserved his harshest criticism for America's evident foes—Syria and Iran—while mildly reproaching its ally Bahrain for its brutal suppression of protesters. Obama the realist did not utter the name of Saudi Arabia in the nearly hour long speech. Not once. Saudi Arabia is too valuable strategically for the administration to lump it together with Egypt and Tunisia. The countries that produce the West's oil got off with a soft slap on the wrist.[60] Again, Obama's foreign policy insists on the recognition of differences and specificities between and among states, and ranks them according to their significance to US national interests. Obviously, as a realist he cares less about consistency and more about successful outcomes and maximizing American bargaining power. Obama's stance toward Saudi Arabia is a case in point.

From the onset of the Arab uprisings, Saudi Arabia, an economic powerhouse and one of America's most loyal friends, opposed Obama's positive approach toward the protesters in Tunisia and Egypt and rebuffed efforts to nudge and influence Gulf countries to institute meaningful reforms and meet the legitimate aspirations of their people.[61] Saudi rulers described the Obama stance as naïve and dangerous. Bahrain became a test of wills between a divided American administration and a determined regional player that wished to assert its power in its neighborhood.

Initially, the Obama foreign policy team cautioned the authoritarian al-Khalifa royal family in Bahrain not to use excessive force against its people. They encouraged King Hamad to undertake serious reforms in order to avert a prolonged political crisis and a bloody armed confrontation. Yet Saudi Arabia feared change in the communal balance of power in neighboring Bahrain, away from the minority-based Sunni royal family and toward the Shiite majority, so it stepped in and put an end to the US effort toward reconciliation there. King Abdullah said that concessions in Bahrain were intolerable. One of his close advisers warned that Bahrain was the "reddest of red lines" for Saudi Arabia.[62] A Saudi GCC-led military force intervened in the small neighboring sheikhdom and allowed local authorities to suppress the protesters. In justifying its military intervention, the Saudis accused Iran of infiltrating the Arab Shiite population and hijacking their political demands for its own geostrategic advantage.[63]

The Obama administration—dependent upon Bahrain with the US Fifth Fleet based there—watched largely in silence as the royal family crushed the uprising.[64] Although initially Obama and his advisers expressed deep concern about the wisdom of the Saudi military intervention, they promptly moved to mend the rift that surfaced during the Egyptian revolution. Downplaying their differences, both camps stressed the common ties that bind them—checking Iranian influence in the Gulf and ensuring security of energy supplies.[65] After meeting with King Abdullah for nearly two hours in April, a meeting that marked the thawing of tensions between the two longtime allies, Defense Secretary Gates acknowledged that he did not even raise the question of Saudi intervention in Bahrain. Reversing himself on the urgent need for the Bahrain royal family to institute structural reforms, Gates urged an "evolutionary" approach. A Defense Department official accompanying Gates stressed, "They're going to have to find their own path," a U-turn for the

Obama administration. Instead, Gates and the Saudi king discussed more pressing issues, such as the sale of more than $60 billion worth of arms to the kingdom, the biggest arms deal signed by the United States, and the modernization of the kingdom's missile defense system. They shared their concerns about Iran and its sinister attempts to exploit the Arab uprisings to its advantage.[66] Gates reportedly told the Saudi king that the Obama administration keenly understands that the kingdom shares vulnerable borders with countries engulfed in revolutionary turmoil—Bahrain, Yemen, and Egypt—and faces internal security risks in its Eastern Province that Iran could exploit. The stability of the kingdom is the keystone of American vital interests in the region, Gates told his Saudis host.[67]

To reinforce the goodwill emerging from Gates's visit, Obama sent Tom Donilon to meet with King Abdullah and to deliver a personal letter to him. In a meeting with the king on April 12, Donilon assured him that, despite previous differences, the United States and Saudi Arabia would work together on securing their common interests. While Donilon discussed the Iranian threat, a constant anxiety for the Kingdom, he did not raise the issue of Bahrain.[68]

Iran, America's regional bogeyman, has colored Obama's view of the democratic revolts in the Arab Middle East. The Obama team has consistently measured every Arab uprising by whether it plays into Iran's hands, an obsession that has led America to squander precious time and resources on a threat that has failed to materialize in any significant way.[69]

Obama's policy of pragmatic realism thus faces a significant test. He could seize this historical moment of self-determination and popular empowerment and craft a strategy that takes into account the change occurring in the region. He could leverage this strategy to reengage the region, and transform America's relations with the Middle East and the Muslim world. But first he has to come up with a clear plan. If he misses this opportunity to recast his engagement with the region, America could find itself with a broken relationship and with its interests completely vulnerable or lost. The region has changed, and Obama's doctrine no longer reflects reality there.[70]

Another case that throws light on Obama's "antidoctrinal doctrine" is Libya. Although some observers linked Obama's decision to support a no-fly zone over Libya to a more muscular Obama Doctrine and a new foreign policy toward the

Middle East, these conclusions are deceptive. Britain and France, concerned for the implications of a failed state nearby and the potential of huge fuel and recon- struction deals, mobilized NATO forces to act. In a last-minute decision, Obama backed NATO's military intervention in Libya because he feared that Qaddafi, un- less deterred, would massacre the rebels in Benghazi. The Defense Department and the generals argued that Libya was not vital to American interests and that the US military was overextended worldwide.

From the beginning of his presidency, Obama has been reluctant to use force except when national security is directly affected, and even in these cases, he has emphasized a drawdown approach instead of an escalation. He is keenly aware that military intervention diminishes America's standing in the Muslim world.[71] When Senator Joseph Lieberman suggested that the intervention in Libya could act as a precedent for armed intervention in Syria, the Obama administration quickly dismissed the linkage and emphasized the differences between the situ- ations in Syria and Libya.[72] Libya is unique because it is largely irrelevant to American national interests, noted Clinton. "We know that a one-size-fits-all ap- proach doesn't make sense in such a diverse region at such a fluid time," Clinton told the US-Islamic World Forum. "Going forward, the United States will be guided by careful consideration of all the circumstances on the ground and by our consistent values and interests," Clinton said.[73]

From a realpolitik perspective, a stronger argument can be made that Ameri- can national security would have been best served by keeping Qaddafi in power, or better served by not supporting a military intervention. The opposition in Libya was seen as a loosely connected force that included elements potentially hostile to the United States. There was also a real danger that a future government in Tripoli would not be as stable as Qaddafi's, not an ally of the United States, and not even democratic.[74] Admiral James Stavridis, supreme allied commander of NATO, even cautioned that there are "flickers" of Al Qaeda within the Libyan opposition.[75]

Obama's decision to back military intervention in Libya was made at a very late hour. The president had been reluctant to go beyond moral condemnations of Libya and targeted financial and arms sanctions against Qaddafi. He hoped that economic sanctions would cause the Qaddafi regime to collapse from within, and he had deep reservations about the effectiveness of a no-fly zone and the cost of expanding America's already substantial military commitments abroad. But after several weeks of indecision and mounting domestic political pressure from the right and the left, Obama decided to act only when the city of Benghazi, the rebels' main stronghold in eastern Libya, was on the verge of falling to Qaddafi forces. The rebels had by that time lost their most substantial gains since the beginning of the uprising in February, and a massacre in Benghazi seemed imminent.[76]

Assessing the impending fall of Benghazi from her hotel room in Paris, Hillary Clinton, who often prefers stability to risky interventions, decided at the last minute to support a military intervention. Leaving the noninterventionist camp led by Robert Gates and joining the camp led by humanitarian interventionist and special adviser Samantha Power, Clinton tipped the balance in the National Security Council and persuaded Obama to support an international coalition that US ambassador to the United Nations Susan Rice was crafting with her French and British counterparts. Agreeing with Power and Rice that gaining support from the Arab League, the Libyan opposition, Qatar, and the United Arab Emirates for joining the coalition would provide the United States with legitimacy and cover for a largely humanitarian-driven mission, Clinton successfully influenced Obama's thinking. The president gave the green light to Susan Rice to support UN Resolution 1973, authorizing a no-fly zone and the use of all necessary force to protect the Libyan people. In the case of Libya, Obama's idealism overrode his more pragmatic inclinations.[77]

Obama conditioned his backing for the no-fly zone on the establishment of an international coalition with an Arab face; the United States would not take a permanent lead role during or after the commencement of hostilities. With a military capability superior to that of France and Britain, initially the United States would spearhead the assault on the Qaddafi regime, but once the no-fly zone could be enforced without the need of direct American participation, the United States would switch to a supporting role. Obama also made it clear that the United States would not deploy ground troops, and that the conflict would be limited in scale and would not serve as a precedent for future engagements.[78]

In justifying military intervention in Libya, Obama made his case in a speech at the National Defense University on 28 March 2011:

Mindful of the risks and costs of military action, we are naturally reluctant to use force
to solve the world's many challenges. But when our interests and values are at stake,
we have a responsibility to act. That's what happened in Libya over the course of these
last six weeks.[79]

No, US vital security interests were not at stake in Libya, but, as citizens of the
world, Obama told his audience:

There will be times, though, when our safety is not directly threatened, but our interests and our values are. Sometimes, the course of history poses challenges that threaten
our common humanity and our common security. . . .These may not be America's
problems alone, but they are important to us . . . and in these circumstances, we know
that the United States, as the world's most powerful nation, will often be called upon
to help.[80]

He stressed the need for collective international action in which the United States
would not bear the whole burden:

In such cases, we should not be afraid to act—but the burden of action should not be
America's alone. As we have in Libya, our task is instead to mobilize the international
community for collective action.[81]

Although Libya is not a core part of the Obama Doctrine or of his new Middle
East strategy, if he eventually defines one, the no-fly zone does again reflect his sit-
on-the-fence idealist-realist tendencies.[82]

Far from showing an invigorated US strategy, the Libyan case sheds further light
on America's retrenchment and its unwillingness to get bogged down in the region's
shifting sands. President Obama rightly feared that an active role would do more
harm than good to the NATO mission, and insisted that an Arab face be put on the
military operation spearheaded mainly by France and Britain. Obama got it right.
Taking ownership of the Libyan operation would have compromised the whole mission, a testament to where the United States finds itself in the Middle East and the
damage that Bush and the neoconservatives inflicted on its standing there. Obama's

low-key approach proved effective by keeping a distance from Libya's raging battles. Ironically, success was achieved by flexing less, not more, military muscle, and allowing nearby powers to lead.

As the previous analysis has shown, Obama's foreign policy defies simplistic ideological and conceptual labeling and characterization. To understand the full story of Obama's Mideast policies and its complexity, we need to examine his position in various cases studies, such as the Arab-Israeli conflict, the war on terror, and pivotal regional states—Turkey, Iran, and Egypt.

CHAPTER 4

ISRAELI-PALESTINIAN PEACE

The Arab-Israeli peace process exposes a wide gap between Obama's words and actions. It also constitutes a striking policy failure. Obama has repeatedly stressed that peace in the region is central to American strategic interests, and he has spent considerable political assets trying to bridge the divide between the Israelis and Palestinians. He has raised expectations at home and in the region about a breakthrough on the peace front because of his soaring rhetoric and his personal story: a progressive young African American president, who as a child lived in a majority-based Muslim Indonesia. Yet he has been unable to convince Israel, America's special ally, to accept a settlement that will serve both its long-term security and the legitimate rights of the Palestinians. He has been the willing victim of a dysfunctional American political system that fetters the hands of presidents.

For many people in the Middle East, including those skeptical of US foreign policy, the contrast between Barack Obama and George W. Bush could not be more striking. Unlike Bush, widely despised for his wars against Muslim countries and his strong bias toward Israel, Obama pledged a new beginning with Muslims and a fair hearing for their legitimate grievances, especially regarding the presence of US forces in their lands and the need for a Palestinian state. Obama attempted to shift the conversation between America and the Muslim world from armed confrontation and hostility to engagement and common interests. As Obama was sworn in, the optimistic belief was that he would transform American foreign policy and bring about peace and reconciliation in the Holy Land. That optimism overlooked the structural-institutional problems in America's political system that, time and again, have undermined the national interest. It also overlooked the reality of Obama as an ambitious politician who wants to be elected to a second presidential term.

The optimism generated by the Obama campaign neglected a fundamental truth: Obama had never claimed that he would pursue a transformational foreign policy. Far from it. As shown previously, throughout his primary and presidential campaigns, Obama aligned himself with the realist tradition in US foreign policy. There was no ambiguity about his stance. Equally important, Obama's statements on the Middle East left some audiences with a mistaken belief that the region topped his list of foreign policy priorities. The reality was much more complex. For the new administration, the Middle East was bleeding the United States militarily and financially and distracting it from a broader and more important set of priorities, including the rise of Asia, the faltering global economy, and nuclear proliferation. While Obama reached out to Muslims and promised to reduce the US military footprint, he and his foreign policy team, mostly realists, did this with the purpose of rebalancing resources and the diplomatic posture in the world away from the region.

Though he wished to gradually refocus policy toward Asia, Obama knew that he could not ignore the Middle East entirely, given America's strong military presence there and dependence on its energy resources. He recognized the centrality of the Arab-Israeli conflict to US relations with Arab countries and the greater Middle East. On his first day in the White House, one early call was to Palestinian president Mahmoud Abbas, to whom he pledged that he would pursue an Israeli-Palestinian peace settlement and help bring about a Palestinian state. Moreover, he linked the establishment of a Palestinian state to national security, thus elevating and prioritizing the drive for Arab-Israeli peace.

The heavy civilian death toll in Gaza that resulted from the Israel invasion in 2008, coupled with an outpouring of public outrage in the Arab and Muslim world, reinforced Obama's conviction about the urgent need to resolve the Arab-Israeli conflict. Since then there has been hardly any progress. The elevation, in March 2009, of Benjamin Netanyahu to prime minister as head of a staunchly right-wing government has stalled any genuine steps toward peace. Netanyahu and his even more inflexible hard-line partners in the Israeli governing coalition do not recognize the need for a peaceful resolution with the Palestinians. They are proponents of the doctrine of permanent conflict. The clearest proof of this uninterest in a peaceful solution is the continued expansion of settlements on the West Bank and the construction of new housing units.[1] Netanyahu resisted pressure for a settlement freeze from the world community, including the Obama administration. He and Obama have had three confrontations on the settlements issue, and Obama backed down each time.

In the context of the grand vision laid out in his Cairo speech, Obama's failure to carry the dispute with Netanyahu to its logical conclusion has bitterly disappointed people in the Arab and Muslim world; it has confirmed a widely held belief that Obama has not wrenched American foreign policy away from the baleful Israel-first school; and it has emboldened Netanyahu and weakened Obama's ability to promote peace. In the view of one commentator, Obama "has been defeated by Netanyahu and by America's pro-Israeli lobbies even more resoundingly than George Bush senior was defeated by Yitzhak Shamir a generation earlier."[2] Abbas, who initially put all his eggs in Obama's basket, reached a similar conclusion. He decided to go to the United Nations to seek recognition of a Palestinian state despite the Obama administration's threats to exercise its veto in the UN Security Council and to end America's financial support for the Palestinian Authority.[3]

As Henry Siegman, the former executive director of the American Jewish Congress, noted: "It is now widely recognized in most Israeli circles—although denied by Israel's government—that the settlements have become so widespread and so deeply implanted in the West Bank as to rule out the possibility of their removal (except for a few isolated and sparsely populated ones) by this or any future Israeli government unless compelled to do so by international intervention, an eventuality until now considered entirely unlikely."[4] Siegman, a powerful voice within the American Jewish community and a critic of Israel's right-wing policies, persuasively argues that for the past four decades Israeli foreign policy has strived to keep the major land prizes in East Jerusalem, the West Bank, and the Golan Heights: "Israeli governments pretend they are seeking a two-state solution, and the United States pretends it believes them."[5]

A former member of the executive committee of the American Israel Public Affairs Committee (AIPAC) for thirty years, Siegman calls on the Obama administration to stand up to the Israel lobby and press for a peace accord now, before it is too late. Obama, says Siegman, must put forward American parameters for bilateral talks based on the 1967 lines with mutually agreed minor territorial swaps and credible security arrangements for both parties. According to Siegman, Obama's proposal must state clearly that rejecting American parameters will have consequences, such as the loss of financial support. Siegman, who has his finger on the pulse of the Jewish community in America, contends that Obama would prevail against the Israel lobby, and a Congress so deeply beholden to that lobby, by speaking truthfully to the American people about the Israeli government's intransigence; by explaining that a genuine and a fair peace settlement would serve the national interest; and by enlisting the support of former presidents Bill Clinton and George W. Bush, whose pro-Israeli credentials are beyond doubt. Siegman notes that American Jewish opinion is more diverse and less hard-line than the self-serving picture presented by AIPAC, which is viewed by Congress and the administration as an authoritative representative of American Jews.[6]

Indeed, polls of young American Jews show that, with the exception of the Orthodox, many of them feel less attached to the land of Israel than do their Baby Boomer parents, who came of age during the era of the 1967 and 1973 wars, when Israel was seen as less of an aggressor and more of a victim. A 2007 poll by Steven Cohen of Hebrew Union College and Ari Kelman of the University of California Davis found that although the majority of American Jews of all ages continue to identify as "pro-Israel," those under thirty-five are less likely to identify as "Zionist." Over 40 percent of American Jews under thirty-five believe that "Israel occupies land belonging to someone else," and over 30 percent report sometimes feeling "ashamed" of Israel's actions.[7] Even young rabbis are, as a cohort, more likely to be critical of Israel than are older rabbis.

According to a poll released by the Hebrew Union College in September 2011—a survey of rabbinical students at New York's Jewish Theological Seminary, the premier institution for training Conservative rabbis—though current students are just as likely as their elders to have studied and lived in Israel and to believe Israel is "very important" to their Judaism, about 70 percent of the young, prospective rabbis report feeling "disturbed" by Israel's treatment of Arab Israelis and Palestinians, compared to only about half of those ordained between 1980 and 1994.[8] The emergence of the successful new pro-Israel and pro-two-state solution lobby group, J-Street, provides further evidence of these trends toward moderation.

In the spring of 2009, Obama pressed for Israel's newly formed coalition government to make concessions for peace and partially freeze settlement construction on the West Bank and in occupied East Jerusalem. Netanyahu's response, which came several months later, was to voice his support for the idea of a Palestinian state, provided that it would be demilitarized and that the Palestinians would recognize Israel as a Jewish state. Despite attempts to pacify the Obama administration, Netanyahu also indicated that settlement construction would and should continue. Rather than standing his ground, Obama praised Netanyahu's token gesture as a positive step toward reaching a peace settlement. Embracing Obama's initial position, Abbas said he would negotiate with the Israelis if they would stop confiscating more Palestinian lands.[9]

At the outset of his presidency, Obama had pressed Israel to meet this legitimate condition for talks and stop the construction of new Jewish settlements. As Oxford historian Avi Shlaim has noted, expecting the Palestinians to negotiate without a complete settlement freeze is like asking two people to negotiate about dividing up a pizza while one of them continues to eat it. Netanyahu, who was well aware of Obama's low popularity in Israel, did not consider it worthwhile to make concessions that could cost him political support at home, and he forthrightly refused to have talks "with conditions." He said he was willing to negotiate but without "pre-set" conditions.[10]

OBAMA TURNS UP THE HEAT ON NETANYAHU

President Obama's second year in office began with no indication that the Arab-Israeli conflict would figure prominently on his foreign policy agenda. By March 2010, his sole achievement had been an agreement for US-mediated indirect talks between Israel and the Palestinian Authority, in addition to an Israeli commitment to "temporarily" suspend settlement building on the West Bank. Undermining the Obama administration's diplomatic initiative, Netanyahu insisted that "substantive" issues concerning security and territorial status should not be part of the talks.[11] However, talks that omitted discussion of an extension of a construction freeze on illegal settlements would be far from meaningful on the core issues of the conflict. As notable Israeli journalist Gideon Levy argued, "What is required is not merely extending the settlement construction freeze—whether or not it includes the occupied areas of Jerusalem—but applying pressure on Israel to begin withdrawing to its own borders."[12] However, without an alternative to these limited talks, Obama reluctantly agreed.

A visit by Vice President Joseph Biden to Israel in March 2010 was expected to symbolize the administration's growing support for the new round of indirect peace talks. Biden was also expected to allay Israeli fears about Iran's nuclear program, though the Obama foreign policy team did not expect a major breakthrough to result from his visit. On the first day of Biden's visit, the Israeli Interior Ministry announced the construction of 1,600 additional housing units in occupied East Jerusalem, a highly contentious and provocative step.[13] Shocked by the announcement, Biden and the White House swiftly condemned the Israeli move as an impediment to peace. In a heated private exchange with Netanyahu, Biden reportedly told him, "This is starting to get dangerous for us," implying that the security of US troops in the greater Middle East was at risk. Obama, who had coordinated Biden's visit, considered Israel's surprise announcement a "slap in the face."[14] The Palestinians immediately issued a statement saying that Israel's announcement jeopardized the American drive for restarting the peace talks.

Although Netanyahu apologized for the announcement's poor timing and claimed that it was accidental, his words did not soothe the White House, especially after he declared that the construction of settlements would continue as planned. Concluding his visit, Biden stressed that Israel's announcement had "inflamed" the Israeli-Palestinian situation. "I, and at the request of President Obama, condemned it immediately and unequivocally," said Biden: "Quite frankly, folks, sometimes only a friend can deliver the hardest truth."[15] The resulting schism between Netanyahu and the Obama administration led George J. Mitchell Jr. to indefinitely postpone his visit to the region. Defense Secretary Robert Gates expressed great frustration at the incident, saying that if he had been Biden he would have cut his Israel visit short as soon as the housing units were approved, adding that he would have told "the prime minister to call Obama when he was serious about negotiations."[16]

In a direct and lengthy phone call with Netanyahu, Secretary of State Hillary Clinton expressed the administration's deep concern and displeasure with Israel's decision to build more Jewish settlements on Palestinian land. According to State

Department spokesperson P. J. Crowley, Clinton made it "clear that the United States considered the announcement to be a deeply negative signal about Israel's approach to the bilateral relationship and counter to the spirit of the vice president's trip." That same day, the Middle East negotiators known as the Quartet (a group established in 2002 as a result of escalating hostilities between Israelis and Palestinians, in an effort to mediate between the two warring camps, and comprised of diplomats from the European Union, the United States, Russia, and the United Nations) released a statement condemning Israel's move as undermining the peace process.[17]

Israel's ambassador to the United States, Michael Oren, reportedly acknowledged that the relationship between the two countries appeared to be at its lowest point since 1975.[18] The Obama administration kept up the heat on Netanyahu with David Axelrod, the president's adviser, firing a powerful salvo. "This [the settlement announcement in East Jerusalem] was an affront, it was an insult but most importantly it undermined this very fragile effort to bring peace to that region."[19] Taken aback by the intensity of the US response, Netanyahu reiterated Israel's commitment to peace.

In an effort to deflect increasing criticism, Netanyahu offered a series of "trust-building measures," including a promise to release Palestinian prisoners, transfer more control of the West Bank to the Palestinian Authority (PA), and slow the speed of construction of Jewish settlements in the Palestinian neighborhoods of East Jerusalem. In return for these "positive" signs, Clinton agreed to send Mitchell back to the region to help restart the peace talks.[20]

In an address in March 2010 to AIPAC, the pro-Israeli lobbying powerhouse, Clinton said that the Jewish state must make "difficult and necessary choices" to achieve peace with its neighbors.[21] She urged Israel to broaden the ten-month suspension of settlement building to include East Jerusalem and stressed that "proximity talks are the first step toward the full negotiations."[22] Speaking to AIPAC after Clinton, Netanyahu (visiting Washington at that time) was defiant: "The Jewish people were building Jerusalem 3,000 years ago and the Jewish people are building Jerusalem today."[23]

While on that visit to Washington at the end of March 2010, Netanyahu met with Obama at the White House to try to find common ground and to improve US-Israeli relations after a tense few weeks.[24] The meeting was brief and futile, with

Obama still angry about the ill-timed announcement of new Israeli settlements during Biden's visit earlier in the month. The president outlined a series of benchmarks that Israel should meet to restart the peace talks. These included the extension of the freeze on settlement construction on the West Bank, cessation of building in East Jerusalem, and the reduction of Israeli military blockades in the occupied Palestinian territories. Obama also sought Netanyahu's approval for the indirect talks to focus on "substantive issues," such as security and final status territorial questions.[25]

Netanyahu refused Obama's demands, arguing that he was constrained by his more hawkish governing allies. Unsatisfied with Netanyahu's intransigence, Obama left Netanyahu in the White House while he had dinner with his family. The typical formalities extended to visiting heads of state were absent, as Netanyahu left without even a photo op with Obama.[26]

Startled by Obama's cold reception, Netanyahu extended his stay for another day and held emergency talks with US officials. But both camps stuck to their guns.[27] Netanyahu refused to concede ground, while Obama made it clear he was in no mood to play the role of a friendly host. In a meeting with congressmen, Netanyahu described Obama's demands as "illogical and unreasonable," claiming that they would only delay the peace talks.[28]

Netanyahu returned to Israel empty-handed, and White House Press Secretary Robert Gibbs characterized the visit as a "dressing down" for the uncompromising Israeli prime minister. The series of meetings between Netanyahu and American leaders had come on the heels of the Democrats' health-care victory, and Netanyahu faced a more confident and reinvigorated Obama.[29]

The Israeli media harshly criticized Netanyahu for his inability to break the deadlock with the United States and depicted the Washington drama as a personal humiliation for the prime minister.[30]

After his return to Israel, Netanyahu met with his senior ministers to discuss Obama's demands. There was no public announcement afterward. Netanyahu's office released a short statement, saying, "The prime minister's position is that there is no change in Israeli policy on Jerusalem."[31] Netanyahu was unyielding. Instead of exerting pressure on Netanyahu to force him to freeze settlement construction and backing his special envoy Mitchell, Obama dropped the matter.[32]

For the Obama foreign policy team, the political costs of standing up to Netanyahu outweighed any long-term strategic advantages. Once again, the American political system imposed constraints on presidential decision making and, once again, prevented progress on the Israeli-Palestinian front. Real or imagined, domestic politics are often used by politicians as a justification for inaction, thus privileging the Israel-first school. The result is to perpetuate the status quo and widen the gulf between the United States and the Arab and Muslim world.

Obama's even-handed approach had evaporated well before Netanyahu's March 2010 visit. Despite his personal connections to the president, George Mitchell's January 2009 appointment as special envoy for Middle East peace was welcomed by independent observers across the ideological spectrum. But as Obama eased into his new position, he slowly allowed the old crowd of Israel-first advisers to take control of the peace process. It is no wonder that Mitchell's attempts to move Israel beyond this point eventually proved futile, especially given Dennis Ross's long history of representing Israel-first special interest groups within and beyond US administrations.

At a joint news conference with Netanyahu in Jerusalem in October 2009, Clinton disingenuously announced that the United States supported the Israeli position. She not only described the prime minister's offer to curb only some settlement construction as "unprecedented" in its "specifics" but also supported Israel's demand that Abbas return to the negotiating table without preconditions. "I want to see both sides as soon as possible begin negotiations," Clinton stressed.[33] What she omitted to mention is that Netanyahu's ten-month freeze was partial. It did not apply to the thousands of housing units on the West Bank that had already been approved, and it did not apply to East Jerusalem.

The response of Abbas was to declare his intention to resign amid charges of "betrayal" by the Americans.[34] Hamas and Fatah, Palestine's rival movements, were provoked into a rare moment of unity in opposition to the call to restart peace talks without freezing settlement construction.[35] Chief Palestinian negotiator Saeb Erekat released a statement venting the frustration of the Palestinian Authority. "If America cannot get Israel to implement a settlement freeze," he asked, "what chance do the Palestinians have of reaching agreement" with Israel on the more complex set of issues involved in final peace-talks?[36]

Egypt and Jordan, Washington's close allies, and the only Arab countries that have peace agreements with Israel, voiced similar concerns. Jordan's King Abdullah

II traveled to Cairo to consult with Mubarak; afterward, the king's official account said that both leaders "insisted on the need for an immediate halt of all Israeli unilateral actions, which undermine the chances of achieving peace, especially the settlement construction."[37]

But it was the secretary-general of the Arab League, Amr Moussa, who best summarized the depth of Arab bitterness and anger over Obama's change of approach on settlements. He told reporters: "[All] of us, including Saudi Arabia, including Egypt, are deeply disappointed . . . with the results, with the fact that Israel can get away with anything without any firm stand that this cannot be done." When asked if Obama's initiative to restart Israeli-Palestinian peace talks had failed, he added the ominous words: "I still wait until we have our meetings and decide what we are going to do. But failure is in the atmosphere all over."[38]

The Obama administration sought to contain the furor generated by Clinton's remarks by reassuring Arab foreign ministers at a meeting in Morocco about Washington's desire to push Netanyahu to do more. Clinton told the assembled ministers that her comments in Jerusalem were meant to encourage Israel to move in the right direction, even if that movement fell short of what the United States wanted. "The Obama administration position on settlements is clear, unequivocal, it has not changed," Clinton stated. "As the president has said on many occasions, the United States does not accept the legitimacy of continued Israeli settlements."[39]

Nevertheless, the Obama administration did not appreciate the contradictions in its own position. The overall effect of the retreat on Jewish settlements eroded America's already fragile authority in the region. The lesson learned by Arabs and Israelis from this episode was that Obama did not possess the political will to push forward his vision of a two-state solution. His capitulation to Israeli and domestic opposition sent the wrong message to both camps and convinced the Palestinian leadership of the futility of relying on the Obama administration to deliver a Palestinian state.

THE SUMMIT OF HOPE?

With the moratorium on settlement building set to expire on 26 September 2010 and with very little progress on the peace front, Obama made a final attempt to reinvigorate the peace talks. He held an unprecedented summit at the White House with Abbas, Netanyahu, Abdullah II of Jordan, and Mubarak of Egypt in early September. These talks marked the first direct negotiations between the Israelis and Palestinians in nearly two years. By persuading Abdullah and Mubarak to attend and by gaining the backing of the Arab League, Obama sought to shift the burden of brokering a peace settlement to the regional states, particularly Egypt, that have a direct stake in the conflict resolution and could provide security guarantees to Israel if and when a Palestinian state is established. The Obama administration hoped that their inclusion would produce better results and shift the blame away from the United States in case of failure.[40]

The White House summit was bound to disappoint. Netanyahu had expressed no desire to partially freeze the construction of new settlements, and most observers dismissed the gathering as a futile exercise in high diplomacy, merely another Annapolis—the scene of Bush's final failed push for peace.[41] The Palestinian Authority was reluctant to engage in direct talks with the Israelis without a freeze on settlement building and a serious discussion of occupied East Jerusalem. President Obama had exerted considerable pressure on Abbas to attend the summit. America's Arab allies, including King Abdullah of Saudi Arabia, threatened to punish the Palestinians by reducing financial aid if Abbas did not make the journey to Washington.[42]

In a rare gesture to build international public support for the peace talks, Mubarak wrote an op-ed piece in the *New York Times,* optimistically titled "A Peace Plan within Our Grasp."[43] Defying the cynics who cursed the darkness, Mubarak heaped praise on Obama: "However, President Obama's determined involvement has revived our hopes for peace and we must seize this opportunity. The broad parameters of a permanent Palestinian-Israeli settlement are already clear: the creation of a Palestinian state in the territories occupied by Israel in 1967 with Jerusalem as a capital for both Israel and Palestine. Previous negotiations have already resolved many of the details on the final status of refugees, borders, Jerusalem and security."[44]

Echoing Mubarak's optimism but deploying soaring rhetoric, Obama stressed in his opening remarks the historic responsibility of those leaders assembled at the White House: "We are but five men, but when we come together, we will not be alone. We will be joined by the generations of those who have gone before." He urged Israel and his Arab partners to "work diligently to fulfil their aspirations." "Too much blood has already been shed, too many hearts have already been broken," he noted, recalling the price of failure. "This moment of opportunity may not return soon again."[45] He and his administration sought to revive the stalled talks by shifting the focus away from technical details surrounding the settlements to the larger final-status issues that would constitute the main aspects of a peace treaty, a task that had eluded his predecessor and Bill Clinton as well.

Obama did not accompany his lofty rhetoric with a threat of consequences if either of the two parties did not accept the delineated terms of a two-state solution. Before the summit, he had met with Netanyahu in hopes of convincing him to extend the moratorium on settlement building and thus allow the talks to focus on the broader thorny questions of borders, refugees, and the status of Jerusalem. Netanyahu refused to compromise and therefore set the summit on a collision course. Obama also tried to persuade Abbas to put aside his demand for a settlement freeze and focus instead on the bigger picture—the final status arrangements. But Abbas in a rebuke to Obama after the latter's optimistic opening marks, forewarned of "the difficulties we're going to face tomorrow" unless Israel froze its settlements.[46]

With the settlements issue stalemated, Netanyahu and Abbas held a day of substantive talks mediated by Clinton at the State Department. Ignoring the expiring moratorium, Clinton impressed on Abbas and Netanyahu that by working out a "framework agreement" on the core issues, the two camps could reach a peace settlement in a year. She stressed that she was fully aware of the difficulties involved in bringing the antagonists together. But, she said, "I fervently believe that the two men sitting on either side of me, that you are the leaders who can make this long-cherished dream a reality."[47]

Although Netanyahu and Abbas concluded the day of talks with a commitment to meet in two weeks for further talks in Sharm el-Sheikh, Egypt, they did not reach any agreement on extending the settlement freeze. Fatah's deputy prime minister and minister of information, Nabil Shaath, warned that "the cloud is still there, the Israelis gave absolutely no hopeful signs that they will continue the moratorium. And in our point of view, that is the litmus test for the Israelis."[48] Echoing a similar warning, chief Palestinian negotiator Saeb Erekat noted that "the key [to peace, i.e., halting settlements] is in their hands."[49]

At the meeting in Sharm el-Sheikh, the settlement cloud hung ominously over the heads of Abbas and Netanyahu and blocked progress.[50] Netanyahu refused to extend the freeze and allowed the deadline on construction to expire without making any concession. Aware of the clock's having run out on the moratorium and at the risk of squandering another opportunity for peace, Obama stepped up diplomatic efforts and pushed the two sides to continue their direct negotiations. He sent Mitchell back to the region to impress on Abbas and Netanyahu the need to remain engaged, while Britain, France, and the United Nations called on Israel to end the building of settlements.

Netanyahu did not oblige. Abbas could no longer negotiate with Netanyahu while the Israelis settled on more Palestinian land, and his position at home became untenable.[51] The Palestinians were fed up with Obama's nonmuscular stance. "We cannot accept the American position that says it is against settlements but does not lead to an end to them," stated Shaath, a top member of the Palestinian negotiating team. "We need a practical position from the United States against settlements. I am surprised that America is unable to stop them."[52]

By failing to exert real pressure on Israel, Obama's summit initiative of September 2010 met a fate similar to the Bush adminstration's efforts at Annapolis in 2007. As a last-ditch effort to revive it in November, Obama naïvely offered Netanyahu a long list of goods and services in return for a mere ninety-day freeze on settlement construction. It included twenty F–35 fighter jets with a $3 billion price tag, a promise to veto any UN resolution that recognized Palestine's independence, and a commitment not to ask again for another construction moratorium on settlements. Netanyahu turned down Obama's generous offer.[53]

That marked the end of the direct talks between the Palestinians and the Israelis—and the end of Obama's peace drive.[54] The high hopes that the president would help broker an Arab-Israeli peace treaty were wrecked on the rocks of harsh domestic political realities in both the United States and Israel. So were Obama's hopes of recalibrating and restructuring America's relations with the greater Middle East. His promises and words were not matched by decisive actions. That reinforced the popular view in the Arab world that the peace process had reached a dead end and that the two-state solution was dead.

THE PALESTINIAN BID

Obama's State Department speech on 18 May 2011 also convinced the Palestinian leadership that the administration wouldn't deliver on its previous pledge to help bring about a Palestinian state. Obama did not lay out new, concrete initiatives to break the standoff between the Israeli and Palestinian camps. Instead, he addressed the Palestinian issue as part of his belated decision to embrace the Arab popular uprisings and position the United States on the right side of history. He walked a fine line between reiterating his strong support for the security of the Jewish state and his preference for a two-state solution. Obama said that the borders between Israel and Palestine "should be based on the 1967 lines with mutually agreed swaps." In a blow to Palestinian aspirations, Obama condemned their strategy of seeking statehood recognition from the UN General Assembly, and he criticized the reconciliation pact between Fatah and Hamas. He also endorsed Israel's demand that a future Palestinian state must be demilitarized.

Three days later, when Netanyahu publicly objected to Obama's mention of the 1967 borders in this speech, Obama qualified his statement. He now told AIPAC that what he meant by "mutually agreed swaps" is "that the parties themselves—Israelis and Palestinians—will negotiate a border that is different than the one that existed on June 4, 1967." In other words, the United States will neither define its preferences for a peace settlement nor insist that the Palestinian state be based on the 1967 lines. It was an important shift in US foreign policy.

It is no wonder then that in reaction Abbas decided to rattle Israel and the United States by pressing for a United Nations declaration of Palestinian statehood. His impassioned UN speech in September 2011 got an exceedingly positive response at home; he was treated like a hero upon his return to Ramallah. Thousands of cheering, flag-waving Palestinians and all the leaders of the PLO and Fatah lined up to shake his hand. Many embraced him. His critics, left and right, gave him credit for keeping his promise when he requested that the Security Council recognize a Palestinian state and for reminding the world of the suffering of the Palestinians and the wrongs and injustices inflicted on them by Israel. Abbas held firm in a speech in Ramallah after his return from the General Assembly session. "We will not accept [negotiations] until legitimacy is the foundation and they cease settlement completely," he told a flag-waving crowd.[55]

Abbas's senior aide, Nabil Shaath, was even more blunt after President Obama met Abbas's speech with a promise to block the Palestinian statehood bid at the Security Council. "Obama prefers to capitulate to pressure from the Zionist lobby but he will lose a lot in the Arab world," said Shaath. "The Palestinians won't pay the price for his reelection. No one could force us to backtrack."[56]

In fact, the Palestinian bid for statehood is both a declaration of independence from American diplomacy and a testament to the failure of that diplomacy (particularly Obama's more recent efforts to broker a peace settlement). After two decades the Palestinians have little to show for it. They know that the United States has a significant role to play in nudging Israel to withdraw from Palestinian territory. But they seem to have given up on America's monopolizing the peace talks. Given the constraints of the American political system, the Palestinian leadership has concluded, Obama does not have the will and resolve to lead.

To avert a showdown at the United Nations, the White House sent two senior diplomats on repeated trips to Jerusalem and Ramallah to try to work out an alternative plan—Dennis B. Ross and David M. Hale, the administration's new special envoy, who had replaced the more prominent Mitchell. Ross and Hale tried to get agreement on a statement, backed by the international community, affirming Obama's proposal in May 2011 to negotiate the establishment of a Palestinian state. That plan called for negotiations based on the pre-1967 lines with mutually agreed land swaps. But Palestinian officials dismissed the American proposal as too little too late and said the vote would go ahead regardless.[57]

"Whoever wrote this thought we are so weak that we cannot even wiggle or that we are stupid," Nabil Shaath, said angrily. "Whatever is to be offered, it is too late."[58]

Abbas also disclosed that Palestinians had been threatened. Another senior official urged Obama to face the moment of "truth." Mohammad Shtayyeh added afterward, "This is a peaceful measure. There is no reason whatsoever for the United States not to support us on this step."[59]

In a last-ditch push to relaunch Israeli-Palestinian peace talks and avert a showdown, envoys from the Middle East negotiators known as the Quartet met in New York at the end of September.[60]

Unfortunately, the Quartet issued a watered-down document that set a timetable, but avoided any of the difficult—and highly contentious—issues that had been the focus of negotiations for months and that continued to divide the Israelis and Palestinians. It did reaffirm "strong support for the vision of Israeli-Palestinian peace" outlined by Obama in his May speech. It included two states separated by the borders that existed in 1967 with "land swaps" to account for Israeli settlements in East Jerusalem and the West Bank. The Quartet called on the Israelis and

Palestinians to meet and agree on an agenda and a schedule for resuming direct negotiations within a month and to come forward with "comprehensive proposals" on territory and security within three months, before the end of 2011. The two sides should make "substantial progress" within six months and complete a final agreement before the end of 2012.[61]

Although Hillary Clinton praised the Quartet's "concrete and detailed proposal," it was not concrete and it did not stand any chance of bringing the two camps together. As soon as the Quartet released its statement, Israel announced that it was going to construct 1,100 new housing units in occupied East Jerusalem. That drew criticism from Clinton. She called Israel's move "counterproductive" to reviving negotiations. She said both sides should avoid provocative actions that undermine trust, particularly in Jerusalem.[62] By now the right-wing government in Israel was used to such vacuous statements from Washington. The Palestinian response was swift. Chief Palestinian negotiator Saeb Erekat said Israel's decision amounts to "1,100 no's to the resumption of peace talks."[63]

Moreover, the American government's feeble stance on the vital question of Jewish settlements would only have a negative effect on Obama's previous attempt to reach out to the Arab and Muslim world and his attempt to contain Iranian influence in the Middle East. The president himself has acknowledged such a link exists between bringing about a Palestinian state and healing the rift with Muslims. In his address in Cairo, Obama stressed the issue: "The United States does not accept the legitimacy of continued Israeli settlements. This construction violates previous agreements and undermines efforts to achieve peace. It is time for these settlements to stop."[64]

Ironically, in September 2010, Obama had opened the door to Palestinian state membership in the United Nations. He stood before the General Assembly and delivered an impassioned call for Palestinian statehood within the next year, to be recognized, he said, in the United Nations—the very same place where one year later Obama tried to foil that same bid. "We should reach for what's best within ourselves," Obama said. "If we do, when we come back here next year, we can have an agreement that will lead to a new member of the United Nations: an independent, sovereign state of Palestine, living in peace with Israel."[65]

In his UN address in September 2011, which earned him the support of prominent pro-Israel Americans, Obama hailed what he called a "time of extraordinary transformation," as he touted the Arab uprisings, yet he opposed the Palestinian right to self-determination. "This has been a remarkable year," Obama said. "Something's happening in our world. The way things have been is not the way they will be. . . . Dictators are on notice." He said the international community will still "have to respond to the calls for change" elsewhere in the region, pointing to the repressive behavior of regimes in Syria and Iran, among others.[66] A day earlier, after meeting with Libya's transnational leader Mustafa Abdel-Jalil at the United Nations, Obama welcomed the new Libya with open arms. "Today the world is saying, in one unmistakable voice, 'We will stand with you as you seize this moment of promise; as you reach for the freedom, the dignity and the opportunity you deserve,'" he said. But Obama was talking about Libyans, not Palestinians, the *New York Times* sarcastically reminded its readers.[67]

At the United Nations, Obama said, Palestinians must make peace with Israel before gaining statehood themselves. Both Israelis and Palestinians have legitimate grievances that should be addressed. "Ultimately, it is Israelis and Palestinians—not us—who must reach agreement on the issues that divide them: on borders and on security; on refugees and Jerusalem," Obama concluded in a gesture designed to reassure Israel and its allies in the United States.[68] Writing in Israel's liberal newspaper *Haaretz*, Akiva Eldar lamented the extent to which Obama has regressed from his previous promising position on the peace process: the UN address should be compared to the speech he gave in Cairo in 2009. At that time he pledged "personally to pursue this outcome with all the patience that the task requires," and said "it is time for all of us to live up to our responsibilities," opined Akiva. "Yesterday he sent the occupied and the occupier, the strong and the weak, to solve the core issues on their own."[69]

Indeed, Netanyahu, whose relationship with Obama has often been tense, expressed appreciation after the speech, calling it a "badge of honor" when both leaders met later in the day. "I am ready to sign on this speech with both hands," said Israel's foreign minister, Avigdor Lieberman, who opposes not only peace with the Palestinians but equal rights for Israeli Arabs. In contrast, the speech was criticized as "a real disappointment" by Hanan Ashrawi, a top Palestinian negotiator. "Listening to [Obama], you would think it was the Palestinians who occupy Israel," she lamented. Ashrawi said Obama had sought to delink the Palestinians from the Arab spring movement's aspirations. "Somehow these principles do not apply, they apply only when Arabs rebel against their own repressive regimes," she said.[70]

While Obama's vision of a two-state solution had crashed on the rock of immovable resistance by Netanyahu, the latter acknowledged that there was "close cooperation" with the United States to make sure the Palestinians' bid was shot down in the UN Security Council, the powerful body that must approve membership.[71] On the one hand, Obama rewarded Netanyahu, who repeatedly rejected his requests to partially freeze the construction of Jewish settlements on Palestinian territories and publicly challenged him by going over his head to Congress. On the other, Obama threatened to punish the Palestinians who followed his script to the letter and hoped to be rewarded with a state of their own. The Israel-first school "endures," said a pro-Israeli US commentator, who reassured his readers that Obama is currently fighting a backroom battle, against great odds, to prevent the United Nations from declaring Palestine a state. The executive director of the American Jewish Committee, David Harris, praised the administration's determined efforts to support Israel and stand up to Palestinian "brinkmanship." Harris slammed as "highly objectionable" and "counterproductive" the public criticism of President Obama by right-wing Zionist groups.[72]

Many in the region view Obama's address in the United Nations and his opposition to the Palestinian bid for statehood as a declaration of an "open war against all Arabs," as one commentator put it. The editor of an influential pan-Arab newspaper, Abd al-Bari Atwan, vehemently criticized Obama's decision to oppose legitimate Palestinian aspirations and to side with Israel against the Palestinian spring. Atwan called on the Arab and Muslim nations to resist American foreign policy, a "hypocritical" and "manipulative" policy that he claims condones "injustice" and "aggression."[73]

Even if Abbas wished to offer more concessions and to return to negotiations without preconditions, he would do so at his own peril, especially given the popularity bump he gained by his UN appearance. The already unpopular Palestinian president would risk a revolt from within his ruling Fatah Party at a time when Hamas was buoyed by the Arab revolutions, especially the ouster of its archenemy—Mubarak. "The Islamist movement had already stressed that Abbas did not represent the Palestinians as a whole and could not sign any peace agreement without a public mandate." Hamas had publicly rejected Abbas's UN plan as a useless stunt aimed at continuing what it called fruitless negotiations with Israel. Mahmoud Zahar, a senior Hamas leader, argued that turning to the United Nations would get Abbas nothing. The *New York Times* reported that another Hamas official, Fawzi Barhoum, "told reporters that Abbas had approached the United Nations unilaterally, without winning support from the group, despite what Mr. Barhoum called the Palestinian president's rhetoric about reconciliation."[74] After Abbas delivered his impassioned plea for the United Nations to give its blessing to the creation of a Palestinian state, Hamas dismissed his "emotional" speech as "empty rhetoric" because Abbas still called for negotiations to resolve the conflict. In contrast, Hamas believes that armed struggle is the most effective means to ending Israel's military occupation.[75]

Despite a concerted campaign by the United States and its European and Arab allies to weaken and marginalize Hamas, the Islamist group has weathered the violent storm and consolidated its authority in Gaza. Hamas will keep Abbas's feet to the fire and prevent him from making concessions that the radical Islamist movement considers tantamount to surrender.

The rise of Hamas came in the Palestinian election of January 2006, when the party won a comfortable parliamentary majority over the previously dominant Fatah. Although the two camps signed a reconciliation pact in May 2011, the relations between them remain tense. Initially, Hamas's election was the result of a miscalculation on the part of the Bush administration, which had pushed for legislative elections to go ahead by January 2006 despite warnings by Fatah that they were not ready. This arguably helped Hamas win control of parliament. However, Bush's miscalculation was to be followed by another, which was more severe. The administration was not willing to allow Hamas—a US-designated terrorist organization—to assume control of the Palestinian territories. Consequently, the administration's policy was to devise a secret plan that would arm Fatah with US weapons, giving it the means to remove the democratically elected Hamas-led government from power.[76]

When events later unfolded, Hamas militarily seized total control of the Gaza Strip and expelled Fatah from the territories. Therefore, Bush's plan backfired in a significant way, and the scale of this failure was magnified as comparisons were made with previous misadventures, including the CIA's 1953 ouster of Prime Minister Mossaddegh in Iran, which set the stage for the 1979 Islamic Revolution, and the aborted 1961 Bay of Pigs invasion, which gave Fidel Castro an excuse to solidify his hold on Cuba.

Officials in the Bush administration believed that Hamas' election and takeover of Gaza was an illegal coup. However, the weight of evidence shows that Fatah, not Hamas, carried out a coup in cahoots with the Bush administration. This putsch highlighted the growing hypocrisy between President Bush's call for democracy in the Arab arena and his policies on the ground.

Therefore, as Fatah and Hamas forge ahead in their efforts to reconstitute a single national leadership, create an interim government, and hold legislative elections, memories of the bloody 2007 civil war remain fresh in the minds of ordinary Palestinians. That war was sparked when the Bush administration, after failing to anticipate Hamas' victory over Fatah in the 2006 Palestinian election, financed an armed force under Fatah strongman Muhammad Dahlan to defeat Hamas. The resulting bloodshed in Gaza left the Islamist movement stronger than ever, and Abbas and his Palestinian Authority have been severely weakened ever since.[77] Abbas' softened approach to the settlement issue and the scandalous revelations in the leaked negotiation documents obtained by Al Jazeera—known as the Palestine Papers—collectively demonstrate the huge challenge that he and Fatah face in the upcoming elections. Abbas has lost significant authority and credibility in the eyes of many Palestinians, because he has not delivered tangible progress on the peace front, and his regime is seen as corrupt. His close alliance with the United States has hurt him and strengthened Hamas' narrative about the futility of making further concessions to the Israelis. The wide-ranging concessions to the Israelis described in the Palestine Papers shocked Palestinian public opinion and supplied Hamas with ammunition that it readily used against Abbas and the Palestinian Authority.

The April 2011 reconciliation agreement between Hamas and Fatah, along with continuing talks, reflects four processes at work: (1) a weakened Palestinian Authority whose leader gambled on President Obama to help deliver a Palestinian state; (2) the failure of American diplomacy to deploy its political and material assets to broker a peace settlement; (3) the revolution in Egypt, which has brought an important shift in the country's foreign policy and approach toward Palestine; and (4) a besieged and exhausted Hamas whose leaders have made a conscious decision to moderate their behavior and to escape isolation. Obviously, Abbas and his aides have concluded that the Israeli leadership is not interested in a genuine settlement and that Netanyahu is committed to the idea of a greater Israel to encompass most of the West Bank—or Judea and Samaria, the biblical names that many Israelis use to refer to the land. Netanyahu, in his September 2011 speech to the United Nations, repeatedly referred to this historic claim. "Jacob and his 12 sons roamed these same hills of Judea and Samaria 4,000 years ago, and there's been a continuous Jewish presence in the land ever since," he told the Assembly.[78]

In his UN address in September 2011, Obama went farther and lectured the Palestinians by saying there are no "shortcuts" to peace and that they must return to negotiations with Netanyahu, even though the latter rejected Obama's pleas to freeze the construction of Jewish settlements in occupied Palestinian territories and past concessions by the Palestinians.[79] The US president treats the Israelis and Palestinians as if they are on equal footings with equal negotiating power, a false premise that tips the balance of power further in Israel's favor. While Obama's 2009 address in Cairo was the high point of an even-handed approach to the Arab-Israeli conflict, his 2011 UN speech represents a major retreat and a stunning triumph of the Israel-first school. The president did not just express US opposition to the Palestinian bid for statehood but directed his team to lobby other nations to do so as well. The dramatic change in Obama's position is very striking because, as an academic at the University of Chicago, he was closely exposed to the Palestinian narrative through Palestinian colleagues who taught there, and had a closer and more direct knowledge of the Palestinian predicament than any of his presidential predecessors, even those seasoned in foreign affairs.

Early in his presidency Obama called the Israeli settlements in the West Bank "illegitimate," and drew criticism from Israel and its American supporters for saying it. In his UN speech there was no mention of Jewish settlements. With fourteen months until voters would decide whether to give him a second term, Obama had no stomach for another battle with a Congress that threatened, if the Palestinian Authority sought United Nations membership, to punish the Palestinians and end American aid to the Palestinian Authority[80]—an act that would create more chaos and instability in the region (Congress acted on that threat and the Obama administration cut funding to UNESCO in October 2011 because member states voted to seat Palestine as a member of that organization). Obama also faced fierce attacks by Republican presidential candidates and pro-Likud Jewish activists who accuse him of fostering a policy of "appeasement" in the Middle East and pushing Israel harder than the Palestinians to make compromises to achieve peace.[81]

OBAMA'S PREDICAMENT AT HOME

The loss of congressional seats in the 2010 midterm elections imposed severe domestic constraints on Obama's ability to exert pressure on Netanyahu to freeze settlements that could restart negotiations with the Palestinians. If the president was reluctant to invest more political capital in brokering an Arab-Israeli peace before the midterm elections, he seemed even more so as he geared up for the presidential election in 2012. Although he had been buoyed by the killing of Osama bin Laden and the defeat of Muammar Qaddafi in 2011, taking political risks would go against his instincts as a politician par excellence.

Of all foreign policy issues, the Arab-Israeli conflict is most organically linked to American domestic politics. Presidents from Nixon to Obama have been fully aware of the high political costs inherent in pursuing an Arab-Israeli peace, and presidents and politicians often think twice before criticizing Israel, as they fear that their strong opinions could pit them against Israel's American supporters at the local level as well as in Congress, and that any misstep could cost them money and votes.[82]

This deeply entrenched caution among American policymakers deters presidents from taking a proactive approach in the search for peace. In his memoirs, James Baker, secretary of state in the administration of George H. W. Bush, writes of the showdown with the Likud hardliner Yitzhak Shamir over the construction of Jewish settlements on Palestinian lands. He concedes that "in a full-fledged fight with AIPAC, the risks to the administration would be substantial."[83] Although Baker boasts that the administration scored a legislative victory over AIPAC in Congress, only the second time that lobby had been defeated, what he omits to mention is the impact of that confrontation on the outcome of the presidential elections in 1992: Bush was defeated by a Democrat, Bill Clinton, who wholeheartedly subscribed to the Israel-first school and who filled his administration with pro-Israel appointees.[84]

Obama in this respect is the rule, not the exception. Long before his UN address in 2011, some of his senior aides, including his top adviser and veteran negotiator Dennis Ross, warned Obama that he was alienating Israeli public opinion, and that he must ingratiate himself better with Israelis; he had to reassure them that he wouldn't shove a peace settlement down their throats. Henry Siegman, the former national director of the American Jewish Congress, highlighted opinion polls that showed that a bare 6–8 percent of the Israeli public supported Obama.[85] However, other sources suggested that Obama's approval rating in Israel could have been as low as 4 percent.[86] The president's popularity rose sharply in Israel after he spoke out forcibly against a Palestinian statehood bid at the United Nations, according to a poll published by the *Jerusalem Post*. The poll found 54 percent of Israelis thought Obama's policy was favorable to Israel, while 19 percent said it was pro-Palestinian. A survey in May 2011 showed 12 percent thought US policy was pro-Israel and 40 percent saw it as pro-Palestinian.[87]

Congressmen, too, know the dangers of upsetting the Israel-first school. In March, 2010, in glaring contrast to the White House's icy demeanor, Congress warmly embraced Netanyahu. On the morning after his snub by Obama, Netanyahu was welcomed by the congressional leadership of the Republican and Democratic parties alike. Distancing herself from the president, Speaker of the House Nancy Pelosi, a Democrat and an Obama ally, told Netanyahu that Congress fully supported him: "We in Congress stand by Israel. In Congress we speak with one voice on the subject of Israel."[88]

New York Democrat Nita Lowey, who chaired the House subcommittee overseeing foreign aid appropriations to Israel (about $3 billion a year), reassured the Israeli leadership that the ten-year memorandum of understanding ($30 billion) was solid. "There is strong bipartisan support for Israel in the Congress that will not falter," Lowey stated. Siding with Netanyahu against her own president and the leader of her own party, she asked sarcastically, "How can he go to the end stage of any discussion and give away the store in the middle of a negotiation?"

Pelosi's and Lowey's lockstep stood in stark contrast to the White House's nuanced stance and showed how deeply special interests are entrenched in Congress. Their response demonstrated clearly the complexity of the American political system and the domestic challenges facing Obama in his effort to advance peace in the Middle East. When it comes to foreign policy in the Arab-Israeli arena, the Congress ties the president's hands and limits his options. Though the presidency is a very powerful institution, Congress wields considerable power and influence of its own. On the Arab-Israeli conflict, it speaks with "one voice," as Pelosi bluntly put it.

Pelosi, like some of Obama's closest Democratic allies, was ready to desert him if he decided to exert real pressure on Netanyahu and so much as threatened to withhold the billions of dollars in military and financial aid that go to Israel. Although in the final analysis Obama would be able to carry such a policy through—as has been accomplished by some of his predecessors, from Eisenhower to Bush senior—that would be very costly politically, and he would sacrifice other important priorities. Historically, the Democrats have been the party with closer links to Israel than their Republican counterparts. That is no longer the case. In fact, the Republicans are much more hawkish and aggressive than the Democrats in backing the Jewish state. Cemented by an unholy alliance between the religious right in America and the right-wing in Israel, the growing bond between the Republicans and the Likud-led coalition has complicated American diplomacy on the Arab-Israeli conflict and weakened the president's authority. More than any other factor, unyielding backing of Israel in Congress impedes presidential decision making and America's ability to lead.[89]

The *New York Times,* a newspaper that cannot be dismissed as anti-Israeli, ran an investigative report in September 2011 that highlighted the extraordinary intersection of American diplomacy and domestic politics, the result of an ever-tightening relationship between the Israeli government and the Republican Party, which, after the 2010 midterm elections, controlled the House of Representatives.[90] For example, when the Obama administration wanted to be certain that Congress would not block $50 million in new aid to the Palestinian Authority in August 2011, it did not turn to moderate Republicans for votes. Instead, the Obama foreign policy team turned to a singularly influential lobbyist: Netanyahu. At the request of the secretary of state and the American embassy, Netanyahu urged dozens of members of Congress who were visiting Israel in August not to object to the aid, which, Netanhyahu said, would be used for training Palestinian police officers who work closely with the Israeli government. Republican representatives acknowledged that they felt more comfortable receiving the explanation from the Israeli prime minister than from the president of the United States. That the financing request first had to be approved by House Republicans—many of them backbenchers who were among eighty-one members of Congress to visit Israel in summer 2011—demonstrates the power of the relationship between the Republican Party and the Israeli government.[91]

According to the *Times,* this close relationship has significantly complicated the administration's diplomatic efforts to establish a Palestinian state, including Obama's ability to exert pressure on Netanyahu to freeze settlement construction on Palestinian lands.[92] Although solid support for Israel has long been a bipartisan fact of American domestic politics, "Netanyahu's popularity in Congress now runs deeper than ever. When he appeared before Congress in the spring, his speech rebutting Mr. Obama's ambitious peace proposals was interrupted by nearly three dozen standing ovations."[93] Representative Eric Cantor, the most powerful pro-Likud member of Congress, noted that "What you have on the Hill is a bipartisan demonstration for the U.S./Israeli relationship, and frankly I think it's in contrast to the signals being sent from the White House." To prove his point about bipartisan congressional support for the Jewish state, Cantor said he had written an op-ed article with Representative Steny H. Hoyer, the Democratic minority whip, expressing their support for the nation.[94] It is no wonder that Netanyahu can challenge Obama and defeat him.

Although domestic politics is a key driver behind Obama's indecisiveness, the chasm of perceptions and views between him and Netanyahu is as important.[95] A close observer of the Washington scene and early supporter of the president lamented that the world had watched Obama lose the battle over Israeli settlement expansion. He compared the defeat to that of the Soviet Union when, at the height of its power, it lost the war of wills over its use of Cuba as a missile platform: "The client state trumped the President of the United States—telegraphing to many around the world that President Obama ultimately didn't have the courage of his convictions and wasn't able to deploy power and statecraft to achieve the outlines of what he called for in his lofty rhetoric. Obama's General Assembly speech has done nothing to reverse the impression that Netanyahu is the alpha dog in the relationship with President Obama—and this is truly tragic and geostrategically consequential."[96]

Although Obama committed himself to making peace between the Israelis and the Palestinians a priority from day one, the relationship with China and the US wars in Afghanistan and Pakistan remain the most important items on his foreign policy agenda. But with social revolutions sweeping the Arab world, the Obama administration is attempting to cope with the unfolding developments in the area and minimize their potential damage to US interests. American foreign policy is focused primarily on managing social and political change and maintaining stability in post-Mubarak Egypt, in Bahrain, Yemen, and the Gulf in general; America's fundamental goal is to prevent reverberations from the popular uprisings from spilling over into Israel, oil production, and counterterrorism operations. Yet, the Obama national security team has not drawn a link between the Arab democratic awakenings and the urgency of establishing an independent Palestinian state and the need for a more proactive US strategy toward the peace process.

In fact, when Netanyahu and his American allies publicly confronted Obama after his speech at the State Department, the Obama foreign policy team retreated and stopped linking the Palestinians' desires to the aspirations of the Arab awakening movements. In his address at the United Nations in September, Obama de-linked the two issues and demanded that the Palestinians negotiate with Israel on Israel's terms first before they become eligible for a state of their own. He called the year of 2011 "a time of transformation." This year alone, he said, "more individuals are claiming their universal right to live in freedom and dignity." He hailed the democratic movements in the Ivory Coast, in Tunisia, in South Sudan. Of Egypt, where President Hosni Mubarak fell after thirty years of autocratic rule, Obama said, "we saw in those protesters the moral force of non-violence that has lit the world from Delhi to Warsaw; from Selma to South Africa—and we knew that change had come to Egypt and to the Arab world." He hailed the Libyan toppling of Qaddafi, and threw US weight behind the protesters in Syria.[97]

But, he said, Palestinians must make peace with Israel before gaining statehood themselves. "The deadlock will only be broken when each side learns to stand in each other's shoes," Obama added. And he issued an oblique challenge to the United Nations itself as an institution which has long been accused of being anti-Israel. The *New York Times* reported that Obama's aides were aware of the incongruity in his position, which would be seen as hypocritical. But the same officials said that since Obama is the president of the United States, he has had to put American interests first.[98]

Did he? A convincing argument can be made that the dramatic shift in Obama's position will undermine US vital interests in the Middle East. Netanyahu's conduct undermines Obama's strategy of outreach to Muslims. As the fundamental fault line in the region and a significant source of tensions between the United States and the Arab-Islamic arena, a festering Palestine conflict will put American lives and interests at risk.

For the first time ever, the US military warned of the repercussions of failure to resolve the Arab-Israeli conflict. Early in 2010, General David Petraeus had indicated that the conflict was one of the "root causes of instability" in the region. "The enduring hostilities between Israel and some of its neighbors present distinct challenges to our ability to advance our interests," the influential general told Congress. "Arab anger over the Palestinian question limits the strength and depth of US partnerships with governments and peoples in the [Middle East] and weakens the legitimacy of moderate regimes in the Arab world," Petraeus said.[99]

Not long thereafter, Arab countries rose in revolt against dictators, and the Palestine question achieved totemic significance for the entire region, as the violent protests in Egypt against Israel showed. The United States has struggled to place itself on the side of those seeking justice and freedom in the current Arab revolts. As noted, it has supported uprisings in Libya and Syria, while looking askance during a crackdown by an ally, Bahrain. Opposition to the Palestinian quest for UN membership intensifies Arab perceptions of American double standards and stirs up anti-US sentiments.[100] The consequences of this double standard for American foreign policy could be serious.

By giving priority to the war on terror and Asia, Obama allowed Netanyahu to prevail. Thus far, the Israeli prime minister has made it clear that he is unwilling to compromise, refusing to offer even a partial freeze of settlement construction on the West Bank and in East Jerusalem. Even after Obama and the Quartet called on both parties to restart peace talks and put negotiations on a faster track in September 2011, Netanyahu said he wouldn't halt construction in settlements in the occupied West Bank in order to lure the Palestinians back to the negotiating table. The American ambassador to Israel, Dan Shapiro, an Obama confidant, agreed with Netanyahu, saying that Washington had never favored making a freeze a condition for negotiations: "We've never set that, in this administration or any other, as a precondition for talks," he told Israeli Army Radio, in response to a question on whether he favored the Palestinian demand for a settlement freeze.[101] Abbas can no longer offer more concessions than he has already made because he won't be able to sell them to a skeptical public, and by pushing Abbas to accommodate Netanyahu, Obama has further weakened the Palestinian leader. Ever since, Abbas has been trying tried to recover his equilibrium and limit the damage to his standing among the Palestinian public.

While all the Arab countries, including the Palestinian leadership, say they are ready and willing to make peace with the Jewish state, the latter resists and creates facts on the ground by building more settlements. A sea change has occurred in the official Arab position regarding peace with Israel, a fact acknowledged by President Obama, his senior aides, and top Republican and Democratic leaders. For example, Robert Gates told President Obama that not only is "Netanyahu ungrateful, but also endangering his country by refusing to grapple with Israel's growing isolation and with the demographic challenges it faces if it keeps control of the West Bank," according to several senior US officials.[102] During the debate over the Palestinian bid for statehood in the United Nations, former President Bill Clinton, well known as one of the most pro-Israeli of American presidents, lamented that Netanyahu had squandered a historic opportunity to reconcile with the entire Arab world, not just the Palestinians. Clinton told *Foreign Policy* magazine that Israel was also on the verge of being recognized by Arab nations, adding that the "king of Saudi Arabia started lining up all the Arab countries to say to the Israelis, 'if you work it out with the Palestinians . . . we will give you immediately not only recognition but a political, economic, and security partnership.'"[103] Clinton added: "This is huge. . . . It's a heck of a deal. That's what happened. Every American needs to know this. That's how we got to where we are."[104] The Israeli ruling elite have neither grasped the historic opportunities offered by the comprehensive peace plan advanced by Saudi Arabia at the 2002 Arab summit in Beirut, which offered Israel full diplomatic recognition and integration in return for withdrawal from occupied Arab terrirories, nor Abbas's readiness to sign a peace deal that ends the conflict between Palestinians and Jews.[105] It is difficult to escape a cynical perspective of Netanyahu's calls for negotiations; it "means that he's just not going to give up the West Bank," Clinton concluded.[106]

A consensus exists among Arab states that the solution lies in the so-called land-for-peace-formula that emerged in 2002. It proposes that Israel must withdraw from the Arab territories that it occupied in 1967, including East Jerusalem, in return for diplomatic recognition by all Arab states. This peace proposal is the best possible settlement of the Arab-Israeli conflict. It shows the depth of change in the views of the Arab regimes toward Israel, though the change is much slower at the grassroots level.

The Arab states have, for the first time since Israel's founding, reached a consensus on recognizing the Jewish state and establishing normal relations with it. These states hope that a peace settlement will also reduce Iranian clout in the Arab arena and weaken its radical allies closer to home, particularly Hamas and Lebanon's Hezbollah.[107]

Rather than engaging with the Arab countries that proposed a comprehensive peace initiative, the Israeli foreign policy and security elite, particularly those with right and centrist viewpoints, ignored them. Instead, they waged a war against Hamas in Gaza.

There was a time when Obama shared Bill Clinton's view. On his visit to Israel and Palestine in 2008, Obama reportedly sounded out Mahmoud Abbas and Israeli leaders about the prospects for reviving the Arab peace initiative advanced at the Arab Summit in Beirut. "The Israelis would be crazy not to accept this initiative," Obama told Abbas, according to the *Sunday Times* of London. "It would give them peace with the Muslim world from Indonesia to Morocco."[108]

The same Obama stood before the General Assembly in 2011 and made the opposing case against Palestinian self-determination. He knew full well that Israel had been offered a historic opportunity to reconcile with its foes and live in peace. That shift in his position shows the extent to which Washington has changed Obama, and reveals the preponderant influence of the American political system on presidential decision making.

HAMAS: A PARTNER OR A SPOILER OF PEACE?

It is a commonly held view in Israel, the United States, and some European quarters that Hamas is a monolith, implacably opposed to peace efforts, an Al Qaeda–like terrorist organization bent on the destruction of Israel. It must therefore be excluded and isolated from diplomatic efforts until it recognizes Israel and renounces violence.

There is substantial evidence that Hamas has evolved and signaled a readiness to recognize Israel, that Israel should talk to Hamas and influence its behavior, and that the United States and Europe should therefore encourage rather than hinder intra-Palestinian reconciliation. The evidence for this view needs also to be critically examined.

Something is stirring within the Hamas body politic, a moderating trend that, if nourished and engaged, could transform Palestinian politics and the Arab-Israeli peace process. There are unmistakable signs that the religiously based radical movement has subtly changed its uncompromising position on Israel. Although low-key and restrained, those shifts indicate that the movement is searching for a formula that addresses the concerns of Western powers and avoids alienating its social base.

This shift, far from being impulsive and unexpected, reflects a gradual evolution over seven years. The big strategic turn occurred in 2005, when Hamas decided to participate in the January 2006 legislative elections and thus tacitly accepted the governing rules of the Palestinian Authority, one of which includes recognition of Israel. Ever since, top Hamas leaders have repeatedly declared they will accept a resolution of the conflict along the 1967 borders but based on a Palestinian referendum and the will of the Palestinian people.

The Damascus-based Khaled Meshaal, head of Hamas's political bureau and considered a hardliner, acknowledged as much in 2008. "We are realists," he said, who recognize that there is "an entity called Israel." Pressed by an Australian journalist on policy changes Hamas might make, Meshaal asserted that the organization has shifted on several key points: "Hamas has already changed—we accepted the national accords for a Palestinian state based on the 1967 borders, and we took part in the 2006 Palestinian elections."[109]

In an interview with *Newsweek* in October 2010, Meshaal affirmed this. "There is a position and program that all Palestinians share. To accept a Palestinian state on the 1967 borders with Jerusalem as the capital. With the right of return. And this state would have real sovereignty, on the land and on the borders. And with no settlements." He said, "When this program is implemented . . . we would respect the will of the Palestinian people."[110] At the signing of the reconciliation agreement between Fatah and Hamas in May 2011, Meshaal emphasized, "We have given peace since Madrid till now 20 years, and I say we are ready to agree among us Palestinians and with Arab support to give an additional chance."[111]

Another senior Hamas leader, Ghazi Hamad, was more specific than Meshaal, telling journalists in January 2009 that Hamas would be satisfied with ending Israeli control over the Palestinian areas occupied in the Six-Day war—the West Bank, Gaza, and East Jerusalem. In other words, Hamas would not hold out for liberation of the land that currently includes Israel.[112]

Before the parliamentary elections of 2006, Hamas was known for its suicide bombers, not its bureaucrats, even though between 2002 and 2006 the organization moved from rejection toward participation in a political framework that is a direct product of the Oslo Accords. After the elections, the shift continued. "It is much more difficult to run a government than to oppose and resist Israeli occupation," a senior Hamas leader told me while on official business in Egypt in 2007. "If we do not provide the goods to our people, they'll disown us." Hamas is not just a political party. It is a social movement, and as such it has a long record of staying in touch with public opinion.[113]

EFFECTS OF THE GAZA WAR OF 2008

The 2008 battle with Israel caused incalculable human suffering and led to increasing public dissatisfaction with Hamas, and the burden of governing a war-torn Gaza has been a key factor in the organization's transformation. However, the shift in its position began before the Gaza war. The deteriorating social conditions in Gaza, and Hamas' weak performance in the fighting, led to a fairly intense soul-searching and reassessment of strategic options.[114]

Hamas' strategic predicament lies in striking a balance between, on the one hand, a new moderating and maturing sensibility and, on the other, insistence on the right and the imperative of armed resistance that is guaranteed under international law. This difficult balance often explains the tensions and contradictions in Hamas's public and private pronouncements.

Indeed, it could be argued that Hamas has moved closer to a vision of peace that is consistent with international law and international consensus (two separate states in historic Palestine, divided more or less as before, with East Jerusalem as the capital of Palestine, and recognition of both by all states in the region) than has the current Likud-led Israeli governing coalition. Netanyahu vehemently opposes the establishment of a genuinely viable and independent Palestinian state in the West Bank and Gaza based on international law and is opposed to giving up any part of Jerusalem—and his governing coalition is more right-wing and pro-settlement than he is.

According to the Palestine Papers obtained by Al Jazeera, the Palestinian negotiating team offered wide-ranging concessions to Israel that go far beyond the declared official position. Yet the documents show that the Israeli leadership dismissed the concessions as inadequate and continued to construct more settlements. More importantly, as Condoleeza Rice's memoir reveals, then-foreign minister Tzipi Livni attempted to prevent an accord during the Bush administration by going behind Prime Minister Ehud Olmert's back before he was indicted for criminal corruption.[115] The truth is that Israeli politicians must have made a conscious decision that keeping Palestinian and Arab lands is more important than constructing a peace with their neighbors. Although Netanyahu insists he is sincere about achieving peace with the Palestinians, his actions—constructing more and more settlements—speak louder than any empty promises. As mentioned previously, American leaders, such as former president Clinton and defense secretary Gates, who are strong supporters of Israel, have said as much. As Clinton noted, Netanyahu is more interested in land grabbing than peacemaking.

Observers might ask, if Hamas is so eager to accept a two-state solution, why doesn't it simply accept the three conditions for engagement required by the diplomatic Quartet: recognition of Israel, renunciation of violence, and acceptance of all previous agreements—primarily the Oslo Accords.

In my interviews with Hamas officials, they stress that while they have made significant concessions, the Quartet has not lifted the punishing sanctions against Hamas, nor has it pressed Israel to end its siege, which has caused a dire humanitarian crisis.[116] In addition, Hamas leaders believe that recognition of Israel is the last card in their hand, and they are reluctant to play it before talks even begin. Their diplomatic starting point will be to demand that Israel recognize the national rights of the Palestinians and withdraw from the occupied territories—but it will not be their final position. Finally, Hamas asks, what are the borders of the state they are supposed to recognize?[117]

In their effort to avoid engaging the Palestinians, the Netanyahu-led government has obfuscated the truth by repeatedly emphasizing that they do not have

Palestinian partners. In fact, Israeli officials have launched a frontal diplomatic assault on the Hamas-Fatah unity pact, which Netanyahu denounced in London in May 2011 as a "mortal blow to peace and a great victory to terrorism."[118] Netanyahu's fundamental aim was to lobby European countries against backing a United Nations resolution that would recognize a Palestinian state and preempt any potential pressure by the US administration before his meeting with Obama in Washington later that month. Ironically, as mentioned before, Hamas criticized Abbas for making the bid for statehood recognition without consulting it in advance. The Israeli campaign bore some fruit. In his May speech before AIPAC, the pro-Israel lobby, President Obama described the Fatah-Hamas agreement as "an enormous obstacle to peace." Repeating the Netanyahu line, Obama said, "No country can be expected to negotiate with a terrorist organization sworn to its destruction."[119] Jacob Sullivan, director of planning and policy at the State Department, said that the formation of a unity Palestinian government would prompt the United States to review the new Palestinian government's standing and review its assistance, a veiled threat directed at Abbas and the Palestinian Authority.[120]

Ironically, after Abbas defied the United States and Israel by making a bid for Palestinian statehood membership at the United Nations, the interests of Hamas and Netanyahu temporarily converged. They reached a historic deal to exchange prisoners. Hamas succeeded in trading over a thousand prisoners in exchange for one Israeli soldier, Gelad Shalit. By concluding the prisoners exchange with Hamas immediately after the UN session, Netanyahu sought to improve his deteriorating standing at home and abroad, as well as to punish Abbas and drive a wedge between the two rival Palestinian groups. Similarly, Hamas hoped to capitalize on the release of prisoners to get traction among Palestinians and show them that the "logic of resistance" is more effective in producing results than Abbas' peace talks.

More importantly, the Arab spring uprisings have already had a moderating influence on Hamas' conduct domestically and regionally. Hamas officials say they feel more empowered by popular support in neighboring countries. For Hamas, in particular, the electoral victory of Islamist parties could be seen as a game-changer. The Islamist movement no longer sees itself as a besieged island in a sea of hostility. Hamas leaders now feel that they have strategic depth. "This is an Islamic area, and once people are given a fair chance to vote for their real representatives, they vote for the Islamists," said Mahmoud Zahar, a senior Hamas leader in Gaza, referring to the ascendance of Islamist parties in recent elections in Egypt, Tunisia, and Morocco. "We feel strengthened by popular support."[121]

Impressed by the electoral victory of Islamist parties in Tunisia, Morocco, and Egypt, Hamas' top leader, Khaled Meshaal, told his counterparts in Gaza that "we need to learn from these experiences in dealing with other parties and social groups, and that one-party rule is outdated," according to a Hamas official. The example of the Islamist parties "opened [our] eyes to make coalitions with other Palestinian factions," said Ghazi Hamad, deputy foreign minister of the government in Gaza. "This will create a new political Islam in which a coalition is the main goal, not to monopolize the regime. No one accepts one political color. The time of one-party rule has passed."[122]

In this regard, at the end of 2011 Meshaal and his team held talks with Abbas and other Fatah officials in Cairo in an effort to implement the reconciliation pact reached in early 2011 and to end the political separation between their two rival groups. Hamas leaders, including Meshaal, say they are ready to merge with Fatah and suspend armed resistance against Israel, a pronounced shift from their earlier position.[123] What this means is that Hamas implicitly accepts a peace settlement based on a two-state solution, even though it has not institutionalized and formalized its decision.

Internally, Hamas has also shown signs of pragmatism and tolerance by ceasing to enforce strict religious rules regarding individual freedoms and behavior, such as bans on women smoking water pipes in public and male coiffeurs styling women's hair and veiling. Hamas leaders acknowledge "mistakes" were made and pledge to correct them. In a memo to Gaza activists, Meshaal's political bureau cautioned that restrictive measures are tarnishing the movement's image, said a Hamas figure. People in Gaza already feel a change in atmosphere, according to human rights activists and even political rivals of Hamas.[124]

OBAMA'S RETREAT

By 2012, it was clear that Obama's speech to the General Assembly in September 2011 was an acknowledgment of failure, a retreat from evenhanded diplomacy, and a triumph for the Israel-first perspective. On that occasion, Obama laid out the dominant Israeli security narrative and hardly uttered a word about what it should do to escape its security dilemma. Instead of saving Israel from itself and defining American preferences and a vision for a peace settlement, he portrayed Israel, which occupies Palestinian lands, as a victim whose very survival is at stake. Therefore, Israel's security, narrowly defined, takes precedence over Palestinian security and even self-determination. "America's commitment to Israel's security is unshakable. Our friendship with Israel is deep and enduring," he stated. "And so we believe that any lasting peace must acknowledge the very real security concerns that Israel faces every single day."[125]

In contrast, in Cairo in 2009, Obama had offered an inclusive vision that encompassed Israeli and Palestinian security alike.[126] But in 2009, the new president was not as encumbered by local politics and institutional constraints as he was in 2011. Obama was now fighting for his political survival, for election to a second presidential term.

Like most of his predecessors, Obama allowed himself to be entrapped by parochial concerns and became hostage to local politics. He shied away from exerting sufficient pressure on Israel, and he lacked the courage to translate his stated convictions into real policies. Despite the early promising months of the Obama presidency and its fresh rhetoric, structural-institutional continuity reasserted itself and co-opted Obama. This institutional continuity largely explains the persistent failure of US foreign policy toward the Arab-Israeli conflict. Historians are likely to judge the Obama presidency as a missed opportunity to resolve the conflict and escape the bonds of the American political system.

CHAPTER 5

THE PIVOTAL STATES

Egypt, Iran, and Turkey

Barack Obama confronts a Middle East where the three pivotal states—Turkey, Iran, and Egypt—are making a serious bid for regional leadership and challenging American dominance. In the last decade the regional landscape has been transformed. Turkey is playing a more active role in its Middle Eastern neighborhood than ever before. Iran has relentlessly struggled to spread its influence in the Persian Gulf and beyond and has spearheaded resistance to what it calls the US-Zionist alliance. The pro-Western Tunisian and Egyptian autocrats have been toppled, and Egypt will likely emerge from its political slumber and cultural decline to regain its lost voice and reassume its old leadership role.

These culturally distinct Muslim states are at the center of a regional system, and their soft power defines and shapes political and cultural trends there. All three states have long histories (however distant) as great empires, and each is polylingual and multireligious, though only Egypt shares the majority Arab identity of the Middle East. In the past ten years, non-Arab Turkey and Iran have spread their influence deep into the Arab heartland because of the general malaise that infects Arab countries, particularly Egypt, the Arab world's most populous state and its capital of cultural production and center of gravity. Egypt's revival as a pluralistic state will be a corrective, a balancing act that allows the Arabs to be a player on the regional and international stage.

Of the three states, Egypt has experienced the greatest change: a revolution still unfolding that has toppled its thirty-two-year-old regime and turned the political system upside down.

Turkey, where the process of democratic consolidation has progressed rapidly during the past decade, is seen as an example, if not a model, by many in the Arab world.

Iran crushed the Green Movement—a liberal opposition grouping that includes diverse but united social and political segments and aims to replace the authoritarian Islamic Republic with a government based on a plurality—after the contested 2009 presidential elections, and it has weathered the powerful democratic storm sweeping the region since the spring of 2011. But the Islamic Republic is vulnerable to internal convulsion because repression has replaced consent as a subtext of relations between ruler and citizen, and it suffers from a debilitating legitimation crisis at home. Furthermore, a fierce power struggle has occurred between the clerical and nonclerical elements within the current government. It has brought into question the position of the Ayatollah himself and could prove very damaging to the regime.[1]

With these three states' increasing assertiveness, the role of the United States must necessarily change. And it has. US influence on these countries is at its lowest point since the beginning of the Cold War in the late 1940s. America's ability to dictate policy in the Middle East has diminished considerably, and it no longer determines the course of events in the region. America's moment is coming to an end. One of the early lessons learned in the course of the Arab uprisings is that, like its clients, the United States was caught off guard and labored hard to keep up with spreading social turmoil in the region. Millions of Arab protesters, driven by their own revolutionary agenda, demanded the immediate ouster of autocratic rulers and paid little attention to pronouncements by the Obama administration. Despite belated efforts by President Obama to ride the Arab democratic wave, his inspirational calls have largely fallen on deaf ears. As noted earlier, in his Ankara and Cairo addresses, Obama raised Arab and Muslim expectations to a fever pitch only to disappoint by failing to bring an end to Israeli occupation of Palestinian lands, the war on terror, and US support for local autocrats.

Even Saudi Arabia, America's most loyal and dependable ally, has unusually challenged the US position vis-à-vis the Arab awakenings.[2] Exemplary in this respect was the uprising in Bahrain. Saudi Arabia disregarded Washington's calls for political dialogue between the Bahrain royal family and the opposition. Along with the United Arab Emirates, it deployed thousands of troops to its neighbor Bahrain, and with their presence the royal family suppressed the Shiite-based protesters. The United States accepted the Saudi fait accompli without uttering a word of disapproval or criticism. Similarly, as shown in chapter 4, with respect to Israel, Prime Minister Benjamin Netanyahu publicly contested Obama's vision for peace as one based on "illusions" and rejected his repeated requests for a partial freeze on settlement construction in the occupied West Bank and East Jerusalem.

More recently, Iraq rebuffed the Obama administration's efforts to keep America troops there after December 31, 2011. For eighteen months, the White House and Pentagon labored to negotiate an agreement with the Iraqis that would override the one signed by President George W. Bush. It provided for the withdrawal of all American troops by December 2011 and granted US soldiers immunity from Iraqi jurisdiction for any crimes they might be accused of. Although Iraqi Prime Minister Nouri al-Maliki tried to arrange for US forces to remain in Iraq under a grant of immunity, he failed to get the necessary majority in Parliament. There exists widespread public opposition to the US military presence in Iraq among nationalists and Islamists who want to take ownership of their country. In particular, the Sadrists (followers of the influential cleric and political leader Muqtada al-Sadr) said they would withdraw their support for the government if Maliki agreed to America's terms.[3] The withdrawal of all uniformed US troops from Iraq clearly shows the limits of America's power and its decline in the region, as well as the significance of awakened Arab public opinion.

As the last US troops left Iraq at the end of December 2011, nearly nine years after President Bush invaded the country and toppled its regime in 2003, President Obama, who as a senator had opposed the war, greeted Iraqi Prime Minister Nuri al-Maliki at the White House as "the elected leader of a sovereign, self-reliant and democratic Iraq."[4] But the reality is much more complex and dangerous. Far from leaving behind a democracy, the United States' legacy is a sectarian-Shiite-based political system, a mutilated society, enforced by a strongman who sanctions no dissent, and who concentrates too much power in his hands. Even before the United States completed its withdrawal, al-Maliki swiftly moved against his Sunni critics, asking lawmakers to withdraw confidence from his deputy, Saleh al-Mutlaq, for making controversial comments and accusing al-Maliki of being a "dictator." The prime minister also issued an arrest warrant for Vice President Tariq al-Hashimi, the country's most senior Sunni official, for allegedly running a hit squad that killed government officials during Iraq's wave of sectarian bloodletting, and reportedly rounded up hundreds of dissidents. Although there is more to al-Maliki's actions than sectarianism, the steps risk tearing at the same Shiite-Sunni fault lines that pushed Iraq to the brink of all-out civil war just a few years ago.[5] Iraq is in tatters with the remnants of Al Qaeda frequently carrying out deadly suicide bombings that pour fuel on a raging fire.

Equally important, the United States leaves Iraq almost empty-handed, with Iran being the power broker there. Instead of consolidating American influence in Iraq and undermining the neighboring clerical regime, the US invasion allowed Iran to build a network of allies, including al-Maliki, who control political life. Iran is by far the dominant external power in Iraq, and its weight will increase now that US troops have exited. The crisis in Syria is a case in point. Before the dust settled on the US withdrawal, al-Maliki said he would not participate in sanctioning the Assad regime, as the Obama administration had urged him to do, and the Tehran–Baghdad road has become Damascus' lifeline. In the raging cold war in the Middle East, Iraq is solidly anchored in the Iranian camp, a far cry denouement from the neoconservatives' fairytale. Barack Obama inherited the mess, and his persistent efforts to maintain a military footprint in Iraq were met with widespread societal and political opposition.

Of all Middle Eastern states, Israel, Saudi Arabia, and Iraq would be least expected to flout US requests because of their dependence on Washington's security umbrella. The fact that they do so indicates the extent to which the leading regional powers assert their independence and pursue policies against US wishes and national interests. Lamenting America's loss of influence in the Middle East, a former US official said: "We resemble more a modern-day Gulliver tied up by tiny tribes and by our own illusions than a smart, tough and fair superpower."[6]

Obama has inherited not only a bitter legacy in the Middle East but also a weakened and bleeding superpower suffering the effects of more than a decade of war and a pressing domestic economic crisis. The US-led invasion and occupation of Iraq, together with the subsequent graphic reports of bloodshed and torture, damaged America's standing and prestige in the region and emboldened some of the states to establish their own spheres of influence. America's friends learned in the Bush years that the United States couldn't be expected to act rationally to preserve the fragile regional balance of power. By acting unilaterally and aggressively against the wishes of international consensus, under the influence of neoconservative advocates, the United States motivated regional allies and foes to take action to protect their interests.

Historically, Kemalist Turkey (a reference to the founding father of contemporary Turkey, Kemal Ataturk)—a loyal Western ally after World War II—was reluctant to actively engage in the Middle East.[7] The end of the Cold War coincided with significant social, economic, and political change within Turkish society that signaled the rise of the Anatolian elites and the decline of the traditional Kemalist secular establishment based in the major cities of western Turkey. The victory of the center-right AKP in the 2002 parliamentary elections formally inaugurated the rise of the post-Islamist governing elite and established Turkey as a key geoeconomic and geopolitical power with a foreign policy vision aimed at transforming its Middle Eastern neighborhood. In the past decade, Turkey has risen into the ranks of pivotal midsize powers. Its bid to enter the European Union has spurred efforts to modernize its economy and further democratize its laws.

Today Turkey is economically and diplomatically invested in the region and commands respect and even envy for possessing one of the largest and most dynamic economies. Turkey's decision to oppose the invasion of Iraq, along with championing the rights of besieged Palestinians in Gaza and the Arab awakenings, has resonated among people in the region and has earned it high praise. Turkey is a long-standing NATO member, and its foreign policy and economic and security interests are oriented toward the West. However, it has recently pursued an independent strategy in the Middle East, particularly toward Iraq, Iran, and the Arab-Israeli conflict. On these issues, Turkey is frequently at odds with its traditional Western allies.

Iran, too, has emerged as an unrivaled superpower in the Gulf and a pivotal player in the Sunni-based Arab states. Its clerical regime is a major beneficiary of the global war on terror, for in that war the United States toppled two of Iran's most bitter enemies—Saddam Hussein and the Taliban. Filling a leadership vacuum in the Arab arena and branding itself as the leader of the resistance to US-Israeli dominance, Iran has made important inroads among Arabs, particularly by supporting the Palestine cause and providing arms and money to Hamas and Hezbollah. Iran thus represents a significant challenge to American vital interests in the Gulf and the Arab-Israeli arena, a challenge that is magnified by overwhelming pressure from its Gulf and Israeli allies to take military action and abort the Iranian nuclear program. Obama has reached a deadlock with regard to Iran and has deployed economic warfare in an effort to bleed the Iranian regime to submission and force it to change its behavior. But so far the administration has resisted the temptation to use force against Iran and has reportedly warned Israel not to do so, even though Obama has said that all options are on the table, including military strikes.

The stringent economic sanctions, imposed by the West under American pressure, have exacted heavy costs from Iranian society and have exacerbated the crisis of legitimacy of the presidency of Mahmoud Ahmadinejad. In contrast to Turkey, which enjoys political legitimacy and economic prosperity at home, the Iranian model has failed politically and economically; it cannot deliver either democracy or prosperity. The 2009 presidential elections exposed a rupture between the authorities and a critical segment of the Iranian people, a segment that revolted against the repression and corruption of the system and the lack of transparency and accountability.[8] The so-called Green Movement, though suppressed, inspired the subsequent Arab revolts, liberating developments whose significance and lessons were not lost on the vibrant Iranian civil society. The Islamic model in Iran faces grave internal trials and intensified external pressure, as well as a deepening institutional crisis between the office of the Supreme Leader, the parliament, and the presidency.

But contrary to the received wisdom in the West, Iran's confrontation with the United States and its allies over its nuclear program is a blessing in disguise; it allows Ayatollah Ali Khamenei, the Supreme Leader, to divert attention from internal difficulties at home and mobilizes nationalist-Islamist pride against the "arrogant" and "domineering" West. The rhetoric of identity politics finds receptive ears among many Iranians who—given the long history of troubled relations—accept the narrative of Western hostility toward the Islamic Republic. This explains why the Iranian regime frequently whips up nationalist-Islamist sentiment and warns of Western threats to the homeland.

Turkey and Iran have emerged alongside Egypt as indispensable powers in the regional system. Iran's resurgence and Turkey's reengagement blur the boundaries between the Arab arena and what was once considered the non-Arab periphery—Turkey and Iran. The Middle East can no longer be treated as distinctly Arab versus non-Arab in terms of its security and economy, and of its future. Although the Arab revolts that began in the spring of 2011 are still unfolding, Egypt is unlikely to have a major impact on the political and strategic landscape in the Middle East in the short term. Of all the Arab states, it has the greatest capacity to act regionally, but it will be tied down for a while getting its house in order and sorting out the relationship between the civilian and military authorities in the nascent political order. The center of political gravity in the region has shifted from the Arab heartland, comprising Egypt and the Fertile Crescent, to the non-Arab periphery of Turkey and Iran. This was becoming clearly discernible before the Arab revolts. It will most likely continue for the foreseeable future.[9]

From the outset of his presidency, Obama recognized the importance of the three pivotal states. He attempted to transcend George W. Bush's legacy, one that embittered friends and turned potential allies into bitter foes. After September 11, 2001, Iran and Turkey backed the United States in its military campaign against the Taliban and Al Qaeda, and the Iranian leadership expressed a desire to open a new chapter of relations with their American counterparts. Instead of extending an open hand, Bush alienated the Iranians by lumping them with the "axis of evil" and ruined an opportunity to rebuild broken relations with the estranged Iranians. In particular, Bush's invasion of Iraq endangered America's relationship with Turkey, one of America's oldest Middle East allies, and allowed Iran to spread its influence in the Gulf and beyond.

With this in mind, the Obama foreign policy team chose Turkey for Obama's first trip to a Muslim country, a symbolic choice designed to mend the frayed US-Turkish relationship and send a clear message about the significance of Turkey as a Muslim democracy. After lengthy deliberation, Obama aides sent the president to Egypt to deliver his much-awaited message of reconciliation to Arabs and Muslims. In a similar vein, in his inaugural address and in a subsequent interview, Obama offered his hand for engagement with Iran, America's longtime foe.

So far Obama has had mixed results while rebranding and recalibrating relations with the three states. Like all of his predecessors, Obama neither acts in an institutional vacuum nor possesses unlimited political resources to restructure and transform American foreign policy, if he desires to do so. In the case of Iran, Obama has faced fierce resistance at home to his stated aim to engage with the Iranian regime and reach accommodation with it. He also discovered that Iranian leaders are deeply suspicious of the United States and are not receptive to his call for engagement, especially if that means dramatically altering their foreign policy and conduct as well. Obama's misfortune is that he inherited a changed Middle East in which the United States now exercises much less influence than before and in which the war on terror has empowered Iran and allowed it to expand its reach. The presence of Ahmadinejad as president did not help either, even though it is the Supreme Leader who determines the direction of Iranian foreign policy.

Obama's initial approach to engagement did not yield positive results, and US-Iranian relations remain as hostile as ever, with the United States and its Western partners imposing more punishing economic and financial sanctions on Iran than during the Bush administration. Obama's reluctance to openly side with the Green Movement hurt his standing with the opposition, while his vigor in imposing sanctions against the regime has not won him any friends among the old guard. However, a major difference between Obama and his predecessor is that Obama has so far successfully neutralized calls by ideologues at home, in Israel, and the Gulf to launch an attack on Iran's nuclear facilities, though he has threatened to strike Iran if it nears the stage of developing a nuclear weapon.

In contrast to Iran, Egypt was not initially a priority on Obama's foreign policy list. He made it clear that he was not interested in promoting democracy and was mainly concerned about maintaining stability, a code word for retaining the status quo. The guardians of the status quo were Mubarak and like-minded Arab autocrats (such as Tunisian President Ben Ali) who pledged to protect US vital interests in a turbulent region, especially Obama's counterterrorism tactics. After a brief interlude, Obama embraced Mubarak as a wise old statesman of the Arab Middle East, a trustworthy ally to whom time and again the United States had turned for advice and support. Whatever reservations Obama had about Mubarak's oppressive and corrupt rule—if any—he did not make them public.[10] In fact, when asked if the US government considered Mubarak a dictator, Obama and Vice President Biden separately said that the Egyptian leader was not a dictator, simply because he was an ally.

Out of the $2 billion in annual US foreign aid to Egypt, only ten percent is allocated for the civilian sector and the rest for the military, the backbone of the repressive Mubarak regime in the past three decades. The United States reached a similar arrangement with Yemeni President Ali Abdullah Salah, who leveraged the "war on terror," including granting permission to the Obama administration to use drone attacks against suspected Al Qaeda in the Arabian Peninsula (AQAP) targets, to get precious arms and money for his beleaguered regime. The United States backs a long list of Middle Eastern autocrats.

From the first year that Ben Ali took power in 1987 until his ouster in January 2011, the United States provided his regime with more than $600 million worth of weapons and military aid, nearly half of which was supplied by the Obama administration. A few months before the Tunisian people ousted Ben Ali, a Pentagon official justified the latest arms deal by saying that it "will contribute to the foreign policy and national security of the US by helping to improve the security of a friendly country that has been and continues to be an important force for economic and military progress in North Africa."[11]

According to his foreign policy team, Obama prefers private, quiet diplomacy as the means of delivering US misgivings to allies such as Mubarak. Obviously, Obama's approach did not convince Mubarak to stop human rights violations and reform the closed authoritarian system. In fact, Mubarak acted as if he had a mandate from the United States to install his son, Gamal, in the presidency. He brought Gamal with him to the White House in September 2010 to attend the summit called by President Obama to restart stalled Palestinian-Israeli peace talks. The Egyptian press opined that Mubarak wanted to officially introduce Gamal to Obama and Netanyahu and get their blessing for the succession from father to son.

Mubarak did not feel any pressure from Obama to mend his ways. His associates boasted that Hillary Clinton was a close friend of Mubarak and his powerful wife, Suzanne, implying that the Obama administration would be friendlier than its predecessor to the Mubarak family. Ironically, despite many troubling signs, the Obama administration and the Mubarak regime were caught off guard when the country imploded. Even then, Obama procrastinated and vacillated before backing the broadly based social revolution that destroyed the Egyptian regime. Once Mubarak was removed from power, Obama ratcheted up his rhetoric in support of an orderly and peaceful democratic transition. He profusely praised the military for securing the peace and for promising to relinquish power to a civilian leadership, though many Egyptians fear that the senior officers in charge are using sinister tactics like that of the Mubarak regime to monopolize authority and rule the country.[12]

Regardless of the composition of the new leadership in Cairo, Egyptian foreign policy will no longer be as pliant as it was under former President Hosni Mubarak. Bowing to the pressure of public opinion, Egypt's interim military leaders have brokered a reconciliation pact between Hamas and Fatah, which is still very much a work in progress, and partially reopened the Rafah border crossing with the Gaza Strip, a blow to the United States and Israel. It is only a matter of time before the new Egypt, with Islamists holding a Parliamentary majority, will inaugurate a new chapter in foreign policy. Post-Mubarak Egypt has given notice that it will reclaim the country's leadership mantle in the Arab world and repair broken relations with Iran.

Far from being transformational, the belated embrace of the Egyptian revolution is an acknowledgment of new realities in Arab politics, an effort to ride the popular wave and to position the United States alongside the winning camp. The Obama administration had little choice but to accept the inevitable. Nevertheless, the Arab revolts, particularly Egypt's and Tunisia's, have shown how little influence the United States exercises in the Middle East. Obama and his foreign policy team struggled to keep up with revolutionary developments that had a life of their own and spun out of control. It would not be an exaggeration to say that the United States was a passive bystander in an unfolding epic struggle, notwithstanding Washington's direct line to higher echelons of the military. For the first time in decades, the Arab arena, including Egypt, its center, seems to be regaining its equilibrium. Out of social and political turmoil, a new Arab order is being born—though it is unclear how democratic, inclusive, and stable it will be, or how long it will take for the transition to take place.

With the revolutionary changes sweeping the region, the ability of the United States to shape future developments is seriously tested. In the case of Egypt, the prospect is clear. Against their own will, Egypt's interim military rulers have already lost the struggle to preserve continuity with Mubarak's foreign policy and have taken steps toward the Palestinians and Israelis that differ from the position of the United States. Egypt's foreign policy shift will be more pronounced and sharp when a civilian government is elected. The rise of Islamists to power will transform Egypt from being a US client state to an assertive player, an actor that pursues an independent foreign policy. Similarly, despite marked improvement in relations between Ankara and Washington after Obama moved into the White House, Turkey has become more assertive in its international relations; it pursues independent, proactive policies toward its Middle Eastern neighbors. Currently, even the US relationships with Saudi Arabia and Israel, anchors of America's Mideast policy, are strained, weighed down by the revolutionary upheaval in the Arab arena and Obama's inability or unwillingness to press his two allies to accept his vision for gradual and peaceful change.[13]

Awakened regional powers now directly challenge the US foreign policy agenda and attempt to fill the power vacuum left by America's retrenchment and relative decline. Therefore, Obama faces more complex challenges than his predecessors in attempting to refashion American relations with the three pivotal states and the Middle East in general. He has discovered the limits of US power in a changing geopolitical environment and has offered nuanced approaches without overhauling or restructuring the Washington consensus on the region. A close reading of Obama's statements shows more consistency than difference with traditional US strategy. There is a gap between Obama's idealistic rhetoric and his actual policies, solidly anchored in new realism. A consensus builder by nature, Obama has seized the middle ground and governed through compromise. He has not broken with the preexisting foreign policy tradition and style. His inspirational and nuanced rhetoric must not obscure the structural continuity of the US approach toward the Middle East, particularly the Arab-Israeli conflict, the significance of the oil-producing Gulf states, the menace of Iran, and the logic behind the war on terror.

EGYPT

The signing of the Camp David Accords with Israel in 1978 made Egypt one of America's most important functional allies. Ever since, successive administrations have seen that nation as a key regional asset in guaranteeing Arab-Israel peace and ending the state of war with the Jewish state. Viewing the Middle East through the Israel lens has colored the attitudes of US policymakers toward Egypt and disposed them to back Anwar Sadat and his successor, Mubarak, who for three decades suppressed legitimate political opposition at home and maintained the peace with Israel. Notably, Egypt was one of the chief mediators in helping to secure a peace agreement between Israel and Jordan in 1994. Conversely, the Mubarak regime did Washington's bidding in counterbalancing the so-called defiance and resistance camp that challenged the US-Israeli dominant status quo in the region. For example, after Hamas won the 2006 parliamentary elections in Palestine and claimed sovereign control over the Gaza Strip, Egypt cooperated with Israel to blockade Gaza and to tilt the balance of power in favor of Fatah, the nationalist rival to Hamas. Mubarak also proved a reliable ally to the United States by securing a safe passage of the West's oil supplies through the Suez Canal and by supporting the US global war on terror, including the invasion and occupation of Iraq and the rendition and torture of terror suspects sent to Egypt by the Bush administration.

Nevertheless, after the September 11 attacks and the commencing of the war on terror, there was a pronounced chilling of US-Egyptian relations. The Bush administration called on Egypt to institute reforms and open up the closed political system and respect human rights. While visiting Cairo in 2005, Secretary of State Condoleezza Rice shocked the Mubarak regime by reprimanding it for not heeding Bush's calls for political and economic liberalization: "It is time to abandon the excuses that are made to avoid the hard work of democracy."[14] The low point in the US-Egyptian relationship was short-lived, however. As Bush got bogged down in Iraq's killing fields and elections empowered religiously based activists, the Muslim Brotherhood, he abandoned his ideological drive to engineer social change in the Arab heartland and reassured Mubarak and other Arab autocrats of his unwavering commitment to their security and survival.

For Bush officials, the tipping point arrived when the Muslim Brotherhood, the most powerful mainstream Islamist organization, won 20 percent of Egyptian parliamentary seats in the November 2005 elections, and Hamas won a decisive majority in the Palestinian elections the following year. Playing on American fears that "radical Islamists" would hijack democratic reforms, Mubarak branded his regime a bulwark against Islamist extremism and a trustworthy ally in the war on terror. He succeeded in easing US pressure on his regime, even though the Cairo-Washington relationship remained tense. That marked the end of Washington's brief moment of flirtation with democracy promotion, a moment driven by a neoconservative ideology related to rationalizing the expansion of the war on terror and constructing a new regional order in the neoconservative image.

With Obama at the helm, Mubarak sought to rekindle the American-Egyptian relationship and obtain backing for his regime. The state-controlled media in Cairo hailed the prospects of a new era of bilateral harmony between the world's sole superpower and Egypt, the region's political linchpin and center of gravity and a safe haven in a turbulent sea. Mubarak was keen to shore up Obama's support, though he was worried that the president would prioritize democratization and press Egypt to improve its poor human rights record and relax its authoritarian rule. The choice of Ankara, rather than Cairo, as the rostrum for Obama's first address to Muslims did not sit well with the Mubarak regime, which viewed it as a rebuff, according to my conversation with several Egyptian officials. Therefore, Mubarak visited Washington and met with Obama and his foreign policy team in 2009 and pushed for continuation of America's hands-off policy on internal Egyptian politics and $2 billion in direct US aid annually. In exchange, Mubarak pledged Egypt's continuing assistance on the Israel-Palestine front and in deterring Iranian influence in the Arab arena. With his health deteriorating and a succession crisis brewing, Mubarak was desperate to secure US support for his rule.

Obama had chosen quiet diplomacy to impress on the Mubarak regime the need to open up a closed political system. For example, a US diplomatic cable noted that "We continue to promote democratic reform in Egypt, including expansion of political freedom and pluralism, and respect for human rights."[15] Despite US concerns, the cable added that the Mubarak government "remains skeptical of our role in democracy promotion, complaining that any efforts to open up will result in empowering the Muslim Brotherhood."[16]

Mubarak's worries were exaggerated; although the Obama administration had privately expressed an interest in political reforms and in putting an end to human rights violations in the Middle East, including Egypt, democracy promotion was not a top priority. Long before his inauguration, Obama had made it clear he would not preach to other nations, signaling a return to realism in US foreign policy with national interests as the driving force.[17] Given his focus on reviving Israeli-Palestinian peace talks and putting a stop to the Iranian nuclear program, Obama, like his predecessors, recognized the importance of Mubarak as an obliging friend. After a slow start, Obama welcomed Mubarak as a reliable strategic partner and ignored his oppressive and failed regime. Opposition voices in Egypt penned Obama's political obituary and abandoned their hopes that he would transform US policy and end support for Arab dictators.[18]

While the Obama administration supported the Mubarak regime, Egyptians suffered the brunt of the Mukhabarat, a police-based state, including martial law, arbitrary arrest and detention, and systematic abuses of human rights. The torture of Khaled Mohamed Saeed, a young Egyptian who was brutally beaten to death by the police in Alexandria in June 2010, symbolized the breakdown of the state and the loss of its legitimacy and authority. For Egyptians, Khaled Saeed became a symbol of the injustice and ruthless repression of the Mubarak regime and a rallying cry for resistance against it. The Obama administration did not rise to the occasion and failed to condemn its ally's gross violation of Egyptians' human rights.

The last straw for Egyptians was the 2010 parliamentary elections in which the National Democratic Party (NDP) gained a sweeping majority of seats and disenfranchised all legitimate opposition, including the most powerful, the Muslim Brotherhood. In 2010, the Brotherhood lost 87 of the 88 seats that it had won in the previous parliamentary elections in 2005, a relatively more transparent contest held under pressure from the Bush administration. Independent observers and human rights activists criticized the NDP for rigging the elections in Mubarak's favor and monopolizing the political space. A widespread revolt simmered throughout Egypt, and calls of defiance echoed from many quarters. The scene was set for all-out confrontation between the Mubarak regime and the people. Once again, the Obama administration did not publicly pressure Mubarak to investigate credible allegations of electoral fraud and did not push him to institute political reforms.

In his regime's last decade, as Mubarak's legitimation crisis deepened at home, his dependence on the United States increased considerably, and he labored hard to be more useful to his superpower patron. Mubarak squeezed Hamas by helping Israel tighten the siege of the Gaza Strip and spearheaded the Sunni-dominated front against Iran. Whatever Washington desired, Mubarak obligingly provided. In the view of the Egyptians, the Mubarak regime acted as a contractor for the United States and Israel, demeaning their country and abandoning its Arab leadership role. By the time Obama was elected, Mubarak had suffered a fatal crisis of legitimacy at home, becoming the sick man of the Middle East and turning into a liability for the United States.

Nevertheless, the Obama foreign policy team, particularly Clinton, neither anticipated the gathering storm in Egypt nor exerted pressure on Mubarak to change his authoritarian ways. Business as usual was the order of the day in the Obama administration. In this context, the social turmoil on 25 January 2011 was a shock to Mubarak and Obama alike. The Obama foreign policy team initially reacted with hesitancy and ambivalence to the unfolding crisis.[19] As the storm gathered, Obama straddled a policy rift within his administration. The *New York Times* reported that the president navigated between the counsel of the traditional foreign policy establishment led by Clinton, Gates, and Biden and that of a new generation of White House aides. While the diplomats in the State and Defense Departments viewed the crisis through the lens of American strategic interests in the region, particularly its threat to the 1979 peace treaty between Egypt and Israel, and its effects on the Middle East peace process, West Wing staff worried that too much preoccupation with stability could put a historic president on the wrong side of history.[20]

For example, Obama's envoy to Cairo, Frank G. Wisner, told a Munich conference on 4 February 2011 that Mubarak was indispensable to Egypt's transition to democracy. Echoing similar sentiments at the same conference, Clinton expressed concern that, given the lack of a political culture in Egypt, a hasty exit by Mubarak could complicate the country's transition to democracy.[21] In contrast, inside the White House, aides such as Denis McDonough, the deputy national security adviser; Benjamin J. Rhodes, who wrote the president's address to the Muslim world in Cairo; and Samantha Power, human rights advocate—all of whom had pushed Obama during his presidential campaign to challenge the assumptions of the foreign policy establishment—expressed their concern that if he did not step up the pressure on Mubarak and encourage the protesters with forceful, and even inspiring, language, he would be accused of abandoning the ideals that he had voiced during his Cairo speech.

According to reports of internal deliberations within the administration, from the beginning of the revolution until the ouster of Mubarak, Obama took a pragmatic view of how to use America's limited influence to effect change in Egypt. Although he was not in disagreement with Wisner and Clinton about how long a transition would take, he apparently feared that saying so openly would expose the United States to accusations of putting its strategic interests first. Right up to the end, Obama implored Mubarak to take the protesters' demands seriously but did not insist that he resign.[22] Despite his subsequent embrace of the protesters, Obama never lost sight of the utility and usefulness of Mubarak in preserving American vital interests in the region. He was clearly preoccupied with how political change in Egypt could affect the Palestine-Israel peace process and benefit Iran. It is no wonder then that the administration alternately described Mubarak as a stalwart ally and as a foe of meaningful political change.[23]

It was not until 1 February, following Mubarak's defiant speech and refusal to resign, that Obama finally instructed his aides to demand that meaningful political reform must begin "now." He did not want his administration to be seen as protecting a dictator against the wishes of a majority of the people, particularly the youth, thus losing Egypt. Barely an hour after Mubarak announced that he would not run for president again, Obama called and told him that he had not gone far enough. "It is time to present to the people of Egypt its next government," Obama reportedly told his Egyptian counterpart, according to a senior official. "The future of your country is at stake."[24] For the first time, Obama commended the military for its "professionalism and patience" after top army generals had declared that they would not use force against the protesters, a turning point in the democratic uprising. "I urge the military to continue its efforts to help ensure that this time of change is peaceful," concluded Obama in an implicit call for a transition to a post-Mubarak government. Obama went a step farther and addressed the young people of Egypt, the spearhead of the revolution: "I want to be clear: We hear your voices. I have an unyielding belief that you will determine your own destiny and seize the promise of a better future for your children and your grandchildren."[25]

Obama's belated policy shift did not appease human rights activists and groups who criticized the administration for hesitancy and for not fully backing democracy advocates in Egypt from the start. On the other hand, Obama's abandonment of Mubarak, one of America's most loyal and valuable regional allies, frightened Arab rulers who feared a similar fate, as well as Israel, which relied on the Egyptian strongman to enforce the Gaza siege and confront Iran, Hamas, and Hezbollah. In particular, the Saudis, terribly disappointed with Obama's betrayal of Mubarak, publicly voiced their displeasure with the new approach, which they interpreted as naïve and harmful to America's trusted allies. Senator John Kerry, the influential chairman of the Foreign Relations Committee, who is very close to the Obama administration, addressed the Saudi concerns: "Our friends are mad at us because we said Mubarak had to go," he told a US Islamic Forum held in Washington. "We didn't say that . . . the Egyptian people did."[26]

What appeared to be a betrayal was, in fact, a calculated move by Obama to cut his losses: Mubarak had become a liability to the United States. Obama's decision to abandon Mubarak heralded no transformation of American foreign policy in the region, a pivotal strategic and economic theater for the United States and the global economy; the administration was selective and discriminating in its approach, treating each country differently and separately. As a senior official noted, "What we have said throughout this is that there is a need for political, economic, and social reform, but the particular approach will be country by country."[27]

The Obama foreign policy team has drawn a red line in the Gulf sand against revolutionary change of the Egyptian and Tunisian variety. Unlike its stance toward Tunisia, Egypt, Libya, Yemen, and Syria, the Obama administration has urged protesters from Bahrain to Morocco to work with existing rulers toward what some officials call "regime alteration" as opposed to "regime change."[28] "Starting with Bahrain, the administration has moved a few notches toward emphasizing stability over majority rule." According to a US official: "Everybody realized that Bahrain was just too important to fail."[29] In fact, Obama administration officials went out of their way to mend the rift in relations with Saudi Arabia, which, along with the United Arab Emirates, sent about 2,000 troops to Bahrain to empower the ruling royal family in its suppression of the democratic uprising in the tiny kingdom— home to the headquarters of the US Fifth Fleet, which patrols the Arabian Sea, the Persian Gulf, and the Red Sea. In a nod to the Saudis, senior US officials, reversing a previous stance, accepted the claim that the Iranians were trying to exploit the situation in Bahrain and the Gulf.[30]

Therefore, the US approach toward Egypt can't be generalized to other countries in the region, even though Obama strongly implied that this would be so after the fall of Mubarak. On 11 February, Obama compared the organizers of the Egyptian uprising to Martin Luther King and Gandhi and lauded its peacefulness and inclusiveness. "We saw mothers and fathers carrying their children on their shoulders to show them what true freedom might look like. . . . We saw people of faith praying together and chanting—'Muslims, Christians, we are one,'" said Obama. "The people of Egypt have spoken, their voices have been heard, and Egypt will never be the same." In the same speech, Obama urged the Egyptian military to ensure that the transition "bring all of Egypt's voices to the table," lift the emergency law, and guarantee elections.[31]

In his May 2011 speech at the State Department laying out his approach toward the Arab awakenings, Obama sought to realign US foreign policy in the Arab region by saying the United States has a stake not just in the stability of nations, "but in the self-determination of individuals." Apparently developing what amounted to a new US approach to the Arab world, Obama said that America would promote substantive political and economic reform across the region—a set of universal rights—and would support transitions to democracy. "Our support for these principles is not a secondary interest—today I am making it clear that it is a top priority that must be translated into concrete actions, and supported by all of the diplomatic, economic and strategic tools at our disposal," stressed Obama.[32] In an unusually blunt note, he reminded his audience that a strategy based solely upon the narrow pursuit of US interests would not bring stability, prosperity, or freedom to the people of the region. "Moreover, failure to speak to the broader aspirations of ordinary people will only feed the suspicion that has festered for years that the United States pursues our interests at their expense," he stated.[33]

The effort began in Egypt and Tunisia, where the "stakes are high," said Obama, to help them stabilize and modernize their economies. He listed few initiatives, however—relieving Egypt of up to $1 billion in debt, for example, and helping the debt-ridden country regain access to markets by guaranteeing $1 billion in borrowing that was needed to finance infrastructure and job creation. Moreover, Obama pledged to help the new authorities recover assets that were stolen during the Mubarak era.[34] In addition, Group of Eight (the G8—Canada, France, Germany, Italy, Japan, the United Kingdom, the United States, and Russia) leaders approved a package worth billions of dollars in aid to Egypt and Tunisia. The G8 tied aid and development cash to progress on institution building and liberal economic reforms by states that have thrown off autocratic rulers, though Egypt's transitional leaders view such liberal economic reforms as risky and fettering their hands.[35] Trying to erase any doubt about US support of the call for change, Obama indirectly acknowledged that his administration has not been consistent in its stance toward allies like Bahrain and Yemen that have suppressed dissent, though he reproached them with only a slap on the wrist. He reserved his harshest criticism for foes such as Libya, Syria, and Iran.

Ironically, while the US media described Obama's speech as a key policy document that heralded a new approach toward the region, few Egyptians and Arabs tuned in, unlike the large audience for his Cairo address. What Obama has offered Egypt, a poor country saddled with more than $30 billion in debts and facing a grave social and economic crisis, is too little, too late.[36] The glow of his Cairo address to the Muslim world has faded. There exists considerable skepticism about US goals and about Obama's ability or willingness to deliver on his promises. He faces an uphill battle. The early returns are not promising, according to several polls taken in Egypt after the fall of Mubarak. For example, a Gallup poll conducted in June 2011 found that 75 percent of Egyptians oppose US aid to political groups, and 68 percent think the United States will try to exert direct influence over their country's political future. Two-thirds of Egyptians disagreed that the United States is serious about encouraging democracy in the Middle East and North Africa, according to Gallup, perhaps an indication of public frustration over the US government's perceived muted or belated support for Arab uprisings.[37]

There are several reasons that underlie the suspicion Egyptian respondents expressed toward the United States. Theoretically, the Arab awakenings provide the United States with an historic opportunity to reverse the deadly cycle of misperceptions and set a new beginning, a new chapter of relations with the people of the region. Nevertheless, it is unclear whether the Obama administration has made a strategic decision to restructure American foreign policy and fully back democratic forces in the Middle East. There are contradictions and inconsistencies in the administration approach toward the region, and Obama's State Department speech did not resolve these tensions. Although the president's rhetoric is impressive and categorical, it is not matched with concrete initiatives and road maps. As the *New York Times* editors noted, "We do not see how Mr. Obama can talk persuasively about transformation in the Arab world without showing Palestinians a peaceful way forward."[38]

The editorial prod seemed necessary. As millions of Arabs had revolted against their dictators and demanded self-determination and called for open society and government in February 2011, the Obama administration vetoed an Arab resolution at the UN Security Council condemning Israeli settlements in the Palestinian territories as an obstacle to peace. The irony is that the resolution—sponsored by at least 130 countries and backed by all other members of the Security Council—is consistent with Obama's official stance on the construction of Jewish settlements. As the first veto exercised by the Obama administration under pressure from Congress and Israel's friends, it alienated Arabs and Muslims with whom he had promised to improve relations. Regardless of which governments emerge out of the rubble of political authoritarianism in the Arab world, they will have assertive foreign policies that will champion Palestinian rights and challenge Israel's hegemony. Neither the Obama administration nor the Israeli government has drawn big lessons from the democratic waves that have shaken the Arab countries to their foundation. Although Palestine is not the major driver behind the great Arab awakening, it resonates deeply among millions of Arabs, a reminder and symbol of injustice and victimization of an Arab population. During Egypt's revolution, reformists' calls were not just for domestic change, but for a new direction in foreign policy, especially one that is more supportive of the Palestinians and other Arab causes. Many Egyptians say they felt humiliated by how their country abandoned its role and marginalized itself in the region.

The quest for collective "dignity," a rallying cry of the Arab revolts in Egypt and elsewhere, calls for an end to political tyranny at home and for justice for Palestinians. In this regard, it must be emphasized that the plight of the Palestinians is a cause that is reemerging as a motivation and focus for Arab protesters on the street. In Egypt, the frequency of pro-Palestinian protests has increased as a growing number of Egyptians believe that Israel is violating international law. Several protests have already taken place outside the Israeli embassy in Cairo, with protesters holding banners that read, "Here is the Palestinian embassy" and waving Palestinian flags. Protesters have also called for unity among Palestinian factions and for the creation of a reconciliation plan, which the Egyptian government has lately been able to forge, though, so far, without producing genuine success. They call for the resistance movement to "stay on the path," as one protest banner read. Notably, Egypt's Coalition of the Youth of the Revolution organized several large protests in support of the Palestinians in Alexandria for 13 May, demanding particularly the opening of the Egypt-Gaza border for food and medical and other humanitarian supplies.

In August 2011 relations between Israel and post-Mubarak Egypt reached a breaking point after Israeli troops responding to a cross-border Palestinian attack killed five Egyptian police officers inside Egyptian territory on the Israeli border. At the time, Egypt nearly withdrew its ambassador from Israel, and Cairo protesters demanded the expulsion of the Israeli ambassador. When the Supreme Council of the Armed Forces, the current ruling authority, did not do so, angry protesters broke into the Israeli Embassy in Cairo, tearing down a concrete barrier around the high-rise building and trapping six staff members inside. The Israeli ambassador, his family, and most of the staff and their dependents—some 80 people—were evacuated out of the country by military aircraft overnight. The rampage, in which hundreds were injured, further worsened already deteriorating ties between Israel and post-Mubarak Egypt. Obama expressed "great concern" about the degenerating situation between America's two allies and assured Netanyahu that the United States was acting "at all levels" to resolve the crisis.[39]

In contrast to Washington and Jerusalem, the message of Egyptian protesters has gotten through to the corridors of power in Cairo. In an interview with the BBC, Nabil el-Arabi, the then Egyptian foreign minister, said he is aware that he must differentiate himself from his predecessors and devise a new foreign policy in harmony with Egyptian aspirations: "We have made it very clear from the beginning of this government that has now been in power for about six weeks, that we are turning a new page in our foreign relations," he stated. "We are reviewing all our major interests in foreign policy."[40] Egypt's shifting foreign policy, which includes its decision to open its border with the Gaza Strip, broker a reconciliation pact between Hamas and Fatah, and upgrade relations with Iran, raised alarm bells in Israel. "We are troubled by recent developments in Egypt," said a senior Israeli official. "These developments can affect Israel's national security at a strategic level."[41] Indeed, with the Islamists gaining a majority in the new parliament and forming a new government, Egypt will no longer do Israel's and America's bidding in its neighborhood, but it will respond to a public opinion sympathetic to the plight of the Palestinians and a desire to break with Mubarak's foreign policy legacy. In this turn away from America, it is likely that Egypt will be the rule, not the exception, in the region.

Yet the Obama administration has invested its hopes in Egypt's current military rulers to maintain the status quo on the Arab-Israeli conflict and to oversee a gradual and peaceful transition of power. Concerns run high in Washington that early elections could bring unfriendly Islamists to power and further strain relations with Israel, reported the *New York Times*. Initially, the Obama foreign policy team was noticeably silent as the Supreme Council of the Armed Forces suppressed legitimate dissent, polished its image, and plotted to stay in power behind the scenes even after a new Parliament is in place. "We will keep the power until we have a president," Maj. Gen. Mahmoud Hegazy, said.[42] The military council had pledged in formal communiqués in March 2011 to hold the presidential election by September. But the ruling generals reversed themselves and said that would now come only after the election of a Parliament, the formation of a constitutional assembly, and the ratification of a new constitution—a process that could stretch into 2013 or longer. As tensions mounted between the military council and civilian political leaders from liberals to Islamists, a growing number of lawyers and activists questioned the willingness of the military, the country's most revered institution before the revolution, to ultimately submit to civilian authority. The military's new plan "is a violation of the constitutional declaration," Tarek el-Bishry, the jurist who led the writing of that declaration, wrote in the Egyptian newspaper *Al Sharouk*, arguing that the now-defunct referendum had been the military's only source of legitimacy.[43]

Activists and politicians are worried that the military will refuse to have its authority and financial interests answerable to an emerging civilian democracy. Egypt's military tribunals; arrests of dissident voices, most recently including popular blogger Alaa Abdel Fattah; and a crackdown by soldiers that killed 24 Coptic Christian demonstrators in October 2011 have led to anger and deepening suspicions among activists. The military's authoritarian actions show how removed Egyptians are from the freedoms and civil liberties they sought in overthrowing Mubarak's thirty-year-long police state. The country's martial law and political disarray are stark contrasts to the situation in Tunisia, where elections were held in October 2011; Tunisia is much closer to transitioning to civilian governance and achieving the pluralistic ideals of the Arab awakenings.[44]

As tensions mounted inside Egypt, the Obama administration signalled approval of the military's slower approach to relinquishing authority to an elected authority. In an appearance with the Egyptian foreign minister, Secretary of State Clinton called the revised plan for elections "an appropriate timetable," though she urged an early end to the emergency law, which has not been lifted by the military after Mubarak's ouster.[45] The Obama foreign policy team seemed oblivious to popular sentiments and rising tensions between the public and the military council. Since the ouster of Mubarak, the US government has used its connections (and substantive military aid) to the ruling generals to demand assurances that the Muslim Brotherhood's role will be limited in any future government, and to attempt to ensure continuity of relations with Israel. In July 2011, the US House Appropriations Committee earmarked $1.55 billion to Egypt on the condition that such aid should in part be used for "border security programs and activities in the Sinai" in order to ensure Israel's security concerns. The House Appropriations Committee directed that Secretary of State Hillary Clinton certify that the government of Egypt "is not controlled by a foreign terrorist organization, or its affiliates or supporters, is implementing the Egypt-Israel Peace Treaty, and is taking steps to detect and destroy the smuggling network and tunnels between Egypt and the Gaza strip," a humiliating demand to a supposedly democratically elected government in Cairo. For example, when the Egyptian authorities acceded in May 2011 to the demand by the Egyptian public to open the Rafah crossing and ease the blockade on Gaza, the crossing was closed again within just three days because of US and Israeli pressure. The status of the Rafah crossing had not changed significantly since the end of the Mubarak era.[46]

Taking sides with the military, the Obama administration now reinforced widely held sentiments in Egypt and the region in general that it is not genuine about supporting democratic transition there. Despite the announcement of a shift in the US approach to the Arab awakenings, the Obama foreign policy team remained wedded to the old idea of maintaining stability and the status quo. The administration continued to be reluctant to take risks on peoples' choices, a testament to the structural and historical continuity in US foreign policy.

As the ruling generals tightened their grip on power, hundreds of thousands of protesters flooded back to Tahrir Square in November 2011, signalling the start of a second phase of the Egyptian revolt, one that targets the Supreme Council of the Armed Forces (SCAF) and its concerted efforts to maintain the status quo. Although initially welcomed as saviors, Egypt's ruling generals miscalculated monstrously by resisting the transition to civilian rule and brutally suppressing peaceful dissent. Instead of delivering on their pledge to relinquish authority in six months after the ouster of Mubarak, the SCAF led by Field Marshal Hussein Tantawi and Chief-of-Staff General Sami Anan plotted to rule from behind the scenes even after a new parliament is in place. Since the toppling of Mubarak, more than 10,000 civilians have been charged and tried swiftly in military courts and face harsh sentences. The SCAF resisted calls to repeal the despised emergency laws of the Mubarak era and have borrowed a page of his book. As the protesters demanded that the SCAF promptly transfer power to a civilian authority, the ruling generals used blood and iron to silence the demonstrators, killing 59 and injuring 1,000. When Egyptians and world opinion expressed shock, the generals were unmoved: "Egypt is not Tahrir Square." Major General Mukhtar el-Mallah, a member of the SCAF, claimed an open-ended mandate to hold power long after the parliamentary vote, declaring at a press conference, "We will not relinquish power because of a slogan-chanting crowd."[47]

Even as the elections showed Islamists, particularly the Muslim Brotherhood, to have won a majority of seats in the parliament, the ruling generals, who defied and suppressed a week of protests, reiterated more forcefully than ever that they do not intend to yield authority to the new parliament; they said they might claim special permanent powers under the new constitution that the new parliament is to write. "The position of the armed forces will remain as it is—it will not change in any new constitution," declared Tantawi, an acknowledgment that does not bode well for relations with the Muslim Brotherhood.[48] At the same time, Tantawi and the SCAF have set a definite date for the transfer to civilian rule by holding presidential elections no later than 30 June 2012. It is no wonder then that many Egyptians remain sceptical about the SCAF's designs and readiness to cede power. The SCAF's actions are not reassuring, and include human rights abuses of detainees, particularly women. Virginity tests were performed on female protesters, a humiliating and degrading tactic designed to terrorize women who dare to protest, and to label them as "prostitutes," in the words of one of the ruling generals. In another effort to discredit the protesters and sow fear among the public, the ruling generals have fed Egyptians a conspiratorial diet of plots hedged by foreign powers to destroy the nation, a tactic often used by the Mubarak regime. Military police raided the offices of dozens of human rights organizations and confiscated their files and computers under the pretext that they serve a foreign agenda.

As civilian casualties mounted in November and the generals discarded public demands for setting up a national unity caretaker government, the White House finally released a statement critical of the SCAF for the first time since the ouster of Mubarak. It said in part, "The United States strongly believes that the new Egyptian government must be empowered with real authority immediately."[49] As the *New York Times* reported, until mid-November the Obama administration had voiced only approval for the generals' slow and shifting timetables for transferring power to civilians.[50] Secretary of State Hillary Clinton went further and said she is "deeply concerned about the continuing reports of violence in Egypt." Female protesters "being attacked, stripped and beaten in the streets" by security forces "disgraces the state and its uniform," Clinton said at Georgetown University in Washington in December 2011.[51] Once again, like Mubarak, the ruling generals reacted by saying they do not accept outside interference in the country's internal affairs, exploiting nationalist sentiments and deep suspicions of foreign meddling in Egypt. In contrast to earlier statements, in which the US government threatened to withhold military aid ($1.3 billion annually) if the SCAF did not enforce the siege of Hamas and limit the role of Islamists in a future government at home, the brutal crackdown against peaceful dissidents and civil society did not elicit any explicit threat from Washington. In fact, the United Sates called on both sides—protesters and the SCAF—to desist from using violence, thus equating the deadly tactics of the powerful military with the civil resistance of the demonstrators.

The Egyptian case speaks volumes about Obama's muddled and unbalanced approach to the region. Caught off guard by the Arab uprisings, he hesitated and then sought to position the United States on the winning side—that of the democratic forces. Once he reached a decision, he used soaring rhetoric to reach out to millions of protesters who demanded real change, but he offered no grand vision or concrete initiatives to translate words into action. Far from being strategic and comprehensive, the policy is tactical and selective. Obama's foreign policy priorities are elsewhere in Asia, particularly in China, America's global rival. The Arab revolts intruded themselves onto the Obama agenda and sucked him deeper into the Middle Eastern sands, particularly Egypt, a country that his administration had thought would remain safely in Mubarak's hands.

In contrast to Iran, Iraq, Pakistan, and Afghanistan, with which the Obama foreign policy team was preoccupied, Egypt in 2009 was seen to be relatively stable and under control. The new administration had neither the desire nor the will to preach democratization and push Mubarak to reform state and society. Obama did not tinker with the status quo as long as it held. But once the Mubarak regime unraveled, the Obama foreign policy team faced difficult policy choices and had to respond promptly to rapidly unfolding developments. The emerging policy is a work-in-progress, a piecemeal approach designed to absorb revolutionary shocks and preserve American interests in the region. The Obama administration no longer has the luxury of distancing itself from the turmoil engulfing Egypt, and its reputation is on the line. As mentioned previously, it has recently been more assertive and critical of some of the human rights violations of the ruling generals. Unless Obama's uplifting rhetoric is matched by concrete initiatives to facilitate Egypt's democratic transition by pressing the Egyptian military, he risks widening the divide between the new democratic forces and US foreign policy and reinforcing the bitter legacy.

The stakes are high for American vital interests in the Middle East and for Obama's presidential legacy as well. Egyptians no longer invest much value and credibility in Obama's words and promises as they did in the early months of his administration. Former supporters at home have become disillusioned with the president and criticize him for being timid, indecisive, and opportunistic. As Zbigniew Brzezinski, an early backer of Obama's presidential bid, lamented: "I greatly admire his insights and understanding. I don't think he really has a policy that's implementing those insights and understandings. The rhetoric is always terribly imperative and categorical: 'You must do this,' 'He must do that,' 'This is unacceptable.'" Brzezinski added, "He doesn't strategize. He sermonizes."[52]

IRAN: FROM BEST FRIENDS TO WORST ENEMIES

Iran was one of America's most important Cold War allies during the era of Reza Pahlavi, shah of Iran. It was viewed as loyal and dependable and, in the words of Jimmy Carter, "an island of stability in one of the most troubled areas of the world."[53] Following the Iranian revolution in 1979, however, the Islamic Republic rejected Iran's old alliance with the "American and Israeli infidels" and pursued an independent foreign policy serving neither East nor West in the international system.[54] In one stroke, Iran went from being America's best friend to being its worst enemy as it challenged US dominance in the Gulf and the Middle East in general. Ayatollah Khomeini's defiance of the United States, particularly during the 1979–1981 hostage crisis, has had a determining effect on US policies toward Iran ever since. Islamic Iran threatened America's vital interests in the Middle East, as well as those of its regional clients. Indeed, the Islamic revolution has had a "profound effect" on the formulation and conduct of US strategy toward the greater Middle East. In the American imagination, revolutionary Islam as practiced by Khomeini came to be associated with terrorism, fascism, and barbarism.[55]

Ever since 1979, the United States has attempted to isolate and deter the Islamic Republic and roll back its revolutionary model. In the 1980s American foreign policy aligned itself with the late Iraqi president Saddam Hussein against the clerical regime in Tehran in an effort to drain the strength of the two rival Gulf powers: Henry Kissinger famously observed in the 1980s, "It's a pity they both can't lose." Still angered by the Iranians' seizure of the US embassy in Tehran and determined to prevent Khomeini from exporting his Islamic revolution to neighboring countries, the Reagan administration shielded Saddam Hussein from a UN investigation of whether Iraq had used chemical weapons. According to a CIA analysis cited by Joost R. Hiltermann, an investigative writer and human rights activist who reconstructed the US-Iraq connection, Saddam Hussein employed chemical weapons "on a scale not seen since World War I," and Iraq became the first nation ever to use nerve agents in battle. Still, the United States sided with Saddam, shared intelligence data on Iran's battle plans, and provided Baghdad with economic aid. To reassure Iraq of its continuing support, the Reagan administration's most influential messenger, Donald Rumsfeld, made two trips to Baghdad in the early 1980s and presented the Iraqi dictator with a gift of golden spurs.[56] Iran's subsequent decision to start a nuclear program stemmed largely from its perception of vulnerability to nonconventional weapons during the war with Iraq and Western complicity with Saddam.

The United States puts a high premium on deterring Iran and limiting its influence regionally. Martin Indyk, Bill Clinton's principal adviser on US policy toward the Middle East in the early 1990s, developed the concept of "dual containment."[57] Key to American strategy in this significant oil-producing area, the policy toward Iran and Iraq consisted of pitting the two Gulf rivals against each other. For example, after the US-led international coalition expelled the Iraqi army from neighboring Kuwait in 1991, President George H. W. Bush and his advisers decided against marching all the way to Baghdad because they viewed Saddam as a deterrent to powerful Iran.[58] Since then the pendulum of US policy has swung from deterrence to rollback. Mutual suspicion and hostility are the norm in US-Iranian relations. While the Iranian regime has sought to expand the circle of friends in its neighborhood and consolidate its power base, successive US administrations have struggled to isolate Iran and keep it isolated. For three decades, playing Iraq off against Iran has been central to the American strategy.

That strategy changed after the attacks of September 11, 2001. Throwing caution to the winds, President George W. Bush dispensed with the norms and rules that guided American foreign policy since the end of World War II, including a balancing act in the Gulf. The swift invasions of Afghanistan and Iraq in 2001 and 2003, respectively, resulting in the ouster of the Taliban and Saddam, eliminated the two regimes that had kept Iran boxed in. That created space for the clerical regime to make a serious bid for regional leadership and challenge US dominance. In particular, America's invasion and occupation of Iraq opened the gates of hell and caused a host of strategic challenges, including civil war and instability in Iraq, a new cold war between the pro-American Sunni-based regimes of Saudi Arabia and Egypt on the one hand and Iran on the other, and a nascent nuclear arms race.

The new cold war has exacted a heavy toll on societal and sectarian coexistence in Middle Eastern societies. From Iraq to Saudi Arabia and from Lebanon to Pakistan, anti-Shiite sentiments spread like wildfire, fueled mainly by the US-led invasion and occupation of Iraq and the subsequent civil war there. Arab Sunni rulers also manipulated sectarianism to counter increasing Iranian influence in their countries. For example, former Egyptian President Hosni Mubarak said publicly that Shiite Arabs are not loyal citizens and thus cannot be trusted. Jordanian King Abdullah II cautioned against the spread of a "Shi'a crescent" across the Sunni Arab world linking Iran, Iraq, and Lebanon.[59] Yemeni President Ali Abdullah Saleh accused Iran of the incitement of sectarian tensions by arming and financing the Houthi (Shiite) insurgency in the north against his regime. The Bahrain royal family made similar accusations against Iran. Senior Sunni clerics in Saudi Arabia, Egypt, and elsewhere whipped up anti-Shiite feelings by claiming that Shiite Iran and its cohorts were converting Sunnis to Shi'ism. Although political rather than doctrinal, a Sunni-Shiite fault line has widened with grave consequences for social harmony and peace.

In addition to the societal fallout of the US-Iranian rivalry in the Middle East, there is a real danger of a region-wide conflict over Iran's nuclear program. Although the Obama administration has chosen economic warfare and covert activities as its weapons of choice against the Islamic Republic, the likelihood of military hostilities cannot be overlooked. Current Israeli leaders threatened to carry out air strikes against Iranian nuclear facilities and have exerted pressure on the US government to prevent Iran from reaching a threshold that would allow it to build a nuclear bomb. There is a massive buildup of armaments in the Gulf and in the region as a whole, a buildup that has triggered a costly and dangerous arms race and intensified regional tensions and rivalries. In 2011, the United States signed arms deals totaling more than $100 billion with Saudi Arabia, United Arab Emirates, Israel, and other countries. The Middle East is already one of the most militarized areas in the world, a recipe for miscalculation and armed confrontation.[60]

Ironically, September 11 offered a brief moment of opportunity to recalibrate America's relations with Iran and to begin the healing of US-Iranian relations, but that opportunity was missed by the Bush foreign policy team. As the world mourned, so did Iran. Many Iranians publicly expressed compassion for the families of the dead in America. Iran offered assistance to the United States in fighting Al Qaeda and indirectly backed the US invasion of Afghanistan.[61] After the US-led invasion of Iraq in the spring of 2003, Iran offered to enter comprehensive talks with the administration in Washington. In a letter sent to the State Department, Tehran proposed complete cooperation with the West on its nuclear program, acknowledgment of Israel, and the end of Iran's backing of Hamas and other groups in Palestine. Despite Iranian gestures of good will and support in Afghanistan and Iraq, President Bush and the neoconservatives did not attempt to reciprocate or mend ties with Iran. Intoxicated by their own worldview of America's supremacy, the Bush foreign policy team shut its eyes and ears to possibilities of cooperation with the Islamic Republic: ideology trumped pragmatism and the American national interest.[62]

Iranian leaders experienced this stinging rejection publicly when Bush labeled Iran, along with Iraq and North Korea, as the "axis of evil" in his State of the Union address in 2002. As Bush turned his back on Iran, Tehran ceased its overtures to Washington. Furthermore, the departure of President Mohammad Khatami, an enlightened voice, and the election of the hypernationalist Mahmoud Ahmadinejad, set the United States and Iran on a collision course. With the United States bogged down in Iraq's killing fields after 2003, Iran seized the moment and directly asserted its leadership in the Gulf and the greater region. It applied pressure on the United States inside Iraq and Afghanistan.[63]

By the time President Bush left office in 2009, the US-Iranian relationship had reached its lowest point in years. On the most contentious issue, the Iranian nuclear program, the Six-Party Talks had largely hit a standstill. Rounds of UN-imposed economic sanctions, a form of war by other means, brought little change in Iranian behavior. Moreover, Iran's assertiveness in Iraq and its backing of Hezbollah during the 2006 Israel-Lebanon war further heightened US concerns and deepened the antipathy to the Islamic Republic. By the time of Obama's inauguration, Iran featured as one of the most pressing national security challenges for the United States, and the new president agreed with this assessment. Considering Bush's actions largely ineffective in changing Tehran's behavior, Obama signaled that he was going to break with its Manichean foreign policy and engage the estranged nation. As a presidential candidate, he repeatedly said the Bush approach of simply pressuring Iran was not working and that he would be willing to talk to the country's leaders to find ways to reduce tensions: that was the only way to rebuild trust and overcome decades of heightened tensions, verbal threats, and the absence of diplomatic engagement that culminated in the confrontational Bush years.[64]

On Inauguration Day and immediately after, Obama sent a message to the Iranian leadership by saying in his first television interview that "if countries like Iran are willing to unclench their fist, they will find an extended hand from us."[65] For the first five months after his inauguration, Obama repeated the same message in an effort to engage the Iranian regime and persuade it to abandon its nuclear ambitious. Yet, despite his positive verbal overtures, from the beginning Obama had decided to maintain economic sanctions against the Ahmadinejad regime in order to keep up the pressure and force it to change its behavior. Barely a month after his inauguration, the Obama administration sent Daniel Glaser, a senior US Treasury official, to Brussels to reassure more than 70 Middle East and nonproliferation experts from all 27 European Union states and institutions that the new administration remained committed to the "dual-track" approach (of simultaneously exerting economic and political pressure and publicly expressing an interest in negotiating) adopted by previous administrations and to "support[ing] the current international framework targeting Iran's illicit conduct through financial measures."[66] Glaser briefed the Europeans and said that "engagement" would be an important aspect of a comprehensive strategy to dissuade Iran from acquiring nuclear weapons. "However, 'engagement' alone is unlikely to succeed," Glaser added. "Diplomacy's best chance of success requires all elements combining pressure and incentives to work simultaneously, not sequentially." Justifying the use of this dual-track policy, Glaser said, "Time was not on our side. . . . The international community must urgently choose between several bad options. . . ."[67] Thus Obama adopted his predecessor's policy toward Iran despite initially distancing himself from it publicly and promising a more nuanced approach.

In an effort to extend a friendly hand to Iranian leaders and persuade them to abandon their nuclear ambitions, Obama made several statements—most notably, on 20 March 2009, to mark the Persian New Year—in which he respectfully addressed "the people and leaders of the Islamic Republic of Iran," and called for a "new beginning" to overcome old divisions between the two countries.[68] However, the Iranian leadership did not respond to Obama's rhetoric of engagement and resented his dual-track approach, which married sweet words with punishing economic sanctions and covert actions to disrupt the Iranian nuclear program. Ayatollah Ali Khamenei dismissed Obama's gesture as empty talk: "They say they extended their arms towards Iran. What kind of hand? If it is an iron hand covered with a velvet glove, then it will not make any good sense." He concluded by saying, "You change, and we will also change our behavior, too."[69]

According to leaked US diplomatic cables, the Obama administration's engagement efforts were halfhearted. President Obama, a pragmatist, believed that, at a minimum, positive language would improve the atmosphere and facilitate negotiations with Iran, even though rhetoric might not necessarily bring the desired results. In other words, Obama was willing to unclench his fist while keeping the pressure on Iran, a strategy that had little chance of success. Neither the Iranians nor America's Middle East allies were willing to play by Obama's nuanced rules.

From the outset, both Israel and Sunni Arab countries, particularly Saudi Arabia, lobbied hard to portray Iran as a present and immediate danger to their security and called on the Obama administration to confront the clerical regime in Tehran militarily. Leaked US diplomatic documents show a concerted effort by America's local allies warning against Iran's evil and expansionist designs, as well as against any rapprochement with their regional nemesis. Israel spearheaded the drive to convince the Obama foreign policy team to maintain a clenched fist. On his visits to the White House, Netanyahu stressed repeatedly that nuclear-armed Iran poses a grave threat to the Jewish state and the entire Western world, and he impressed on Obama the risks of appeasement. Seeking to divert attention from peace talks with the Palestinians, Netanyahu linked progress with the Palestinians to a pledge by the Obama administration to remain firm on Iran. Even more, the United States has had to deal with the growing threat of Israel's launching a preemptive military strike on Iran's nuclear sites, and it has had to walk the tough line of publicly stressing the importance of diplomatic engagement with Iran while at the same time assuring the Israelis that engagement won't be at the expense of Israel's security.[70]

In a similar vein, the Wikileaks cables show clearly that pro-US Arab rulers urged the Obama foreign policy team to maintain a hard-line stance against Iran and to keep the military option on the table. Behind closed doors with US diplomats, Arab leaders, particularly in the Gulf, spoke candidly about their fears of Iran's growing influence in the region and revealed a level of animosity toward their Shiite neighbor that contrasted radically with their public pronouncements. In the view of the Gulf ruling elite, Iran has replaced Israel as the new enemy. For example, Saudi Arabia's King Abdullah told US leaders that Iran posed a grave threat to the kingdom. In a diplomatic cable, the king reportedly made repeated calls for the United States to attack Iran and "cut off the head of the snake."[71]

Similarly, the crown prince of Abu Dhabi, Mohammed bin Zayed, reportedly urged American officials to "develop a 'plan B'" and "to act quickly" to counterbalance rising Iranian influence.[72] In another more important diplomatic cable summarizing a working dinner meeting in July 2009, Bin Zayed compared the current situation in the Gulf with that of the pre–World War II period in Europe by saying, "Ahmedinejad is Hitler."[73] Likewise, Bahrain's King Hamad bin Isa al-Khalifa is cited in one of the leaked cables as calling on the United States to take "action to terminate [Iran's] nuclear program, by whatever means necessary." Al-Khalifa stated further: "The danger of letting it go on is greater than the danger of stopping it [by military means]."[74] Contrary to the received wisdom, Qatar's prime minister Hamad bin Jassim al-Thani told his US interlocutors that his country did not trust Iran and was not interested in developing a friendly relationship with it. In a revealing diplomatic cable, al-Thani is cited as describing the Qatari-Iranian relationship as one in which "they lie to us, and we lie to them." Moreover, the leaked diplomatic documents note that the Qatari government had told Iran to "listen to the West's proposals or there will be military action."[75]

Though not surprising, the leaked sample of hostile statements against Iran by pro-American Middle Eastern allies inevitably heightened tensions between the United States and its allies on one side and Iran and its partners on the other. The leaked diplomatic cables also further undermined the legitimacy and authority of pro-Western Arab rulers in the eyes of their citizens: the gulf between Arab rulers' public and private statements provided cannon fodder to their critics and exposed them as lackeys of the United States.[76]

The end result is that Obama's initial positive public gestures toward Iran were neutralized by his hard line on economic sanctions and Iran's nuclear enrichment program. Iranian leaders say they are skeptical because Obama has not altered America's hostile policies toward Iran and is determined to ratchet up the pressure. For instance, the Obama administration offered China and Russia incentives in order to keep them from voting against more stringent UN Security Council sanctions on Iran. In the case of China, the United States pushed for a Saudi-brokered deal on oil supplies to replace China's reliance on Iranian oil. Rewarding Russia, the Obama administration agreed to revamp a European missile shield and to allay Moscow's fears about NATO's encroachment on its sphere of influence. As Glaser noted, "the U.S. closely consults Russia and China, who must play their parts."[77]

Although Obama did not break with his predecessor's basic approach to Iran, he did send an important message to Iranian leaders that he was different, and that he was willing to open a new chapter of relations with their country. He also said he wanted neither to "interfere" in the country's internal affairs nor to threaten the survival of their regime. When the 2009 presidential election in Iran triggered large demonstrations, Obama did not back the nascent pro-democracy movement, which was rallying behind Mir-Hossein Mousavi, the leading opposition candidate in an election that was widely disputed. Obama kept his distance, providing only mild rhetorical support. In an interview with CNBC after the protests began, to the chagrin of human rights groups and many liberal voices within the president's own party, Obama said that "the difference between Ahmadinejad and Mousavi in terms of their actual policies may not be as great as has been advertised."[78] Still trying to engage the Iranian government, the Obama foreign policy team refrained from siding with the protesters despite fierce criticism from conservatives and Republicans who demanded that the administration fully back the pro-democracy movement.[79]

Nevertheless, Iranian leaders accused the West, including the United States, of stirring up the protesters and backing the Green Movement that they brutally suppressed. The disputed presidential election and the suppression of the protests represented a turning point in relations between the Obama administration and the Iranian government, resulting in an escalation of tensions and a return to the policy of confrontation.

What to make of Obama's hardening stance toward Iran? The current Iranian leadership has been slow and reluctant to respond to Obama's positive gestures. There is no trust left between Washington and Tehran, and suspicion and hostility permeate their relationship. Ayatollah Khamenei and President Ahmadinejad rebuffed Obama's repeated public gestures on engagement and did not reciprocate. Instead of offering constructive initiatives to recalibrate US-Iranian relations and facilitate Obama's task, the Iranian leaders acted as if nothing had changed in Washington and showed contempt for the new president.[80]

The Iranian leadership seems to be paralyzed by a fierce rivalry between the unelected office of the Supreme Leader Khamenei and the elected presidency of Ahmadinejad. In a wide-ranging speech in October 2011, Khamenei said that Iran could do away with the post of a directly elected president, a warning to Ahmadinejad against overstepping the executive's limited powers. "Presently, the country's ruling political system is a presidential one in which the president is directly elected by the people," he told an audience of academics in the western province of Kermanshah. "However, if one day, probably in the distant future, it is deemed that the parliamentary system is more appropriate for the election of officials (holding) executive power, there would be no problem in altering the current structure," he concluded in the speech broadcast on state television.[81] Khamenei's comments had already been echoed by some of his supporters in Parliament and other politicians. Within the context of Iranian domestic politics, Ahmadinejad is the reformist, trying to clip the wings of the Islamic clergy. Hard-line conservatives constantly accuse him of being in the thrall of "deviant" advisers who want to undermine the role of the clergy, including the office of the Supreme Leader. Members of Parliament threatened to impeach Ahmadinejad over his refusal to comply with parliamentary legislation.[82] From Syria to the United States, the bitter top-level power struggle between the president and the Supreme Leader has complicated the country's international relations and sent mixed signals.

There are also few in Iran who support Washington's demand that the country halt its nuclear program. Iranian leaders from the ultraright to the ultraleft support the development of the nuclear program and view it as an expression of Iranian nationalism. Nevertheless, over the years Ahmadinejad has made several initiatives as serious opening bids for a negotiating settlement of the nuclear issue. He proposed the establishment of an international consortium to enrich uranium, and he accepted a Turkish-Brazilian deal to have the Russians enrich uranium for Iran. Ahmadinejad has also made an offer that would cap Iran's enrichment at the 5 percent level. The Obama administration dismissed Ahmadinejad's offers as a delaying tactic to allow Iran time to build a nuclear weapon. US officials say that Iran is racing to do so. In October 2011, the US government accused the Quds Force of the Islamic Revolutionary Guard Corps of a plot to assassinate the Saudi ambassador to the United States, Adel al-Jubeir, right in Washington, D.C., in a place where large numbers of innocent bystanders could have been killed. To punish Iran and to further isolate it, the Obama administration pressed United Nations nuclear inspectors to release classified intelligence information showing that Iran is designing and experimenting with nuclear weapons technology. For the first time, the International Atomic Energy Agency (IAEA) released a report that described, in detail, the evidence it has collected suggesting that Iranian scientists have experimented with warhead designs, nuclear detonation systems, and specialized triggering devices that can be explained only as work on a nuclear weapon.[83]

The publication of the report by the United Nation's watchdog group precipitated a debate that had been dormant during the Arab awakenings about how aggressively the United States and its allies, particularly Israel, should act to halt Iran's suspected weapons program. Widespread media reports in Israel suggested that Netanyahu is once again considering a strike on Iran's nuclear complexes, while Obama said that he and his allies would maintain "unprecedented international pressure" on Tehran to keep it from producing a nuclear weapon.[84] As the drums of war grew louder in Israel, in interviews and speeches before and after Netanyahu's visit to the White House in March 2012, Obama tried to quiet the loose war talk, while arguing that he will order the US military to destroy Iran's nuclear program if economic sanctions fail to compel Tehran to shelve its nuclear ambitions. Seeking during a presidential election year to persuade the Israeli prime minister to postpone whatever plans he may have to bomb Iran's nuclear facilities in the coming months, Obama declared that "the United States will always have Israel's back." Although the US president struck a consistently pro-Israel posture, he cautioned Israel against a premature strike against Iran, an attack that might help the Islamic Republic and the beleaguered Syrian regime: "At a time when there is not a lot of sympathy for Iran and its only real ally, [Syria,] is on the ropes, do we want a distraction in which suddenly Iran can portray itself as a victim?"[85]

Obviously, the Obama foreign policy security team is anxious that Netanyahu might militarily preempt Iran during the US presidential elections, thus presenting the administration with a fait accompli. In an interview with the *Atlantic* magazine, Obama walked a fine line, backing Israel while warning Netanyahu against miscalculation. He said Netanyahu has a "profound responsibility to protect" Israelis, given the Holocaust and anti-Semitism, and added "that the prime minister is also head of a modern state that is mindful of the profound costs of any military action, and in our consultations with the Israeli government, I think they take those costs, and potential unintended consequences, very seriously."[86]

At a subsequent press conference, Obama excoriated the "bluster" and "big talk" by Republican presidential hopefuls about bombing Iran. "When I see the casualness with which some of these folks talk about war, I'm reminded of the costs involved in war," he said, adding: "This is not a game. And there's nothing casual about it." There would be consequences for both Israel and America, he cautioned, "if action is taken prematurely."[87]

Meanwhile, the United States and its European allies have been waging all-out economic war against the Tehran government and imposing punishing sanctions against its oil and banking sectors, including the central bank. Iranians are suffering, and economic pain can be felt on the streets in soaring prices for state-subsidized goods and a collapse of the rial currency, which lost 40 percent of its value against the dollar between November and December 2011. The price of food staples has increased by up to 40 percent in recent months, Reuters reported. Ahmadinejad told Parliament that the latest sanctions were "the most extensive . . . sanctions ever" and that "this is the heaviest economic onslaught on a nation in history . . . every day, all our banking and trade activities and our agreements are being monitored and blocked."[88] In March 2012, Obama said that sanctions organized by his administration have put Iran in a "world of hurt," and that economic duress might soon force the regime in Tehran to rethink its efforts to pursue a nuclear weapons program.[89]

With regard to a military option, the Obama administration's position is no longer ambiguous. In a speech before the annual convention of AIPAC, the pro-Israel lobbying group, in March 2012, Obama said: "Iran's leaders should know that I do not have a policy of containment; I have a policy to prevent Iran from obtaining a nuclear weapon." But the US president has not accepted Israel's key demand that military action be taken before Iran acquires the ability to manufacture a bomb, as opposed to before it actually builds one.[90]

US strategy is based on strangulation of the Iranian economy. What this means, Obama told the *Atlantic* magazine, is that "We do believe there is still a window that allows for a diplomatic resolution to this issue."[91] For example, at a summit meeting in Cannes, France, at the end of October 2011, Obama and NATO allies refrained from any talk of military strikes and said they remained focused on economic sanctions and other forms of diplomatic pressure, including enforcement of several UN Security Council resolutions that demand that Iran stop all uranium enrichment. The secretary-general of NATO, Anders Fogh Rasmussen, said that "NATO has no intention whatsoever to intervene in Iran, and NATO is not engaged as an alliance in the Iran question," according to the Associated Press. However, the British newspaper *The Guardian* reported that Britain's armed forces were stepping up their contingency planning for military action along with the United States against Iran.[92] *The Guardian* added that the British Ministry of Defense "believes the U.S. may decide to fast-forward plans for targeted missile strikes at some key Iranian facilities."[93]

Speaking at the pro-Israeli Washington Institute for Near East policy, Dennis Ross—recently resigned as Obama's special adviser on the Middle East, and whose portfolio included Iran—stressed that the administration is committed to preventing Iran from acquiring a nuclear weapon, using all means, including military strikes. "The administration prides itself on a certain reality that it does what it says," Ross said, referring to Obama's making good on his pledge to capture or kill Osama bin

Laden. Regarding Iran, Ross noted that when Obama "says all options remain on the table, it doesn't mean that force is his first choice, but it means that's an option that he intends to exercise."[94] A few weeks later, the US president stated specifically that "all options are on the table," and that the final option is the "military component." Obama told the *Atlantic* that both Iran and Israel should take seriously the possibility of American action against Iran's nuclear facilities: "I think that the Israeli government recognizes that, as president of the United States, I don't bluff."[95]

There is an irreconcilable divide between Iran and the Western powers. The Iranian leadership said that all the documents suggesting that it was attempting to create a nuclear weapon that could fit atop an Iranian missile are "fabrications" designed to justify an attack. The *New York Times* noted that the country has been the target of covert attacks, including the assassinations of some nuclear scientists and the use of a computer worm that disabled some of Iran's nuclear centrifuges. The Iranian government published its own evidence of Western terrorist plots against Iran, while its leaders repeat constantly that they would never develop nuclear weapons.[96] In a recent interview with Seymour Hersh in the *New Yorker* magazine, Mohamed ElBaradei, the former head of the IAEA, said he had never "seen a shred of evidence that Iran has been weaponizing, in terms of building nuclear-weapons facilities and using enriched materials."[97]

After the publication of the report by the IAEA and the subsequent belligerent talk, Hersh, who has been reporting on Iran and the bomb for *The New Yorker* for the past decade, concluded that there is no new incriminating evidence in the report indicating that Iran is really building a bomb. He based his conclusion on several interviews with top nuclear engineers and arms control specialists and former US intelligence officials who have spent years researching the Iranian nuclear program. In fact, Hersh asserts that the recent charges against Iran are politically motivated and that the new Director General of the IAEA, Yukiya Amano of Japan, who replaced ElBaradei, is acting at the behest of US wishes, an alarming charge reminiscent of the accusations leveled against Iraq regarding its alleged possession of nonconventional weapons before the US invasion in 2003.[98]

In 2012, as Obama prepares for the next campaign, confronting Iran has replaced engagement, and a concerted effort is being made to limit Iranian influence in the region and prevent it from developing nuclear capabilities. The Obama administration has given up on reaching a rapprochement with the clerical regime and has reverted to the rhetorical devices and policies of its predecessor—economic warfare and pressure. Obama has made it clear that the goal was not to contain Iran, but to prevent the Islamic Republic from acquiring nuclear arms. Dennis Ross acknowledged that the White House would like to see a regime change in Tehran, though it is currently focusing on ways to stop Iran's nuclear program.[99] In a way, the US-Iranian relationship is as low now as it was at the end of the Bush presidency, if not lower.[100] US officials speak of Iran straightforwardly. "The biggest threat to the United States and to our interests and to our friends . . . has come into focus and it's Iran," said a US military official, addressing a forum in Washington.[101] The official conceded that he did not believe Iran wanted to provoke a conflict and that he did not know if the Islamic Republic had decided to build a nuclear weapon.[102]

The wave of democratic uprisings that has swept the region since the spring of 2011 has added further tension to an already bitter relationship. Obama's response to the Arab revolts shows the extent of the shift in his approach toward Iran and the region in general. White House aides stood idly by while the Ahmadinejad regime brutally suppressed the Green Movement in 2009, but in the wake of the Arab uprisings, Obama has adopted a muscular tone on Iran's violations of human rights and increasing authoritarianism.[103] Responding to Iran's crackdown against protesters at home after Mubarak's ouster in January 2011, Obama lambasted the Iranian regime: "It's ironic that the Iranian regime is pretending to celebrate what happened in Egypt. . . . They acted in direct contrast to what happened in Egypt by using force against demonstrators."[104]

From the outset of the Arab awakenings, President Obama and his national security team have been fixated on how revolutionary changes in Egypt and Tunisia will cause turmoil in various Arab states and turn them to their own advantage. Israel and Saudi Arabia, both sworn enemies of the Islamic Republic, sounded the alarm and claimed that Iran will be the main beneficiary of Arab uprisings.

For the Obama administration, the Gulf has been a different matter from Egypt and Tunisia because American vital interests are deeply involved there and the Iranian threat looms large. Notably, Bahrain, a tiny Gulf sheikdom, has become a flash point, a casualty of the US-Iranian rivalry. At the beginning of the Bahrain uprising, Obama senior officials did not accept the official Saudi and Bahrain claims that Iran had fomented the trouble in the small sheikdom. Secretary of Defense Gates bluntly called on America's Gulf ally to introduce substantive reforms and to preempt Iran from exploiting tensions there, an acknowledgment that the pro-democracy movement in Bahrain is indigenous, homegrown, and not inspired or driven by Iran. However, after intensive lobbying by Saudi Arabia and other Gulf countries, the Obama administration reversed course and suggested that pro-Iranian elements might attempt to hijack the Shiite-led protests in Bahrain and install an anti-US government beholden to the Islamic Republic. Therefore, for the United States, Bahrain, unlike Egypt, was just too important to fall. The Iranian lens colored the attitudes of the Obama administration toward Bahrain and distorted its vision, although Saudi resistance to change in the Gulf was key to swaying the US position.[105] In the end, the Saudis took action themselves and preempted the Obama administration, a decision that testifies to the new assertiveness of the Saudi Kingdom.

President Obama has blamed Iran for assisting Syria in the suppression of the uprising that has shaken the regime of Bashar al-Assad. In his first comments on the Syrian crisis, in April 2011, Obama pointed out the Iran-Syria connection: "Instead of listening to their own people, President Assad is blaming outsiders while seeking Iranian assistance in repressing Syria's citizens through the same brutal tactics that have been used by his Iranian allies," and Islamic Republic Revolutionary Guards have been named simultaneously in US and EU sanctions that target Syrian regime officials.[106] In his State Department speech on the Arab uprisings, in which he tried to align the United States with the aspirations of the people, Obama drew a sketch of Iran as a model for repressive states like Syria and the stirring of freedom by Iranians as an example to follow for the Arab people:

> So far, Syria has followed its Iranian ally, seeking assistance from Tehran in the tactics of suppression. And this speaks to the hypocrisy of the Iranian regime, which says it stands for the rights of protesters abroad, yet represses its own people at home. Let's remember that the first peaceful protests in the region were in the streets of Tehran, where the government brutalized women and men, and threw innocent people into jail. We still hear the chants echo from the rooftops of Tehran. The image of a young woman dying in the streets is still seared in our memory. And we will continue to insist

that the Iranian people deserve their universal rights, and a government that does not smother their aspirations.[107]

As the Syrian crisis reached a climax in 2012, Obama viewed the likelihood of Assad's ouster as an additional opportunity to encircle and weaken the Iranian regime. He said that a transition to "a peaceful and stable and representative Syrian government" from the pro-Iranian Assad regime would be "a profound loss for Iran," a statement that shows the uprising in Syria has become embroiled in the new cold war in the Middle East.[108]

Obama no longer seeks engagement with the Islamic Republic, or even containment of the long-term foe. Confrontation and economic strangulation are the name of the game. In the State Department address, Obama reiterated America's major grievances against the Islamic Republic—Iran's intolerance and repressive measures, as well as its illicit nuclear program and its support of terror—which was a marked departure from his statements both as a presidential candidate and in his early months in office when he openly refrained from backing the 2009 Green Movement lest he offend the Ahmadinejad regime, which he was trying to engage. Two years later, Obama invested the Green Movement with meanings that transcended Iran and deployed it as a sword over the heads of Iranian leaders. In fact, Obama's recent statements on Iran do not differ much from Bush's and can be read as a call for regime change in Tehran.

There is no denying that Obama's original desire to recalibrate US-Iranian relations has not borne fruit. The paradigm of "engagement" has suffered a fatal blow, replaced with the paradigm of confrontation. The case of Iran shows clearly that Obama's policy design crashed on the rocks of institutional resistance at home and the suspicion of US designs in Tehran that has developed since the Iranian Revolution. Moreover, Iran's regional rivals, particularly Israel, have exerted pressure on the Obama administration in an effort to stiffen its resolve. Even before his inauguration, the new president faced stiff resistance both from Republicans who opposed any rapprochement with the mullahs and from within his own party—Democrats who believed that engagement would give Iran time and space to develop nuclear weapons and threaten Israel's security. There also existed considerable skepticism among officials in the Defense Department and the intelligence community about

Iran's willingness to abandon its nuclear program, and a belief that Iranian leaders would use engagement as a cover to advance their nuclear ambitions. On Iran, Obama was swimming against the current at home.

His foreign policy stance toward Iran did not survive his first year in the White House, a testament to the emergence of a new era of hegemonic transition and rising geopolitical and geoeconomic powers and realities in the Middle East.

"THE NEW TURKEY"

Turkey's shift toward the Middle East in the last decade and its emergence as a geoeconomic and geopolitical powerhouse is an outgrowth of the rapidly altered domestic context, the changing regional environment, and the waning of US influence. Turkey's refusal to allow US troops to transit its territory in the 2003 invasion of Iraq is a case in point. And, despite intensive lobbying by the Obama administration, Turkey voted against tightening sanctions against Iran in June 2010. While US officials viewed Turkey's action as undermining their efforts to build an international consensus on Iranian nuclear ambitions, their Turkish counterparts saw it as Washington undercutting their efforts to find a solution to the enrichment issue after the United States had indicated support for the Turkish-Brazilian initiative to allow Russia to enrich uranium for Iran. Rejecting the paradigm of containment that the United States and the European Union have justified as promoting security in the Middle East, the new Turkey embraced an open-ended dialogue with the Islamic Republic and cultivated an economic relationship with its next-door neighbor without the threat of coercion. From the Turkish perspective, America's securitized approach in the region is misplaced and counterproductive, a source of instability and a recipe for confrontation. Ankara prefers cooperation over confrontation with Tehran and has resisted Obama's efforts to get it to join in the anti-Iranian coalition.[109]

With the coming to power of a post-Islamist, culturally conservative, market-oriented Justice and Development Party (AKP) governing elite, Turkey has pursued an independent foreign policy and sought to deepen economic and cultural links with its Middle Eastern neighbors. More often than not, the Turkish governing elite has challenged US-sponsored policies in Iraq, Palestine, Israel, Syria, and Iran, policies that aimed at altering fragile power balances in the Middle East with the goal of imposing Western dominance. Therefore, since 2003, US-Turkish relations have become fluid and tense because of the rise of Turkey as a pivotal geoeconomic and geopolitical power, and because the US foreign policy elite has not come to terms with Turkey's new active role and its quest to lead by example. There are deep unspoken tensions between the United States and its formerly pliant ally, an ally whose worldview and regional and international orientation underwent a radical shift after September 11.[110]

The certainty and clarity that characterized Turkey's international relations during the Cold War—firmly siding with the anti-Soviet camp—have disappeared as bipolarity has been replaced with an evolving multipolar world and increasing fragmentation within the West itself. Now Turkey's military strength rivals that of Israel, its political system has stabilized into a relatively functioning democracy, and it has situated itself as an economic giant that dwarfs most other economies in the region.[111] In 2009, US Secretary of State Hillary Clinton described Turkey as an emerging global power along the lines of China, India, and Brazil.[112]

With an ambitious ideological agenda to social engineer transformational change in the Middle East, the neocons in the Bush administration initially welcomed the new Turkish elites and saw them as agents of change that could assist in democratizing the region. However, Turkey's vision, which emphasized soft (diplomatic) power, dialogue, and economic cooperation, had little in common with the neocons' imperial design, which relied on hard (military) power and top-down enforced liberalizing reforms.[113]

The Turkish Grand National Assembly's negative vote on logistical support for the US-led invasion of Iraq in 2003 was the first in a series of acts in which it opposed US policies in the Middle East and roiled relations with Washington. For instance, during his visit to Turkey in April 2003, Paul Wolfowitz publicly scolded the leadership for not joining the US-led coalition against Iraq and said that he wished the Turkish military would play a more prominent role.[114] Ever since, Turkey has charted an independent course in its neighborhood and has resisted US actions that clash with its interests. Turkey's boldness caused much soul-searching among the US foreign policy establishment about what went wrong and who "lost" Turkey, a patronizing attitude that views Turkey as a client as opposed to a free actor having its own legacies and interests.[115] Steven Cook, a senior fellow at the Council on Foreign Relations, went so far as to ask, "How do we keep the Turks in their lane?"[116]

From the beginning of his presidency, Obama recognized Turkey as the most pivotal pro-United States country in the Muslim world, essential to his foreign policy agenda to repair America's relations with Muslims. The president viewed the US-Turkish relationship as a "model partnership," an ideal for other Muslim countries. He saw Turkey as a showcase of a progressive, economically strong, stable, vibrant democracy that shares common values with the United States, a country that enjoys strong links and connections with both the Christian West and the Muslim world. Obama credited the enduring relationship between the United States and Turkey as a testament to the way in which American foreign policy fosters prosperity, democracy, and progress in the region. It is no surprise then that, shortly after assuming office, Obama traveled to Ankara and delivered his first address to Muslims from the floor of the Turkish Parliament, a choice that testifies to the significance of Turkey in Obama's outreach strategy.

Welcomed like a rock star by Turkish parliamentarians, Obama told his captivated audience that this was his first trip overseas as president of the United States:

> Some people have asked me if I chose to continue my travels to Ankara and Istanbul to send a message to the world. And my answer is simple: *Evet*—yes. Turkey is a critical ally. Turkey is an important part of Europe. And Turkey and the United States must stand together—work together—to overcome the challenges of our time.[117]

He emphasized the resilience and endurance of the US-Turkish relationship, even though the two countries at times do not see eye to eye:

> The United States and Turkey have not always agreed on every issue, and that's to be expected—no two nations do. But we have stood together through many challenges over the last 60 years. And because of the strength of our alliance and the endurance of our friendship, both America and Turkey are stronger and the world is more secure.[118]

Obama sought to repair the damage done by Bush's poor stewardship of the US-Turkish relationship, particularly the reverberations of the Iraq War, and to renew the friendship with a valuable friend. With American troops deeply engaged in the region and with a pressing economic crisis back home, a frozen Arab-Israeli peace process, a rising Iran, and social and political uprisings throughout the Arab world, the Obama administration desperately needs a friendly Turkey to maintain its national interests in the greater Middle East. Moreover, Obama's war in Afghanistan-Pakistan and the withdrawal of US troops from Iraq have put more strains on America's capabilities and maneuverability, as well as on relations with Muslim peoples and societies.[119]

Obama has spent more time in consultation with Erdogan (with whom he's developed a close personal relationship), than with other world leaders, a fact that reflects the significance of Turkey in US strategy in the region and beyond. Turkey has provided the United States with cultural and strategic depth. For example, as a long-standing NATO member, Turkey has played a supporting role in Afghanistan and northern Iraq, and until recently served as a strategic mediator between Iran and the West and between Israel and Syria. As the debate heated up in the United States about Turkey's "drift" eastward in 2011, Erdogan agreed to station a radar in the country as part of NATO's American-designed missile defense system to protect against potential Iranian attacks. A senior US official told the *New York Times* that it is "the most significant military co-operation between Washington and Ankara since 2003." It was widely seen as part of a major boost in Turkey's 59-year-old membership in NATO.[120] Far from seeking a revisionist foreign policy in terms of its relations with the United States, the new Turkish ruling elite accept the realist interpretation of Middle Eastern politics advanced by the US establishment, though they reject the neoconservatives' prioritizing of relations with Israel. There is much more continuity in US-Turkish relations than meets the eye.[121] Indeed, many US diplomats quietly say that Turkey's eastern turn is a welcome and beneficial development—in good part because it heralded the eclipse of Iran's much more dangerous influence over the Arab states.[122] For example, now Turkey is spearheading opposition to the Assad regime and has implicitly threatened to confront it. The Obama administration has poured praise on Turkey for taking the lead against Assad and has coordinated strategy with Ankara.

Nevertheless, the Western powers, including the United States, can no longer take Turkey for granted. In the last decade, the conduct and actions of the new Turkish ruling elite have betrayed aspirations for independent leadership and recognition on the international arena; Turkey has slowly shifted its focus from joining the European Union, and has moved to improve its relations with its Middle Eastern neighbors. After the Europeans constantly delayed approval of its quest for membership, Turkey now feels that it has to find "best friends" elsewhere. As Obama aptly noted, "[The EU membership issue] is inevitably destined to impact on the way Turkish people see Europe. If they do not feel part of the European family, then obviously they're going to look elsewhere for alliances and affiliations."[123]

Likewise, countries in the region, impressed by Turkey's economic success and political confidence and vibrancy, have shown a great interest in the new rising power next door. This shift has been reflected in the increased movement of capital, goods, and people between Turkey and its neighbors. Notably, Jordan, Lebanon, and Syria have pushed for an integrated economic free-trade zone with Turkey, which will boost the energy, investment, and tourism sectors of all these states. (The uprising in Syria seems to have dealt a fatal blow to its relationship with Turkey.) Moreover, Gulf citizens are showing a greater interest in exploring, visiting, and investing in Turkey. Thus, Turkey has returned gallantly to the Middle East. So gallantly in fact, that some analysts argue that the old Ottoman soul of Turkey has been reawakened.[124]

As Ankara has developed closer links and interests with its neighbors, it has become more actively engaged in the regional conflicts it once avoided. For example, in contrast to the current Anatolian ruling elite, the Kemalist secular establishment beginning in the 1920s largely refrained from active involvement in the Arab-Israeli arena and instead focused more on its connections with Europe, the Cyprus conflict, and strong economic ties with Israel, its second largest trading partner. Similarly, the Kemalist elites did not take sides in the contentious post-1979 revolutionary politics of Iran that pitted the Islamic Republic against the United States. Recep Tayyip Erdogan's ascension to the premiership in 2003 marked a departure from Turkey's exclusive love affair with the West, which is witnessing internal convulsions of its own. The love affair has not completely soured, as some commentators claim, and Turkey's commitment to NATO and the EU remains strong.[125] What has changed is that the new Turkey asserts itself as a more independent actor rather than as a subservient client of the West, thus reflecting the popular views in Turkey. The new Turkey pursues its vital national interests, defined as economic prosperity and peace, and has been willing to say "no" to its long-term Western partners, including the United States.

Although Obama officials have attempted to "modernize" the relationship with Ankara and accepted the many faces of the new Turkey, after three years they felt frustrated and at a loss as they tried to make sense of the self-described "emerging power."[126] The president's visit to Ankara sought to reset and strengthen the US-Turkish relationship and orient it to a more positive future. In his efforts to restructure US-Turkish relations, Obama, like his predecessor, has encountered serious challenges that stem from the lack of trust and candor and the clash of interests.[127]

In particular, as mentioned earlier, Iran tops the list of contentious foreign policy issues between Washington and Ankara, though this might be changing as Iran and Turkey find themselves on opposite sides in Syria and elsewhere. According to dozens of diplomatic cables released by Wikileaks, the biggest disagreement between the two countries is over Iran's nuclear ambitions. One diplomatic cable from October 2009 shows an angry exchange between the US ambassador to Ankara, James Jeffrey, and a senior Turkish diplomat. Jeffrey vehemently attacks Erdogan's remarks that Iranian nuclear ambitions are merely "gossip." According to this cable: "Holding a copy of President Obama's Pittsburgh Summit condemnation of Iran's nuclear ambitions, the ambassador Sinirlioglu [under secretary of the Turkish Foreign Ministry Feridun Sinirlioglu] asked if this was the 'gossip' to which Erdogan had referred."[128] Another diplomatic cable in February 2010 details a meeting between William Burns, the US under secretary of state for political affairs, and Sinirlioglu in which Burns cautions his Turkish counterpart against complacency and inaction: "Turkish interests would suffer if Israel were to act militarily to forestall Iran's acquisition of nuclear weapons or if Egypt and Saudi Arabia were to seek nuclear arsenals of their own." Sinirlioglu looked "visibly disheartened" by Burns's statement, and conceded the need for a "unified message" on Iran's nuclear ambitions, according to the same cable.[129]

American officials are frustrated by their inability to persuade their Turkish counterparts to adopt a tough, unified stance against Iran. In May 2010, Turkey's nuclear diplomacy with Iran, in cooperation with Brazil, further strained the relationship between the United States and Turkey. Brazil and Turkey convinced Iran that it should take part in a limited nuclear fuel swap with Russia, a move that angered the Obama administration and its European allies, who saw the agreement as giving Iran an easy way out and allowing it to break international consensus on sanctions. After US officials publicly aired their displeasure with Turkey's nuclear diplomacy with Iran, Ankara accused the US of double-dealing diplomacy because in private the Obama administration had approved the talks. Turkey's position on Iran represents a radical departure from that of its Western partners.

Deteriorating relations between Israel and Turkey have created more tensions between Washington and Ankara. Israel's attack on the flotilla that was seeking to penetrate the siege of Gaza during the waning days of the Bush presidency and the start of Obama's term marked the beginning of a rupture between Israel and Turkey, and that imbroglio fractured the US-Turkish relationship further. Defying diplomatic protocol, Turkish Prime Minister Erdogan and Israeli President Shimon Peres had a heated and sharp public exchange in 2009 at the usually calm and sedate gathering of the World Economic Forum in Davos, Switzerland.[130] In May 2010 Israeli commandos attacked a Turkish aid flotilla heading to Gaza and killed eight Turks and one Turkish-American. That deadly raid poured fuel on a raging fire. Ever since, Erdogan has linked normalization of relations with the Jewish state to Israel's making a public apology for the deadly raid and moderating its aggressive behavior.[131] After Israel refused to apologize for the killing of Turkish civilians, Erdogan withdrew his ambassador and suspended the country's military cooperation and froze all trade ties with Israel. While touring the newly liberated capitals of Egypt, Tunisia, and Libya in September 2011, Erdogan vehemently criticized Israel, calling it "the West's spoiled child," and voiced strong support for a Palestinian state. "Israel will no longer be able to do what it wants in the Mediterranean," Erdogan told an audience in Tunis, "and you'll be seeing Turkish warships in this sea," a message intended for Israeli ears and others as well.[132] In a strongly worded criticism, the *New York Times* editorial board wrote that Erdogan's "increasingly shrill denunciations of Israel are a danger to the region as well as to Turkey" and called on him to "weigh his words more carefully."[133]

The Obama administration finds itself in an awkward position, having to mediate between the two. His advisers feel frustrated with Netanyahu after he rejected a sound, American-mediated deal to close the book on Israel's reckless assault on the Gaza aid flotilla. But they feel uneasy and concerned about Turkey's prioritizing of its disagreement with Israel. The Obama administration fears that Turkey, under Erdogan, has taken the clash with Israel to a dangerous level.[134] In contrast, the Turkish government is bitter about America's pro-Israel bias, a blinder that, in its opinion, fuels regional instability and conflict.[135]

The falling-out with Israel has caused a firestorm of criticism of Turkey within the various domestic constituencies of American foreign policy.[136] Neoconservatives and pro-Israel voices have launched a concerted campaign to demonize Erdogan and the AKP, his governing party, and have equated Turkey's distancing itself from Israel with a turn toward an "Islamist agenda."[137] Commentators and members of Congress have questioned whether Turkey can be a reliable ally and whether Washington should maintain close relations with Ankara. The *Wall Street Journal* lamented "the fall of Turkey," and Niall Ferguson, a conservative academic with ties to neocons, has gone so far as to say that "the Erdogan government is a cleverly run one which soft pedals in its negotiations with the West, but is no doubt taking Turkey away from the West in the direction of a neo-Ottoman policy."[138]

Similar views are aired by US diplomats in the field. Leaked diplomatic cables reveal persistent anxieties among American officials about Erdogan's Islamist worldview and the fear that his aim is to transform Turkey into an Islamist state. In a meeting in October 2009 between the US ambassador James Jeffrey and the Israeli ambassador Gabby Levy, the two diplomats complained that Erdogan is a "fundamentalist." As Levy notes, "[Erdogan] hates us religiously and his hatred is spreading." Levy warns of an "anti-Israeli shift in Turkish foreign policy" manifested by the Turkish government's "recent elevation of its relations with Syria and its quest for observer status in the Arab League." Erdogan "simply hates Israel," Levy concluded.[139] Another cable from a US diplomat in March 2005 describes Erdogan as "isolated," relying on "his charisma, instincts, and the filtering of advisors who pull conspiracy theories off the web or are lost in neo-Ottoman Islamist fantasies."[140]

Despite the concerted domestic campaign inside the United States to portray the new Turkish ruling elite as dangerous and unreliable, there is a shared feeling among Obama aides that the "new Turkey" is a vital counterweight to Iran's ambitions in the region, and a useful asset to the NATO operation in Afghanistan and elsewhere.[141] Obama knows that US influence in the region rests on stable relations with rising geoeconomic and geopolitical powers such as Turkey. He has rebuffed policy advocates in Washington who view the US-Turkish relationship through the narrow Israel lens.[142] Clinton's statement about Turkey's emerging as a global power reflects this spirit. With the Arab uprisings, Turkey has become more valuable to the United States as an ally that provides inspiration, a successful example of political and economic transition and development, and institutional assistance to its neighbors along with a pro-Western orientation.

It is worth stressing that the decline of Turkey's relations with Israel and its intensifying links with Iran and other Middle Eastern neighbors should not be seen as a new wave of neo-Ottomanism, as some neoconservative commentators would have it. Erdogan has vehemently denied any desire to revive the Ottoman legacy.[143] It is also misleading to draw a connection between Turkey's new assertiveness as some sort of Islamic imperialism by pointing to Erdogan, a former Islamist and devout believer. This could never be further from the truth. His key message to Egyptians, delivered in a national television interview, is that they should abolish their old sharia-based constitution and become a secular state. "In Turkey, constitutional secularism is defined as the state remaining equidistant to all religious," he said. "In a secular regime people are free to be religious or not."[144] And if there was any ambiguity, the Turkish leader then told Egyptians that the most important thing Arabs should learn from Turkey is secularism—a term that has negative connotations in Egypt and the Arab world in general. "I recommend a secular constitution for Egypt," he said. "Do not fear secularism because it does not mean being an enemy of religion. I hope the new regime in Egypt will be secular. I hope that after these remarks of mine the way the Egyptian people look at secularism will change."[145] That message precipitated a heated debate across the Arab world, and provoked angry responses from the Muslim Brotherhood and other Islamist groups, who nevertheless still sought to associate themselves with Erdogan.

A new anti-Israel coalition is now coalescing around Turkey, according to the received wisdom in Israel and among its supporters in the United States.[146] The reality is that the new Turkey simply differs from the United States and Israel on a host of regional issues, such as the plight of the Palestinians, Iran, and the use of force to bring about change in governments' conduct. The current Turkish ruling elite rebuff their former superpower patron when the latter's policies clash with their own interests.[147]

Turkey's rise in the ranks of geoeconomic and geopolitical powers has coincided with America's waning influence in the Middle East and in the international system, as well as a changed regional landscape. There is nothing uniquely Islamist about Turkish foreign policy and regional diplomacy except insofar as the new Anatolian post-Islamist elite respond to the aspirations and demands of their constituencies, who are socially conservative and religious nationalists. Like their Western counterparts, the Turkish elite play by the rules of the democratic game and domestic politics that impose constraints on foreign policy. Public opinion has become a major variable in the shaping of Turkish foreign policy.[148]

As the US ambassador to Turkey noted, "Does all this mean that the country is becoming more focused on the Islamist world and its Muslim tradition in its foreign policy? Absolutely. Does it mean that it is 'abandoning' or wants to abandon its traditional Western orientation and willingness to cooperate with us? Absolutely not."[149] Turkey's stance on Libya is a case in point. Initially, Erdogan opposed the imposition of a no-fly zone over Libya and expressed concerns about Western intentions there. However, after a direct appeal to and consultation with Erdogan, Obama secured Turkey's support, which proved pivotal in allowing NATO to take the lead in enforcing the no-fly zone and providing legitimacy for the mission in Libya.[150]

US critics of Turkey's approach to the Middle East fail to consider the country's historical evolution and the emergence of a new ruling elite with different sensibilities and a more nuanced worldview than its predecessor. While Turkey continues to look westward to advance its national interests, it has deepened its engagement with the Middle East and taken a leadership position. The architect of Turkey's international relations, Foreign Minister Ahmet Davutoglu, has stressed that his country's major source of power is its identity, which is rooted in its historical and geographic richness. He called for enhancing Turkey's "strategic depth" by establishing "zero problem relations with neighbors" and expanding its sphere of influence in the Middle East. Although Davutoglu's vision has met with only mixed success, Turkey is a preeminent player in the region and has captured the imagination of millions of citizens in neighboring countries.[151]

For example, Turkey was more forthcoming and aggressive than the United States in calling on Mubarak to step down from power when the revolution broke out in Egypt in early 2011. In a speech to the Turkish Parliament on 1 February 2011, Erdogan emphasized, "I am saying this clearly: You must be the first to take a step for Egypt's peace, security, and stability."[152] Similarly, despite the existence of a close relationship between Erdogan and Bashar al-Assad, Turkey publicly criticized the Syrian regime for suppressing the popular protests that have swept the country since spring 2011 and called on Assad to either meet the legitimate democratic demands of his citizens or step down. In a major blow to Assad, Erdogan imposed economic and military sanctions on the Syrian regime and welcomed the Syrian opposition to Turkey. Now Erdogan is pitted in a fierce struggle against his former ally and "friend" Assad. Erdogan has allied himself with the Syrian opposition in a drive to unseat Assad. In contrast, Turkey remained silent on popular protests in Iran, a calculation based on the complexity of the Iranian scene and Turkey's inability to dent it, a position similar to that taken by the Obama administration after the disputed 2009 presidential election in Iran.

Turkey's recent discovery of the Middle East is a testament to the rise of the country as a pivotal power in its own right, a development that has brought nuanced changes in its foreign affairs. The new Turkish elites feel confidently equipped to chart their own policies toward the region without dictation from Washington and European capitals.

American critics who accuse Turkey of drifting from the West and charting an independent foreign policy overlook the sea change that has occurred in the regional landscape and the international system—the rise of geopolitical and geoeconomic powers like Turkey (based on recent economic gains and the strength of its democracy) and the serious decline of American power. These critics have hardly anything to say about the transformation of US foreign policy after September 11, a rupture that wrecked the fragile balance of power in the greater Middle East and shattered confidence in the American strategy of pivotal regional actors. In particular, the US debacle in Iraq, along with the subsequent reverberations, exacted a heavy toll on its reputation, moral stature, and political influence worldwide. In a way, the Iraq war may come to be seen as a watershed in the downward slide of the United States from its once preeminent place in a unipolar international system. Even its closest friends such as Turkey look at it askance and fear that it lost its way.[153]

September 11 sowed the seeds of the decline of US influence in the Middle East and the increased assertiveness of regional powers, particularly Turkey and Iran. Instead of dismissing the new directions in Turkish foreign policy as a "drift" from the West and an embrace of Islamism, Western critics should place them in the context of a global power shift away from a unipolar world dominated by the United States to an evolving multipolar world with new geoeconomic and geopolitical powers. As an emerging global power, Turkey has already positioned itself as a pivotal player in the Middle East. With the revolutionary turmoil sweeping its neighborhood, Turkey's role, weight, and influence are bound to expand and increase.

CHAPTER 6

THE WAR ON TERROR

More than a decade after September 11, 2001, and after the death of Osama bin Laden in May 2011, Al Qaeda is still largely shrouded in myth, generally portrayed as force multipliers, lurking everywhere, ceaselessly plotting to kill innocent people en masse. Every terrorist incident—no matter how amateurish—is widely reported and treated as if performed by masterminds, reinforcing anxiety and paranoia about terrorism generally and Al Qaeda specifically. Moreover, some Western—particularly American—politicians embrace this distorted view of Al Qaeda's threat capability; it affords political opportunities and enhances their ability to shape foreign policy and national security strategy.

THE BUSH LEGACY

While the Bush administration catered to this monolithic and mostly ideological perception of Al Qaeda's omnipotence and invincibility—and indeed promoted it—President Obama has walked a fine line between changing his predecessor's language and terms on the "war on terror" and adopting "a new strategic approach" that exemplifies the structural continuities in US foreign policy. It is an approach designed to reassure Americans that, "faced with that persistent and evolving terrorist threat," the president and his administration will be "unrelenting, unwavering, and unyielding in [their] efforts to defeat, disrupt, and dismantle Al Qaeda and its allies."[1]

By effectively defining the terms of the terrorism narrative, Bush set the limits of American foreign policy. His rhetoric continues to shape its perspective, and Americans continue to experience, remember, and explain September 11 through this rhetorical lens.[2] President Obama has discovered the staying power of that narrative and the challenge of recalibrating it.

Despite a number of books encouraging greater and more sophisticated discussion—John Mueller's *Overblown,* Peter Beinert's *Icarus Syndrome,* and Sandra Silberstein's *War of Words*—neat concepts and convenient theoretical premises continue to dominate, and the terrorism narrative has become deeply entrenched within American political culture and the national psyche. Now active policies from Washington or self-interested advocacy parties no longer appear to provide the main momentum for this worldview; the response to the challenge and threat of terrorism has become an ideology of its own. Consequently, there is very little chance of reevaluating the country's overall strategy, particularly the expansion of the national security complex—even for a president who has a "vivid" sense of American economic decline—except, perhaps, on the rhetorical level, where Obama's discourse does represent a break with the inflammatory rhetoric of his predecessor.

Time and again, the president and his senior advisers have stressed that the United States is not engaged in a "global war" against either "jihadists" or "militant Islamic radicalism," Bush's preferred ideological label for Al Qaeda and its allies. Instead, the Obama National Security Strategy (NSS) released in May 2010 defines "a far-reaching network of hatred and violence," a less hyperbolic and more ideologically neutral phrase.[3] According to Obama's top counterterrorism adviser, John Brennan, the new terminology aims at counteracting the notion that the United States is in conflict with the rest of the world—and that Al Qaeda is a global entity capable of replacing sovereign nation-states.[4]

Obama has offered a more nuanced and realistic interpretation of the fight against Al Qaeda, as he did in a commencement speech to the 2010 graduating class at the United States Military Academy at West Point in which he previewed key elements of his NSS:

> Al Qaeda and its affiliates are small men on the wrong side of history. They lead no nation. They lead no religion. We need not give in to fear every time a terrorist tries to scare us. We should not discard our freedoms because extremists try to exploit

them. . . . Terrorists want to scare us. New Yorkers just go about their lives unafraid. Extremists want a war between America and Islam. But Muslims are part of our national life, including those who serve in our United States Army.[5]

Although like his predecessors Obama explicitly reserves to the United States the right to act unilaterally and to use military force preemptively, he pledged to shape a new "international order" based on engagement, diplomacy, and collaboration with traditional allies and new and rising influential actors.[6]

This approach represents a departure from the rigid and simplistic rhetoric that had previously characterized the debate on terrorism. Absolute security does not exist. Yet American and Western politicians have generally shied away from informing their citizens that, regardless of how vigilant and alert security systems are designed to be, they are by no means fail-safe. A determined, suicidal enemy will likely find a way to penetrate any defense.

In a series of speeches laying out the new thinking, Brennan has made it clear that rather than looking at allies and other nations through the narrow "prism of terrorism," as Bush did—they are either with us or against us—the Obama administration hopes to engage the Muslim world on a broader range of issues, such as education, public health, economic development, responsive government, and women's health. Brennan noted: "Why should a great and powerful nation like the United States allow its relationship with more than a billion Muslims around the world to be defined by the narrow hatred and nihilistic actions of an exceptionally small minority of Muslims?"[7]

The Obama administration thus appears to promote a more balanced and nuanced portrait of the terrorist challenge facing the country as well as a willingness to educate the public and address the exaggerated fears held by many Americans. Yet its rhetoric is at odds with institutional reality. Although the term "war on terror" is no longer used, it still dominates as an amorphous state of mind.[8] Obama's national security advisers have been unable to break free from this mind-set because of Republican criticism that the president is weak on national security, and because of a fear that a terrorist attack could undermine the Obama presidency. Preparing Americans for potentially bad news, US attorney general Eric Holder admitted that the danger of homegrown terrorists "keeps [him] up at night." In an interview with ABC's *Good Morning America,* Holder warned Americans that the terror threat is

206 Obama and the Middle East

grave and immediate. "What I am trying to do in this interview is to make people aware of the fact that the threat is real, the threat is different, the threat is constant," he said. "The threat has changed from simply worrying about foreigners coming here, to worrying about people in the United States, American citizens—raised here, born here, and who, for whatever reason, have decided that they are going to become radicalized and take up arms against the nation in which they were born," Holder added.[9]

Even after the killing of Bin Laden and the dismantling of his organization in Pakistan-Afghanistan, Obama aides keep reminding the American public that the war is not over yet and that the threat of terrorism persists. Speaking at Offutt Air Base, Nebraska, Obama's newly appointed defense secretary Leon Panetta used the continuing threat of Al Qaeda as a justification not to exceed the president's proposed $400 billion cuts to the Defense Department over ten years.[10] Ironically, two months earlier, Panetta had said that the United States is "within reach of strategically defeating al Qaeda," as he traveled to Afghanistan for his first visit there as secretary of defense. The success of the raid on Bin Laden's compound in Abbottabad, Pakistan, along with "operations that we conducted at the CIA," has undermined Al Qaeda's ability to carry out 9/11-type attacks, Panetta told reporters traveling with him. According to Panetta's logic, although the remants of Al Qaeda were on the run and "near collapse," the United States must remain militarily mobilized to meet new potential threats by Al Qaeda.[11]

Similarly, in September 2011 a US drone killed Anwar al-Awlaki, a radicalized American-born Yemeni preacher, and Samir Khan, a twenty-five-year-old American editor of *Inspire*, an English-language web magazine of a local branch in Yemen called Al Qaeda in the Arabian Peninsula (AQAP). The magazine seemed designed to galvanize potential recruits in Western societies, particularly in the United States. Although Awlaki's death is a blow to AQAP, the group remains "a significant threat" to America, according to FBI Director Robert Mueller and National Counterterrorism Center Director Matthew Olsen. "Without question, his death has dealt a major blow to the external operations of Al Qaeda's most operational affiliate, yet we assess that Al Qaeda in the Arabian Peninsula remains a significant threat to the homeland," Olsen told the House Permanent Select Committee on Intelligence.[12] Far from "a significant threat," AQAP, a tiny group which includes between 50 and

300 members, poses, at most, a security irritant to Yemen and the United States. Since September 11, American policymakers have either wittingly or unwittingly hyped the threat posed by Al Qaeda, thus sitrring up unneccesary fear among the American public.

THE INSTITUTIONAL REALITY: STRUCTURAL CONTINUITY

On numerous occsions President Obama and Secretary of State Clinton have issued statements about the danger posed by Al Qaeda, including a potential nuclear threat. They have emphasized the administration's desire to remain on the offensive, to be aggressive, and to maintain a muscular opposition to extremists. One goal of these statements is to preempt critics on the American right. Confusing tactical security measures with strategic threats, the Obama administration has consequently elevated Al Qaeda into a player worthy of attention on the world stage.

Clinton said that, "for most of us," Al Qaeda and its affiliates—"trans-national non-state networks"—represented a more potent threat to national security than a nuclear-armed Iran or North Korea.[13] Although Clinton meant by "most of us" the foreign policy and security establishment, she implied that the entire West faced a strategic threat from Al Qaeda.

President Obama has also emphasized the danger posed by rogue terror groups over that posed by North Korea and Iran. Efforts by Al Qaeda to acquire atomic weapons represented "the single biggest threat to U.S. security—both short-term, medium-term and long-term."[14] "We know that organizations like Al Qaeda are in the process of trying to secure a nuclear weapon—a weapon of mass destruction that they have no compunction at using."[15] Appearing alongside South African President Jacob Zuma, Obama added, "if there was ever a detonation in New York City or London or Johannesburg, the ramifications economically, politically and from a security perspective would be devastating."[16]

These pronouncements show that the "terrorism narrative"—the notion that the West remains under constant and imminent threat of attack—has become institutionalized among policy makers, government officials, and the general public. American neoconservatives can largely be credited with this shift in attitude. Indeed, the neoconservatives' most enduring legacy in US foreign policy is not the

Iraq War, but rather the transformation of the American psyche after September 11. Americans have internalized the fear of terrorism; as evils go, it has become the new Red Scare.

In truth, the only conceivable way Al Qaeda could obtain a nuclear device is by building one. For a group that has never displayed any technical sophistication in its attacks, this would involve a monumentally steep learning curve. Even if Al Qaeda were to acquire the technical sophistication to build a nuclear bomb—and here we enter the sphere of science fiction—it lacks the structural capacity to develop such a weapon, let alone the necessary ingredients.[17]

Moreover, financing a nuclear bomb is beyond Al Qaeda's reach. Peter Zimmerman, a nuclear physicist, and Jeffrey Lewis, a nuclear specialist at the John F. Kennedy School of Government, conservatively estimate the cost of building a bomb at $10 million, in addition to having the scientific know-how and the time and the space—precious assets unavailable for a small group like Al Qaeda.[18] At the height of its prowess in the 1990s, Al Qaeda's entire budget for weapons of mass destruction (WMDs) was estimated at a mere fraction of that: $3,000.[19]

In the (unlikely) event that Al Qaeda obtained the right materials and finances, the odds are stacked heavily against success. John Mueller, an expert on Al Qaeda's atomic potential, notes that the organization would have to address no fewer than twenty different technical scenarios to complete and deploy one bomb, a challenge for a country like Iran. Mueller says that, even if one were to allow Al Qaeda the benefit of, say, a 30 percent chance of overcoming each one of these twenty scenarios, the odds are one in over three billion for a single success. The fact is: Al Qaeda no longer exists as an effective organization. It does not possess the scientific and human resources and financial capabilities and safe havens to carry out complex experiments.[20]

It therefore remains a mystery how a roving band of extremists—on the run and under constant fire in Pakistan's lawless tribal areas along the Afghan border— might be "in the process of trying to secure a nuclear weapon," and once they had done so, of detonating it in a major Western city. The evidence of Al Qaeda's strategic reach and capability seems to foreclose any need for hard evidence and discussion. Nonetheless, the media faithfully report the alarming refrain without subjecting the evidence to critical scrutiny and analysis, thus indirectly reinforcing widely held perceptions of Al Qaeda's prowess.

When the Soviet Union was in its final stage of decline, the majority of the US foreign policy establishment—the Republican camp, in particular, though also mainstream intellectual and media commentators—firmly believed that the Soviets were expanding their influence and posing new threats to the West. US intelligence assessments were often doctored to confirm this alarmist view. Even when the evidence of Soviet weakness was presented, it was dismissed as a ploy by Moscow to dupe the West into lowering its guard.

The parallels between the then-dominant view of the Soviet Union during the Cold War and the present-day Al Qaeda are apparent. Many current US officials were Soviet specialists, just as were many of Bush's foreign policy and national security team, including Cheney and Rumsfeld, and defense secretary Robert Gates, who now view the war on terror through the lens of the Cold War. There is no better way to illustrate the continuity between the Cold War and the war on terror than the priority that Obama's national security team assigns to terrorism. During the Cold War, when the president—the commander in chief—traveled away from the White House, his advisers on Soviet and nuclear affairs accompanied him everywhere like a shadow. Now his counterterrorism advisers do so. In the official US worldview, the menace of terrorism has replaced the Soviet threat.

In short, for many Western government officials and policymakers, terrorism has become "Level A."[21] And, so far, the cost of waging the war on terror has been exorbitant; it will soon top $5 trillion. There is no clear end in sight.[22]

Not unlike the military-industrial complex, against which Dwight Eisenhower warned just over fifty years ago and which centered on making billion-dollar delivery systems to launch nuclear weapons to deter the Soviet Union, a new "national security complex" has been constructed since September 11, 2001.[23] A two-year investigation by the *Washington Post* discovered a "Top Secret America" that has mushroomed in ten years to include some 1,271 government organizations and nearly 2,000 private companies, working on counterterrorism in 10,000 locations across the United States, with at least 854,000 people—or nearly one and one-half times the population of Washington—holding top-secret security clearance (even janitors have top-secret clearances because they work in top-secret installations). The annual US intelligence budget has risen from $40 billion a year in 2001 to more than $80 billion today, a figure that does not include a number of military activities or domestic counterterrorism programs.

That $80 billion far exceeds the $51 billion spent on the State Department and foreign aid programs in 2010.[24]

According to the *Post* series, published in the summer of 2010, "[t]he top-secret world the government created in response to the terrorist attacks of September 11, 2001, has become so large, so unwieldy, and so secretive that no one knows how much money it costs, how many people it employs, how many programs exist within it or exactly how many agencies do the same work."[25]

The study captures the massive expansion of the national security complex: "Twenty-four organizations were created by the end of 2001, including the Office of Homeland Security and the Foreign Terrorist Asset Tracking Task Force. In 2002, 37 more were created to track weapons of mass destruction, collect threat tips and coordinate the new focus on counterterrorism. That was followed the next year by 36 new organizations; and 26 after that; and 31 more; and 32 more; and 20 or more each in 2007, 2008, and 2009."[26]

Massive as it is, the post-September 11 security bureaucracy remains mostly invisible to the people it is meant to protect. It is also extremely inefficient. No fewer than fifty-one federal agencies and military commands, operating in fifteen cities, track the flow of money to and from terrorist networks. Their reports recycle the same facts and overwhelm anyone's ability to analyze them. Every day, collection systems at the National Security Agency intercept and store 1.7 billion emails, phone calls, and other types of communications, a fraction of which are sorted. The complex publishes 50,000 reports each year—a volume so great that many are routinely ignored. The government has recently begun to integrate the latest technology in an effort at "data mining" this huge amount of information. In an interview with the *Washington Post,* Gates acknowledged the "challenge" and "difficulty" of obtaining precise data.[27]

Despite the phenomenal expansion of the intelligence machine, the *Post* points out, it has failed to detect the few serious attacks and plots against the US homeland, such as the November 2009 Fort Hood, Texas, shooting that left thirteen dead, or the Christmas Day 2009 underwear bomber—thwarted not by one of the almost one million individuals with top-secret clearances employed to find lone terrorists, but by an alert airline passenger who saw smoke coming from a seatmate. In May 2010, an alert vendor in Times Square called the police after he saw smoke coming out of a parked SUV, where a naturalized Pakistani-American named Faisal Shahzad had placed a bomb.

Particularly alarming was the failure to prevent the Christmas Day bomber, Umar Farouk Abdulmutallab, from boarding an American airliner in Amsterdam despite warnings of a potential attack originating from Yemen by a Nigerian national. "A systemic failure has occurred, and I consider that totally unacceptable," Obama said, referring to what authorities allege was Abdulmutallab's failed attempt to blow up a Northwest Airlines plane preparing to land in Detroit.[28]

The US government had sufficient information to have uncovered this plot and potentially to have disrupted it, but the intelligence community failed to interpret it. "We need to learn from this episode and act quickly to fix the flaws in our system because our security is at stake and lives are at stake," Obama concluded.[29]

According to the *Post,* while intelligence officials have told Congress that the system has gotten so big that the lines of responsibility have become hopelessly blurred, the response has been to throw more money at it and to create another organization. Before he resigned, director of national intelligence Admiral Dennis C. Blair told Congress that he needed more money and more analysts to prevent another mistake. Similarly, the Department of Homeland Security has asked for air marshals, more body scanners, and more analysts, though it cannot find enough qualified people to fill the current positions for which it has funding.[30] Obama has said that he will not freeze spending on national security, making it likely that requests for more money and personnel will be honored. Undoubtedly, Al Qaeda is big business—the biggest business in Washington.

History may provide some perspective. Nothing like the US national security complex existed even at the height of the Cold War, when the United States and the Soviet Union fought worldwide wars by proxy, from Vietnam to Afghanistan. At the height of its power, the USSR possessed almost 10,000 nuclear bombs, an army of millions of men, and thousands of fighter jets, submarines, armored vehicles, and tanks that could have destroyed the United States and its Western allies several times over. At its peak in the late 1990s, Al Qaeda's membership numbered around 3,000 fighters. There are no brigades, fighter jets, and heavy tanks in Al Qaeda's armory, let alone WMDs.

THE OBAMA REALITY

The American political landscape has become so toxic and polarized that the mere mention of reassessing strategy against Al Qaeda is treated as a sign of weakness. The administration is perfectly aware of this. Yet Al Qaeda still looms large over American foreign policy. The Obama administration has not deviated significantly from the earlier overall strategy: it has intensified the war in Afghanistan and Pakistan and has preserved many controversial Bush programs, such as the so-called secret surveillance and the Guantánamo military commissions. Although it ordered black sites closed, it is impossible, without having access to highly classified information, to know how much has actually changed in the way the intelligence services capture and detain terrorist suspects.[31]

Obama's advisers stress the president's commitment to wage war against Al Qaeda and its allies, such as the Taliban in Afghanistan, Pakistan, and Yemen. They remind Americans that he is fighting the "right war." They also emphasize that Obama has escalated covert operations in Pakistan against Al Qaeda and the Taliban. They do not mention that the administration's weapon of choice is the CIA's Predator drone. Nor that Obama ordered more drone attacks in his first year in office than President Bush did in two full presidential terms.[32] Obama also expanded the use of drones to include low-level targets such as foot soldiers and even drug lords who give money to the Taliban—a remarkably aggressive definition of "material support" to terrorism. Although drone strikes have killed scores of Al Qaeda and Taliban fighters, they have also incinerated, since 2004, more than 1,000 civilians, including women and children. In addition, based on an analysis of US government sources, since the drone attacks intensified in the summer of 2008, the CIA has killed many more low-level fighters than mid-to-high-level Al Qaeda and Taliban leaders.[33]

In 2010, the Predators fired more than one hundred missiles in Pakistan, more than twice the number of strikes in Afghanistan, the recognized war theater. In Pakistan, drone strikes became almost a daily affair, a more than fourfold increase from the Bush years. The *New York Times* and the *Wall Street Journal* reported in the fall of 2010 that the Obama administration was even diverting more aerial drones and weaponry from the Afghan battlefront to significantly expand the CIA's campaign against militants in their Pakistani havens, which put more strains on

US-Pakistani relations and intensified tensions between the two allies. (The United States has also sent more drones to Yemen and appears to be escalating its attacks there.) In 2009 and 2010, the Pentagon and the CIA ramped up their purchases of Predators, which were not being built fast enough to meet the rapid rise in demand in other theaters as well.[34]

The Obama administration has therefore effectively escalated the war on terror in the Afghanistan-Pakistan theater and Yemen and targeted the remnants of Al Qaeda as well as what it calls its "extremist allies" in these countries, a highly ambitious plan. Obama's national security team seems to group Al Qaeda with the Taliban, particularly the Pakistani Taliban. In contrast to its predecessor, the Obama administration has focused more on killing individual terrorists than on capturing them. The killing of Al-Awlaki, an American citizen, is a case in point. The administration has its rationale for drone attacks, stressing that it has degraded the capabilities of the Pakistani Taliban and Al Qaeda without needing to put troops in harm's way on Pakistani soil. Administration officials and terrorism experts argue that the benefits outweigh any inherent human, political, and legal costs. After Bin Laden's death, American officials continued to defend drone attacks as instrumental in the destruction of Al Qaeda's central network in Pakistan and Afghanistan, as evidence of the efficacy and foresight of Obama's military escalation. Al Qaeda's networks in the region, said John Brennan, had been delivered "severe body blows" with Bin Laden's death.[35] In a wide-ranging interview with the Associated Press, Brennan credited aggressive US action against militants across the region as the main reason the intelligence community had detected no active terror plots before the tenth anniversary of the September 11 attacks. He described that as proof that the Obama administration has found "the right formula" to fight intelligence and counterterrorist forces with host nations from Pakistan to Iraq to Yemen, that is, fighting beside them. The goal is to keep Al Qaeda off balance, unable to replace the seasoned lieutenants and managers that the United States eliminates.[36]

When asked about potential repercussions, Brennan brushed off some of the relationship crises, from Pakistan's strident objections to drone strikes, to the revolts across the Arab world that swept from power US counterterror allies in places like Egypt. While he praised Yemen's cooperation with US military and intelligence personnel—who number in the hundreds and who have been working with Yemeni counterterrorism forces—he called Yemen a "tinderbox" that could erupt into a civil war.[37] But this kind of calculus ignores the damage the attacks have inflicted on America's reputation in the Muslim world and the "possibilities of blowback," about which the CIA, which directs the Predator strikes, has warned. Predator attacks have inflamed anti-American rage among Afghans and Pakistanis, including elite members of the security services and the urban middle class, who feel their country is impotent to stand against its powerful patron. There is a widespread perception among Pakistani elites, including the military, that the drone attacks violate Pakistan's sovereignty. Many Pakistanis, including some who live in the West, view the escalating war as an attack on their Muslim identity.[38]

The Pakistani Taliban and other militants are moving to exploit this anger, vowing to carry out suicide bombings in major American cities. It is no coincidence that large numbers of Pakistanis and Afghans are behind terror plots, a spillover of the escalation of the war on terror in their countries. Drone attacks have become a rallying cry and feed the flow of volunteers into a small, loose network that is hard to trace, even harder than the shadowy Al Qaeda. Jeffrey Addicott, former legal adviser to Army Special Operations, said that the drone strategy is "creating more enemies than we're killing or capturing."[39]

The Obama administration has so far been unwilling to acknowledge the link between the escalation of hostilities in Afghanistan and Pakistan and the rising incidence of homegrown radicalization. Instead, the administration has accused the Pakistani Taliban of facilitating, directing, and probably financing the Times Square plot, even though the suspect, Faisal Shahzad, has said he went to the Taliban for help, not the other way around.[40]

In Shahzad's court appearance, in which he pleaded guilty, US District Judge Miriam Cedarbaum asked him whether he was sure he wanted to plead guilty. Shahzad replied that he wanted "to plead guilty and 100 times more" to let the United Sates know that if it did not get out of Iraq and Afghanistan, halt drone attacks, and stop meddling in Muslim lands, "we will be attacking the U.S."[41] Pressed by Judge Cedarbaum to explain his motivation, Shahzad answered, "Well, the drone hits in Afghanistan and Iraq, they don't see children, they don't see anybody. They kill women, children, they kill everybody. It's a war, and in war, they kill people. They're killing all Muslims."[42]

White House counterterrorism chief Brennan dismissed the notion that Shahzad was motivated by anger at the CIA's Predator strikes. He argued that the suspect was "captured by the murderous rhetoric of Al Qaeda and TTP [Tehrik-e-Taliban Pakistan] that looks at the United States as an enemy."[43] Yet in private deliberations, according to an account by Bob Woodward, Obama's national security team appears to be aware that their policy in Afghanistan and Pakistan helps fuel radicalization and terrorism. During a daily briefing in May 2009, Admiral Blair warned the president that twenty radicals with American and European passports were being trained in Pakistani safe havens to return to their homelands to commit "high-profile acts of terrorism."[44]

After the briefing, according to Woodward, Obama's chief of staff, Rahm Emanuel, summoned Blair to his office in the corner of the West Wing and reproached him: "'You're just trying to put this on us, so it's not your fault.' . . . "'No, no,' Blair replied, 'I'm trying to tell you. I'm the President's intelligence officer and I'm worried about this, and I think I owe it to him—and you—to tell him.'"[45]

More ominously, in a response to some lawmakers who suggested that those accused of terrorism, such as Shahzad, should not have the same rights as suspects charged with less serious crimes, Attorney General Holder said that the Obama administration would have to work with Congress to see whether modifications were needed. He added that the administration would suggest some changes to Congress that recognized the reality that terrorism is a rising risk for the United Sates.[46] "We want to work with Congress to come up with a way in which we make our public safety exception more flexible and again more consistent with the threat we face," Holder said.[47]

The attorney general has indicated that he would support a bill proposed by House Judiciary Committee member Adam Schiff. It would create "terrorism exceptions" to Miranda warnings. The bill would allow investigators, with the approval of the attorney general or the director of national intelligence, to question terrorism suspects for up to forty-eight hours before they are informed of their constitutionally mandated rights to remain silent and to have an attorney. A federal judge could extend this for another forty-eight hours. Investigators could therefore potentially question a suspect for up to four days without their Miranda rights being read to them, and their testimony could still be admitted as evidence in court.[48]

For an administration that insists that it has changed course and rhetorically seeks to distance itself from its predecessor, it is remarkable how little has actually changed. Although the legal basis for the Obama administration's policies is substantially firmer than was the basis for Bush's policies, global perceptions of American national security have not changed significantly.[49] Despite the administration's verbal commitment to the rule of law and constitutional values, its tacit blessing of this legislation is alarming. It shows how little it takes—a single failed bombing attempt—to sacrifice basic values on the altar of security.

That was not the maximum deviation from the rule of law. In heated testimony on Capitol Hill, Republican lawmakers directed hostile questions at Holder. They suggested that he and the Obama administration had taken a lackluster approach to terrorism, that the administration viewed Al Qaeda's challenge more as crime fighting than war fighting.

Not at all, according to Holder. Challenged on one particular point, he pledged that the alleged mastermind of September 11, Khalid Sheikh Mohammed, would never be released from US custody—regardless of the outcome of his trial. Holder was asked what the administration would do if a civilian judge ordered Mohammed released. "If that were to be the case, he would not be released," Holder said. "I am not qualifying it. He would not be released."[50] Holder's response seems both to contradict the administration's stated rationale for holding public trials for Mohammed and other terror suspects in civilian courts and to undermine the credibility of its new approach.

"So why are we trying him? Am I missing something?" asked Republican representative John Culberson of Texas. "Why put him on trial if the government is going to hold him anyway?" he added.[51] Holder tried to reassure Culberson by saying that no civilian court would ever release Mohammed.

Congressman Culberson persisted: "The approach of the Obama administration is that this [is] a law enforcement action—it is not, we are at war. Texans understand that when you are at war the goal is to hunt down your enemy and either kill them or capture them."[52] Holder responded that he was aware that the nation was at war. But, he added, the administration's placing some suspects on trial in civilian federal courts was an important tool in the broader waging of that war.[53]

The attorney general's response illustrates the administration's muddled and cosmetic approach to the war on terror and its unwillingness to confront its critics on the right. The exchange shows the gap that exists between Obama's nuanced and rosy rhetoric and the political reality. There are structural continuities in American national security that Obama does not seem to be able or willing to change. The politics of terrorism fetter Obama's hands and impose political costs and constraints that work against any real change in American foreign policy.

In response to similar questions, Secretary of State Clinton has likewise refrained from specifically mentioning unmanned drones, but she has often stated that a war is raging in Pakistan and that the United States is helping to defeat extremists who threaten vital American interests and those of its regional allies—an implicit affirmation of the use of drone technology in Pakistan.[54] A senior aide to Clinton was more explicit. State Department counsel Harold Koh defended the drone attacks as legal under existing law and said they could not be considered "unlawful extrajudicial killing." According to Koh, "recent events have shown Al Qaeda has not abandoned its intent to attack the United States, and indeed continues to attack us. Thus, in this ongoing armed conflict, the United States has the authority, under international law, and the responsibility to its citizens, to use force, including lethal force, to defend itself, including by targeting persons such as high-level al Qaeda leaders who are planning attacks."[55]

The United Nations has disputed the legality of Predator attacks. In June 2010, Philip Alston, the UN's senior official for extrajudicial executions, said that the United States should explain the legal rationale for the CIA's drone war in northwest Pakistan, which he characterized as "a vaguely defined license to kill" that has created "a major accountability vacuum." He pointed out that the CIA does not subject itself to any sort of public review when things go awry, and he urged the Obama administration to disclose the number of civilians killed in the drone strikes.[56]

The call fell on deaf ears. On a surprise visit to Afghanistan in March 2010, President Obama defended the decision to escalate the war in the region and told US troops that their victory against Al Qaeda and its extremist allies—the Taliban—was imperative to America's safety. "Your services are absolutely necessary, absolutely necessary to America's safety and security," Obama told a crowd of about 2,000 troops and civilians at Bagram Air Base. "Those folks back home are relying on you. We can't forget why we're here."[57]

"We did not choose this war," Obama reminded the troops. He recalled the September 11 attacks and warned that Al Qaeda was still using the region to plan terrorist strikes against the United States and its Western allies. "We are going to disrupt and dismantle, defeat and destroy Al Qaeda and its extremist allies." The line has become a central plank of his National Security Strategy in the war on terror.[58]

Nuanced and defensible though they are when compared to policy under Bush, the Obama administration's actions reveal that Al Qaeda continues to dominate the terrorist narrative. In particular, the exponential escalation of drone attacks during the Obama presidency is one reason that former Bush White House official Richard Falkenrath can say with justification that the Obama administration is "rhetorically dissimilar but substantively almost indistinguishable" from its predecessor.[59] Comparing Bush's and Obama's exercise of presidential power, the *New York Times* reached a similar conclusion: Obama has outraged civil libertarians by keeping in place the outlines of many Bush-era policies, like indefinite detention and military commissions for terrorism suspects. And—in the Libya air war and the targeted killing of Anwar al-Awlaki, a Yemeni-American cleric who received a great deal of media coverage for his purported ability to radicalize young Muslims living in Western societies and incite them to commit murder, such as the Christmas Day bomber and the US army major who shot thirteen of his comrades in Fort Hood, Texas—Obama went beyond Mr. Bush's executive-power record.[60] More than any other organization, Al Qaeda has taken hold of the American imagination—or at least the imaginations of Western policy makers—and will not let go.

MAKING SENSE OF US POLICY

In his provocative book *Overblown: How Politicians and the Terrorism Industry Inflate National Security Threats, and Why We Believe Them,* John Mueller, a scholar of US foreign policy, examined the transformation of American political culture under the Bush administration. He argued that, after 2001, fear of terrorism as an existential threat became as institutionalized as fear of the great ideological threats of the twentieth century—communism and fascism—were in their own time. According to Mueller, the twenty-four-hour news cycle, the entertainment industry, the national security community, academics, and politicians have all played complementary roles in hyperinflating terrorism as the evil and plague of the twenty-first century. This hyperinflation not only overshadows the true nature of the threat itself, but has also caused major strategic and costly blunders in American foreign policy.[61]

Mueller's hypothesis builds on a wider body of literature which argues that the experience of World War II is pivotal to unlocking the riddle of American foreign policy and the national culture that reinforces it. Politicians and opinion makers sometimes view conflicts with other nations and even non-state actors through the lens of the titanic struggle against fascism and then communism. Once at war, American leaders fall back on history, which they have internalized, and divide the world into polarities of good and evil. They consider every conflict existential, a matter of life and death, a fight to the end. This helps explain why American foreign policy and political culture are often consumed by exaggeration, overreaction, and a crusading impulse. Reflecting on the Cold War rivalry between the United States and the Soviet Union, Columbia University international relations professor Warner Schilling perceptively noted more than forty years ago that at the summit of US foreign policy, one always finds "simplicity" and "spook," or misunderstanding and ignorance, in plain English.[62] Similarly, Robert Jervis, a theorist of international relations, argued in the mid-1970s that "those who remember the past are condemned to making the opposite mistakes."[63] American foreign policy is entrapped in its own self-constructed anxiety about the risks and dangers of terrorism.[64] Similarly, policy makers seem to view their conflict with Al Qaeda through the lens of a massive global struggle.

In *The Icarus Syndrome: A History of American Hubris,* journalist and academic Peter Beinart contributes to the broader debate about how overreaction and simplification in the face of fear and opportunity often shape America's national culture and foreign policy.[65] With simplification and overreaction comes excessive fear, and foreign policy acts are often justified as a response to that fear. But the level of fear varies, in turn, depending on how policy makers perceive a particular threat. According to Beinart, a threat may be perceived differently in different times and circumstances: "How threatened American policymakers feel is often a function of how much power they have. The more confident our leaders and thinkers become about the hammer of American force, the more likely they are to find nails."[66]

Post-9/11 policy makers were confident about America's preeminent military, economic, and ideological position in the world. As a result, they experienced and perceived the terrorist threat with added gravity. Had the attack occurred at a time when America's position in the world was less secure, such as in 1979, 1985, or 1993, American leaders would likely have acted with more caution, perspective, and, naturally, less fear.[67]

In *War of Words: Language, Politics, and 9/11,* linguist Sandra Silberstein argues that the ways in which rhetoric is employed in moments of national emergency define a state's response. September 11 was a unique experience in American history, and as a result President Bush did not have a precedent from which to draw lessons. Presented with a tabula rasa, he utilized rhetoric that encouraged a hyperextreme response.[68] "In the aftermath, an act of terror became a war; New York became 'America's city,' with Rudy Giuliani as 'mayor of the world,'" Silberstein writes. "Patriotism became consumerism, dissent was discouraged, and Americans became students, newly schooled in strategic geography and Islam. Perhaps, most importantly, public language (re)created a national identity."[69]

In the US view, the attacks of September 11 constitute a turning point in contemporary American history and have been internalized by official Washington and ordinary citizens alike. Al Qaeda and Osama bin Laden shattered Americans' peace of mind. Americans watched helplessly as the Twin Towers collapsed on their television screens. Al Qaeda and Bin Laden accomplished something that the powerful Soviet Union had never achieved: they attacked the homeland and caused Americans to question their personal safety, even in contexts as ordinary as shopping at their local grocery store or picking up their children from school.

It is easy to dismiss the impact of psychology on the making of American foreign policy; statistical realities cannot match the emotional toll such an event has taken on the psyche of a nation. More than a decade later, few Americans and Westerners realize the degree to which their fear of terrorism and terrorists is misplaced. But there can be no closure so long as ideology and reality remain confused.

Ayman al-Zawahiri, Bin Laden's second-in-command and now his successor, and the organization's local allies are perfectly aware of the power of fear. What stature they have depends upon it. Spreading fear is the most effective means of staying in business. In an editorial in *Inspire,* AQAP claimed responsibility for its attempts to bomb two United-States–bound cargo planes in October 2010, boasting that what they called Operation Hemorrhage was cheap and easy, costing only $4,200 to carry out. "On the other hand this . . . will without a doubt cost America and other Western countries billions of dollars in new security measures. This is what we call leverage," the AQAP editors boasted, saying the operation had been in operation for three months.[70]

AQAP unveiled what it called its "strategy of a thousand cuts," which will "bleed the enemy to death"; the goal, said the group's head of foreign operations, was to cause economic damage and foment fear among Westerners:

> From the start our objective was economic. . . . It was determined that the success of the operation was to be based on two factors: The first is that the packages pass through the latest security equipment.
>
> The second, the spread of fear that would cause the West to invest billions of dollars in new security procedures. We will continue with similar operations and we do not mind at all in this stage if they are intercepted, it is such a good bargain for us to spread fear amongst the enemy and keep him on his toes in exchange of a few months of work and a few thousand bucks.[71]

That is Al Qaeda's current war game, one that effectively gives the remaining foot soldiers of the organization an upper hand in their struggle against the most powerful country in the world. Despite suffering a catastrophic military setback and facing a debilitating crisis of legitimacy and lack of acceptance among Muslims, Al Qaeda has taken hold of the American imagination.

AL QAEDA'S ACTUAL STRENGTH

With Bin Laden's death, it has become more clear that it is this imagination and the misplaced policies it has inspired—not the actual organization—that pose the greatest challenge to the United States. In fact, Western intelligence agencies now believe that there are roughly only 300 (now fewer than 100) surviving members of Al Qaeda, based mainly in Pakistan and Afghanistan, into which the United States has poured nearly 100,000 troops.[72] Most of Al Qaeda's skilled operatives and midlevel field lieutenants have been either killed or captured, depleting the ranks of seasoned fighters and effective managers and depriving the organization of significant operational capability. Cooks, drivers, bodyguards, and foot soldiers now make up the bulk of Al Qaeda's membership. Even the White House counterterrorism chief has finally acknowledged this fact by saying that Al Qaeda is in a steady slide. On the ropes. Taking shots to the body and head, a reference to US killing of its top lieutenants and managers. US pressure has degraded the Al Qaeda original network. "There's no longer a management grooming program there. They don't stay in place long enough," Brennan told the Associated Press.[73]

Al Qaeda's centralized command-and-control has been dismantled and its top remaining leaders have gone deeper and deeper underground, choosing personal safety over operational efficacy—even according to US intelligence. In his last five years, hiding in Abbottabad, Bin Laden reportedly relied almost exclusively on one sole courier to communicate with the outside world.[74] Suicide bombers remain Al Qaeda's weapon of choice, but its ability to project power and carry out complex attacks along the September 11 lines has also been degraded considerably. After reviewing computer files and documents seized at Bin Laden's compound, American officials say that the evidence suggests that while he continued, until his death, to encourage his followers to strike inside the United States, his instructions were "aspirational" rather than explicit in detail. Despite repeated threats to attack the US homeland, Bin Laden and Zawahiri failed to do so, undermining their credibility and authority in the eyes of their small base.

Nevertheless, Al Qaeda and other similar factions might succeed in carrying out an attack in the not too distant future because of the escalation of conflict in Afghanistan and Pakistan and the consequent radicalization wave affecting tiny elements of these two communities in the West. Most of the recent arrests have been young Pakistani and Afghan men. There is, too, the motive to avenge the killing of Bin Laden, along with Al-Awlaki, which they view as an assassination, effectively cold-blooded murder. But the possibility of a successful attack, troubling as it is, must not blind us to the gradual and steady dismantling of Al Qaeda's military apparatus and the limited nature of the challenge now posed by Al Qaeda.

Similarly, the actions of local Al Qaeda branches in Iraq, Saudi Arabia, Yemen, the Maghreb, and elsewhere have exposed the organization's loss of operational control and damaged its outreach efforts to Muslims. Indiscriminate targeting of civilians has turned Muslim opinion against Al Qaeda, its tactics, and ideology. For most Muslims, Al Qaeda stands accused of having brought ruin to the *ummah* (global community).[75] Some insist that Al Qaeda is an American invention, a pretext to intervene in Muslim lands.

In other words, Al Qaeda, long before Bin Laden's death, had lost the struggle for Muslim hearts and minds, a fact that is more evident in the wake of the Arab popular uprisings, as fewer skilled recruits are drawn to the organization, and it finds fewer shelters.

Contrary to the received wisdom in the West, there never was any swell of Muslim public support for Bin Laden and his transnational jihadi contingent. More of a fringe phenomenon than a popular social movement, transnational jihad has never enjoyed a big constituency in Muslim societies.[76] The majority of Arabs and Muslims were (and are) highly critical of US and Western foreign policies, but only a small segment condones and sanctions a direct war with the West, in particular the killing of noncombatants. No prominent Muslim theorists or ideologues have called for attacking the West. The struggle within—an intracivilizational rift between secular nationalists on the one hand and religious nationalists on the other—has overshadowed and eclipsed the struggle without a so-called clash of cultures and civilizations.

After September 11, Bin Laden, Zawahiri, and their cohorts discovered that neither domestic jihadis nor the *ummah* had any desire to join their caravan. Indeed, influential opinion makers, clerics, and chiefs of domestic jihadis warned that Al Qaeda's reckless conduct risked embroiling Muslims in unnecessary, costly wars and endangered the very survival of the Islamist movement. With the exception of one or two pockets of refugee camps, the Muslim world did not hail September 11 as a triumph but considered it a catastrophe.

Since September 11, I have argued that, contrary to received wisdom in the West, Muslim opinion has embraced neither Al Qaeda's extremist ideology nor its murderous tactics and that Bin Laden and his cohorts did not speak for the mainstream Islamists who represent the majority of religiously based activists, let alone for the *ummah*.

The democratic revolutions that swept the Middle East in early 2011 show clearly that Al Qaeda is a nonentity, a fringe that exercises no influence over political life in Arab lands. The mass social movements that toppled the Tunisian and Egyptian dictators have exposed the holes in the deeply entrenched terrorism narrative. Al Qaeda is the biggest loser because the peaceful protest movements have exposed the bankruptcy of the organization's central tenets—that nonviolent change is difficult, that terrorism is the only effective means to oust autocratic rulers, and that democracy is an "evil principle," a "heresy," and a false deity. Millions of Arabs have spoken out about the significance of politics and democratic activism, eschewing Bin Laden's rejection of the political. Ayman al-Zawahiri has spent more than two decades preaching to Egyptians that only armed subversion or a military coup would topple the Mubarak regime. The power of the Egyptian people has proved him wrong.

The broad-based peaceful revolutions have also discredited Al Qaeda's fundamental claim that the Islamist vanguard will spearhead revolutionary change in Muslim societies. On the whole, the revolts have been peaceful, nonideological, and led by the embattled middle class, including a rainbow coalition of men and women of all ages and political colors: liberal-leaning centrists, democrats, leftists, nationalists, and Islamists. Clerics and mullahs are not key drivers; there is no Ayatollah Khomeini waiting in the wings to hijack the revolution and seize power.

It is true that religious-based activists, such as the Ennahdha (Renaissance) party, the Muslim Brotherhood and the Salafis, and independent Islamists, will be a dominant force in the post-autocratic order—as elections in Tunisia, Morocco, and Egypt have already shown. But mainstream Islamists of the Muslim Brotherhood variety have little in common with Al Qaeda. The Muslim Brotherhood has evolved considerably. It renounced violence in the early 1970s. For more than four decades, Brotherhood leaders labored to join the political space and gain legal status. They learned the art of compromise and pragmatism through hardship and persecution. Ideology takes a back seat to the interests and political well-being of the Brotherhood and Ennahdah. More than ever, their message targets specific constituencies and interest groups—a sign of an ideological shift to pragmatism.

After their impressive performance in the first round of Egypt's parliamentary elections, the Brotherhood publicly stressed its commitment to pluralism and protecting individual rights.[77] The two top leaders of the Brotherhood's newly formed Freedom and Justice Party, Mohammad Mursi and Essam el-Arian, say that if they win they will form a national unity government with other parties. After it gained a majority in the Tunisian parliament at the end of 2011, Ennahdah established a broadly based unity coalition to oversee the transition to pluralism. Addressing assertions often made by their secular opponents, they insisted that the party "would hand over power if we lose" because the public will no longer tolerate dictatorship.

El-Arian pledged that Freedom and Justice will not add terminology to the Egyptian national constitution to make explicit old demands that all legislation comply with sharia law. Article 2 of the constitution already states that the "principal source of legislation is Islamic jurisprudence."[78]

The Arab revolts have left Bin Laden's vanguard behind. Jihadis like Zawahiri spent a lifetime criticizing the Brotherhood, including its sister Hamas, of betrayal, of sacrificing theological purity on the altar of a bankrupt political ideology called democracy. Al Qaeda is highly critical of the Brotherhood, who in its opinion, accepts the rules of politics and participates in the "evil" democratic game. As to Salafis, Al Qaeda has hardly anything to say about them, partly because they are an enigma, unknown, ultra-traditional, and quietist. Far from endearing the Salafis to Al Qaeda, their participation in the parliamentary elections will earn them its wrath.

The US terrorism narrative has suffered an equally hard blow. The question is not why the Arabs and Muslims hate America so much, as the conventional wisdom would have it after September 11, but why Western pundits and policy makers underestimated and dismissed the genuine yearnings of millions of Arabs and Muslims for universal values such as human rights, the rule of law, an open and pluralistic society, and individual freedom and liberty. Although Middle Easterners are critical of US foreign policy, the Arab revolts show that they admire universal values of a free and democratic society and separation of powers. Unlike protesters during the Islamic Revolution in Iran in the late 1970s, modern Egyptians, Tunisians, Libyans, and others neither burned American and Western flags nor blamed Western colonialism for their predicament. Domestic concerns and grievances—jobs and freedoms, not anti-American sentiments or foreign policy—mainly fuel the Arab revolts; Al Qaeda's jihadist agenda is distinguished by its very absence.[79]

Nonetheless, the dominant opinion in Western official circles was that Bin Laden did in fact speak for a significant segment of Muslims and for Islamists of all colors. No distinction was made between domestic jihadis and transnational Al Qaeda types, nor between Al Qaeda and politically based Islamists such as the powerful Muslim Brotherhood, Palestinian Hamas, or Hezbollah. The conclusion reached was that the West faced an immediate and present danger that had to be met with full force. Accordingly, a global war on terror was launched with the double aim of destroying Al Qaeda and rogue Middle Eastern regimes and engineering democracy.[80] In one stroke, this turned Bin Laden and Zawahiri's dangerous but inconsequential insurgency into a geostrategic threat and elevated them to the ranks of global actors.

The war on terror was a boon to Bin Laden and Zawahiri, who attempted to rally Muslim opinion against the invasion and occupation of Iraq and act as the spearhead of the *ummah*'s armed resistance. From 2003 until 2006, their defiant message fell on receptive ears, particularly among politically radicalized religious activists outraged by what they saw as the occupation of Muslim territories. From London to Algiers and from Islamabad to Sanaa, young Muslim men tried to journey to Iraq and fight alongside members of Al Qaeda Between the Two Rivers, a group that embraced Bin Laden's ideology but maintained its independence.

In my travels in Arab and Muslim cities, towns, and villages, I met many young men—Libyans, Tunisians, Syrians, Palestinians, Jordanians, Lebanese, Saudis, Yemenis, Algerians, Moroccans, Pakistanis, and others—who relayed stories of their failed efforts to travel to Iraq and join the "martyrs'" brigade. America was waging a "crusade" against Islam, and Al Qaeda was a vanguard of Islamic resistance. None of these young men bought the premise that the invasion and occupation of Iraq had anything to do with September 11.

Immediately after the US invasion and occupation of Iraq, Bin Laden and Zawahiri tailored their rhetoric to fit the angry Arab mood. Their success was fleeting, however. Al Qaeda again proved to be its own worst enemy. Iraq clearly showed the limits of transnational jihadism of Al Qaeda's variety.

Al Qaeda lost Iraq, and Abu Musab al-Zarqawi, chief of Al Qaeda in Iraq, was the reason. Zarqawi, who was killed in a US attack in June 2006, terrorized Iraqis and fueled all-out sectarian war. His methods, particularly dispatching multiple car and suicide bombings against indiscriminate civilian targets, killed and maimed thousands and turned nearly all Iraqis against his organization and against Al Qaeda in general. He also sent suicide squads to his native country, Jordan, and in one instance turned a wedding into a funeral.[81] To cut his losses, and to distance himself from his reckless lieutenant, Bin Laden publicly apologized to Muslims for the mistakes and misdeeds perpetrated by his men and reminded them that even the Prophet had made mistakes. But Bin Laden's apology was too late. Sunni Iraqis had turned against Bin Laden's men with a vengeance, and the reverberations of that civil war are still felt in Iraq and beyond.

All of this information is more or less public record now. Yet the politics of terrorism in the West sustains Al Qaeda, at least the idea of Al Qaeda. American's political culture in particular remains obsessed with Al Qaeda, and the terrorism narrative continues to resonate both with ordinary Americans and with top military commanders in charge of national security. "You can't find a four-star general without a security detail," said one three-star general posted in Washington after years of service abroad. "Fear has caused everyone to have [platoons of personal bodyguards and staff]."[82] Defense Secretary Gates acknowledged the problem in an interview in September 2010. Since the Twin Towers collapsed, "what little discipline existed in the Defense Department when it came to spending has gone completely out of the window," he says. Gates argued that the bureaucracy had "swelled to cumbersome and top-heavy proportions, grown over-reliant on contractors, and grown accustomed to operating with little consideration to cost."[83]

THE CULTURAL REVERBERATIONS OF THE WAR ON TERROR

The politics of terrorism have driven military adventurism, a mushrooming national debt, and the militarizing of domestic affairs—torture, military tribunals, and the massive expansion of the national security machine.[84] They have also exposed deep cultural, legal, and philosophical fault lines within Western societies. They have given rise to attempts to demonize Muslims and portray them as aliens, a fifth column. Though driven by powerful far-right grassroots groups, Islamophobia, sometimes called the "new anti-Semitism," has gone mainstream. In Europe, the alarm over the Islamicization of the continent, masquerading as the demographic crisis in which Muslims outbreed their Christian counterparts, has become commonplace, reflected in the literature, ranging from more sophisticated treatments like Christopher Caldwell's *Reflections on the Revolution in Europe: Immigration, Islam, and the West* to cruder polemics like Mark Steyn's *America Alone: The End of the World as We Know It* and Bat Ye'or's *Eurabia: The Euro-Arab Axis*.[85] These two long polemics are sparse on strong, reasoned arguments, but abound with hyperbole, exaggeration, and fear mongering.

Many surveys and public opinion polls have suggested that an increasing number of Western citizens accept the fringe's depiction of Muslims. According to a nationwide poll conducted by Cornell University, nearly half of all Americans (44 percent) say that the government should restrict the civil liberties of American Muslims.[86] There is a growing cottage industry of Western commentators and politicians who thrive on bashing Islam. The war on terror has provided a substantial level of cover for their views.[87] Shortly after the September 11, 2001, attacks, ABC News found that 39 percent of the American public had a negative view of Islam; ten years later, pollsters James Zogby and Shibley Telhami found that 61 percent of Americans hold a negative view, a pronounced negative shift in public perception.[88] For a glimpse of this venomous rhetoric, read a now-notorious blog post by Martin Peretz, the *New Republic*'s editor in chief, which stated, "Frankly, Muslim life is cheap, most notably to Muslims." Peretz added: "I wonder whether I need honor these people and pretend they are worthy of the privileges of the First Amendment, which I have in my gut the sense that they will abuse."[89] Although Peretz apologized twice for this outburst, he nevertheless defended his assertion that Muslim life is cheap. "This is a statement of fact, not value," he said.[90] Writing in the *Jewish Daily Forward*, Matthew Duss of the Center for American Progress noted that hatred of Arabs/Muslims has had a permanent home not only in the *New Republic*, one of America's oldest and most respected liberal magazines, but in many pro-Israeli forums that stoke fear of Islam for political profit.[91]

Fox News, the home, of course, of Sean Hannity, and several nationally syndicated talk radio hosts, including Rush Limbaugh and Michael Savage, has frequently promoted Islamophobia on the national stage. In an interview on *The View*, a popular ABC television talk show, Bill O'Reilly, a Fox News host, declared that "Muslims killed us on 9/11."[92] Moreover, prominent politicians such as former Speaker of the House Newt Gingrich, Congressman Peter King, and Senator Saxby Chambliss legitimize the demonization of Muslims with dark and misleading language. Critical groups of Evangelical Christianity and prominent religious leaders such as Pat Robertson, John Hagee, and Franklin Graham, to name just a few, have contributed to the intensification and escalation of this phenomenon throughout the United States.

A similar debate is raging across Europe. A plurality of Swiss voted against the construction of mosques even though the Muslim community in Switzerland numbers only 400,000, most of whom are not Arabs or Africans but Europeans from Bosnia, Albania, and Kosovo;[93] by the spring of 2011 Belgium and France had both passed legislation making it illegal to wear the burqa and other Islamic face covering.[94]

Anti-Muslim sentiment in European countries that possess sizable Muslim minorities, coupled with anti-immigrant fervor resulting from difficult economic conditions and high unemployment, has raised serious questions about the future of multicultural and multireligious Western societies. Exploiting the bitter debate, Bin Laden and Zawahiri released several audiotapes condemning discrimination against Muslims and vowing to attack European countries that insult Islam and its Prophet. The irony is that Islam bashers provided Bin Laden and his associates with more murderous fodder for their cannons.

Similarly, the cultural reverberations of the war on terror have put America's values of religious tolerance and individual freedom under stress. As of 2011, there were between 2.5 and 7 million Muslims in the United States (out of a total population of 300 million), a third of whom are African American. Confrontations have broken out over proposed mosques in Tennessee, California, Georgia, Kentucky, Wisconsin, and Illinois, as well as in Sheepshead Bay in Brooklyn and Midland Beach on Staten Island in New York City.[95] Islamophobes seized on a proposed mosque and Islamic center in Lower Manhattan to stir up anti-Muslim sentiment. Presidential hopeful Newt Gingrich spearheaded opposition to building such a mosque as long as Saudi Arabia bars construction of churches and synagogues. To do so "a few blocks from the site where Islamist extremists killed more than 3,000 Americans," Gingrich opined, is a "political act" of "triumphalism."[96] He justified his opposition by drawing an analogy with the Holocaust: "Nazis don't have the right to put up a sign next to the Holocaust museum in Washington," he said.[97]

Moreover, in a major speech at the influential conservative American Enterprise Institute (AEI) in Washington in July 2010, Gingrich warned his listeners that "sharia," or Islamic law, is on the verge of taking over America. "I believe sharia is a mortal threat to the survival of freedom in the United States," he thundered.[98] Widely touted as a major address on the failings of the Obama administration and national security, Gingrich's remarks cleverly used the terrorism narrative to stoke fear of "the other" and recapture his role as a national Republican leader. Obama is wrong to say that Afghanistan is the "central front" in the struggle against Al

Qaeda and its extremist allies, he added. "The central front is the United States," he said, and it is there, along with the "second front" in Europe—that the final battle against sharia and Islam will be fought and won.[99] The former Speaker of the House said he intended to propose a law that "no court anywhere in the United States under any circumstances is allowed to consider sharia as a replacement for American law, period."[100]

Beyond the homeland, Gingrich called for a new Cold War, a long struggle against radical Islam, and the toppling of regimes in Iran, North Korea (he did not say what North Korea has to do with radical Islam), and others. He suggested that there are no fewer than seven simultaneous fronts in the greater Middle East for his new Cold War, beginning with Iran, Saudi Arabia, Pakistan, Afghanistan, Iraq, Egypt, and Israel's "borderlands," meaning Palestinian Hamas and Lebanon's Hezbollah.[101]

It is easy to dismiss Gingrich's speech, as some progressive writers have, as full of "hateful, vile garbage [that] makes Joe McCarthy look measured and responsible."[102] The sad reality is that this presidential hopeful is tapping into and nourishing a powerful anti-Muslim current, an anti-immigrant sentiment, echoing through the United States. Oklahoma legislators, fearing the imposition of Islamic law or sharia in Oklahoma courts, a bizarre threat, have even asked voters to amend the state constitution to forbid it.[103] As *The Economist* noted, the "odd thing is that no one has ever proposed making appeals to *sharia* in America."[104] More and more citizens believe they must defend themselves because the government has failed them by passively allowing Muslim subversion. In Florence, Kentucky, protesters against a proposed mosque tried to mobilize opposition by calling on Americans "to stop the takeover of our country, our government is not protecting us."[105]

A decade of growing anti-Muslim sentiment has taken its toll. In 2010, Gallup's Muslim West Facts Project published the results of a major poll about American prejudices toward Islam. They showed a causal link between rising anti-Islam and the politics of terrorism. The most significant finding is also the least surprising: a slight majority of Americans—53 percent—stated that their opinion of the faith is either "not too favorable"—22 percent—or "not favorable at all"—31 percent. Americans in 2010 were more than twice as likely to express negative feelings toward Muslims than toward Buddhists, Christians, or Jews. A majority of Americans—66 percent—disagreed with the statement that most Muslims are accepting of other religions and also admitted that they know either very little—40 percent—about Islam, or nothing at all—23 percent.[106] Putting the best face on Gallup's finding, *Boston Globe* columnist James Carroll said that Muslims are wildly misperceived and wrongly judged, but that Americans are "at war, and afraid," and therefore that "exaggerated fears fuel themselves, and the dynamic of prejudice can be a riptide."[107] He compared the blanket stereotyping of Muslims to an unseen current that has run below the surface of Western culture for a millennium.[108]

The "M-word" has become a pejorative term in America, suggested *USA Today* in an article covering the reasons that a growing number of Americans believed President Obama is a Muslim.[109] Some 18 percent said the president was a Muslim, up from 11 percent in March 2009, according to a Pew Research survey on Religion and Public Life released in August 2010.[110] A *Newsweek* poll found that 52 percent of Republicans believed that it was either "definitely true" or "probably true" that "Barack Obama sympathizes with the goals of Islamic fundamentalists who want to impose Islamic law around the world."[111] Despite the efforts by the president's team to downplay the astonishing findings, *USA Today* zeroed in on the M-word and asked whether it is "mockery—or worse—to call someone a Muslim only when you dislike, fear, or disagree with the person? The way to put someone down in polite company? . . . Is the M-word becoming the political slur that gets through the social filters?"[112]

"Our enemies struck at our heart, but did they also warp our identity?" queried *New York Times* columnist Maureen Dowd, a critic of the American political scene.[113]

CONCLUSION

"IN FOR A PENNY, IN FOR A POUND"?

After more than three years in office, Obama has shown in his foreign policy in the Middle East more continuity with the past than real change. He has adopted a centrist-realist approach toward the region, an approach consistent with the dominant US foreign policy orientation. His administration aims at retaining the status quo with a few minor corrections. Even as a presidential candidate, he identified himself with traditional foreign policy realists, like George H. W. Bush. He stressed that, in his administration, foreign policy in the Middle East and elsewhere would be driven by the national interest and would focus on attaining stability, as opposed to his predecessor's ideology of proselytizing for democracy and freehandedly deploying force in international affairs. Obama has consistently refrained from offering an expansive foreign policy vision and has preferred to be guided by practical considerations and shifting tides. His White House aides emphasize that he is a nonideological, pragmatic politician interested only in what works. When asked to describe the Obama doctrine, the president has chosen not to respond directly, but he explained that he believes the United States must act with other countries. "[Mine is] an American leadership that recognizes the rise of countries like China, India and Brazil. It's a U.S. leadership that recognizes our limits in terms of resources and capacity."[1]

When Barack Obama assumed office, he, along with his foreign policy team, recognized the enormousness of the bitter legacy he had inherited in the Middle East, a legacy that implicated America in the dealings of oppressive autocrats and costly wars in Iraq and Afghanistan, as well as serious regional challenges by Pakistan and Iran, global terrorism, and a troubled legacy that associated America with words like "torture." As a new president, Obama also faced an economic recession at home, and the ascendance of China and India abroad portended a shift from unipolarity to multipolarity in the international system. In contrast to his conservative opponents, Obama and his aides had a "vivid" sense of American decline relative to the new rising powers and wanted to rebalance foreign policy priorities away from the Middle East to the Pacific Ocean and Asia. Putting America's fiscal house in order and renewing its long-term economic strength topped Obama's agenda. That meant reducing the nation's commitments abroad, especially in the Middle East, where they have extended beyond vital national interests.

Before extracting US troops from Muslim lands, the Obama foreign policy team wanted to bring a measure of stability to America's relations within the region. From day one, Obama reached out to Muslims in an effort to restore the trust shattered during the Bush administration. He pledged to reduce the US military footprint and help bring about a Palestinian state. Preferring engagement to confrontation, Obama challenged the leadership of Iran to meet him diplomatically halfway. In his first six months in the White House, the new president made all the right moves and said all the right words. His uplifting rhetoric raised expectations in and outside the region that he would reset relations between America and the world, particularly the Muslim world, and pursue an evenhanded approach toward the Arab-Israeli conflict.

However, Obama singularly failed to translate his hopes and promises into concrete policy. In contrast to the claims of his Republican detractors, Obama has not departed from the Washington foreign policy consensus. As the previous analysis has shown, Obama's foreign policy has been consistently anchored in pragmatic responses to problems abroad, but deep political dysfunctions in domestic politics have prevented decision makers from taking bold and forward-thinking initiatives in the new Middle East. Obama surrounded himself with like-minded realists, not forward-thinking strategists; Hillary Clinton, Joe Biden, Robert Gates, and Leon Panetta view the world through a narrow lens and complement and reinforce their commander in chief's worldview. While he reversed some of the worst ideological excesses of the George W. Bush administration's foreign policy, he only brought the

United States back to the cautious middle; he did not implement his own ambitious rhetoric. Measuring Obama's Middle East policy against his predecessor, and his damage control duties, Obama moved the United States from its underwater position. His Turkey policy has shored up ties with a rising geostrategic power; his outreach to Muslims has been largely positive, though harmed by inconsistencies; his Israel-Palestine policy is a dismal failure; his Iran policy an uncertain gamble; his counterterrorism strategies technically successful; his goal of removing US troops from Iraq and Afghanistan has borne fruit; and his approaches toward the Arab awakening, a mixed bag.

Although Obama understands the complex issues of the Middle East on an intellectual level, he has shown himself to be too timid when he gets into trouble. He is far from being a risk taker, and he governs by consensus at home and by the national interest abroad. Given his sensibilities as a decision maker and the advisers with whom he surrounds himself, it is difficult to imagine how Obama's ambitious promises could have been fulfilled. He was not disposed by sentiment and training to pursue a transformational foreign policy against the wishes of the dominant foreign policy narrative. It is no wonder then that Obama often retreated when faced with internal and external challenges to his policies. For example, from the start of his administration Obama invested considerable political capital trying to help broker an Israeli-Palestinian peace settlement. He initially insisted that Israel freeze the construction of Jewish settlements on occupied Palestinian lands. Obama even confronted Israeli Prime Minister Benjamin Netanyahu and impressed on him the need to discuss final status issues with the Palestinians. But when Netanyahu refused to stop building settlements and publicly defied Obama, Obama backed down and allowed the Israeli prime minister to score a political victory.

More than Obama's political timidity, America's current dysfunctional political culture imposes severe constraints on his ability to pursue an evenhanded approach toward the Palestine question, which remains an enduring and preeminent issue, even as regional war and regional revolution threaten the decade-old pursuit of stability. US politicians, including Obama, are trapped in a political culture that promotes conformity and group-think on Israel and strongly discourages dissenting voices. After a promising start, the new president dared not to exert real pressure on Israel to stop the construction of settlements on the West Bank and to negotiate in good faith with the Palestinians. For example, when Palestinian president Abbas, after being disappointed by the failure of US diplomacy, took his case to the United Nations and sought recognition of a Palestinian state, Obama threatened to veto that quest in the Security Council and to punish the Palestinian Authority by ending America's financial aid. In 2009 in Cairo, the newly inaugurated president offered an inclusive vision for Israeli-Palestinian peace and security; in September 2011 at the General Assembly, Obama laid out the dominant Israeli security perspective, which, in his new view, overrides Palestinian security and even self-determination. The Cairo speech was the high point of an evenhanded approach to the Arab-Israeli conflict; the UN speech represented a triumph for the Israel-first school.

Why the dramatic shift in Obama's position? "Domestic politics interceded," Zbigniew Brzezinski, a former national security adviser to President Jimmy Carter, stated bluntly.[2] In 2009, the new Obama was not as encumbered by national politics as he was in 2011, when he began fighting for a second presidential term. He and his advisers have convinced themselves that challenging the institutional status quo would mean a loss of votes, money, and—ultimately—office. As a politician, Obama has played it safe and catered to special interest groups, even though his aides say that the president has done so because of the national interest. In fact, as Obama had stated at the start of his tenure, a resolution of the Palestine-Israeli conflict would serve America's national interests more by strengthening moderate, progressive, and democratic voices in the region. Yet, like his predecessors, Obama allowed the politician to prevail over the statesman, a long pattern of presidential behavior that explains why US Mideast policy persistently fails. Time and again in the Arab-Israeli arena, poisonous domestic politics in America takes precedence over strategic considerations, thereby undermining US credibility and influence. Obama's conduct thus testifies to the structural-institutional continuity of US foreign policy. More than in any other region in the world, presidential policy in the Middle East is hampered by institutional, bureaucratic, and domestic politics. They are a toxic mix.

Obama's retreat on Israeli-Palestinian peace could not have occurred at a worse moment, for it came during the transition from authoritarianism to democracy in the Arab world, a moment of self-determination that Obama embraced, though belatedly. On the one hand, Obama recognized the significance of the moment in the Arab world as "a time of transformations" and called on the world to respond to the calls for change elsewhere in the region, particularly in Syria. On the other hand, he disconnected the Arab world's pursuit of dignity and freedom from the Palestinian's pursuit of those same ideals. By doing so he risked being seen as "hypocritical," according to the *New York Times,* even as he alienated the rising forces to whom he was reaching out. Despite his endeavors to be on the right side of history in the Middle East, Obama thereby joined the long list of presidents who, by failing to courageously contend against political power with political power, were accused of double standards, and who, in the end, compromised the national interest.

There is a real danger that by underestimating the importance of Palestine for the newly revitalized Arab civil societies, the United States might find itself confronted by them. As the Arab revolutions establish a new order, Palestine, far from fading away, will be fundamental in Arab politics. The newly dominant social and political forces, particularly Islamists, prioritize the Palestinian cause, and they will increase pressure on Israel to withdraw from the occupied territories. For example, in their first meeting with Deputy Secretary of State William Burns, the second-ranking diplomat in the State Department, after they had won more than 40 percent of the seats in Egypt's parliamentary elections, leaders of the Muslim Brotherhood's political party, the Freedom and Justice Movement, called on the United States to pursue a more balanced approach toward the Arab-Israeli conflict and stressed the significance of Palestine in the US-Egyptian relationship. Mohammed Morsi, head of the party, urged the United States to "reconsider" its policies in the region, favoring people's choices as reflected by the Arab uprisings instead of dictatorial regimes, because that proved to be "not in its best interest."[3] The likelihood of an escalation of tensions between Israel and its Arab neighbors should not be overlooked. The Israeli embassy incident of 2011 may only be a taste of things to come. The status quo will be difficult to maintain, and it will strain relations between the United States and emerging Arab democracies.

Turkish President Abdullah Gul is right in saying that the future of the movement for democracy in the Middle East depends on creating a lasting Israeli-Palestinian peace and a broader peace between Israel and its neighbors. Since the plight of the Palestinians was a root cause of the unrest in the region, and a pretext for tyranny on behalf of the dictatorial regimes, Gul argues that "whether these uprisings lead to democracy and peace or to [further] tyranny and conflict will depend on forging a lasting Israeli-Palestinian peace agreement."[4] Like Gul, former US National Security Adviser Brent Scowcroft, a realist like Obama, cautioned that "the nature of the new Middle East cannot be known until the festering sore of the occupied territories is removed."[5]

It is worth noting that Obama inherited an altered regional environment in which local actors frequently challenge the United States and feel more empowered in an incipient multipolar world. The short-lived unipolar system in which the United Stated dominated international relations has come to an end. A global redistribution of power has curtailed America's freedom of maneuver and exposed its relative decline. The Iraq debacle has not only undermined America's moral standing and credibility but also its deterrent strategy. America is neither feared nor trusted to act rationally and wisely to preserve world peace. Although Obama has labored to rebuild trust lost during the Bush years, the genie is out. Increasing evidence shows that ambitious regional powers, driven by awakened public opinion and civil society, no longer show deference to the great powers, particularly the United States. These countries—from Iraq to Afghanistan to Turkey to Iran— pursue autonomous and assertive policies that frequently clash with US interests. Netanyahu's defiance of Obama is more or less a case of US domestic politics and Obama's political timidity and ambitions. But Abbas's decision to seek UN recognition of a Palestinian state against the express wishes and threats of the United States is a declaration of independence from American diplomacy, a radical departure from the old pattern of acquiescence and subservience. Driven by a galvanized public opinion and declining personal fortunes, Abbas, who initially relied wholly on Obama, cut his losses and turned elsewhere for support. Although in the end aggressive American lobbying undercut Abbas's design, the Obama administration's explicit threats of punitive measures did not change the conduct of the Palestinian Authority, a small non-state actor dependent on American foreign aid, with meager material assets and options.

The United States can no longer take for granted the loyalty of its allies and the compliance of its foes. Iraq is a case in point. After intense negotiations with Iraqi leaders for more than a year, the Obama administration had little choice but to withdraw all US troops from the war-torn country. Iraqi Prime Minister Nuri al-Maliki could not accede to America's demand and grant legal immunity to American soldiers if they violated the country's laws, though Maliki would have liked to do so. Fierce popular opposition inside Iraq to continuing the American military presence forced his hand. Afterward, the Obama foreign policy team portrayed the military withdrawal from Iraq as the fulfilment of the president's pledge when he campaigned for office. Nevertheless, until the last few days of the American troops' presence in Iraq in late December 2011, American officials pressed their case. Ironically, the Iraqi leadership, which had been empowered by the toppling of the Saddam Hussein regime, demurred. Iraqi public opinion has turned against the United States with a vengeance. Of all Middle Eastern countries, one would have expected Iraq, a state in transition that suffers from a severe political and security crisis, to welcome Obama's decision to keep a sizable military force there. The stakes are big for the United States in Iraq, a country that the Bush administration used as a laboratory of social engineering and empire building. A river of blood was shed, together with almost a trillion dollars in direct US costs, to turn Iraq into a functioning model, an ideological rival, to the Islamic Republic in Iran.

As US troops exited Iraq almost a decade after the invasion and occupation of the country, they left behind a sectarian-based system, not a functioning democracy, and a fragmented political elite. The prospects of Iraq's revival as a pivotal Gulf power are slim. In the meantime, the country is squarely in the Iranian orbit of influence, doing its bidding in Syria and backing the besieged Assad regime in direct opposition to a US strategy whose goal is to oust Assad. Violence has escalated to a dangerous level in Iraq, and political rivalries have paralyzed the state, threatening its integrity and national unity. A decade on, the legacy of America's war in Iraq has shattered prospects for communal coexistence in the Middle East and damaged vital American interests in the wider region. Nevertheless, through its recognition of the limits of US power and cutting its losses in Iraq and elsewhere, Obama's decision making contrasts sharply with that of his predecessor. As a realist whose foreign policy priorities lie in the Asia-Pacific region, Obama does not believe that a military presence in Iraq serves the national interest, even though he accepted initially the military establishment's advice to keep an armed force there.

Similarly, after initially deferring to the military and ordering an eighteen-month troop buildup in Afghanistan, Obama began to disengage militarily from the broken country and to entertain a political horizon that includes the Taliban. With the killing of Osama bin Laden and the emasculation of the remnants of his organization in Pakistan, Obama is able to talk and act seriously on drawing down forces in Afghanistan. In June 2011, he announced that the United States would begin pulling out 10,000 troops by the end of 2011 and an additional 23,000 by the end of the summer of 2012, leaving 70,000 troops in Afghanistan. The war of necessity, or the right war, as Obama contrasted the Afghan conflict with that of Iraq during the presidential campaign, is no longer necessary or affordable, given the dismal state of the US economy and the vast challenges in Afghanistan. A consensus exists within foreign policy circles that there is no military solution to the Afghan conflict and that the Taliban must be included in a future settlement that allows American troops to return home. The Obama administration reportedly has tried to speed up the peace talk process with the Taliban in hopes of announcing substantial progress at a NATO summit in May 2012. As the administration reduces its military force in Afghanistan, it will hand over control of the mission there entirely to Special Forces and clandestine CIA operatives.[6] By replacing soldiers on the ground with drone attacks and special operations on a large scale, the realist and pragmatist president is fulfilling his promises to end Bush's wars while keeping the military establishment satisfied.

Given the dysfunctional nature of the current political culture in America, Obama has been a breath of fresh air. The difference between Obama's competence and his predecessor's is night and day. Obama's actions are consistent with his key foreign policy agenda—one that has not been without its share of successes, especially compared with the record of his predecessor. The end goal has been to reprioritize relations with Asia and reduce US commitments in the Middle East. What he has done in his first presidential term is to slowly and gradually reduce the military presence in the Muslim world and mend the rift of the Bush years without incurring huge material and political costs. Treading lightly, Obama does not want to be entangled in the region's raging conflicts and get burned at home. He and his foreign policy team feel that the United States has overextended itself and suffered both a colossal loss of moral authority as well as opportunity costs, costs that would have been better spent elsewhere.

For example, instead of taking the lead in the military confrontation against Qaddafi, Obama insisted that European powers and the Arab League take ownership of the operation. Throughout the conflict and despite vocal criticism by Republican detractors, Obama took a backseat to the leadership of Britain and

France. He proved his critics on both the right and left wrong, though for different reasons. Obama scored a political victory in Libya because he showed restraint and kept a low profile, a fact lost on his detractors, and, to lesser extent, his supporters. Obama knew that America was unpopular among Arabs, who suspect it of harboring colonial designs on their societies, and he knew too that the American military was overextended. In Libya, Obama exercised self-control because he is aware of the size of the challenges he inherited and the limits of US power. Similarly in Syria, Obama pushed back against military intervention there when pressed by a journalist to explain why Assad was being allowed to crush an uprising in the city of Homs, while Qaddafi was not. "I said at the time with respect to Libya that we would be making these decisions on a case-by-case basis based on how unified the international community was, what our capacities were," Obama said. "But not every situation is gonna allow for the kind of military solution we saw [in Libya]."[7]

In contrast to his ideologically driven predecessor, Obama is not a liberal interventionist; he is less inclined to use force to advance "causes." Obama sets strict limits on the use of the military, only employing it to strictly serve the national interest. While he wages a fierce counterterrorism campaign against Al Qaeda and like-minded groups worldwide, he has drawn down the forces in Iraq and Afghanistan. The Obama administration did not consider Libya (and Syria) strategically important to US vital interests; it lacked a clear understanding of the composition of the anti-Qaddafi coalition (and had no exit strategy in Syria). It insisted on a unified international response and that its European allies, which have more vested interests in the North African country, should do the heavy lifting.

While Obama shows more continuity than discontinuity with regard to US foreign policy toward the Middle East, he has attempted to normalize America's relations with Muslims and make a break with the Bush legacy of moral crusading and social engineering. More than any of his recent predecessors, Obama has recognized the complexity of social and political conditions in the region. He has sought (within the permissible parameters of the US foreign policy debate) to reorient and recalibrate American policy and he has met with failure and some success.

For example, although the Obama foreign policy team was outmaneuvered by Netanyahu on the settlements and retreated in disarray, and although Obama initially wavered before abandoning pro-US Arab authoritarian rulers, he, more than any of his senior foreign policy aides, recognized the significance of the Arab awakenings and the need for America to be forward-looking and responsive to the aspirations of the protesters. In a speech at the Department of State in May 2011, Obama announced an important policy shift, saying that the United States would now be guided by support for democratic transitions and reform. Yet, despite many positive steps that have placed America on the right side of the historical wave of political change, Obama has not invested enough political and financial capital in assisting transitioning Arab societies in the development of their shattered economies and institutions through neutral multilateral, nongovernmental organizations, including the United Nations. In fact, the Obama administration has sent mixed messages to the ruling generals, particularly in Egypt, who have struggled to preserve the status quo at any cost. Still, Obama is right to keep a low profile and allow the people in the region to take ownership of their destiny. By doing so, he neutralizes lingering suspicions by Tunisians, Egyptians, Libyans, and others that "the West" would hijack the moment and, once again, deprive them of self-determination. In a way, Obama has begun a subtle process of normalization with Middle Eastern states and societies, a process designed to deactivate cultural minefields that historically have crippled US foreign relations with the peoples of the region. If successful, Obama will lay to rest a widespread belief that America is omnipotent, lurking everywhere, always meddling in the region's internal affairs.

Perhaps Obama's greatest political achievement in the Middle East lay in nourishing an exceptionally close strategic relationship with Turkey and its outspoken, charismatic prime minister, Recep Tayyib Erdogan. From the outset, Obama recognized Turkey's pivotal role in its neighborhood as a force for moderation and stability. Despite the concerted effort of American right-wing circles to portray Erdogan as a radical Islamist and staunchly anti-Israeli, Obama did not allow this partisan noise and dissonance to poison America's relations with the new Turkey. The Obama administration has co-opted the new rising geostrategic and geoeconomic power and leveraged its influence. In fact, the president has spent more time in direct meetings and on the phone with the Turkish prime minister than with any other leader in the world.

In the cases of Libya and Syria, the Obama administration has coordinated its actions with Turkey. Given the complexity of the Syrian crisis and US policy constraints, Obama is now more than ever relying on Erdogan to exert real pressure on Assad and force him out. Of all outside powers, Turkey, which until recently had a warm relationship with the Assad regime, is the only state that has implicitly threatened to use force there (to establish a humanitarian buffer zone inside the country) if the UN Security Council sanctions such a move. Obama aides say they are pleased that Turkey has actively backed the democratic uprisings in various Arab countries and has served as an example for millions of Arabs, particularly rising Islamist parties there. Obama's nuanced multilateral approach contrasts sharply with his predecessor's unilateralism. Although the Obama administration has differed with Turkey on a number of issues, particularly on Israel and Iran, it practices quiet diplomacy and does not allow policy differences to stand in the way of the two countries' strategic partnership; it recognizes the rise of a geostrategic and geoeconomic power and coordinates policy to tackle regional crises. Far from viewing Turkey's assertiveness and independent posture as a threat, Obama sees Erdogan overall as an asset who might fill the leadership vacuum in this turbulent neighborhood and allow the United States to shift foreign policy focus elsewhere.

If the working relationship with Turkey is Obama's greatest foreign policy achievement, his approach toward Iran is his greatest gamble. His early promise of diplomatic engagement has been replaced by confrontation. As 2011 drew to a close, the United States and Iran found themselves on a warpath. In December 2011 Congress passed a defense authorization bill that included bilateral sanctions on the Central Bank of Iran. Although Obama expressed reservations, he signed it into law. According to Gary Sick, a former American official and a prominent analyst on Iran, by cutting off from the US financial system any foreign banks that continue to transact business with the Central Bank of Iran, this latest sanctions package is intended to prevent Iran from receiving payment for its oil—the equivalent of an act of war and effectively a financial blockade of Iran's oil ports that would deprive the country of more than half its budgetary revenues.[8] Faced with economic warfare, Iran has held naval maneuvers in the Strait of Hormuz and threatened to close it to commerce, leading to a sharp escalation in the thirty-year war of words between Washington and Tehran. There is a real danger that Iranian or American strategies of brinksmanship will lead to a miscalculation that triggers a war that would be disastrous to all.[9] If Iran were to use its full economic and military leverage, it would of course suffer a tremendous blow; but it would go down fighting, sending the world economy into a tailspin.

Obama has stressed that he believes that the recent unprecedented economic sanctions imposed on Iran can curb its nuclear program if they are given more time to work. At the same time, the president has asked the Pentagon to come up with military options for a possible strike against Iran's nuclear program, US officials say. According to the *Wall Street Journal,* the Pentagon is pushing ahead with contingency planning, including the building of the largest conventional "bunker buster" bombs, costing hundreds of millions of dollars each and capable of destroying Iran's most heavily fortified underground facilities.[10] Obama's Iran gamble is fraught with risks and dangers. If three decades of sanctions against Iran may serve as a guide, the new punishing measures are unlikely to force Iranian leaders to shut down their nuclear program. In fact, the Iranians have recently doubled their efforts to amass more low-enriched uranium and begun enrichment at a facility deep underground.[11] The danger is that if sanctions fail to change Iran's conduct of the nuclear program, Obama has no exit strategy. He might have to confront a military option.

In hindsight, the odds were against Obama's early offer of engagement to the Iranian leadership—"a single roll of the dice," according to a senior State Department official.[12] There is insufficient political will and a lack of trust between the United States and Iran. The thirty-year-old enmity between the two states has become institutionalized. For example, as tensions intensified between Iran and the United States and its allies in early 2012, Iran's supreme leader Ayatollah Ali Khamenei warned that any military strike "will be ten times more detrimental to the United States" than to his nation. He reminded Iranians: "We should not fall for the smile on the face of the enemy," Khamenei said. "We have had our experience the last 30 years. . . . We should not be cheated by their false promises and words, they break their promises very easily . . . they feel no shame . . . they simply utter lies."[13] And in the United States, from the outset, Obama faced stiff institutional resistance to his vision of engagement, including powerful members of his own Democratic Party, and allowed the political right to define the metrics of success on Iran. As a shrewd analyst on Iran noted, Obama has bought the idea that a "strong" policy toward Tehran must be tough, punishing, and confrontational, thus permitting the debate to take place on the right's turf. He simply did not educate the American public on the relative stakes involved in diplomatically engaging the Iranians as opposed to the costs of a prolonged confrontation.[14]

The Israeli government used high-level Democratic donors to exert additional pressure on Obama to forsake diplomacy with Iran.[15] As the US presidential campaign heated up in 2012, Benjamin Netanyahu exerted increasing pressure on Obama to lay the trip wire for military action against Iran, though the US president deflected the attempt. Neighboring states in the Persian Gulf also added their voices to Israel's. In other words, the political costs for attempting to resolve tensions with Iran were excessive and the political space too narrow to justify embarking on the bumpy path to peace with Iran.[16] As noted in chapter 5, internal tensions and rivalries among Iranian leaders, coupled with deep suspicions of Washington, paralyzed Tehran's decision-making process and squandered the unprecedented opportunity offered by the Obama administration to embark on a cautious reconciliation program.

There is an inherent danger that the Obama administration's approach in the Middle East reflects a vacuum in global leadership, a vacuum that is weakening the ability of post-autocratic governments to overcome the structural economic and institutional challenges that they have inherited from autocratic rulers. Unlike their Latin American and East European counterparts in the 1990s, the Arabs are on their own, with meager international assistance. Egyptian officials bitterly complain that most of the foreign aid pledged after the ouster of Mubarak, especially that promised by Arab Gulf states, has not been delivered. The Egyptian and Tunisian economies are in tatters and face severe vulnerabilities in the coming years. Other Arab economies, such as Yemen, Syria, and, to a lesser extent, Libya, have almost collapsed. The United States, together with the European Union, Japan, China, and the oil-producing Arab countries, should lead and impress on its allies the need to make structural investments in these transitioning Arab societies.

The challenge facing US foreign policy is to strike a balance between keeping a healthy distance from the Arab region's political and social turmoil and providing leadership and a set of global initiatives to smooth the transition to economic viability, solvency, and pluralism. If the United States and Europe are pressed for cash, there is significant unspent money in the Gulf states, tens of billions of US dollars, that can be prudently invested, as opposed to being handed out, in the reconstruction of newly freed societies. The returns on this investment would be high for all sides; the money would help promote a better world and improve the quality of life of millions of poor Arabs. As previously argued, the Obama administration has shied away from taking a leadership role in the non-oil-producing Arab countries, because of the failed interventionist record of George W. Bush and because its foreign policy priorities lie elsewhere in Asia. Possibly, the coming to power of elected governments in Tunisia and Egypt would bring about a reassessment of US strategy. Assisting the new leaders in obtaining resources would allow them to restructure their economies along more equitable lines.

Even if Obama resists the temptation to go to war, as he has done so far, he will end 2012 with a hard-line position on Iran similar to that of his hawkish predecessor. Time and again, the Middle East intrudes unexpectedly and dangerously into the foreign policy agenda of American presidents. Obama is no exception. The Arab awakenings and Iran have forced Obama's hand and complicated his foreign policy agenda. There are storms gathering on the horizon—not just in Iran, but also in Iraq, Syria, Afghanistan, and Pakistan. Obama inherited these dangers from his predecessors, and they pose severe risks to his presidency. As a former US foreign policy official put it: "America's stock is lower than it's ever been, its partners are gone, along with the familiar bad guys, and it's not at all clear who or what will take the place of those partners. We confront not just an Arab Spring but an array of uncertainties complex enough to run many years to come."[17] The uncertainties stem from an altered regional environment and a global redistribution of power away from a unipolar system dominated by the United States to an international system with multiple power centers. America's predicament in the Middle East is stark, a bitter inheritance more than a half century in the making, and springing from systemic failures to view the region from the inside and to limit the excessive role of domestic politics and special interests. These points may be obvious, but like other plain truths they bear repeating and demystifying. One of this book's major conclusions is that the United States may have reached the end of its moment in the Middle East.

Obama has attempted to mend the widening rift between America and the Middle East and recalibrate relations with it. The jury is still out. His administration is wary of making substantive investments there, preferring retrenchment and selective commitments. The Arab awakenings forced Obama's hand and caused him to become more engaged in the area. As a realist, nonideological president, his central goal is to minimize the damage to vital American interests and manage the transition. But as pro-US Arab dictators fall and new political forces take their place, the Obama administration has recalibrated its approach in recognition of new realities. For example, when religious-based activists or Islamists won a majority of parliamentary seats in Tunisia, Morocco, and Egypt, the administration reversed a decades-long policy and engaged the previously shunned actors. This was a testament to its pragmatism and realism. Yet the Obama administration has shown no such flexibility toward similar Islamist parties that confront Israel, such as the Palestinians' Hamas and Lebanon's Hezbollah, because that would cost him political support at home. Since Obama's presidency began, he has had to do damage control on the Bush administration's failed policies; because of this, his successes have been less apparent, and his failures clearly evident.

Liberated from the policy straitjacket of Bush's wars, and freed from the timid expediency demanded by a looming re-election campaign, a second-term Obama could potentially shed his political inhibitions and escape the trappings of special interest groups in an effort to establish America's progressive leadership in the New Middle East. As the old British saying goes—"in for a penny, in for a pound"—now is a time for courage, leadership, and bold moves in the region. Obama has successfully moved the United States out of the ditch that George W. Bush left the country in. But the test of this president will be whether or not he can realign US foreign policy with progressive and democratic voices in the region and translate his words into concrete policies.

NOTES

INTRODUCTION

1. Fareed Zakaria, *The Post-American World* (New York: W. W. Norton, 2008).
2. Ibid.
3. Ibid.
4. Rashid Khalidi, *Sowing Crisis: The Cold War and American Dominance in the Middle East* (Boston: Beacon Press, 2009); Odd Arne Westad, *The Global Cold War: Third World Interventions and the Making of Our Times* (London: Cambridge University Press, 2007).
5. Mohamed Heikal, *The Cairo Documents: The Inside Story of Nasser and His Relationship with World Leaders, Rebels, and Statesmen* (New York: Doubleday, 1973); Anthony Nutting, *Nasser* (New York: E. P. Dutton, 1972).
6. Ewen MacAskill, "Mubarak Claims Obama 'Does Not Understand Egyptian Culture,'" *The Guardian*, 4 February 2011, http://www.guardian.co.uk/world/2011/feb/04/mubarak-stands-fast.
7. "Egypt Protests: US Call to Hosni Mubarak's Government," BBC News, 9 February 2011, http://www.bbc.co.uk/news/world-middle-east-12400422.
8. "Qaddafi Unplugged and Uncensored: Recollections of My Life—Mu'ummar Qaddafi by Col. Mu'ummar Qaddafi, trans. Sam Hamod (9 April 2011), http://www.informationclearinghouse.info/article27856.htm#idc-cover.
9. "Interview Crown Prince Abdullah," "House of Saud," *Frontline*, Public Broadcasting Service, 8 February 2005, http://www.pbs.org/wgbh/pages/frontline/shows/saud/interviews/abdullah.html.
10. Andrew Hammond, "Saudi Clerics Condemn Protests as Un-Islamic," *FaithWorld*, Reuters, 7 March 2011, http://blogs.reuters.com/faithworld/2011/03/07/saudi-clerics-condemn-protests-as-un-islamic.
11. Cited by Yahya Sadowski, "The New Orientalism and Democracy Debate," *Middle East Report* 23 (July-August 1993): 14.
12. Cited by Martin Kramer, *Arab Awakening and Islamic Revival: The Politics of Ideas in the Middle East* (New Brunswick, N.J.: Transaction Publishers, 1996), 269.
13. See Daniel Brumberg, "The Trap of Liberalized Autocracy," *Journal of Democracy* 13, no. 4 (October 2004): 56-68; and Glenn E. Robinson, "Defensive Democratization in Jordan," *International Journal of Middle East Studies* 30, no. 3 (August, 1998): 387-410.
14. George W. Bush, "Remarks by President George W. Bush at the 20th Anniversary of the National Endowment for Democracy," 6 November 2003, National Endowment for Democracy, http://www.ned.org/george-w-bush/remarks-by-president-george-w-bush-at-the-20th-anniversary.
15. Daniel E. Zoughbie, "The Ends of History: George W. Bush's Political Theology and the Israeli-Palestinian Conflict" (DPhil, University of Oxford, 2011).
16. John Tirman, "Wikileaks Releases Damning—but Misleading—Documents on Iraq," Iraq: The Human Cost, http://web.mit.edu/humancostiraq/index.html.
17. World Public Opinion.org, "Muslim Public Opinion on US Policy, Attacks on Civilians and Al Qaeda," 24 April 2007, Program on International Policy Attitudes, University of Maryland, http://www.worldpublicopinion.org/pipa/pdf/apr07/START_Apr07_rpt.pdf.

18. Thom Shanker, "Warning against Wars Like Iraq and Afghanistan," *New York Times*, 25 February 2011, http://www.nytimes.com/2011/02/26/world/26gates.html.

19. Office of the Press Secretary, "Remarks by the President on a New Beginning," 4 June 2009, The White House, http://www.whitehouse.gov/the-press-office/remarks-president-cairo-university-6-04-09.

20. Ryan Lizza, "The Consequentialist: How the Arab Spring Remade Obama's Foreign Policy," *New Yorker*, 2 May 2011, http://www.newyorker.com/reporting/2011/05/02/110502fa_fact_lizza#ixzz1UHMhJeLO.

21. Office of the Press Secretary, "Remarks by President Obama to the Turkish Parliament," 6 April 2009, http://www.whitehouse.gov/the_press_office/Remarks-By-President-Obama-To-The-Turkish-Parliament.

22. "Obama Interview: The Transcript," BBC News, 2 June 2009, http://www.bbc.co.uk/worldservice/news/2009/06/090602_obama_transcript.shtml.

23. Lizza, "The Consequentialist."

24. Charles M. Blow, "Decline of American Exceptionalism," *New York Times*, 18 November 2011.

25. Lizza, ibid.

26. Cited by Lizza, ibid.

27. Ibid.

28. Margaret Talev, "Obama's Asia Focus Driven by Economy, Demographics," Bloomberg News, 11 November 2011; Fareed Zakaria, "The Strategist," *Time*, 30 January 2012.

29. Researchers at Brown University recently estimated that the costs of the wars in Iraq, Afghanistan, and US assistance to the Pakistani military total between $3.2 and $4 trillion. ("Costs of War," Watson Institute for International Studies, Brown University, http://costsofwar.org.)In their forthcoming book, *Terror, Security, and Money* (New York: Oxford University Press), Mark Stewart and John Mueller calculate that the enhanced costs of the war on terror—increased costs of domestic security beyond those in place on 10 September 2001—have totaled more than $1 trillion. The costs for overseas ventures like the Afghanistan and Iraq wars, part of the war on terror, have so far come to at least an additional $2 trillion and may well be twice that.

   Joseph Stiglitz and Linda Bilmes estimate that the direct and indirect costs of the Iraq war will top $3 trillion, and they say that their estimates are conservative: at least $600 billion would be needed for the lifetime health-care costs for injured US soldiers, $400 billion due to loss of workers to the economy, both injured and those serving in the National Guard, $600 billion for interest on money borrowed to finance the war, and $1–$2 trillion is the macroeconomic impact of the war. See Linda Bilmes and Joseph Stiglitz, *The Three Trillion Dollar War: The True Cost of the Iraq Conflict* (New York: W. W. Norton, 2008). Congress has allocated $1.05 trillion to the Iraq and Afghanistan wars. See "Notes and Sources: Cost of War Counter," National Priorities Project, http://www.nationalpriorities.org/cost_of_war_counter_notes.

   As of 2008, the United States has spent more than $300 billion on a new post–September 11 Department of Homeland Security, a second "defense" department. The $300 billion does not include what local and state governments and private businesses have spent on homeland security. In addition, the cumulative increased cost of counterterrorism for the United States since September 11 (the federal, state, local, and private expenditures as well as opportunity costs) has topped $1 trillion. See J. Mueller, "Terrorphobia: Our False Sense of Insecurity," *American Interest* (May/June 2008), http://www.the-american-interest.com/article.cfm?piece=418.

   In addition, according to Stewart and Mueller, "An assessment of increased United States federal homeland security expenditure since 2001 and expected lives saved as a result of such expenditure suggests that the annual cost ranges from $64 million to $600 million (or even more) per life saved, greatly in excess of the regulatory safety goal of $1 million to $10 million per life saved. As such, it clearly and dramatically fails a cost-benefit analysis. In addition, the opportunity cost of these expenditures, amounting to $32 billion per year, is considerable, and it is highly likely that far more lives would have been saved if the money (or even a portion of it) had been invested instead in a wide range of more cost-effective risk mitigation programs." "Assessing the Costs and Benefits of United States Homeland Security Spending," Research Report No. 265.04.08, Centre for Infrastructure and Reliability, University of Newcastle, Australia.

   Since September 11, the US defense budget for foreign counterterrorism has increased considerably. It is hard to find comprehensive data on foreign aid related to counterterrorism, especially key "frontline" states in the "War on Terror"—Pakistan, Afghanistan, Yemen, Turkey, Jordan, Lebanon, Indonesia, Philippines, and others—a category of security assistance used during the Cold War to provide support to key geopolitical allies. For example, the level of development assistance "nearly tripled from approximately $10 billion in 2000 to $28.5 billion in 2005. In October 2009, President Obama allocated $7.5 billion for Pakistan." See Stephen Kaufman, "Bush's Budget Request Would Continue Increase in Foreign Aid: USAID Administrator Says U.S. Aid Has Nearly Tripled Since 2000," America.gov, 5 February 2007, http://www.america.gov/st/washfile-english/2007/February /20070205173017esnamfuak8.193606e-02.html#ixzz0i9F93xof; Jim Lobe, "U.S. Foreign Aid Budget Takes on Cold War Cast," Inter Press Service (IPS News), 3 February 2004, http://www.ipsnews .net/interna.asp?idnews=22232 ; "Obama Signs Big Pakistan Aid Bill," BBC News, 15 October 2009, http://news.bbc.co.uk/1/hi/world/americas/8309643.stm.

30. "Clinton, Gates: U.S. in Afghanistan for Long Haul," CNN, 5 October 2009, http://articles.cnn .com/2009-10-05/politics/clinton.gates_1_afghanistan-taliban-state-hillary-clinton?_s=PM:POLITICS; "US Vows No Change in Afghan Strategy," *AFP,* 27 February 2012.

31. David D. Kirpatrick and Steven Lee Myers, "Overtures to Egypt's Islamists Reverse Longtime U.S. Policy," *New York Times,* 3 January 2012.

32. Ibid.

33. Aaron David Miller, "Arab Spring, American Winter," *Los Angeles Times,* 13 November 2011.

34. Ibid.

35. Melvyn Leffler, *A Preponderance of Power: National Security, the Truman Administration, and the Cold War* (Stanford, Calif.: Stanford University Press, 1992).

36. Warren Bass, *Support Any Friend: Kennedy's Middle East and the Making of the U.S.-Israel Alliance* (New York: Oxford University Press, 2004); Talking Outline: Saudi-UAR Relations, 4 October 1962, box 158, in the John F. Kennedy National Security Files, the Middle East: National Security Files, 1961-1963, microfilmed from the holding of the J. F. Kennedy Library (Frederick, Md.: University Publications of America, 1989), reel 3 out of 3. [Henceforth, this series will be referred to as JFK Files, 1961-1963]. Malcom H. Kerr, *America's Middle East Policy: Kissinger, Carter, and the Future* (Institute for Palestine Studies, June 1980).

37. Fred Halliday, *The Middle East in International Relations: Power, Politics, and Ideology* (Cambridge: Cambridge University Press, 2005); Shibley Telhami, *The Stakes: America and the Middle East* (New York: Basic Books, 2002).

38. Avi Shlaim, *War and Peace in the Middle East: A Critique of American Policy* (New York: Penguin Books, 1994).

39. Henry Kissinger, *White House Years* (Boston: Little, Brown, 1979).

40. Ibid., 1279.

41. Ibid., 1291.

42. Adeed Dawisha and Karen Dawisha (eds), *The Soviet Union in the Middle East: Policies and Perspectives* (London: Heinemann, 1982).

43. Shlaim, *War and Peace in the Middle East.*

44. Cited by Noam Chomsky, *Middle East Illusions: Including Peace in the Middle East? Reflections on Justice and Nationhood* (Lanham, Md.: Rowman & Littlefield, 2004), 177.

45. Barak Ravid, Avi Issacharoff, and Natasha Mosgovaya, "After His Stint at UN, Abbas Is Politically Stronger than Ever," *Haaretz,* 26 September 2011.

46. Kerr, *America's Middle East Policy.*

47. George W. Ball, *Diplomacy for a Crowded World* (Boston: Little, Brown, 1976), 121.

48. Ball, *Diplomacy;* Kerr, *America's Middle East Policy.*

49. Rashid Khalidi, *Sowing Crisis: The Cold War and American Dominance in the Middle East* (Boston: Beacon Press, 2010).

50. Robert D. Kaplan, *The Arabists: The Romance of an American Elite* (New York: Free Press, 1993).

51. Martin Kramer, "Endangered Species: The Arabists," *Commentary* (February 1994).

52. US Ambassador to Israel and Assistant Secretary of State for Near East Affairs during the Clinton Administration. In 1993, he was the first to outline the "dual containment" strategy, a US foreign policy that aimed at containing Iraq and Iran, then viewed as Israel's two most important strategic adversaries.

53. Deputy National Security Adviser for Global Democracy Strategy and National Security Council Senior Director for Near East and North African Affairs during the George W. Bush administration.

Abrams designed the policy for undermining the democratically elected Hamas government and for US training of Fatah security services. (http://conflictsforum.org/2007/elliot-abrams-uncivil-war/)

54. Served as the director of policy planning in the State Department under George H. W. Bush; was the special Middle East coordinator under Clinton and is currently a special adviser for the Persian Gulf and Southwest Asia to Secretary of State Hillary Clinton. One former colleague accused Ross of acting as "Israel's lawyer."

55. Bolton served as the Third Under Secretary for Arms Control and International Security and then as US ambassador to the United Nations under George W. Bush. He is known for outspoken statements in favor of those on the right in Israeli internal politics and is a founding member of the Friends of Israel Initiative, which sees Israel as the first line of defense in terms of Western civilization. "Defending Israel means defending the values that made and sustain our Western civilization," according to the initiative. (http://www.friendsofisraelinitiative.org/article.php?c=57).

56. Friedberg, who served as a deputy assistant to Vice President Dick Cheney for national security affairs, called John Mearsheimer and Stephen Walt's critical study of the Israeli lobby study "a slanderous and infalsifiable allegation of treason." (*Foreign Policy*, July/August 2006, http://mearsheimer.uchicago.edu /pdfs/A0042.pdf).

57. A senior aide on national security to Vice President Cheney, Hannah is thought to have a played a major role in gathering the intelligence used to justify the invasion of Iraq.

58. Perle worked in the Reagan administration as an assistant secretary of defense and on the Defense Policy Board Advisory Committee under George H. W. Bush and Bill Clinton. In the George W. Bush administration, he was the chairman of the same board. His 2004 book, *An End to Evil: How to Win the War on Terror*, prescribed abandonment of the Israeli-Palestinian peace process and invasion of Syria as ways to defend the United States against terrorism. He also chaired a study group, including David Wurmser and Douglas Feith, that produced *A Clean Break*, a 1996 paper for incoming Israeli prime minister Benjamin Netanyahu that recommended the removal of Saddam Hussein, armed battles in Lebanon, and the invasion of Syria. "Richard Perle," American Enterprise Institute, http://www.aei .org/scholar/richard-perle-1/; David Frum and Richard Perle, *An End to Evil: How to Win the War on Terror* (New York: Random House, 2003); "A Clean Break: A New Strategy for Securing the Realm," American Enterprise Institute.

59. Wolfowitz was deputy secretary of defense under the George W. Bush administration and was said to be the first to mention the possibility of an invasion of Iraq following the 9/11 attacks.

60. Feith served as under secretary of defense for policy under George W. Bush and was one of the architects of the Iraqi invasion.

61. Wurmser served as Middle East adviser to Vice President Dick Cheney and as a special assistant to John Bolton at the State Department. Wurmser has researched and coauthored several influential Israel-first papers, including *A Clean Break* and *Ending Syria's Occupation of Lebanon: The U.S. Role*, which argued that Syria was developing weapons of mass destruction. (http://www.meforum.org/research/lsg.php)

62. Levitt served as deputy assistant secretary for intelligence and analysis at the Department of the Treasury and pushed for Iranian financial sanctions as a way to curb the country's nuclear ambitions.

63. Kerr, *America's Middle East Policy*.

64. Ibid., 30.

65. This has not always been the case. In the Cold War, the role of the presidency and the president in the making of American foreign policy toward the Middle East was pivotal. The personality of the president matters, especially his worldview, set of beliefs, perceptions of the domestic and international environment, and the senior advisers with whom he surrounds himself. For example, as will be shown in chapter 1, Harry Truman's role in the UN decision to partition historic Palestine into two states—Jewish and Arab—was fundamental. Influenced by a small coterie of White House aides and domestic political calculations, Truman overruled broad institutional and bureaucratic opposition to the establishment of the Jewish state. See Richard E. Neustadt, *Presidential Power and the Modern Presidents: The Politics of Leadership from Roosevelt to Reagan* (New York: Free Press, 1991); Arthur M. Schlesinger Jr., *The Imperial Presidency* (New York: Mariner Books, 2004); and George C. Edwards III, *The Strategic President: Persuasion and Opportunity in Presidential Leadership* (Princeton, N.J.: Princeton University Press, 2009).

Similarly, President Dwight Eisenhower and his secretary of state played a key role in Middle East policymaking. During the Suez crisis in 1956, not unlike his predecessor, Eisenhower dismissed institutional dissonance and resistance and insisted successfully that Israel withdraw from the Sinai without conditions. When Israel refused to evacuate the Gaza Strip, an Egyptian-administered sector of Palestine, Eisenhower "went to the country" and ordered the American delegation to the United Nations to prepare a resolution to censure Israel. As added pressure, the president contemplated suspension of any private aid to Israel from the United States. As a result, in March 1957 Israel agreed to withdraw her forces from Gaza. See George Lenczowski, *American Presidents and the Middle East* (Durham, N.C.: Duke University Press, 1990), 44-45.

Moreover, to convince Israeli Prime Minister David Ben-Gurion that the United States meant business, Eisenhower gave strict orders to the State Department to inform Israel that his handling of the Suez crisis would not be constrained by domestic politics: "We should handle our affairs exactly as though we did not have a Jew in America. The welfare and best interests of our country were to be the sole criteria on which we operated." (See Secretary Dulles's Office, Department of State, Washington, 31 October 1956; 302nd Meeting of the NSC, 1 November 1956; and President Eisenhower to Swede Hazlett, Washington, 2 November 1956, in FRUS, Suez Crisis, 1956, vol. 16, 891-92, 905-6, 944.)

In 1967 before, during, and after the Six-Day War President Lyndon B. Johnson lent significant support to Israel and punished Nasser, whom he loathed and considered an ally of Soviet Communism. Johnson's pro-Israeli and anti-Nasser sentiments proved decisive in determining American foreign policy in the region for years to come, particularly a critical tilt toward the Jewish state.

Similarly, the personality and predilections of President Richard M. Nixon and his top foreign policy adviser, Henry Kissinger, were instrumental in shaping the US approach toward the Middle East. From the US-Israeli special relationship to shuttle diplomacy after the 1973 October war, Nixon and Kissinger's role was instrumental. Nixon delegated authority to Kissinger that allowed the latter to exercise considerable influence over the making of foreign policy. See Alistair Horne, *Kissinger: 1973, the Crucial Year* (New York: Simon & Schuster, 2009).

The ability of the president and his senior advisers to act freely depends not just on a less constraining domestic environment but also on regional and global developments. As noted previously, the 1973 October war forced Nixon and Kissinger to revise their basic policy premise that regional stability and political settlement depended on Israeli military might. The early 1970s witnessed the consolidation of Israel's lobby in the United States and the intensification of institutional pressure on presidential foreign policy decision making toward the Middle East, particularly the Arab-Israeli conflict. US Mideast policy became deeply entangled in domestic politics, and presidents ever since have come under immense pressure from Congress and Israel's friends to provide unwavering support to the Jewish state. See John J. Mearsheimer and Stephen M. Walt, *The Israel Lobby and U.S. Foreign Policy* (New York: Farrar, Straus and Giroux, 2008).

The irony is that with the exception of a few minor incidents, all US presidents from Truman to Obama have fully backed Israel. All stress that there is no daylight between America and the Jewish state and pledge to maintain its military superiority over all its Arab neighbours. For example, Israeli prime minister Menachem Begin said that there had never been an administration as favorable to Israel as the Reagan administration. It is worth mentioning that Reagan's secretary of state, Alexander Haig, gave Begin and his defense minister, Ariel Sharon, a green light to invade Lebanon in 1982. Begin's successors consider President George W. Bush as more pro-Israeli than Reagan and other US presidents. That goes to show the difficulty facing any president, including Obama, who attempts to break with the consensus on the Arab-Israeli conflict within the American foreign policy establishment.

There have been a few rare examples in which US presidents have exhibited leadership and invested political capital in an effort to force Israel to change its conduct. In the Suez crisis President Eisenhower's actions against Israel are a case in point. Eisenhower's political friends warned the president of the dangers that his unrelenting pressure on Israel presented in view of the approaching elections in November 1956. In his memoirs, Eisenhower recalls that two weeks before Israel's attack on Egypt, he sent a personal letter to Ben-Gurion to make his position absolutely clear:

Both Foster and I suspected that Ben-Gurion might be contemplating military action during these pre-elections days in the United States because of his possible overestimate of my desire to avoid offending the many voters who might have either sentimental or blood relations with Israel. I emphatically corrected any misapprehension of this kind he might have. (See

Eisenhower, *Mandate for Change, 1953-1956: The White House Years* [New York: Doubleday, 1963], 56.

Presidents Carter and George Herbert Walker Bush also bickered with Israel over the peace process and marshaled all their political resources to prevail only partially. One of the most contentious issues for President George Bush was Netanyahu's insistence on a 10 billion dollar US loan guarantee despite his refusal to take substantive steps to support the peace process. Reinforcing his secretary of state James Baker's negotiating position, George H. W. Bush asked Congress to delay consideration of this loan guarantee until Israel made concessions on settlement building. Netanyahu refused to make any concessions on settlements, and this stalemate lasted from the spring of 1991 to the summer of 1992, when Netanyahu's government was voted out of office. See Clyde R. Mark, "Israel: US Foreign Assistance," *CRS Issue Brief for Congress,* December 2001, http://www.fas.org/sgp/crs/mideast /IB85066.pdf, 3.

The reality is that since the late 1960s the US foreign policy establishment, including the presidency, Congress, and special interests, shares a common belief, a relative consensus, that the interests of Israel and the United States are nearly identical, that Israel is a strategic asset and, like America, a frontier democratic state in a sea of Arab and Palestinian reaction and extremism. Widely disseminated and promoted in the last four decades, this narrative, which marries realist and cultural factors alike, resonates with the US public and is deeply entrenched in intellectual circles. There exists a strong residual belief among the power elite, not limited to the Jewish community, in the vitality of America's special relationship with Israel and of an American obligation not to impose political solutions on her that she considers unacceptable, though this belief might be changing. See Kerr, *America's Middle East Policy.* The result is that challenging the dominant narrative on the Arab-Israel conflict would be politically costly and risky. Even if they deem it critical to the national interest, presidents, including Obama, would have to think twice before applying pressure on Israel to accept a peace settlement based on international law.

CHAPTER 1

1. Address by President Woodrow Wilson before a joint session of Congress on 8 January 1918.
2. *King-Crane Commission Report,* 28 August 1919. The text above, accessed from http://www.mideast-web.org/kingcrane.htm, is available at numerous other sites.
3. Eugene L. Rogan, "The Emergence of the Modern Middle East into the Modern State System," in *International Relations of the Middle East,* ed. Louise Fawcett (Oxford: Oxford University Press, 2005), 27.
4. Ussama Makdisi, *Faith Misplaced: The Broken Promise of U.S.-Arab Relations: 1820-2001* (New York: Public Affairs, 2010), 164.
5. Philip K. Hitti, "America in the Eyes of an Easterner," in *America in an Arab Mirror: Images of Arab Travel Literature: An Anthology,* ed. and trans. Kamal Abdel-Malek (New York: Palgrave Macmillan, 2000), 49.
6. George Wadsworth, U.S. Minister to Syria-Lebanon, to President Truman on behalf of himself and Ministers to Egypt, Saudi Arabia, and Jerusalem, Conference of Chiefs of Mission with the President, 10 November 1945, *FRUS* [*Foreign Relations of the United States*], The Near East and Africa, 1945, vol. 8, 13-15.
7. Makdisi, *Faith Misplaced,* 12; "The Case Against a Jewish State in Palestine: Albert Hourani's Statement to the Anglo-American Committee of Enquiry of 1946," *Journal of Palestine Studies* 35 (2005): 90.
8. Makdisi, *Faith Misplaced,* 4-5.
9. Quoted from Truman's memoirs by George Lenczowski, *American Presidents and the Middle East* (Durham, N.C.: Duke University Press, 1990), 27.
10. Ibid., 174.
11. "The American Conscience and the Palestine Question" [in Arabic], *Al-Risala* (October 1946). See also John Calvert, *Sayyid Qutb and the Origins of Radical Islamism* (New York: Columbia University Press, 2010).

12. Ibid.

13. Telegram from James Keeley, Minister in Syria, to US Secretary of State in Washington, 19 July 1950, *FRUS,* The Near East, South Asia and Africa, 1950, vol. 5, 1213.

14. However, at this juncture, not all Arabs viewed America through Qutb's prism. The June 1967 Arab-Israeli War and Israel's 1982 invasion of Lebanon were turning points.

15. James Moore, US Ambassador to Syria, to Washington, 7.5. 1955, *FRUS,* vol. 13, 525.

16. George Antonius, *The Arab Awakening: The Story of the Arab National Movement* (New York: Capricorn, 1965), 442.

17. Telegram from James Keeley, Minister in Syria, to US Secretary of State in Washington, 24 February 1950, *FRUS,* The Near East, South Asia and Africa, 1950, vol. 5, 1205.

18. Hafez al-Assad, interview with Patrick Seale, Damascus, May 1985. Cited in Seale, *Asad of Syria: The Struggle for the Middle East* (Berkeley: University of California Press, 35).

19. Irene L. Gendzier, *Notes From the Minefield: United States Intervention in Lebanon and the Middle East, 1945-1958* (Boulder, Colo.: Westview Press, 1999), 21-22. See also David W. Lesch, *The Middle East and the United States: A Historical and Political Reassessment* (Boulder, Colo.: Westview Press, 1999), 1.

20. Louise d'Estrange Fawcett, *Iran and the Cold War: The Azerbaijan Crisis of 1946* (Cambridge: Cambridge University Press, 1992).

21. Melvyn Leffler, *A Preponderance of Power: National Security, the Truman Administration, and the Cold War* (Stanford, Calif.: Stanford University Press, 1992).

22. John Lewis Gaddis, "Reconsiderations: Was the Truman Doctrine a Real Turning Point?" *Foreign Affairs* 52, no. 1 (1974): 386-402.

23. Rashid Khalidi, *Sowing Crisis: The Cold War and American Dominance in the Middle East* (Boston: Beacon Press, 2009). Odd Arne Westad, *The Global Cold War: Third World Interventions and the Making of Our Times* (London: Cambridge University Press, 2007).

24. Khalidi, *Sowing Crisis.*

25. Quoted in Douglas Little, "Cold War and Covert Action: The United States and Syria, 1945-1958," *Middle East Journal* 44, no. 1 (Winter 1990): 55-56, cited in David Lesch, *Syria and the United States: Eisenhower's Cold War in the Middle East* (Boulder, Colo.: Westview Press 1992).

26. A 1952 memo by the Acting Regional Adviser Near East Office Harold B. Hoskins to the Assistant Secretary of State Henry Byroade: Memo, 7 April 1952, FRUS, 1952-54, vol 9, part I (Washington, D.C., 1986), 204-13.

27. Dwight D. Eisenhower, *The White House Years,* vol. 1, *Mandate for Change, 1953-1956* (New York: Doubleday, 1963), 162.

28. Dean Acheson, *Present at the Creation* (New York: W. W. Norton, 1969), 682; Lenczowski, *American Presidents and the Middle East,* 14-15.

29. Acheson, *Present at the Creation,* 679.

30. Steve March, "Continuity and Change: Reinterpreting the Policies of the Truman and Eisenhower Administrations toward Iran, 1950-1954," *Journal of Cold War Studies* 7, no. 3 (Summer 2005): 79-123.

31. Kermit Roosevelt, *Countercoup: The Struggle for the Control of Iran* (New York: McGraw-Hill, 1979), 8. See also George Lenczowski, *Russia and the West in Iran* (Ithaca, N.Y.: Cornell University Press, 1949), 10-11.

32. Roosevelt, *Countercoup,* 11-12.

33. Ibid., 8.

34. Lenczowski, *American Presidents and the Middle East,* 38.

35. Ibid., 39. For an analysis of the CIA's official history of the coup, see Mark J. Gasiorowski, "The CIA Looks Back at the 1953 Coup in Iran," *Middle East Report (MERIP)* 216 (Autumn, 2000): 4-5.

36. Eisenhower, *White House Years,* 1, 164.

37. Ibid., 165; Lenczowski, *American Presidents and the Middle East,* 40.

38. Eisenhower, *White House Years,* 1, 162; Lenczowski, *American Presidents and the Middle East,* 36-37.

39. "The Iranian Accord" (editorial), *New York Times,* 6 August 1954.

40. Stephen Kinzer, *All the Shah's Men: An American Coup and the Roots of Middle East Terror* (New York: Wiley, 2003).

41. Lesch, *Syria and the United States,* 104-20.

42. Ambassador in Egypt (Caffery) to the Department of State, Cairo, 18 September 1952; and the Secretary of State to the Secretary of Defense (Lovett), Washington, 21 November 1952, in *FRUS, 1952-1954*, vol. 9, part 2, 1860-61, 1889.

43. Anthony Nutting, *No End of a Lesson: The Story of Suez* (London: Constable, 1967), 47.

44. A Conference with the President, White House, Washington, 27 July 1956; and the Department of State to the Secretary of State, at Lima, Washington, 28 July 1956 in *FRUS, Suez Crisis, 1956*, vol. 16, 12, 25.

45. Keith Kyle, "Britain and the Crisis, 1955-1956," in *Suez 1956: The Crisis and Its Consequences,* ed. William Roger Louis and Roger Owen (Oxford: Clarendon Press, 1989), 109.

46. Strobe Talbot, ed., *Khrushchev Remembers* (London: Book Club Associates, 1971), 431-32.

47. Mohamed Heikal, *Sphinx and Commissar: The Rise and Fall of Soviet Influence in the Arab World* (London: Collins, 1978), 53.

48. Cited by Walter Z. Laqueur, ed., *Communism and Nationalism in the Middle East* (London: Routledge and Kegan Paul, 1956), 262.

49. Ibid.; Kennett Love, *Suez: The Twice Fought War* (New York: McGraw-Hill, 1969), 235.

50. The Embassy in Egypt to the Department of State, 19 April 1956, in *FRUS, 1956*, vol 15, 557-58.

51. Diary Entries by the President, Washington, 13, 28 March 1956; and Memorandum of Discussion at the 279th Meeting of the NSC, Washington, 8 March 1956, in *FRUS, 1956*, vol. 15, 329, 342, 425.

52. Memorandum of a conversation, White House, Subject: United States Policy in the Near East, Washington, 28 March 1956; and the Department of State to the Embassy in Egypt, 3 April 1956, in *FRUS, 1956*, vol. 15, 423, 453.

53. Department of State, Subject: U.S.-Egyptian Relations, Washington, 17 May 1956; Rountree to the Secretary of State, 23 May 1956; and the Embassy in Egypt to the Department of State, Cairo, 23 May 1956, in *FRUS, 1956*, vol. 15, 645-50, 664, 670.

54. Rountree to the Secretary of State, Subject: Aswan High Dam, Washington, 6 June 1956, in *FRUS, 1956*, vol. 15, 717; interview with Eugene Black, president of IBRD, in Muhammed Abd el-Wahab Sayed-Ahmed, *Nasser and American Foreign Policy, 1952-1956* (London: Laam, 1989), 120; William Burns, *Economic Aid and American Foreign Policy toward Egypt, 1955-1981* (New York: State University of New York Press, 1985), 76.

55. Mohamed Heikal, *Nasser: The Cairo Documents* (London: New English Library, 1972), 70; *The Collected Speeches, Declarations and Statements of President Nasser, 1952-58* [in Arabic], vol. 1 (Cairo, n.d), 638; Anwar El-Sadat, *My Son: This Is Your Uncle Gamal* [in Arabic] (Cairo, n.d.), 164-65, 169.

56. The Middle East resolution, which later became known as the Eisenhower Doctrine, was adopted by the Senate and the House of Representatives on 5 and 7 March 1957. Eisenhower signed the resolution into law on 9 March. Editorial Note, in *FRUS, Arab-Israeli Dispute, 1957*, vol. 17, 83-87.

57. Conversation between the President and the Secretary of State, Secretary Dulles's Room, Walter Reed Hospital, Washington, 12 November 1956; and the President to the Secretary of State, Augusta, Georgia, 12 December 1956, in *FRUS, Arab-Israeli Dispute, 1957*, vol. 17, 1114, 1297. See also J. C. Campbell, *Defense of the Middle East: Problems of American Policy* (New York: Harper, 1958), 128-29; and Burns, *Economic Aid and American Policy toward Egypt*, 108.

58. The Secretary of State to the Department of State, Karachi, 8 March 1956; the Acting Secretary of State to the Secretary of State, Washington, 12 March 1956; Diary Entry by the President, Washington, 13 March 1956; the Director of the Office of Near Eastern Affairs (Wilkins), Subject: United States Policy in the Near East, Washington, 14 March 1956; and Memorandum of a Conference with the President, White House, Washington, 28 March 1956, in *FRUS, Arab-Israeli Dispute, 1957*, vol. 17, 325-326, 341, 343, 355, 362, 422-423.

59. Malcom H. Kerr, *The Arab Cold War: Gamal 'Abd al-Nasir and His Rivals, 1958-1970*, 3rd ed. (London: Oxford University Press, 1971).

60. Dwight Eisenhower, *The White House Years*, vol. 2, *Waging Peace, 1956-1961* (New York: Doubleday, 1965), 114-16; Conference with the President, 20 November 1956, in *FRUS, Suez Crisis, 1956*, vol. 16, 1153.

61. Eisenhower, *The White House Years*, 114-16; The President to the Secretary of State, 12 December 1956, in *FRUS, Suez Crisis, 1956*, vol. 16, 1297; Sherman Adams, *First-Hand Report: The Inside Story*

of the Eisenhower Administration (London: Hutchinson, 1962), 223; Robert W. Stookey, *America and the Arab States: An Uneasy Encounter* (London: Wiley, 1975), 161.

62. Talking Outline: Saudi-UAR Relations, 4 October 1962, box 158, in the John F. Kennedy National Security Files, the Middle East: National Security Files, 1961-1963, microfilmed from the holding of the J. F. Kennedy Library (Frederick, Md.: University Publications of America, 1989), reel 3 out of 3. [Henceforth, this series will be referred to as JFK Files, 1961-1963]. Cairo to Department of State, Subject: US-UAR Relations: I. Areas of Maneuver, 11 April 1964, in the Lyndon B. Johnson National Security Files, the Middle East: National Security Files, 1963-1969, microfilmed from the holdings of the L. B. Johnson Library, Austin, Texas (Frederick, Md.: University Publications of America, 1989), reel 7 out of 8. [Henceforth, this series will be referred to as LBJ Files, 1963-1969].

63. Burns, *Economic Aid and American Policy toward Egypt*, 146.

64. Moshe Maoz, *Syria and Israel: From War to Peacemaking?* (Oxford: Oxford University Press, 1995), 86.

65. *The Collected Speeches, Declarations and Statements of President Nasser, 1962-64* [in Arabic], vol. 4 (Cairo, n.d), 527-30; *The Struggle of the Ba'th: The National Leadership, 1963-1966, from the Ramadan and March Revolution until 23 February 1966* (Beirut, 1971), vol. 10 [in Arabic], 214, 236; Ahmed Shukairi, *On the Road to Defeat: With Kings and Presidents* (Beirut, 1972), vol. 1 [in Arabic], 204-5, 208-9.

66. Department of State to Embassy Cairo, no. 4292, 17 March 1964, in LBJ Files, 1963-1969, reel 7 out of 8; Cairo to Secretary of State, no. 2660, 11 May 1964; Cairo to Secretary of State, no. 2585, 3 May 1964; and Cairo to Secretary of State, no. 2586, 4 May 1964, in LBJ Files, 1963-1969, reel 7 out of 8; Cairo to Secretary of State, no. 2660, 11 May 1964.

67. Lyndon Baines Johnson, *The Vantage Point: Perspectives of the Presidency, 1963-1969* (New York: Holt, Rinehart and Winston, 1971), 290; Mahmoud Riad, *The Struggle for Peace in the Middle East* (London: Quartet Books, 1981), 15; Mahmoud Riad, *Memoirs: America and the Arabs* (Beirut: Dar al-Mustaqbal al-Arabic, 1986), vol. 3 [in Arabic], 34-35; Heikal, *1967: The Years of Upheaval, the Thirty Years War* (Cairo, 1988), vol. 1 [in Arabic], 727-28, 736. Heikal, *Nasser: The Cairo Documents*, 203; Ahmed Ahmed Youssef, *The Egyptian Role in Yemen, 1962-1967* (Cairo, 1981) [in Arabic], 314; Nutting, *Nasser*, 344; Burns, *Economic Aid and American Policy toward Egypt*, 152.

68. Cairo to Department of State, Subject: US-UAR Relations, 11 April 1964, in LBJ Files, 1963-1969, reel 7 out of 8.

69. London to Secretary of State, no. 4713, 25 March 1964, in LBJ Files, 1963-1969, reel 7 out of 8.

70. London to Secretary of State, no. 4713, 25 March 1964; and Cairo to Secretary of State, no. 3410, 29 March 1965, in LBJ Files, 1963-1969, reel 7 out of 8. Cairo to Secretary of State, no. 2660, 11 May 1964; John S. Badeau, *The American Approach to the Arab World* (New York: Published for the Council on Foreign Relations by Harper & Row, 1968), 147.

71. George Lenczowski, *American Presidents and the Middle East*, 113.

72. Makdisi, *Faith Misplaced*, 299.

73. William B. Quandt, *Decade of Decisions: American Policy toward the Arab-Israeli Conflict, 1967-1976* (Berkeley: University of California Press, 1977), 71.

74. Abba Eban, *An Autobiography* (New York: Random House, 1977), 272, 362, 400. See also, in Eban, a statement by Israeli cabinet minister Moshe Shapira to Abba Eban after the cessation of hostilities.

75. Johnson, *Vantage Point*, 299-300; Lenczowski, *American Presidents and the Middle East*, 113.

76. Cairo to Secretary of State, no. 3292, 7 June 1967, in LBJ Files, 1963-1969, reel 1 out of 8; CIA, Memorandum for Walt W. Rostow, 6 June 1967; Harriman to the President, no. 6577, 8 June 1967, and Department of State to Embassy London, no. 208887, 7 June 1967; and NSC, Memorandum of Walt Rostow, Subject: Reactions to your paper of 7 June 1967, 8 June 1967; and Richard Helms, CIA, to Walt Rostow, Subject: Israeli Objectives in the Current Crisis—Soviet Policy Miscalculation, 6 June 1967, in LBJ Files, 1963-1969, reel 1 out of 8; Lenczowski, *American Presidents and the Middle East*, 112-13.

77. Lenczowski, *American Presidents and the Middle East*, 115.

78. Ibid., 282.

79. Quandt, *Decade of Decisions*, 123-26.

80. Henry Kissinger, *White House Years* (Boston: Little, Brown, and Co, 1979).

81. Ibid., 124-27.
82. Ibid., 200-201.
83. Lenczowski, *American Presidents and the Middle East,* 112-15.
84. Quandt, *Decade of Decisions,* 200-202; Lenczowski, *American Presidents and the Middle East,* 138-39.
85. George Lenczowski, *Middle East Oil in a Revolutionary Age* (Washington, D.C.: American Enterprise Institute, 1976), 13.
86. Lenczowski, *American Presidents and the Middle East,* 139.
87. Malcolm H. Kerr, *America's Middle East Policy: Kissinger, Carter and the Future* (Beirut, Lebanon: Institute for Palestine Studies, 1980), IPS Papers, no. 14.
88. Ze'ev Schiff and Ehud Ya'ari, *Israel's Lebanon War* (New York: Touchstone, 1985); Rashid Khalidi, *Under Siege: P.L.O. Decision Making During the 1982 War* (New York: Columbia University Press, 1987).
89. David Hirst, *Beware of Small States: Lebanon, Battleground of the Middle East* (London: Faber and Faber, 2010), 136.
90. Ibid., 137.
91. Ibid., 116, 160. See also the Kahan Commission's report, which found Sharon "indirectly responsible" for Sabra/Shatilla and forced him to resign (Yitzhak Kahan, Aharon Barak, and Yona Erfat, "Report of the Commission of Inquiry into the Events at the Refugee Camps in Beirut," 8 February 1984, in Israel's Foreign Relations Selected Documents, vol. 8, Israeli Foreign Ministry, http://www.mfa.gov. il/MFA/Foreign%20Relations/Israels%20Foreign%20Relations%20since%201947/1982-%20of%20 Inquiry%20into%20the%20e.
92. Hirst, *Beware of Small States,* 183.
93. Quoted by Augustus Richard Norton, *Hezbollah: A Short History* (Princeton, N.J.: Princeton University Press, 2007), 33.
94. Usama bin Laden, "Full transcript of Usama bin Laden's Speech in Videotape Sent to Al Jazeera," Aljazeera.net (online publication), 30 October 2004. Accessed through "Transcript: Translation of Bin Laden's Videotaped Message," *Washington Post* website, published on 1 November 2004, accessed on February 13, 2011, http://www.washingtonpost.com/wp-dyn/articles/A16990-2004Nov1.html. In *Messages to the World: The Statements of Osama Bin Laden,* edited and introduced by Bruce Lawrence (London: Verso, 2005), Bruce Lawrence says, "Bin Laden dates his own political awakening from 1973, when an American airlift ensured Israeli victory over Egypt and Syria in the Yom Kippur War," xii.
95. Robert S. Litwak, *Détente and the Nixon Doctrine: American Foreign Policy and the Pursuit of Stability, 1969-1976* (Cambridge: Cambridge University Press, 1984).
96. Zbigniew Brzezinski, *Power and Principle: Memoirs of the National Security Adviser, 1977-1981* (New York: Farrar, Straus and Giroux, 1983), 354, 398.
97. Robin Wright, *Sacred Rage: The Wrath of Militant Islam* (New York: Simon & Schuster, 1985), 270; Gary Sick, *All Fall Down: America's Tragic Encounter with Iran* (New York: Random House, 1985), 187.
98. Cited in Brzezinski, *Power and Principle,* 151-53. Uri Lubrani, the former Israeli ambassador to Iran, recalls that after the revolution, he called for carrying out a coup against the clergy by working with the Iranian army; he said he believed the coup could work by killing a few thousand people. Cited in Noam Chomsky, *The Fateful Triangle: The United States, Israel, and the Palestinians,* updated edition (Cambridge, Mass.: South End Press, 1999), 458.
99. Jimmy Carter, *Keeping Faith: Memoirs of a President* (New York: Bantam Books, 1982), 451, 453; Hamilton Jordan, *Crisis: The Last Year of the Carter Presidency* (New York: G. P. Putnam, 1982), 39.
100. Sick, *All Fall Down,* 164, 219-20.
101. Ibid., 164-66; Harold Saunders, "The Crisis Begins," in *American Hostages in Iran: The Conduct of a Crisis,* ed. Warren Christopher (New Haven, Conn.: Yale University Press, 1985), 47, 52.
102. Ibid., 164.
103. Ibid., 164-66.
104. Ibid., 167-68.
105. In the words of the late Ayatollah Ruhollah Khomeini in his speech on 5 November 1979. The term "Great Satan" (Shaytan-e Bozorg) was originally used by the Iranian leader Khomeini to describe the United States, which he accused of imperialism and sponsoring corruption throughout the world. Israel has also been depicted as "the Little Snake."

106. Sick, *All Fall Down*, 233; Saunders, "Diplomacy and Pressure, November 1979–May 1980," in Christopher, *American Hostages in Iran*, 91.
107. Brzezinski, *Power and Principle*, 484, 533.
108. Cited in ibid., 482-84 See also Sick, *All Fall Down*, 206.
109. Cited in Sick, *All Fall Down*, 210.
110. Shireen T. Hunter, *Iran and the World* (Bloomington: Indiana University Press, 1990), 59-60.
111. Gary Sick, "Military Options and Constraints," in Christopher, *American Hostages in Iran*, 151.
112. Weekly Compilation of Presidential Documents, US Government Printing Office, vol. 16, no. 4, 28 January 1980, 194-96.
113. Ahmed Rashid, "The Rise of Bin Laden," *New York Review of Books*, 27 May 2004; Steve Coll, *Ghost Wars: The Secret History of the CIA, Afghanistan, and Bin Laden, from the Soviet Invasion to September 10, 2001* (New York: Penguin Press, 2004).
114. Brzezinski, *Power and Principle*, 470-78, 485, 489.
115. Too much was at stake—not just for the "free world," as US officials were fond of saying, but also for their bureaucratic careers and lifelong investment in anticommunism—to either decline to play the game or suspend it temporarily.
116. Ahmed al-Khatib, "Second Revisions of Tanzim al-Jihad: Sayyid Fadl, Mufti al-Jihad, Responds to Zawahiri's "Exoneration": Al-Qa'ida's Second-in-Command Is a 'Hypocrite,'" no. 3, 21, 11, 2001. See *al-Masri al-Yawm* [Egyptian newspaper], no. 10, 29 November 2008.
117. Fawaz A. Gerges, *The Far Enemy: Why Jihad Went Global* (Cambridge: Cambridge University Press, 2009), chap. 3 and 4.
118. Peter L. Bergen, *Holy War, Inc.: Inside the Secret World of Osama bin Laden* (New York: Free Press, 2001), 81-82.
119. *Messages to the World: The Statements of Osama Bin Laden*, edited and introduced by Bruce Lawrence (London: Verso, 2005), 25.
120. "Declaration of War Against the Americans Occupying the Land of the Two Holy Places," *Al-Quds al-Arabi* [in Arabic], 23 August 1996. For an English translation, see "The Response after the September 11 Terrorist Attacks," *NewsHour with Jim Lehrer*, Public Broadcasting Service, http://www.pbs.org/newshour/terrorism/international/fatwa_1996.html.
121. Barack Obama, "Renewing American Leadership," *Foreign Affairs* (July/August 2007).
122. Ibid.

CHAPTER 2

1. "The National Security Strategy," September 2002, The White House of George W. Bush, http://georgewbush-whitehouse.archives.gov/nsc/nss/2002/; and "President Bush's Second Inaugural Address," 20 January 2005, NPR, http://www.npr.org/templates/story/story.php?storyId=4460172.
2. Condoleezza Rice, "A Balance of Power that Favors Freedom," Wriston Lecture, 1 October 2002, Manhattan Institute for Policy Research, http://www.manhattan-institute.org/html/wl2002.htm.
3. Letter to President Clinton, Project for a New American Century, 26 January 1998, http://www.newamericancentury.org/iraqclintonletter.htm.
4. Richard A. Clarke, "Memorandum for Condoleeza Rice," 25 January 2001, National Security Council, The White House, http://www.gwu.edu/~nsarchiv/NSAEBB/NSAEBB147/clarke%20memo.pdf.
5. Michael Hirsh, "Bush and the World," *Foreign Affairs* 81, no. 5 (September-October 2002): 18-43; Condoleezza Rice, "Rethinking the National Interest: American Realism for a New World," *Foreign Affairs* 87, no. 2 (July-August 2008); James Mann, *Rise of the Vulcans: The History of Bush's War Cabinet* (New York: Viking, 2004); Ron Suskind, *The One Percent Doctrine: Deep Inside America's Pursuit of Its Enemies Since 9/11* (New York: Simon & Schuster, 2006); Bob Woodward, *Plan of Attack* (New York: Simon & Schuster, 2004).
6. Woodward, *Plan of Attack*; Bob Woodward, *Bush at War* (New York: Simon & Schuster, 2002).
7. Jonathan Monten, "The Roots of the Bush Doctrine: Power, Nationalism, and Democracy Promotion in U.S. Strategy," *International Security* 29, no. 4 (Spring 2005): 112-56; Walter Russell Mead, *Power, Terror, Peace, and War: America's Grand Strategy in a World at Risk* (New York: Knopf, 2004); Joseph S. Nye Jr., "US Power and Strategy after Iraq," *Foreign Affairs* 82, no. 4 (July/August 2003):

60-73. For a strong overview of neoconservatism, consult Francis Fukuyama, *America at the Cross-roads: Democracy, Power, and the Neoconservative Legacy* (New Haven, Conn.: Yale University Press, 2006).

8. George W. Bush, *Decision Points* (New York: Broadway, 2010), 154.
9. Jessica P. Ashooh, "Beltway Battles: Ideology and Infighting in US Foreign Policy toward the Middle East 2001-2006" (DPhil, University of Oxford, 2011); Daniel Zoughbie, "The Ends of History: George W. Bush's Political Theology and the Israeli-Palestinian Conflict" (DPhil, University of Oxford, 2011),
10. Daniel Zoughbie, "Ends of History."
11. Robert G. Kaufman, *In Defense of the Bush Doctrine* (Lexington: University Press of Kentucky, 2007); Norman Podhoretz, *World War IV: The Long Struggle Against Islamofascism* (New York: Doubleday, 2007); John Bolton, *Surrender Is Not an Option: Defending America at the United Nations and Abroad* (New York: Threshold Editions, 2007); Natan Sharansky with Ron Dermer, *The Case for Democracy: The Power of Freedom to Overcome Tyranny and Terror* (New York: Public Affairs, 2006); Fukuyama, *America at the Crossroads*; Robert Jervis, "Understanding the Bush Doctrine," *Political Science Quarterly* 118, no. 3 (Fall 2003): 365-88; Robert Jervis, "Why the Bush Doctrine Cannot Be Sustained," *Political Science Quarterly* 120, no. 3 (Fall 2005): 351-77; Robert Jervis, "The Compulsive Empire," *Foreign Policy* 137 (July-August 2003): 82-87.
12. Daniel Zoughbie, "Ends of History."
13. Ibid., 397.
14. Ibid.
15. "National Security Strategy of the United States of America, September 2002," The White House, http://www.whitehouse.gov/nsc/nss.pdf.
16. "National Security Strategy of the United States of America, September 2002," The White House, http://www.whitehouse.gov/nsc/nss.pdf; Daniel Zoughbie, "Ends of History."
17. Daniel Zoughbie, "Ends of History."
18. Avi Shlaim, *Israel and Palestine: Reappraisals, Revisions, Refutations* (London: Verso, 2009).
19. Zoughbie, "Ends of History," 69.
20. Shlaim, *Israel and Palestine*.
21. George Packer, *The Assassins' Gate: America in Iraq* (New York: Farrar, Straus and Giroux, 2005); Charles Krauthammer, "The Axis of Petulance," *Washington Post*, 1 March 2002; William Kristol and Robert Kagan, "Bombing Iraq Isn't Enough," *New York Times*, 30 January 1998; Paul Wolfowitz, "Rebuilding the Anti-Saddam Coalition," *Wall Street Journal*, 18 November 1997; Project for the New American Century, Letter to President Bill Clinton, 26 January 1998.
22. George Packer, *The Assassins' Gate*.
23. Dick Cheney began his political career working for Donald Rumsfeld, a former member of Congress, and later served five terms in Congress himself. When Rumsfeld became chief of staff to President Gerald Ford, Cheney again joined the White House staff. He succeeded Rumsfeld as Ford's chief of staff when Rumsfeld became secretary of defense. Later, Cheney became the new defense secretary under George H. W. Bush. Rumsfeld turned to a private business career but returned as secretary of defense when Cheney became vice president in 2001.
24. Richard A. Clarke, *Against All Enemies: Inside America's War on Terror* (London: New Press, 2004), 247-91;Woodward, *Plan of Attack*.
25. Packer, *The Assassins' Gate*.
26. Daniel Zoughbie, "Ends of History."
27. Woodward, *Plan of Attack*, 25.
28. Woodward, *Bush at War*, 49-50.
29. Bush, *Decision Points*, 228.
30. Martin Chulo and Helen Pidd, "Curveball: How US Was Duped by Iraqi Fantasist Looking to Topple Saddam," *Guardian*, 15 February 2011.
31. Bush, *Decision Points*, 228.
32. Douglas J. Feith, *War and Decision: Inside the Pentagon at the Dawn of the War on Terrorism* (New York: HarperCollins, 2008), 181-228.
33. Ibid.

34. Bush, *Decision Points.*
35. Todd Purdum, "Bush Officials Say the Time Has Come for Action on Iraq," *New York Times,* 9 September 2002.
36. Joseph C. Wilson, "What I Didn't Find in Africa," *New York Times,* 6 July 2003, http://www.nytimes.com/2003/07/06/opinion/what-i-didn-t-find-in-africa.html.
37. Bush, *Decision Points,* 229.
38. Ibid., 230.
39. Woodward, *Plan of Attack.*
40. Ibid., 150-151.
41. Ibid., 271.
42. Bush, *Decision Points,* 248.
43. Woodward, *Plan of Attack,* 86-87.
44. Bush, *Decision Points,* 397.
45. Packer, *The Assassins' Gate.*
46. Bush, *Decision Points,* 232.
47. Packer, *The Assassins' Gate.*
48. Barton Gellman, *Angler: The Cheney Vice Presidency* (New York: Penguin, 2008).
49. Woodward, *Plan of Attack,* 428.
50. Zoughbie, "Ends of History."
51. "Chronology: The Evolution of the Bush Doctrine," *Frontline: The War behind Closed Doors,* PBS, http://www.pbs.org/wgbh/pages/frontline/shows/iraq/etc/cron.html. See "Liberal Education, Liberty, and Education Today," delivered in Phillips Auditorium at Hillsdale College, 11 November 2001, for a full transcript of Victor David Hanson's speech.
52. For a strong overview of the Iraq war, consult the following books by Thomas E. Ricks: *Fiasco: The American Military Adventure in Iraq* (New York: Penguin, 2006) and *The Gamble: General David Petraeus and the American Military Adventure in Iraq, 2006-2008* (New York: Penguin, 2009). For an assessment of the regime change in Iraq, consult Toby Dodge, *Iraq's Future: The Aftermath of Regime Change* (New York: Routledge, 2005); and Ali A. Allawi, *The Occupation of Iraq: Winning the War, Losing the Peace* (New Haven, Conn.: Yale University Press, 2008). For an excellent overview of the Gulf region and international politics since 9/11, consult F. Gregory Gause, *The International Relations of the Persian Gulf* (Cambridge: Cambridge University Press, 2009).
53. Zoughbie, "Ends of History," 106.
54. Woodward, *Plan of Attack,* 283.
55. Ricks, *Fiasco;* Bob Woodward, *State of Denial* (New York: Simon & Schuster, 2006).
56. Ricks, *Gamble;* Nir Rosen, *Aftermath: Following the Bloodshed of America's Wars in the Muslim World* (New York: Nation Books, 2010).
57. David Rose, "Neo Culpa," *Vanity Fair,* January 2007.
58. Dick Cheney, *In My Time: A Personal and Political Memoir* (New York: Threshold Editions, 2011); Thom Shanker and Elizabeth Bumiller, "Looking Back, Gates Says He's Grown Wary of 'Wars of Choice,'" *New York Times,* 18 June 2011, http://www.nytimes.com/2011/06/19/us/politics/19gates.html?pagewanted=all.
59. Bush, *Decision Points,* 267.
60. Ibid., 397.

CHAPTER 3

1. http://www.nytimes.com/2007/12/04/us/politics/04transcript-debate.html?pagewanted=7.
2. Part 3 of CNN Democratic Presidential Debate, CNN, 21 January 2008, http://www.cnn.com/2008/POLITICS/01/21/debate.transcript3/index.html.
3. Ibid.
4. The CNN Democratic Presidential Debate in Texas, CNN, 21 February 2008, http://www.cnn.com/2008/POLITICS/02/21/debate.transcript/index.html.
5. "President Barack Obama's Inaugural Address," Office of the Press Secretary, The White House, 21 January 2009, http://www.whitehouse.gov/blog/inaugural-address/.

6. Ryan Lizza, "The Consequentialist," *New Yorker*, 2 May 2011, http://www.newyorker.com/reporting/2011/05/02/110502fa_fact_lizza?currentPage=1.

7. Fareed Zakaria, "Post-Imperial Presidency," *Newsweek*, 14 December 2009, http://www.newsweek.com/id/225824; Fareed Zakaria, "Stop Searching for an Obama Doctrine," *Washington Post*, 6 July 2011; Justin Logan, "How Washington Changed Obama," *Politico*, 27 April 2011.

8. Niall Ferguson, "Wanted: A Grand Strategy for America," *Newsweek*, 14 February 2011, http://www.newsweek.com/2011/02/13/wanted-a-grand-strategy-for-america.html.

9. Robert Kagan, "Obama's Year One: Contra," *World Affairs*, January/February 2010.

10. Zbigniew Brezzinski, "From Hope to Audacity," *Foreign Affairs*, January/February 2010.

11. Fareed Zakaria, "Stop Searching for an Obama Doctrine."

12. Lizza, "Consequentialist."

13. Ibid.; David Remnick, "Behind the Curtain," *New Yorker*, 5 September 2011.

14. Cited in Lizza, "Consequentialist."

15. Helene Cooper, Mark Landler, and David E. Sanger, "In U.S. Signals to Egypt, Obama Straddled a Rift," *New York Times*, 12 February 2011, http://www.nytimes.com/2011/02/13/world/middleeast/13diplomacy.html; Sam Stein, "Obama's Restraint Doctrine: How the President's Egypt Policy Has Managed to Please No One at All," *Huffington Post*, 3 February 2011, http://www.huffingtonpost.com/2011/02/02/obamas-restraint-doctrine_n_817796.html; Marcus Baram, "Obama Administration Cut Funding To Promote Democracy in Egypt, Disappointing Human Rights Activists," *Huffington Post*, 29 January 2011, http://www.huffingtonpost.com/2011/01/28/obama-cut-egypt-funding_n_815731.html; Barbara Slavin, "Obama's Middle East Democracy Problem," *Foreign Policy*, 5 March 2010, http://www.foreignpolicy.com/articles/2010/03/05/obamas_middle_east_democracy_problem.

16. David Frum, "David Frum's Diary," 3 November 2007, http://frum.nationalreview.com/post/?q=ODczZGIwMmFkZmU2MjhkNmNlNzQ4YjNkOGI5ZWU3Y2Q=.

17. "Remarks by the President on a New Beginning," Office of the Press Secretary, White House, 4 June 2009, http://www.whitehouse.gov/the_press_office/Remarks-by-the-President-at-Cairo-University-6-04-09/.

18. Bob Woodward, *Obama's Wars* (New York: Simon & Schuster, 2010); Cooper, Landler, and Sanger, "In U.S. Signals to Egypt."

19. Lizza, "Consequentialist."

20. Sam Stein, "Obama Defends Cabinet: The Change Will Come From Me," *HuffingtonPost*, 26 November 2008.

21. Woodward, *Obama's Wars;* Cooper, Landler, and Sanger, "In U.S. Signals to Egypt."

22. Ibid.

23. Ibid.; Robert Dreyfuss, "Obama's Evolving Foreign Policy," *Nation*, 21 July 2008, http://www.thenation.com/doc/20080721/dreyfuss.

24. Text of Barack Obama's Nobel Prize Lecture, 10 December 2009, http://www.nobelprize.org/nobel_prizes/peace/laureates/2009/obama-lecture_en.html.

25. "National Security Strategy," The White House, May 2010, http://www.whitehouse.gov/sites/default/files/rss_viewer/national_security_strategy.pdf.

26. Barack Obama, "Renewing American Leadership," *Foreign Affairs* 86, no. 4 (July/August 2007): 2-16.

27. Lizza, "Consequentialist."

28. "National Security Strategy," The White House, May 2010, http://www.whitehouse.gov/sites/default/files/rss_viewer/national_security_strategy.pdf.

29. Ibid.

30. The notable exception is the Carter administration, which first advocated a foreign policy that prioritized human rights, but soon found in its engagement in the Middle East that a human rights foreign policy could not be easily sustained.

31. "National Security Strategy," The White House, May 2010, http://www.whitehouse.gov/sites/default/files/rss_viewer/national_security_strategy.pdf.

32. Ibid.

33. Fawaz Gerges, *The Far Enemy: Why Jihad Went Global* (Cambridge: Cambridge University Press, 2005).

34. "Extracts: Bush Speech on Terror," BBC News, 19 March 2004, http://news.bbc.co.uk/1/hi/world/americas/3551455.stm.

35. Steven W. Hook, and John Spanier, *American Foreign Policy Since World War II* (Washington, D.C.: CQ Press, 2007), 325.

36. "Transcript: President Bush's Speech on the War on Terrorism," *Washington Post*, 30 October 2005, http://www.washingtonpost.com/wp-dyn/content/article/2005/11/30/AR2005113000667.html.

37. Fawaz Gerges, *The Rise and Fall of Al Qaeda* (New York: Oxford University Press, 2011).

38. John L. Esposito and Dalia Mogahed, "Who Speaks for Islam: What a Billion Muslims Really Think?" (Gallup Press, 2008); see also Pew Surveys from 2001 to 2008, "Global Public Opinion in the Bush Years (2001-2008)," Pew Global Attitudes Project, Pew Research Center, 18 December 2008, http://www.pewglobal.org/2008/12/18/global-public-opinion-in-the-bush-years-2001-2008.

39. "Remarks by President Obama to the Turkish Parliament," Office of the Press Secretary, White House, 6 April 2009, http://www.whitehouse.gov/the_press_office/Remarks-By-President-Obama-To-The-Turkish-Parliament.

40. Ibid.

41. "Remarks by the President on a New Beginning," Office of the Press Secretary, White House, 4 June 2009, http://www.whitehouse.gov/the_press_office/Remarks-by-the-President-at-Cairo-University-6-04-09/

42. Ibid.

43. Ibid.

44. Ibid.

45. John J. Mearsheimer and Stephen M. Walt, *The Israel Lobby and U.S. Foreign Policy* (New York: Farrar, Straus and Giroux, 2007).

46. Charles Krauthammer, "The Settlements Myth," *Washington Post*, 5 June 2009, http://www.washingtonpost.com/wp-dyn/content/article/2009/06/04/AR2009060403811.html.

47. "Remarks by the President on a New Beginning."

48. See Barack Obama, *Dreams From My Father: A Story of Race and Inheritance*, rev. ed. (New York: Three Rivers Press, 2004).

49. Ibid.

50. Ibid.

51. Ibid.

52. "National Security Strategy," The White House, May 2010, http://www.whitehouse.gov/sites/default/files/rss_viewer/national_security_strategy.pdf.

53. Barbara Slavin, "Obama's Middle East Democracy Problem," *Foreign Policy*, 5 March 2010, http://www.foreignpolicy.com/articles/2010/03/05/obamas_middle_east_democracy_problem.

54. "National Security Strategy," The White House, May 2010.

55. Niall Ferguson, "Wanted: A Grand Strategy for America," *Newsweek*, 14 February 2011, http://www.newsweek.com/2011/02/13/wanted-a-grand-strategy-for-america.html.

56. Foud Ajami, "A Cold-Blooded Foreign Policy," http://online.wsj.com/article/SB10001424052748704152804574628134281062714.html?mod=rss_Today%27s_Most_Popular#articleTabs%3.

57. Lizza, "Consequentialist."

58. Ibid.

59. Ibid.

60. Mark Landler and Helen Cooper, "Obama Seeks a Course of Pragmatism in the Middle East," *New York Times*, 10 March 2011, http://www.nytimes.com/2011/03/11/world/africa/11policy.html?ref=helenecooper; "Why Washington Is at a Loss over Syria," 2 April 2011, BBC News, http://www.bbc.co.uk/news/world-us-canada-12943622.

61. Helene Cooper and Mark Landler, "Interests of Saudi Arabia and Iran Collide, with the U.S. in the Middle," *New York Times*, 18 March 2011, http://query.nytimes.com/gst/fullpage.html?res=9F0CE4D81531F93BA25750C0A9679D8B63&ref=helenecooper; Mai Yamani, "Guarding the Fortress," *World Today* 67, no. 4; David E. Sanger and Eric Schmitt, "U.S.-Saudi Tensions Intensify with Mideast Turmoil," *New York Times*, 14 March 2011, http://www.nytimes.com/2011/03/15/world/middleeast/15saudi.html?scp=5&sq=saudi%20arabia%20us&st=cse. Vali Nasr, "Will the Saudis Kill the Arab Spring," *Bloomberg*, 23 May 2011.

62. Karen DeYoung, "Top White House Aide Delivers Obama Letter to Saudi King," *Washington Post*, 12 April 2011, http://www.washingtonpost.com/world/top-white-house-aide-delivers-obama-letter-to-saudi-king/2011/04/08/AF5KD9SD_print.html.

63. Elisabeth Bumiller, "Gates Tells Bahrain's King that 'Baby Steps' to Reform Aren't Enough," *New York Times*, 12 March 2011, http://www.nytimes.com/2011/03/13/world/middleeast/13military.html?scp=23&sq=bahrain&st=cse; Ethan Bronner, "Two Protesters Dead as Bahrain Declares State of Emergency," *New York Times*, 15 March 2011, http://www.nytimes.com/2011/03/16/world/middleeast/16bahrain.html; Ethan Bronner and Michelle Slackman, "Saudi Troops Enter Bahrain to Help Put Down Unrest," *New York Times*, 14 March 2011, http://www.nytimes.com/2011/03/15/world/middleeast/15bahrain.html?scp=16&sq=bahrain&st=cse.

64. Bronner and Slackman, "Saudi Troops"; Sanger and Schmitt, "U.S.-Saudi Tensions Intensify"; Alexander Cooley and Daniel H. Nexon, "Bahrain's Base Politics," Snapshots, *Foreign Affairs*, 5 April 2011, http://www.foreignaffairs.com/articles/67700/alexander-cooley-and-daniel-h-nexon/bahrains-base-politics; Michael Slackman, "The Proxy Battle in Bahrain," *New York Times*, 19 March 2011, http://www.nytimes.com/2011/03/20/weekinreview/20proxy.html?scp=13&sq=bahrain&st=cse; Clifford Kraus, "Bahrain's Rulers Tighten Their Grip on Battered Opposition," *New York Times*, 6 April 2011, http://www.nytimes.com/2011/04/07/world/middleeast/07bahrain.html?scp=4&sq=bahrain&st=cse; Elisabeth Bumiller, "Defense Chief Is on Mission to Mend Saudi Relations," *New York Times*, 6 April 2011, http://www.nytimes.com/2011/04/07/world/middleeast/07military.html?scp=1&sq=gates%20saudi%20arabia&st=cse.

65. Sanger and Schmitt, "U.S.-Saudi Tensions Intensify."

66. Craig Timberg, "Gates Has 'Warm' Meeting with Saudi Arabia's King Abdullah," *Washington Post*, 6 April 2011, http://www.washingtonpost.com/world/defense-secretary-gates-arrives-in-saudi-arabia-for-meeting-with-king-abdullah/2011/04/06/AFV6iXnC_story.html.

67. DeYoung, "Top White House Aide," *Washington Post*, 12 April 2011.

68. Ibid.

69. David E. Sanger, "The Larger Game in the Middle East: Iran," *New York Times*, 2 April 2011, http://www.nytimes.com/2011/04/03/weekinreview/03sanger.html?scp=4&sq=iran%20&st=cse; "Clinton Warns Iran over Meddling in Persian Gulf," *Al Aribiya*, 19 March 2011, http://www.alarabiya.net/articles/2011/03/19/142232.html; "Gates Sees Iran Meddling in Bahrain," 7 April 2011, *United Press International*, http://www.upi.com/Top_News/Special/2011/04/07/Gates-sees-Iran-meddling-in-Bahrain/UPI-91361302187995/.

70. Will Inboden, "Waiting for an 'Obama Doctrine,'" *Foreign Policy*, 4 March 2011, http://shadow.foreignpolicy.com/posts/2011/03/04/waiting_for_an_obama_doctrine; Jonathan Masters, "Democracy Promotion and the Obama Doctrine," Council on Foreign Relations, 8 April 2011, http://www.cfr.org/us-strategy-and-politics/democracy-promotion-obama-doctrine/p24621; Lisa Anderson, "Demystifying the Arab Spring," *Foreign Affairs*, May/June 2011; Daniel Drezner, "Does Obama Have a Grand Strategy?," *Foreign Affairs*, July/August 2011.

71. Stephen Biddle, Daniel L. Byman, Wesley K. Clark, Alexis Crow, Nile Gardiner, Malou Innocent, Josef Joffe, and Danielle Pletka, "Room for Debate: Is There an Obama Doctrine?" *New York Times*, 29 March 2011, http://www.nytimes.com/roomfordebate/2011/03/29/is-there-really-an-obama-doctrine?scp=1&sq=room%20for%20debate%20obama%20doctrine&st=cse; Robert Dreyfuss, "Obama's 'Doctrine' and Libya and Iran," *Nation*, 30 March 2011; Daniel W. Drezner, "Let's Define Our Foreign Policy Terms, Shall We?" *Foreign Policy*, 29 March 2011, http://drezner.foreignpolicy.com/category/wordpress_tag/obama.

72. "Lieberman Suggests No-Fly Zone an Option in Syria If Violence Escalates," Fox News, 27 March 2011, http://www.foxnews.com/politics/2011/03/27/lieberman-suggests-fly-zone-option-syria-violence-escalates/; Jim Young, "Clinton Rules Out U.S. Syria Involvement," Reuters, 5 April 2011, http://www.reuters.com/article/2011/03/27/us-syria-usa-idUSTRE72Q1X920110327.

73. Jay Solomon, "Clinton Pushes Arab Reforms," *Wall Street Journal*, 13 April 2011, http://online.wsj.com/article/SB10001424052748704336504576259312835815994.html.

74. Jason Pack, "The Two Faces of Libya's Rebels," *Foreign Policy*, 5 April 2011, http://www.foreignpolicy.com/articles/2011/04/05/the_two_faces_of_libyas_rebels; Joseph Felter and Brian Fishman, "The Enemies of Our Enemy," *Foreign Policy*, 30 March 2011, http://www.foreignpolicy.com/articles/2011/03/30/the_enemies_of_our_enemy.

75. Missy Ryan and Susan Cornwell, "Intelligence on Libya Rebels Shows 'Flickers' of Qaeda," Reuters, 29 March 2011, http://www.reuters.com/article/2011/03/29/us-libya-usa-intelligence-idUST RE72S43P20110329.

76. Niall Ferguson, "The Big Dither," *Daily Beast,* 20 March 2011, http://www.thedailybeast.com/blogs -and-stories/2011-03-20/niall-ferguson-obamas-indecision-about-libya/; John Mueller, "The Iraq Syndrome Revisited," Postscripts, *Foreign Affairs,* 28 March 2011, http://www.foreignaffairs.com /articles/67681/john-mueller/the-iraq-syndrome-revisited; "Does the World Belong in Libya's War?" *Foreign Policy,* 18 March 2011, http://www.foreignpolicy.com/articles/2011/03/18/does_the_world _belong_in_libyas_war?page=0,7; Andrew J. Bacevich, Richard Fontaine, Rachel Kleinfeld, Paul R. Pillar, Kori Schake, and Micah Zenko, "Room for Debate: What Is the U.S. Plan for Libya?" *New York Times,* 23 March 2011, http://www.nytimes.com/roomfordebate/2011/03/22/what-is-the-us-plan -for-libya/; Dirk Vandevalle, "How Not to Intervene in Libya," *Foreign Policy,* 10 March 2011, http: //www.foreignpolicy.com/articles/2011/03/10/how_not_to_intervene_in_libya; "Libya: Barack Obama Announces Gaddafi Sanctions," BBC News, 26 February 2011, http://www.bbc.co.uk/news/world -africa-12585949; David D. Kirkpatrick and Kareem Fahim, "Qaddafi Warns of Assault on Benghazi as U.N. Vote Nears," *New York Times,* 17 March 2011, http://www.nytimes.com/2011/03/18 /world/africa/18libya.html?scp=3&sq=susan%20rice%20libya%20un&st=cse; United Nations Security Council, "Resolution 1973," United Nations, 17 March 2011, http://daccess-ods.un.org /TMP/6276748.html.

77. Josh Rogin, "How Obama Turned on a Dime toward War," *Foreign Policy,* 18 March 2011, http: //thecable.foreignpolicy.com/posts/2011/03/18/how_obama_turned_on_a_dime_toward_war; Helene Cooper and Steven Lee Myers, "Obama Takes Hard Line with Libya after Shift by Clinton," *New York Times,* 18 March 2011, http://www.nytimes.com/2011/03/19/world/africa/19policy.html?scp =1&sq=clinton%20obama%20libya&st=cse; Sheryl Gay Stolberg, "Still Crusading, but Now on the Inside," *New York Times,* 29 March 2011, http://www.nytimes.com/2011/03/30/world/30power .html?scp=2&sq=samantha%20power&st=cse; Mark Landler and Dan Bilefsky, "Specter of Rebel Rout Helps Shift U.S. Policy on Libya," *New York Times,* 16 March 2011, http://www.ny times.com/2011/03/17/world/africa/17diplomacy.html?scp=10&sq=susan%20rice%20libya%20 un&st=cse.

78. Office of the Press Secretary, "Remarks by the President on Libya," The White House, 19 March 2011, http://www.whitehouse.gov/the-press-office/2011/03/19/remarks-president-libya; Josh Rogin, "Obama: Libya Attack Will Have Limited Goals," *Foreign Policy,* 18 March 2011, http://thecable .foreignpolicy.com/posts/2011/03/18/obama_libya_attack_will_have_limited_goals; David D. Kirkpatrick, Steven Erlanger, and Elisabeth Bumiller, "Allies Open Air Assault on Qaddafi's Forces in Libya," *New York Times,* 19 March 2011, http://www.nytimes.com/2011/03/20/world/africa/20libya .html?pagewanted=1&sq=obama%20libya%20brazil&st=cse&scp=9; Thom Shanker and Helene Cooper, "Doctrine for Libya: Not Carved in Stone," *New York Times,* 29 March 2011, http://www .nytimes.com/2011/03/30/world/africa/30doctrine.html?scp=1&sq=obama%20doctrine&st=cse.

79. Office of the Press Secretary, "Remarks by the President in Address to the Nation on Libya," The White House, 28 March 2011, http://www.whitehouse.gov/the-press-office/2011/03/28/remarks -president-address-nation-libya.

80. Ibid.

81. Ibid.

82. Stephen M. Walt, "Why Obama's Libya Speech Didn't Matter," *Foreign Policy,* 29 March 2011, http: //walt.foreignpolicy.com/posts/2011/03/29/why_obamas_libya_speech_didnt_matter; Michael W. Doyle, "The Folly of Protection," in Gideon Rose (ed.), *The New Arab Revolt: What Happened, What It Means, and What Comes Next* (New York: Council on Foreign Relations/Foreign Affairs, 2011); Snapshots, *Foreign Affairs,* March 20, 2011, http://www.foreignaffairs.com/articles/67666/michael-w -doyle/the-folly-of-protection; Richard K. Betts, "The Delusion of Impartial Intervention," *Foreign Affairs* 73, no. 6, November/December 1994): 20-33.

CHAPTER 4

1. "The Report on Israeli Settlement," Foundation for Middle East Peace, http://www.fmep.org/reports/; "Reports," Peace Now, http://peacenow.org.il/eng/content/reports.

2. Patrick Seale, "Obama's Collapse to Israeli Pressure," Agence Global, 24 May 2011; Seale, "America's Terrible Decade," MEC Analytical Group, 6 September 2011.

3. Steven Lee Myers and Mark Landler, "U.S. Is Appealing to Palestinians to Stall U.N. Vote," *New York Times*, 3 September 2011; Henry Siegman, "September Madness," Foreign Policy Middle East Channel, 15 September 2011, http://mideast.foreignpolicy.com/posts/2011/09/15/september_madness.

4. Henry Siegman, "Imposing Mideast Peace," *Nation*, 7 January 2010, http://www.thenation.com/doc/20100125/siegman.

5. Henry Siegman, "Can Obama Beat the Israel Lobby?" *Nation*, 25 May 2011.

6. Ibid. David Paul Kuhn, author of *The Neglected Voter: White Men and the Democratic Dilemma*, cites empirical evidence showing that American Jews don't vote on Israel: A majority of Jews, like Americans overall, said the economy was their top issue, according to two polls by Gerstein in 2010. Israel ranked near the bottom. Only about a tenth of Jews named Israel as their top issue. That does not mean Jews adore Obama's Middle East policy, Kuhn concludes. Gerstein found that seven in ten Jews agree with Obama's Israel policies but half of them disagreed with his "execution." See Khun, "Obama Doesn't Have a 'Jewish Problem'—He Has a People Problem," *Atlantic*, 17 September 2011, http://www.theatlantic.com/politics/archive/2011/09/obama-doesnt-have-a-jewish-problem-he-has-a-people-problem/245250/.

7. Dana Goldstein, "Why Fewer Young American Jews Share Their Parents' View of Israel," *Time*, 29 September 2011.

8. Ibid.

9. "Israel PM Calls for Demilitarized Palestinian State," CNN, 14 June 2009, http://edition.cnn.com/2009/WORLD/meast/06/14/israel.netanyahu/; "Abbas: No Peace Talks without Full Settlement Freeze," *Haaretz*, 31 August 2009, http://www.haaretz.com/hasen/spages/1111369.html.

10. Barak Ravid, "Netanyahu: Israel and U.S. Have Resolved Settlements Row," *Haaretz*, 19 October 2009, http://www.haaretz.com/hasen/spages/1121965.html.

11. Francis Matthews, "Netanyahu Dodges Real Issues," *Gulf News*, 18 March 2010, http://m.gulfnews.com/opinions/columnists/netanyahu-dodges-real-issues-1.599190.

12. Gideon Levy, "U.S. Tough Love Is the Kind Israel Needs," *Haaretz*, 18 March 2010, http://www.haaretz.com/print-edition/opinion/u-s-tough-love-is-the-kind-israel-needs-1.264946.

13. "Biden Condemns Israel's Approval of Plan to Build New Settlements in East Jerusalem," *Huffington Post*, 3 March 2009, http://www.huffingtonpost.com/2010/03/09/biden-urges-israel-to-tak_n_491309.html.

14. "Netanyahu Publicly Apologizes to Biden, but Refuses to Scrap Settlement Plan," *Huffington Post*, 11 March 2010, http://www.huffingtonpost.com/2010/03/11/netanyahu-publicly-apolog_n_495201.html.

15. Ibid.

16. Barak Ravid, "'Gates Called Netanyahu an Ungrateful Ally to U.S. and a Danger to Israel,'" *Haaretz*, 6 August 2011.

17. Matthew Lee, "Clinton Slams Israel's Settlement Plans: 'Deeply Negative Signal,'" *Huffington Post*, 12 March 2010, http://www.huffingtonpost.com/2010/03/12/clinton-delivers-strong-m_n_497052.html.

18. "Ties Between Israel and US 'Worst in 35 Years,'" BBC News, 15 March 2010, http://news.bbc.co.uk/2/hi/middle_east/8567706.stm.

19. "Obama Aide Condemns 'Destructive' Israeli Homes Plan," BBC News, 14 March 2010, http://news.bbc.co.uk/2/hi/middle_east/8566992.stm.

20. Mark Weiss, "Deal Paves Way for Resumption of Middle East Talks," *Irish Times*, 20 March 2010, http://www.irishtimes.com/newspaper/world/2010/0320/1224266708325.html.

21. "Hillary Clinton Warns Israel Faces 'Difficult' Choices," BBC News, 22 March 2010, http://news.bbc.co.uk/2/hi/middle_east/8579766.stm.

22. Ibid.

23. Ibid.

24. Giles Whittell and James Hilder, "Binyamin Netanyahu Humiliated After Barack Obama 'Dumped Him for Dinner,'" *The Times* (London), 26 March 2010, http://www.timesonline.co.uk/tol/news/world/us_and_americas/article7076431.ece.

25. Ibid.

26. Ibid.

27. Helene Cooper and Isabel Kershner, "U.S. Fails to Persuade Israel on Housing Plan," *New York Times*, 25 March 2010, http://www.nytimes.com/2010/03/26/world/middleeast/26diplo.html.

28. "Netanyahu Holds Talks with Obama Amid Settlement Row," BBC News, 24 March 2010, http://news.bbc.co.uk/2/hi/middle_east/8583589.stm.

29. Ibid.

30. Christophe Schmidt, "US Standing Firm in Row with Israel," Agence France Presse, 25 March 2010, http://www.google.com/hostednews/afp/article/ALeqM5jzz864Nxn2DSRDW2ioDNWvKZz3iA.

31. Amy Teibel, "2 Israeli Soldiers, 1 Palestinian Killed in Gaza," Associated Press, 26 March 2010, http://news.yahoo.com/s/ap/20100326/ap_on_re_mi_ea/ml_israel_palestinians.

32. Robert Dreyfuss, "Statesman Obama Beats Boorish Netanyahu," *Nation*, 25 May 2011.

33. "Clinton Urges New Mid-East Talks," BBC News, 1 November 2009, http://news.bbc.co.uk/1/hi/8335211.stm.

34. "Abbas Makes His Move," *New York Times*, 5 November 2009, http://roomfordebate.blogs.nytimes.com/2009/11/05/abbas-makes-his-move/.

35. Fawaz Gerges, "America-Israel: Dangerous Disarray," *Open Democracy*, 27 November 2009, http://www.opendemocracy.net/fawaz-gerges/america-and-israel-palestine-dangerous-disarray.

36. "Palestinians in Statehood Warning," BBC News, 4 November 2009, http://news.bbc.co.uk/1/hi/world/middle_east/8341929.stm.

37. "Palestinians Say Clinton Is Hurting Peace Talks," MSNBC, 1 November 2009, http://www.msnbc.msn.com/id/33560578/ns/world_news-mideastn_africa/.

38. "Clinton: Israel's Settlement Offer Falls Short of U.S. Wishes," *Haaretz*, 11 February 2009, http://www.haaretz.com/news/clinton-israel-s-settlement-offer-falls-short-of-u-s-wishes-1.4937.

39. Laura Rozen, "Clinton Walks Back Israel Settlements Remarks," *Politico*, 2 November 2009, http://www.politico.com/blogs/laurarozen/1109/Clinton_walks_back_Israel_settlements_remarks.html.

40. Helene Cooper and Mark Landler, "Leaders Call for Peace as Mideast Talks Begin," *New York Times*, 1 September 2010, http://www.nytimes.com/2010/09/02/world/middleeast/02diplo.html?scp=4&sq=israel&st=nyt.

41. The Annapolis Conference—a Middle East peace conference held at the US Naval Academy in Annapolis, Maryland, on 27 November 2007—was organized by the Bush administration and spearheaded by then-secretary of state Condoleezza Rice as the power broker. Attendees included Palestinian president Mahmoud Abbas, Israeli prime minister Ehud Olmert, and President George W. Bush. The aim of the conference was to produce a substantive document resolving the Israeli-Palestinian conflict in line with Bush's "Roadmap for Peace." Importantly, the conference represented the first time in which the idea of a "two-state solution" was a mutually agreed upon concept for addressing the conflict and concluded with a joint statement signed by all parties. Hamas called on Palestinian leaders to boycott the Annapolis Conference. Stephen M. Walt, "Direct Talks Déjà Vu," *Foreign Policy*, 30 October 2010, http://walt.foreignpolicy.com/posts/2010/08/29/direct_talks_deja_vu; Josh Ruebner, "Top Ten Reasons for Skepticism on Israeli-Palestinian Talks," Mondoweiss, 26 August 2010, http://mondoweiss.net/2010/08/top-ten-reasons-for-skepticism-on-israeli-palestinian-talks.html; James Traub, "Mixed Irish Blessing," *Foreign Policy*, 27 August 2010, http://www.foreignpolicy.com/articles/2010/08/27/mixed_irish_blessing.

42. Cooper and Landler, "Leaders Call for Peace as Mideast Talks Begin."

43. Hosni Mubarak, "A Peace Plan within Our Grasp," *New York Times*, 31 August 2010, http://www.nytimes.com/2010/09/01/opinion/01mubarak.html?scp=7&sq=israel&st=nyt.

44. Ibid. See former prime minister Ehud Olmert's reflections on how close the positions of the two camps on peace talks were: Ethan Bronner, "Olmert Memoir Cites Near Deal for Mideast Peace," *New York Times*, 27 January 2011, http://www.nytimes.com/2011/01/28/world/middleeast/28mideast.html.

45. Cooper and Landler, "Leaders Call for Peace as Mideast Talks Begin."

46. Ibid.

47. Landler and Cooper, "Settlements in West Bank Are Clouding Peace Talks," *New York Times*, 2 September 2010, http://www.nytimes.com/2010/09/03/world/middleeast/03diplo.html?scp=12&sq=israel&st=nyt.

48. Ibid.

49. Ethan Bronner, "Mideast Leaders Hopeful After Opening of Talks," *New York Times,* 5 September 2010, http://www.nytimes.com/2010/09/06/world/middleeast/06mideast.html?scp=5&sq=peace+talks +egypt&st=nyt.

50. Mark Landler, "Israelis and Palestinians Add a Meeting as Peace Talks Dig into Divisive Issues," *New York Times,* 15 September 2010, http://query.nytimes.com/gst/fullpage.html?res=9502E4D6103B F936A2575AC0A9669D8B63&scp=8&sq=peace+talks+egypt&st=nyt.

51. Ethan Bronner and Mark Landler, "Diplomats Try to Save Mideast Talks," *New York Times,* 27 September 2010, http://www.nytimes.com/2010/09/28/world/middleeast/28mideast.html?scp=10&sq =peace+talks+egypt&st=nyt.

52. Ibid.

53. Elliot Abrams and Michael Singh, "Obama's Peace Process to Nowhere," *Foreign Policy,* 20 November 2010, http://www.foreignpolicy.com/articles/2010/11/19/obamas_peace_process_to_nowhere.

54. James Traub, "The White House Waits," *New York Times,* 7 February 2011, http://www.nytimes .com/2011/02/13/magazine/13IsraelSidebar-t.html.

55. Dan Murphy, "The Latest Quartet Proposal to Pressure Abbas? Going Nowhere," *Christian Science Monitor,* 26 September 2011; Ravid, Issacharoff, and Mosgovaya, "After His Stint at UN, Abbas Is Politically Stronger Than Ever," *Haaretz,* 26 September 2011, http://www.haaretz.com/print-edition /news/after-his-stint-at-un-abbas-is-politically-stronger-than-ever-1.386682.

56. Murphy, "The Latest Quartet Proposal to Pressure Abbas? Going Nowhere."

57. Ethan Bronner and Isabel Kershner, "Abbas Says He Will Seek Palestinian State at the Security Council," *New York Times,* 16 September 2011; Myers and Landler, "U.S. Is Appealing to Palestinians to Stall U.N. Vote"; Mohammed Daraghmeh and Tarek El-Tablawy, "Palestinians Will Submit UN Membership Letter," Associated Press, 19 September 2011.

58. Myers and Landler, "U.S. Is Appealing to Palestinians to Stall U.N. Vote."

59. Bronner and Kershner, "Abbas Says He Will Seek Palestinian State at the Security Council."

60. "Mideast Quartet Envoys to Meet in New York on Sunday," Reuters, 17 September 2011; Daraghmeh and El-Tablawy, "Palestinians Will Submit UN Membership Letter."

61. Neil MacFarquhar and Steven Myers, "Palestinians Request U.N. Status; Powers Press for Talks," *New York Times,* 23 September 2011.

62. "UN Security Council to Consider Palestinian Statehood Bid," Voice of America, 28 September 2011.

63. Ibid.

64. Office of the Press Secretary, "Remarks by the President on a New Beginning," 4 June 2009, The White House, http://www.whitehouse.gov/the-press-office/remarks-president-cairo-university-6-04-09.

65. Helene Cooper, "Obama, at U.N., Explains Rationale for Opposing Palestinian Statehood Bid," *New York Times,* 21 September 2011.

66. Cooper, "Obama, at U.N., Explains Rationale for Opposing Palestinian Statehood Bid."

67. Helene Cooper and Neil Macfarquhar, "Obama Praises Libya's Post-Revolution Leaders at the United Nations," *New York Times,* 21 September 2011.

68. For a transcript of Obama's UN speech, see: http://www.politico.com/news/stories/0911/64026.html #ixzz1Z8seQCTY.

69. Akiva Eldar, "Obama's Passivity Could Lead to the Loss of a Palestinian Partner," *Haaretz,* 22 September 2011.

70. Cooper, "Obama, at U.N., Explains Rationale for Opposing Palestinian Statehood Bid"; Scott Wilson and William Branigin, "Obama Tells U.N. He Sees 'No Shortcut' to Israeli-Palestinian Peace," *Washington Post,* 21 September 2011; Eric Alterman, "The Obama Presidency Invites Contempt," *Nation,* 3 October 2011.

71. Amy Teibel, "Israel PM: Palestinian Statehood Bid Will Fail," Associated Press, 18 September 2011.

72. Elka Looks, "AJC Slams Pro-Israel Group over Anti-Obama Ad in NY Times," *Haaretz,* 20 September 2011; Khun, "Obama Doesn't Have a 'Jewish Problem.'"

73. Abd al-Bari Atwan, "Abbas: A Powerful Speech . . . We Await Its Translation to Action," *A-Quds Al-Arabi,* 23 September 2011 [in Arabic], http://alquds.co.uk/index.asp?fname=today%5C23z999 .htm&arc=data%5C2011%5C09%5C09-23%5C23z999.htm.

74. Bronner and Kershner, "Abbas Says He Will Seek Palestinian State at the Security Council."

75. "Hamas Considers Abbas' Speech without Substance," *Al-Quds Al-Arabi,* 23 September 2011.

76. David Rose, "The Gaza Bombshell," *Vanity Fair*, April 2008, http://www.vanityfair.com/politics/features/2008/04/gaza20080.

77. Ibid.; "Poll: Abbas Approval Rating Plummets," *Majlis*, 18 October 2009, http://www.themajlis.org/2009/10/18/poll-abbas-approval-rating-plummets.

78. Speech by PM Netanyahu at the United Nations General Assembly (September 23, 2011), Jewish Virtual Library (a division of the American–Israeli Cooperative Enterprise).

79. Netanyahu is responsible for the inability to reach a peace deal that would end the conflict between Israel and the Palestinians, former president Bill Clinton disclosed. Speaking on the sidelines of the Clinton Global Initiative conference in New York, Clinton, a well-known strong supporter of Israel, was quoted by *Foreign Policy* magazine as claiming that Netanyahu lost interest in the peace process as soon as two basic Israeli demands seemed to come into reach: a viable Palestinian leadership and the possibility of normalizing ties with the Arab world.

   "The real cynics believe that the Netanyahu's government's continued call for negotiations over borders and such means that he's just not going to give up the West Bank," Clinton added. See "Bill Clinton: Netanyahu Isn't Interested in Mideast Peace Deal," *Haaretz*, 23 September 2011.

80. The US has suspended West Bank development projects worth tens of millions of dollars after Congress froze funding to dissuade the Palestinians from seeking UN recognition of an independent state, according to Palestinian officials. The Obama administration also cut funding to UNESCO because member states voted to seat Palestine as a member of the organization. http://www.washingtonpost.com/world/middle-east/us-funding-cuts-prompted-by-palestinian-membership-in-unesco-threaten-pro-democracy-projects/2011/11/23/gIQA3UdqnN_story.html; http://www.haaretz.com/news/diplomacy-defense/palestinians-economy-affected-by-u-s-congress-aid-cut-pa-officials-say-1.387961; http://thecable.foreignpolicy.com/posts/2011/11/04/state_dept_we_are_trying_to_save_palestinian_authority_aid_funding.

81. "UNESCO Votes to Admit Palestine; U.S. Cuts Off Funding," *Washington Post*, 31 October 2011, http://www.washingtonpost.com/world/national-security/unesco-votes-to-admit-palestine-over-us-objections/2011/10/31/gIQAMleYZM_story.html; Wilson, "At U.N., Obama's Rejection of Palestinian Bid Offers Strongest Embrace of Israel"; Bronner and Kershner, "Abbas Says He Will Seek Palestinian State at the Security Council"; "Perry Blames Obama 'Appeasement' for Palestinian Statehood Bid," Fox News, 20 September 2011, http://www.foxnews.com/politics/2011/09/20/perry-criticizes-obama-over-police-on-israel/#ixzz1YVmqaaE0.

82. John J. Mearsheimer and Stephen M. Walt, *The Israel Lobby and U.S. Foreign Policy* (New York: Farrar, Straus and Giroux, 2007).

83. James Baker, *The Politics of Diplomacy: Revolution, War, and Peace, 1989–1992* (New York, Putnam and Sons, 1995), 551.

84. Avi Shlaim, *The Iron Wall: Israel and the Arab World* (W. W. Norton and Company, 2011), 532.

85. Henry Siegman quoted in Bradley Burston, "Why Do Israelis Dislike Barack Obama?" *Haaretz*, 2 November 2009, http://www.haaretz.com/news/why-do-israelis-dislike-barack-obama-1.4930; Editorial, "Diplomacy 101," *New York Times*, 27 November 2009, http://www.nytimes.com/2009/11/28/opinion/28sat1.html

86. Ibid.

87. "Obama Popularity in Israel Surges after U.N. Speech: Poll," Reuters, 28 September 2011.

88. Matti Friedman and Matthew Lee, "Obama and Israeli PM Meet Amid Dispute," *Washington Post*, 24 March 2010, http://www.washingtonpost.com/wp-dyn/content/article/2010/03/23/AR2010032301731.html?referrer=emailarticle.

89. Mearsheimer and Walt, *Israel Lobby and U.S. Foreign Policy*; Stephen M. Walt, "Did 'The Israel Lobby' Change Anything?" *Foreign Policy*, 25 March 2011, http://www.foreignpolicy.com/articles/2011/03/25/did_the_israel_lobby_change_anything?sms_ss=twitter&at_xt=4d9a077708a52b3d,0.

90. Jenniffer Steinhauer and Steven Lee Myers, "House G.O.P Finds a Growing Bond with Netanyahu," *New York Times*, 21 September 2011.

91. Ibid.

92. Ibid.

93. Ibid.

94. Ibid.

95. Aaron David Miller, "Obama and 'the Jewish Lobby of One,'" *Los Angeles Times,* 29 April 2011.
96. Steve Clemons, "Obama Tells Palestinians to Stay in Back of the Bus," *Atlantic,* 22 September 2011, http://www.theatlantic.com/international/archive/2011/09/obama-tells-palestinians-to-stay-in-back -of-the-bus/245487/.
97. Text of Obama's AIPAC Speech, National Journal, 22 May 2011; Cooper, "Obama, at U.N., Explains Rationale for Opposing Palestinian Statehood Bid."
98. Ibid.
99. US General David Petraeus quoted after addressing Congress in Hilary Leila Krieger, "Arab-Israeli Conflict Hurts US," *Jerusalem Post,* 18 March 2010, http://www.jpost.com/International/Article .aspx?id=171255.
100. Bronner and Kershner, "Abbas Says He Will Seek Palestinian State at the Security Council."
101. "US against Israeli Settlement Halt as Condition for Talks," Reuters, 27 September 2011.
102. Ravid, "Gates Called Netanyahu an Ungrateful Ally to U.S. and a Danger to Israel."
103. "Bill Clinton: Netanyahu Isn't Interested."
104. Ibid.
105. Friedman and Lee, "Obama and Israeli PM Meet Amid Dispute."
106. "Bill Clinton: Netanyahu Isn't Interested."
107. Ian Black, "Time to Resurrect the Arab Peace Plan," *Guardian,* 18 October 2008, http://www .guardian.co.uk/world/2008/oct/18/middle-east; Text of Arab Peace Initiative, http://www.al-bab .com/Arab/docs/league/peace02.htm.
108. Uzi Mahnaimi and Sarah Baxter, "Barack Obama Links Israel Peace Plan to 1967 Borders Deal," *Times* (London), 16 November 2008, http://www.timesonline.co.uk/tol/news/world/middle_east /article5162537.ece.
109. Paul McGeough, *Kill Khalid: The Failed Mossad Assasination of Khalid Mishal and the Rise of Hamas* (New York: New Press, 2009). See also Henry Siegman, "Hamas: the Last Chance for Peace?," *New York Review of Books,* 27 April 2006, http://www.nybooks.com/articles/archives/2006/apr/27/hamas -the-last-chance-for-peace/; and David Hinckley, "Jimmy Carter: Hamas Is Willing to Accept Israel as Its Neighbor," *New York Daily News,* 21 April 2008, http://articles.nydailynews.com/2008-04-21 /news/17895235_1_hamas-spokesman-hamas-officials-hamas-leaders.
110. Babak Dehghanpisheh, "A Place for Mr. Meshaal," *Newsweek,* 18 October 2010, http://www .newsweek.com/2010/10/18/is-hamas-ready-for-peace-with-israel.html.
111. Reuters, "Hamas Says Prepared to Give Peace with Israel 'Another Chance,'" *Haaretz,* 4 May 2011, http://www.haaretz.com/news/diplomacy-defense/hamas-says-prepared-to-give-peace-with-israel -another-chance-1.359836.
112. "Hamas Ready to Accept 1967 Borders," *Al Jazeera,* 22 April 2008, http://english.aljazeera.net/news /middleeast/2008/04/2008615098393788.html.
113. Jeroen Gunning, *Hamas in Politics: Democracy, Religion, Violence* (London: Hurst, 2007).
114. According to leading scholars on Hamas, the transformation of its position began before the 2009 Gaza attack. See Jeroen Gunning, "Hamas: Talk to Them," *OpenDemocracy,* 18 April 2008, http: //www.opendemocracy.net/article/conflicts/middle_east/hamas_talk_to_them; Ghassan Khatib, "Hamas's Shortsighted Manoeuvre," *OpenDemocracy,* 18 June 2007, http://www.opendemocracy.net /conflicts/israel_palestine/hamas_shortsighted_manoeuvre; Khaled Hroub, "Hamas's Path to Rein- vention," *OpenDemocracy,* 9 October 2006, http://www.opendemocracy.net/conflict-middle_east _politics/hamas_3982.jsp.
115. Condoleeza Rice, *No Higher Honor: A Memoir of My Years in Washington* (New York: Crown Publishers, 2011).
116. Oxfam, Joint report from Amnesty International UK, CARE International UK, Christian Aid, CA- FOD, Medecins du Monde UK, Oxfam, Save the Children UK, and Trocaire, "The Gaza Strip: A Humanitarian Implosion," March 2008, http://www.oxfam.org.uk/resources/policy/conflict_disasters /gaza_implosion.html.
117. Fawaz Gerges, "The Transformation of Hamas," *Nation,* 25 January 2010, http://www.thenation.com /doc/20100125/gerges.
118. Alan Cowell, "Palestinians and Israelis Seek Support in Europe," *New York Times,* 5 May 2011.

119. Joby Warrick, "Obama Seeks to Reassure Israel on Mideast Policy in Speech at AIPAC Conference," *Washington Post*, 22 May 2011. Text of Obama's AIPAC Speech, *National Journal*, 22 May 2011.

120. Joshua Mitnick, Matt Bradley, and Jay Solomon, "Egypt Policy Toward Gaza, Hamas Vexes Israel," *Wall Street Journal*, 30 April 2011.

121. Joel Greenberg, "Hamas Adjusts to Arab Spring," *Washington Post*, 22 December 2011.

122. Karin Laub and Mohammed Daraghmeh, "Hamas in Gaza Says It's Learning from Arab Spring," Associated Press, 11 December 2011.

123. "Mashaal: Reconciliation Is our Choice and Destiny" [in Arabic], *Al Jazeera*, 27 December 2011.

124. Laub and Daraghmeh, "Hamas in Gaza Says It's Learning from Arab Spring"; Greenberg, "Hamas Adjusts to Arab Spring."

125. Cooper, "Obama, at U.N., Explains Rationale for Opposing Palestinian Statehood Bid."

126. "Text: Obama's Speech in Cairo," *New York Times*, 4 June 2009.

CHAPTER 5

1. Robert Dreyfuss, "Inside Iran's Fight for Supremacy," *The Diplomat*, 2 June 2011, http://the-diplomat .com/2011/06/02/inside-iran%E2%80%99s-fight-for-supremacy/; Reza Marashi and Jason Rezaian, "Iran: The Next Generation," *National Interest*, 29 June 2011, http://nationalinterest.org/commentary /irans-next-generation-5541.

2. Vali Nasr, "Will the Saudis Kill the Arab Spring?" Bloomberg, 23 May 2011, http://www.bloomberg .com/news/2011-05-23/will-the-saudis-kill-the-arab-spring-.html.

3. Patrick Markey, "Analysis: Iraq U.S. Troop Deal Drifts over Immunity," Reuters, 16 October 2011, http: //www.reuters.com/article/2011/10/16/us-iraq-usa-idUSTRE79F17720111016; "Iraq's Sadr Condemns U.S. 'Occupiers,'" UPI, 11 October 2011, http://www.upi.com/Top_News/Special/2011/10/11 /Iraqs-Sadr-condemns-US-occupiers/UPI-47021318343036/?spt=hs&or=tn.

4. Mohammed Tawfeeq and Arwa Damon, "Political Turmoil in Iraq as U.S. Pulls Out,"CNN, 18 December 2011.

5. "Evading Arrest, Iraq VP Denies Hit Squad Claim," Associated Press, 20 December 2011.

6. Aaron David Miller, "Arab Spring, American Winter," *Los Angeles Times*, 13 November 2011.

7. Basheer M. Nafi, "The Arabs and Modern Turkey: A Century of Changing Perceptions," *Insight Turkey* 11, no. 1 (2009): 63-82, http://www.setav.org/ups/dosya/53100.pdf.

8. Nader Hashemi and Danny Postel, eds., *The People Reloaded: The Green Movement and the Struggle for Iran's Future* (New York: Melville House, 2011).

9. See the perceptive article by Mohammed Ayoob, "Beyond the Democratic Wave: A Turko-Persian Future?" *Middle East Policy* 18, no. 2 (Summer 2011): 110-119.

10. Justin Webb, "An Interview with President Obama," BBC News, 1 June 2009, http://www.bbc.co.uk /blogs/thereporters/justinwebb/2009/06/an_interview_with_president_ob.html.

11. Spencer Ackerman, "U.S. Had Helo Deal with Ousted Tunisian Dictator," *Wired*, 14 January 2011, http://www.wired.com/dangerroom/2011/01/u-s-copter-sales-cant-save-wiki-ousted-tunisian-dictator; Esam Al-Amin, "Back to Tahrir Square," *Journal of Foreign Relations*, 24 November 2011, http: //www.jofr.org/2011/11/24/back-to-tahrir-square/#.TwSuU5iKrXk.

12. "Obama's Remarks on the Resignation of Mubarak," *New York Times*, 1 February 2011, http://www .nytimes.com/2011/02/12/world/middleeast/12diplo-text.html.

13. Nawaf Obaid, "Amid the Arab Spring, a U.S.-Saudi Split," *Washington Post*, 16 May 2011, http: //www.washingtonpost.com/opinions/amid-the-arab-spring-a-us-saudi-split/2011/05/13/AFMy8Q4 G_story.html.

14. "Remarks of Secretary of State Condoleezza Rice at the American University of Cairo," *The Arabist*, 20 June 2005, http://www.arabist.net/blog/2005/6/20/condoleezza-rices-remarks-from-her-cairo-speech -at-auc.html.

15. From the lead up to FBI Director Robert Mueller's visit to Cairo in February 2010. 10CAIRO179, SCENESETTER FOR FBI DIRECTOR MUELLER, http://wikileaks.org/cable/2010/02/10CAIRO 179.html.

16. 10CAIRO179, SCENESETTER FOR FBI DIRECTOR MUELLER, http://wikileaks.org/cable/2010/02/10CAIRO179.html.

17. Ryan Lizza, "The Consequentialist," *New Yorker*, 2 May 2011, http://www.newyorker.com/reporting/2011/05/02/110502fa_fact_lizza?currentPage=1.

18. James Zogby, *Arab Voices: What They Are Saying to Us, and Why It Matters* (New York: Palgrave Macmillan, 2010).

19. "Exclusive: Biden Discusses Unrest in Egypt, Keeping U.S. Competitive," The Rundown, *PBS NewsHour*, 27 January 2011, http://www.pbs.org/newshour/rundown/2011/01/exclusive-biden-discusses-unrest-in-egypt-keeping-us-competitive.html.

20. Helene Cooper, Mark Landler, and David E. Sanger, "In U.S. Signals to Egypt, Obama Straddled a Rift," *New York Times*, 12 February 2011.

21. Ibid.

22. Ibid.

23. Ibid.

24. Ibid.

25. "Transcript of Obama's Remarks on Egypt," The Washington Wire, *Washington Post*, 1 February 2011, http://blogs.wsj.com/washwire/2011/02/01/transcript-of-obamas-remarks-on-egypt-2/.

26. Karen DeYoung, "Top White House Aide Delivers Obama Letter to Saudi King," *Washington Post*, 12 April 2011.

27. Entous and Barnes, "U.S. Wavers on 'Regime Change.'"

28. Ibid.

29. Ibid.

30. Ibid.; Lobe, "U.S. Keeps Quiet over Bahrain Repression."

31. "Obama Delivers Remarks on Egypt," *Washington Post*, 11 February 2011, http://projects.washingtonpost.com/obama-speeches/speech/559/.

32. "Obama's Mideast Speech," 19 May 2011, *New York Times*, http://www.nytimes.com/2011/05/20/world/middleeast/20prexy-text.html?pagewanted=all.

33. Ibid.

34. Ibid.

35. Brian Love and Catherine Bremer, "G8 Leaders to Tie Arab Spring Aid to Reforms," Reuters, 27 May 2011.

36. "Endemic unemployment ranks among the most problematic issues, particularly during the current period of economic slowdown. Despite reforms initiated under Mubarak starting in 2004, the Egyptian economy had continued to suffer from serious structural deficits when the revolution forced the leader out seven years later. As a result of high unemployment, rising costs of fuel and energy subsidies, and out-of-control pension spending, the economy was an inefficient, distorted bureaucracy in need of further reform.

"With the revolutions, however, the economy deteriorated further. Closed businesses reportedly cost $310 million each day; tourism sector income, the second largest revenue source, declined; and the stock market lost nearly one-fifth of its value. Meanwhile, around 20 percent of the Egyptian population continued to live in poverty, reliant on a transitional government facing elections and unlikely to enact the painful changes necessary for long-term economic reform. What was needed from Obama was a pledge of targeted financial support to assist in the establishment of an efficient economy. Instead, the president offered a much-heralded $2 billion pledge from the United States focused on the private sector, bond guarantees, and debt swapping with no support to buoy the country's public finances." See Chris McGreal, "Egypt: Bread Shortages, Hunger, and Unrest," *The Guardian*, 27 May 2008, http://www.guardian.co.uk/environment/2008/may/27/food.egypt; "Egyptians Protest over Minimum Wage," *Al Jazeera*, 2 May 2010, http://english.aljazeera.net/news/middleeast/2010/05/201052161957263202.html; Samir Sulayman, *The Autumn of Dictatorship: Fiscal Crisis and Political Change in Egypt under Mubarak*, trans. Peter Daniel (Stanford, Calif.: Stanford University Press, 2011); Data: Egypt, http://data.worldbank.org/country/egypt-arab-republic; David Schenker, *Egypt's Enduring Challenges: Shaping the Post-Mubarak Environment*, Policy Focus no. 110 (Washington D.C.: Policy Focus, April 2011), http://www.washingtoninstitute.org/templateC04.php?CID=341; "How Can the U.S. and International Finance Institutions Best Engage Egypt's Civil

Society?" Global Views, Policy Papers 2011-06. (Washington D.C.: Global Views, June 2011), http://www.brookings.edu/papers/2011/06_egypt_civil_society.aspx; Steffen Hertog, "The Perils of Economic Populism in the Mideast," Bloomberg, July 2011, http://www.bloomberg.com/news/2011-07-07/perils-of-economic-populism-in-the-mideast-commentary-by-steffen-hertog.html.

37. For the latest Gallup poll, "Egypt from Tahrir to Transition," see Hannah Allam, "U.S. Fares Poorly in First Modern Polling of Egyptian Views," McClatchy Newspapers, 25 June 2011, http://www.mcclatchydc.com/2011/06/25/v-print/116485/us-fares-poorly-in-first-modern.html.

38. "President Obama and the Arab Spring," Editorial, New York Times, 17 May 2011, http://www.nytimes.com/2011/05/18/opinion/18wed1.html?scp=1&sq=president%20obama%20and%20the%20arab%20spring&st=cse.

39. "Egyptians Break into Israeli Embassy in Cairo," Associated Press, 10 September 2011.

40. "New Egyptian Minister Promises Shifts in Foreign Policy," BBC News, 23 April 2011.

41. Joshua Mitnick, Matt Bradley, and Jay Solomon, "Egypt Policy toward Gaza, Hamas Vexes Israel," Wall Street Journal, 30 April 2011.

42. David D. Kirpatrick, "Egypt's Military Expands Power, Raising Alarms," New York Times, 14 October 2011.

43. Ibid.

44. Jeffrey Fleishman and Amro Hassan, "Egypt Military Giving Signs of Not Wanting to Relinquish Power," Los Angeles Times, 3 November, 2011.

45. Ibid.

46. Al-Amin, "Back to Tahrir Square."

47. David D. Kirkpatrick, "Egypt Military and Protesters Dig in for a Long Standoff," New York Times, 25 November 2011.

48. David D. Kirkpatrick, "Long Lines Form as Egyptians Vote in Historic Election," New York Times, 28 November 2011.

49. David D. Kirkpatrick, "New Clashes Underscore Standoff in Egypt," New York Times, 26 November 2011.

50. Ibid.

51. Maram Mazen, "Egypt Clashes Enter Fifth Day after U.S., UN Condemn Violence," Bloomberg Businessweek, 20 December 2011.

52. Lizza, "The Consequentialist."

53. On the eve of the Iranian Revolution (31 December 1977), President Jimmy Carter traveled to Iran and, at an official state dinner in his honor, toasted the shah with the following words, which came back to haunt him: "Iran, because of the great leadership of the shah, is an island of stability in one of the more troubled areas of the world. This is a great tribute to you, your majesty, and to your leadership, and to the respect and the admiration and love which your people give to you." (Quoted in Glenn Kessler, "History Lesson: Why Letting Go Is So Hard to Do," 2 May 2011, The Fact Checker, Washington Post, http://voices.washingtonpost.com/fact-checker/2011/02/history_lesson_why_letting_go.html).

54. Richard Cottam, Iran and the United States: A Cold War Case Study (Pittsburgh, Pa.: University of Pittsburgh Press, 1988); Bill James, The Eagle and the Lion: The Tragedy of American-Iranian Relations (New Haven, Conn.: Yale University Press, 1989); Nikki R. Keddie and Mark J. Gasiorowski, eds., Neither East nor West: Iran, the Soviet Union, and the United States (New Haven, Conn.: Yale University Press, 1990); Gary Sick, All Fall Down: America's Tragic Encounter with Iran (London: I. B. Tauris, 1985).

55. Jimmy Carter, Keeping Faith: Memoirs of a President (New York: Bantam Books, 1982); Sick, All Fall Down; George Lenczowski, American Presidents and the Middle East (Durham, N.C.: Duke University Press, 1990); William O. Beeman, The "Great Satan" vs. the "Mad Mullahs": How the United States and Iran Demonize Each Other (Westport, Conn. Praeger, 2005).

56. Joost R. Hiltermann, A Poisonous Affair: America, Iraq, and the Gassing of Halabja (New York: Cambridge University Press, 2007).

57. Martin Indyk, "Challenges to US Interests in the Middle East: Obstacles and Opportunities," The Soref Symposium (Washington, D.C.: Washington Institute for Near East Policy, May 18-19, 1993), 4.

58. George Bush and Brent Scowcroft, A World Transformed (New York: Knopf, 1998).

59. Nicolas Blanford, "Shia Crescent Pierces Heart of Arab World," The Times (London), 17 July 2006, http://www.timesonline.co.uk/tol/news/world/middle_east/article688836.ece.

60. James Hackett, ed., *The Military Balance 2011: The Annual Assessment of Global Military Capabilities and Defence Economics,* The International Institute for Strategic Studies (London: Routledge, 2011), chap. 7.

61. Gareth Porter, "How Neo-Cons Sabotaged Iran's Help on al Qaeda," 21 February 2006, http://ipsnews.net/news.asp?idnews=32249; "Iran and Afghanistan," Institute for the Study of War, http://www.understandingwar.org/themenode/iran-and-afghanistan.

62. Glenn Kessler, "In 2003, U.S. Spurned Iran's Offer of Dialogue," *Washington Post,* 18 June 2006, http://www.washingtonpost.com/wp-dyn/content/article/2006/06/17/AR2006061700727.html; Gareth Porter, "Iran Proposal to U.S. Offered Peace With Israel," *IPS,* 24 May 2006, http://ipsnews.net/news.asp?idnews=33348.

63. Ray Takeyh, *Guardians of the Revolution: Iran and the World in the Age of the Ayatollahs* (Oxford: Oxford University Press, 2009); Stephen Kinzer, *Reset Middle East: Old Friends and New Alliances; Saudi Arabia, Israel, Turkey, Iran* (London: I. B. Tauris, 2010).

64. "Obama Promises New Track on Iran," BBC News, 11 January 2009, http://news.bbc.co.uk/1/hi/7822961.stm; Jackie Northam, "Obama Administration Shifts Its Tactics On Iran," National Public Radio, 13 February 2010, http://www.npr.org/templates/story/story.php?storyId=123663806.

65. "Obama Reaches Out to Muslim World," BBC News, 27 January 2009, http://news.bbc.co.uk/1/hi/world/middle_east/7852650.stm.

66. 09BRUSSELS536, IRAN SANCTIONS: AA/S GLASER BRIEFS EU ON PRIORITY, http://wikileaks.org /cable/2009/04/09BRUSSELS536.html.

67. Ibid.

68. "Obama's Videotaped Remarks in Celebration of Nowruz (Persian New Year), March 2009," Council on Foreign Relations, 20 March 2009, http://www.cfr.org/iran/obamas-videotaped-remarks-celebration-nowruz-persian-new-year-march-2009/p18890.

69. "Iranian Leader: Obama's Rhetoric Not Enough," CNN, 21 March 2009, http://articles.cnn.com/2009-03-21/world/iran.us.obama_1_iaea-official-islamic-republic-news-agency-ayatollah-ali-khamenei?_s=PM:WORLD.

70. Jeffrey Goldberg, "Netanyahu to Obama: Stop Iran—Or I Will," *Atlantic,* March 2009, http://www.theatlantic.com/magazine/archive/2009/03/netanyahu-to-obama-stop-iran-or-i-will/7390/.

71. 08RIYADH649, SAUDI KING ABDULLAH AND SENIOR PRINCES ON SAUDI, http://wikileaks.org/cable/2008/04/08RIYADH649.html.

72. 09ABUDHABI736, CROWN PRINCE SOUNDS ALARM ON IRAN, http://wikileaks.org/cable/2009/07/09ABUDHABI736.html.

73. 09ABUDHABI754, S) MbZ HOSTS GULF SECURITY DINNER WITH ISA ASD VERSHBOW AND, http://wikileaks.org /cable/2009/07/09ABUDHABI754.html.

74. 09MANAMA642, GENERAL PETRAEUS WITH KING HAMAD: IRAQ, http://wikileaks.org/cable/2009/11/09MANAMA642.html.

75. 09DOHA728, QATAR,S PRIME MINISTER ON IRAN: "THEY LIE TO US," http://wikileaks.org/cable/2009/12/09DOHA728.html.

76. Ahmed Saleh al-Faqih, "The Scandel of the Arab Regimes in Wikileaks Documents" [in Arabic], in *aleshteraki.net,* 05 December 2010, http://www.aleshteraki.net/articles.php?id=1885.; Al-Jazeera-Arabic Talk Show, with Faisal Kassim, Areeb al-Rantawi, and Hassan Yousif, "Is Wikileaks a Scandal for America, or Another Kind of Conspiracy?" in *aljazeera.net,* 14 December 2010, http://www.aljazeera.net/NR/exeres/5FB98E2B-3BAA-4A0A-A03B-0689A0C81631.

77. 09BRUSSELS536, IRAN SANCTIONS: AA/S GLASER BRIEFS EU ON PRIORITY, http://wikileaks.org/cable/2009/04/09BRUSSELS536.html.

78. Quoted in Lizza, "The Consequentialist."

79. Ibid.

80. Mohsen M. Milani, "Tehran's Take," *Foreign Affairs,* July/August 2009; Robin Pomeroy, "Iran Rebuffs Obama's Call to Free US Detainees," *The Independent,* 1 August 2010, http://www.independent.co.uk/news/world/middle-east/iran-rebuffs-obamas-call-to-free-us-detainees-2040993.html; Ken Timmerman, "Obama Policy on Iran a Failure, Experts Say," *Newsmax.com,* 10 December 2010, http://www.newsmax.com/KenTimmerman/nuclear-iran-orde-kittrie/2010/12/10/id/379555.

81. "Ayatollah Khamenei: Iran Could Scrap Directly Elected President," Reuters, 16 October 2011.

82. Ibid.; Saeed Kamali Dehghan, "Mahmoud Ahmadinejad: The Last President of Iran?" *The Guardian* (Comment Is Free), 4 November 2011.

83. David E. Sanger and Mark Lander, "To Isolate Iran, U.S. Presses Inspectors on Nuclear Data," *New York Times*, 15 October 2011; Isabel Kershner and David E. Sanger, "Israel Faces Questions About News Reports of Eyeing Iran Strike," *New York Times*, 3 November 2011.

84. Ibid.

85. Jefferey Goldberg, "Obama to Iran and Israel: 'As President of the United States, I Don't Bluff,'" *Atlantic*, 2 March 2012. http://www.theatlantic.com/international/archive/2012/03/obama-to-iran-and -israel-as-president-of-the-united-states-i-dont-bluff/253875/; Mark Landler, "Obama Cites 'Window' for Diplomacy on Iran Bomb," *New York Times*, 5 March 2012.

86. Goldberg, "Obama to Iran and Israel."

87. Kathleen Hennessey, "Obama: GOP 'Beating the Drums of War' on Iran," *Los Angeles Times*, 6 March 2012.

88. Justyna Pawlak and Parisa Hafezi, "EU Plans Embargo of Iranian Crude," Reuters, 5 January 2012; Parisa Hafezi, "Iran threatens U.S. Navy as Sanctions Hit Economy," Reuters, 3 January 2012.

89. Goldberg, "Obama to Iran and Israel."

90. Landler, "Obama Cites 'Window' for Diplomacy on Iran Bomb."

91. Goldberg, "Obama to Iran and Israel."

92. Nick Hopkins, "UK Military Steps Up Plans for Iran Attack Amid Fresh Nuclear Fears," *The Guardian*, 2 November 2011, http://www.guardian.co.uk/world/2011/nov/02/uk-military-iran-attack-nuclear.

93. Kershner and Sanger, "Israel Faces Questions about News Reports of Eyeing Iran Strike."

94. "Ross: Iran Nukes Pose Danger of Nuclear War," JTA, 13 December 2011.

95. Goldberg, "Obama to Iran and Israel."

96. Sanger and Lander, "To Isolate Iran, U.S. Presses Inspectors on Nuclear Data"; Kershner and Sanger, "Israel Faces Questions About News Reports of Eyeing Iran Strike."

97. Seymour M. Hersh, "Iran and the Bomb: How Real Is the Nuclear Threat," *New Yorker*, 6 June 2011, http://www.newyorker.com/reporting/2011/06/06/110606fa_fact_hersh; Fareed Zakaria, "To Deal with Iran's Nuclear Future, Go Back to 2008," *Washington Post*, 26 October 2011; Richard Dalton, "Iran Is Not in Breach of International Law," *The Guardian*, 9 June 2011, http://www.guardian.co.uk/com-mentisfree/2011/jun/09/iran-nuclear-power-un-threat-peace; Anthony H. Cordesman and Abdullah Toukan, "Options for Dealing with Iran's Nuclear Program," Center for Strategic and International Studies, 23 March 2010, http://csis.org/publication/options-dealing-iran%E2%80%99-nuclear-program.

98. Seymour M. Hersh, "Iran and the I.A.E.A," *New Yorker*, 18 November 2011.

99. Vitzhak Benhorin, "Ross: Obama Won't Hesitate to Use Force against Iran," Ynetnews, 13 December 2011.

100. David E. Sanger, "The Larger Game in the Middle East: Iran," *New York Times*, 2 April 2011, http://www.nytimes.com/2011/04/03/weekinreview/03sanger.html?_r=1&scp=1&sq=iran%20factor &st=cse.

101. Reporters were allowed to cover the event on condition the official not be identified. "U.S., Israel Talk Tough Ahead of Iran Nuclear Report."

102. Ibid.

103. Bari Weiss and Douglas Feith, "Denying the Green Revolution," *Wall Street Journal*, 23 October 2009, http://online.wsj.com/article/SB10001424052748704224004574489772874564430.html.

104. Neil MacFarquhar, "Iran's Leader Derides Protests; Lawmakers Urge Death for Opposition Leaders," *New York Times*, 15 February 2011, http://www.nytimes.com/2011/02/16/world/middleeast/16iran .html.

105. Elisabeth Bumiller, "Defense Chief Is on Mission to Mend Saudi Relations," *New York Times*, 6 April 2011, http://www.nytimes.com/2011/04/07/world/middleeast/07military.html?scp=1&sq=obama%2 0bahrain%20gates&st=cse.

106. "Syrian Forces 'Open Fire on Mourners,'" Sky News, 23 April 2011, http://news.sky.com/skynews /Article/201104115977762.

107. Office of the Press Secretary, "Remarks by the President on the Middle East and North Africa," The White House, 19 May 2011, http://www.whitehouse.gov/the-press-office/2011/05/19/remarks -president-middle-east-and-north-africa.

108. Goldberg, "Obama to Iran and Israel."
109. Emiliano Alessandri, "Turkey and the United States," in *Turkey's Global Strategy* (London School of Economics: IDEA Reports, May 2011).
110. Graham E. Fuller, *The New Turkish Republic: Turkey as a Pivotal State in the Muslim World* (Washington, D.C.: United States Institute of Peace Press, 2007); Alessandri, "Turkey and the United States."
111. Kinzer, *Reset Middle East.*
112. Daniel Dombey and Gideon Rachman, "Mapped Out," *Financial Times,* 3 June 2010, http://www.ft.com/cms/s/0/0375c750-6ea7-11df-ad16-00144feabdc0.html#axzz1Ui1t7PRj.
113. Alessandri, "Turkey and the United States"; Fuller, *The New Turkish Republic.*
114. http://www.amazon.com/Islam-Challenge-Democracy-Boston-Review/dp/0691119384; Khaled Abou El Fadl, "Islam and the Challenge of Democracy," *Boston Review* (April/May 2003), http://bostonreview.net/BR28.2/abou.html.
115. Philip H. Gordon and Omer Taspinar, *Winning Turkey: How America, Europe, and Turkey Can Revive a Fading Relationship* (Washington, D.C.: Brookings Institution Press, 2008); Alessandri, "Turkey and the United States."
116. Sabrina Tavernise and Michael Slackman, "Turkey Goes from Pliable Ally to Thorn for U.S.," *New York Times,* 8 June 2010, http://www.nytimes.com/2010/06/09/world/middleeast/09turkey.html.
117. Office of the Press Secretary, "Remarks by President Obama to the Turkish Parliament," The White House, 6 April 2009, http://www.whitehouse.gov/the-press-office/remarks-president-obama-turkish-parliament.
118. Ibid.
119. Kinzer, *Reset Middle East.*
120. Thom Shanker, "U.S. Hails Deal with Turkey on Missile Shield," *New York Times,* 15 September 2011, http://www.nytimes.com/2011/09/16/world/europe/turkey-accepts-missile-radar-for-nato-defense-against-iran.html.
121. Hasan Kösebalaban, *Turkish Foreign Policy: Islam, Nationalism, and Globalization* (New York: Palgrave Macmillan, 2011).
122. Doug Saunders, "Why the West Quietly Cheers Turkey's Rise," *Globe and Mail,* 17 September 2011.
123. Paolo Valentino, "Obama Says Turkey Should Be Full Member of Europe," *Corriere Della Sera,* 18 July 2010, http://www.corriere.it/International/english/articoli/2010/07/08/Barack-Obama-exclusive-interview-Corriere-della-Sera.shtml.
124. Hugh Pope, "Pax Ottomana?" *Foreign Affairs,* November/December 2010.
125. Kösebalaban, *Turkish Foreign Policy.*
126. Gordon and Taspinar, *Winning Turkey;* Alessandri, "Turkey and the United States."
127. Pelin Turgut, "Turkey Sees a Greater Role in Obama's Foreign Policy," *Time,* 11 March 2009, http://www.time.com/time/world/article/0,8599,1884042,00.html.
128. Wikileaks Cable, 09ANKARA1583, WORKING ERDOGAN BACK INTO THE FOLD ON IRAN, http://wikileaks.org /cable/2009/11/09ANKARA1583.html.
129. 10ANKARA302, U/S BURNS' FEBRUARY 18 MEETINGS WITH U/S, http://wikileaks.org/cable/2010/02/10ANKARA302.html.
130. Katrin Bennhold, "Leaders of Turkey and Israel Clash at Davos Panel," *New York Times,* 29 January 2009, http://www.nytimes.com/2009/01/30/world/europe/30clash.html.
131. Sabrina Tavernise, "Raid Jeopardizes Turkey Relations," *New York Times,* 31 May 2010, http://www.nytimes.com/2010/06/01/world/middleeast/01turkey.html; Pelin Turgut, "Friends No More? Why Turkey and Israel Have Fallen Out," *Time,* 14 October 2009, http://www.time.com/time/world/article/0,8599,1930203,00.html.
132. David D. Kirkpatrick, "Premier of Turkey Takes Role in Region," *New York Times,* 12 September 2011, http://www.nytimes.com/2011/09/13/world/middleeast/13egypt.html; Cecile Feuillatre, "Turkish PM Visits Birthplace of Arab Spring," AFP, 15 September 2011, http://www.google.com/hostednews/afp/article/ALeqM5i5YTkKlErh05uT4PySda3HLKPDbg?docId=CNG.c3d28c9ce20f22f00e7bae9c0b328b07.4e1.
133. "Turkey's Leadership," *New York Times,* 21 September 2011.
134. Ibid.
135. Fuller, *The New Turkish Republic.*

136. Laura Rozen, "Obama's Turkey Bind," *Politico,* 21 June 2010, http://www.politico.com/news/stories /0610/38806.html.

137. Benny Morris, "Turkey's Islamic Revolution," *National Interest,* 1 August 2011, http://nationalinterest .org/commentary/turkeys-islamic-revolution-5685.

138. Ted Galen Carpenter, "Falling Out," *National Interest,* 23 April 2010, http://nationalinterest.org/article /falling-out-3460; Steven A. Cook, "How Do You Say 'Frenemy' in Turkish?" *Foreign Policy,* 1 June 2010, http://www.foreignpolicy.com/articles/2010/06/01/how_do_you_say_frenemy_in_Turkish; Cengiz Çandar, "Who's Calling Turkey a Police State?" *The Guardian,* 28 March 2011, http://www .guardian.co.uk/commentisfree/2011/mar/28/turkey-freedom-speech-turkish-government.

139. 09ANKARA1549, ISRAELI AMBASSADOR TRACES HIS PROBLEMS TO ERDOGAN, http: //wikileaks.org/cable/2009/10/09ANKARA1549.html.

140. 05ANKARA1730, TURKEY ADRIFT, http://wikileaks.org/cable/2005/03/05ANKARA1730.html.

141. Paula Wolfson, "Obama, Erdogan Discuss Afghanistan, Iran," *Voice of America,* 7 December 2009, http://www.voanews.com/english/news/Obama-Erdogan-Discuss-Afghanistan-Iran-78727157.html.

142. 10ANKARA87, WHAT LIES BENEATH ANKARA'S NEW FOREIGN POLICY, http://wikileaks .org/cable/2010/01/10ANKARA87.html.

143. Kösebalaban, *Turkish Foreign Policy.*

144. Saunders, "Why the West Quietly Cheers Turkey's Rise."

145. Ibid.

146. Yavuz Baydar, "Apologize and Move On," *Today's Zaman,* 21 July 2011, http://www.todayszaman .com/mobile_detailc.action?newsId=251197.

147. Kinzer, *Reset Middle East;* Pope, "Pax Ottomana?"

148. Kösebalaban, *Turkish Foreign Policy.*

149. Ibid.

150. "Erdogan, Obama Agree Gaddafi Must Step Down, Depart Libya," *Today's Zaman,* 27 April 2011, http://www.todayszaman.com/news-242153-erdogan-obama-agree-gaddafi-must-step-down-depart -libya.html.

151. Kösebalaban, *Turkish Foreign Policy.*

152. "Prime Minister Recep Tayyip Erdogan Joins Call for Egypt's Mubarak to Make Big Changes," Babylon & Beyond, *Los Angeles Times,* 1 February 2011, http://latimesblogs.latimes.com/babylonbeyond /2011/02/turkey-recep-tayyip-erdogan-egypt-hosni-mubarak.html.

153. Patrick Seale, "America's Defeat in Iraq and Beyond," Agence Global, 1 November 2011; Immanuel Wallerstein, "U.S. Withdrawal and Defeat in Iraq," Agence Global, 1 November 2011.

CHAPTER 6

1. "A New Approach to Safeguarding Americans," Remarks by John O. Brennan, assistant to the president for homeland security and counterterrorism—as prepared for delivery (Center for Strategic and International Studies, Washington, D.C.), The White House, Office of the Press Secretary, 6 August 2009.

2. Ibid.

3. "National Security Strategy," May 2010, The White House, http://www.whitehouse.gov/sites/default /files/rss_viewer/national_security_strategy.pdf.

4. "A New Approach to Safeguarding Americans," Remarks by John O. Brennan.

5. "Remarks by the President at the United States Military Academy at West Point Commencement," The White House, Office of the Press Secretary, 22 May 2010, http://www.whitehouse.gov/the-press -office/remarks-president-united-states-military-academy-west-point-commencement.

6. "National Security Strategy," May 2010.

7. "A New Approach to Safeguarding Americans," Remarks by John O. Brennan.

8. In terms of language, Obama's national security advisers have removed terms such as "Islamic radicalism" from a new document outlining national security strategy and will use the new version to emphasize that the United States does not view Muslims through the lens of terrorism. Distancing themselves from the Bush National Security Strategy, which outlined his doctrine of preventive war and which states, "The struggle against militant Islamic radicalism is the great ideological conflict of the early

years of the 21st century," Obama's advisers say that changing terminology is part of a larger effort, one that seeks to change how the United States talks to the Muslim world, as well as what it talks about, from technology transfer to health care, education, and business startups. See Matt Apuzzo, "Not All Terrorism: Obama Tries to Change Subject," Associated Press, 7 April 2010.

9. Lucy Madison, "Attorney General Eric Holder: Threat of Homegrown Terrorism 'Keeps Me Up at Night,'" ABC News, 23 December 2010. In an interview in January 2009, former Vice President Dick Cheney said he was concerned that the Obama national security team was not ready to deal with the new threats facing the United States in the post-September 11 era. He noted that there "are a lot of people who did good work and were honorable civil servants and public servants during the Clinton administration coming back in. One of the things I worry about, though, is they'll assume they can pick up right where they left off. And the fact is the world has changed in major ways since January of '01 when we took over. And that break in service of some eight years, I think, they will find has been a period of time when the threat to the nation has changed in fairly dramatic ways." See "Political Punch: Cheney Assails Obama Decision to Close Gitmo; Expresses Concern That Democrats About to Take Over Don't Realize World Has Changed," ABC News, 13 January 2009, http://blogs.abcnews.com /politicalpunch/2009/01/cheney-assails.html.

   In a speech to the American Enterprise Institute in May 2009, Cheney questioned Obama's decision to close Guantánamo Bay and his approach to national security. He said, "What's more, to completely rule out enhanced interrogation methods in the future is unwise in the extreme. It is recklessness cloaked in righteousness, and would make the American people less safe." According to Cheney, "There is never a good time to compromise when the lives and safety of the American people are in the balance." Criticizing Obama's approach in the fight against terrorism in general, Cheney said that "behind the overwrought reaction to enhanced interrogations is a broader misconception about the threats that still face our country. You can sense the problem in the emergence of euphemisms that strive to put an imaginary distance between the American people and the terrorist enemy. Apparently using the term 'war' where terrorists are concerned is starting to feel a bit dated. So henceforth we're advised by the administration to think of the fight against terrorists as, quote, 'Overseas contingency operations.'" See "Transcript of Former Vice President Dick Cheney's Speech on Interrogation," Delivered at the American Enterprise Institute, 21 May 2009, About.com Guide by Justin Quinn, http: //usconservatives.about.com/od/capitalpunishment/a/Cheney_AEI_Speech.htm.

10. Steve Clemons, "Leon Panetta Hypes al Qaeda to Ward Off More Defense Cuts," *Atlantic,* 17 August 2011.

11. Mary Walsh, "Panetta: U.S. 'Within Reach' of Defeating al Qaeda," CBS News, 9 July 2011.

12. "After Awlaki's Death, Al Qaeda Still a Major Threat," ABCNews.com, 6 October 2011.

13. Eamon Javers, "Clinton: Al Qaeda More 'Agile,'" *Politico,* 2 July 2010, http://www.politico.com/news/ stories/0210/32633.html (with video clip).

14. Ross Colvin and Caren Bohan, "Obama: Al Qaeda Bid to Go Nuclear Is Top Threat," Reuters, 12 April 2010.

15. Ibid.

16. Ibid.

17. Lucy Madison, "Attorney General Eric Holder: Threat of Homegrown Terrorism 'Keeps Me Up At Night,'" CBC News, 23 December 2010.

18. Peter D. Zimmerman and Jeffrey G. Lewis, "The Bomb in the Backyard," *Foreign Policy* 85, no. 6 (November/December 2006): 32-39. According to John Mueller, Zimmerman and Lewis understate the costs wildly: the conspirators would be lucky to buy off three people with the paltry sum of $10 million. Moreover, the terrorists would be required to expose their ultimate goals to at least some of the corrupted, and at that point (if not earlier) they would become potential extortion victims. They could not afford to abandon unreliable people who know their goals (though they could attempt to kill them), and such people would enjoy essentially monopolistic powers whenever they wanted to escalate their price. The cost of the operation in bribes alone could easily become ten times the sum suggested by Zimmerman and Lewis. And even at that, Mueller notes, there would be, of course, a considerable risk that those so purchased would, at an exquisitely opportune moment of their own choosing, decide to take the money and run—perhaps to the authorities representing desperate governments with essentially bottomless bankrolls and an overwhelming incentive to expend resources to arrest the atomic

plot and to capture or kill the scheming perpetrators. See John Mueller, *Atomic Obsession* (New York: Oxford University Press, 2010), 178.

19. Mueller, *Atomic Obsession,* 155-236.

20. Ibid.

21. On level "A" threat, see Ashton B. Carter and William J. Perry, *Preventive Defense: A New Security Strategy for America* (Washington, D.C.: Brookings Institution Press, 1999), 11-15; and Joseph S. Nye Jr., "Redefining the National Interest," *Foreign Affairs* 78, no. 4 (July-August 1999).

22. In their forthcoming book, *Terror, Security, and Money* (New York: Oxford University Press) Mark Stewart and John Mueller calculate that the enhanced costs of the war on terror—increased costs of domestic security beyond those in place on 10 September 2001—have accumulated to more than $1 trillion. The costs for overseas ventures like the Afghanistan and Iraq wars, part of the war on terror, have so far come to at least $2 trillion additional and may well be twice that.

Joseph Stiglitz and Linda Bilmes estimate that the direct and indirect costs of the Iraq war will top $3 trillion, and say that their estimates are conservative: at least $600 billion would be needed for the lifetime health-care costs for injured US soldiers, $400 billion resulting for the loss of workers to the economy, both injured and those serving in the National Guard, $600 billion interest for money borrowed to finance the war, and $1–$2 trillion for the macroeconomic impact of the war. See Joseph Stiglitz and Linda Bilmes, *The Three Trillion Dollar War: The True Cost of the Iraq Conflict* (New York: W. W. Norton, 2008).

Congress has allocated $1.05 trillion to the Iraq and Afghanistan wars. See "Notes and Sources: Cost of War Counter," National Priorities Project, http://www.nationalpriorities.org/cost _of_war_counter_notes.

As of 2008, the United States had spent more than $300 billion on a new post-September 11 Department of Homeland Security, a second "defense" department. The $300 billion bill does not include what local and state governments and private businesses have spent on homeland security. In addition, the cumulative increased cost of counterterrorism for the United States since September 11 (the federal, state, local, and private expenditures as well as opportunity costs) has topped $1 trillion. See Mueller, "Terrorphobia: Our False Sense of Insecurity," *The American Interest,* May/June 2008, http://www.the-american-interest.com/article.cfm?piece=418.

In addition, "An assessment of increased United States federal homeland security expenditure since 2001 and expected lives saved as a result of such expenditure suggests that the annual cost ranges from $64 million to $600 million (or even more) per life saved, greatly in excess of the regulatory safety goal of $1 million–$10 million per life saved. As such, it clearly and dramatically fails a cost-benefit analysis. In addition, the opportunity cost of these expenditures, amounting to $32 billion per year, is considerable, and it is highly likely that far more lives would have been saved if the money (or even a portion of it) had been invested instead in a wide range of more cost-effective risk mitigation programs." See M. G. Stewart and J. Mueller, "Assessing the Costs and Benefits of United States Homeland Security Spending," Research Report No. 265.04.08, Centre for Infrastructure and Reliability, University of Newcastle, Australia.

Since September 11, the US defense budget for foreign counterterrorism has increased considerably. It is hard to find comprehensive data on foreign aid related to counterterrorism, especially key "front-line" states in the "war on terror"—Pakistan, Afghanistan, Yemen, Turkey, Jordan, Lebanon, Indonesia, Philippines, and others—a category of security assistance used during the Cold War to provide support to key geopolitical allies. For example, the level of development assistance "nearly tripled from approximately $10 billion in 2000 to $28.5 billion in 2005. In October 2009, President Obama allocated $7.5 billion for Pakistan." See Stephen Kaufman, "Bush's Budget Request Would Continue Increase in Foreign Aid: USAID Administrator Says U.S. Aid Has Nearly Tripled since 2000," *America.gov,* 5 February 2007, http://www.america.gov/st/washfile-english/2007/February /20070205173017esnamfuak8.193606e-02.html#ixzz0i9F93xof; Jim Lobe, "U.S.: Foreign Aid Budget Takes on Cold War Cast," *IPS,* 3 February 2004, http://www.ipsnews.net/interna.asp?idnews=22232; "Obama Signs Big Pakistan Aid Bill," BBC News, 15 October 2009, http://news.bbc.co.uk/1/hi /world/americas/8309643.stm.

23. There is a tremendous volume in the foreign policy literature on bureaucracies and their natural tendency to grow and multiply over time. Scholars argue that government bureaucracies develop

internal pressures for self-aggrandizement and expansion. See William A. Niskanen Jr., *Bureaucracy and Representative Government* (Chicago: Aldine-Atherton, 1971); Hugh Heclo and Aaron B. Wildavsky, *The Private Government of Public Money: Community and Policy inside British Politics* (London: Macmillan, 1974); Anthony Downs, "A Theory of Bureaucracy," Rand Paper, 1964; Daniel Tarschys, "The Growth of Public Expenditures: Nine Modes of Explanation," *Scandinavian Political Studies* 10 (1975).

24. Dana Priest and William Arkin, "Top-Secret America: A Hidden World, Growing beyond Control," *Washington Post,* 18 July 2010 (part 1). See also "Top-Secret America: National Security Inc.," *Washington Post,* 20 July 2010 (part 2); "Top-Secret America: The Secrets Next Door," *Washington Post,* 20 July 2010 (part 3); Kimberly Dozier, "Total U.S. Intelligence Bill Tops $80 Billion," Associated Press, 28 October 2010.

25. Priest and Arkin, "Top-Secret America."

26. Ibid.

27. Ibid.

28. "Obama: Human, Systemic Failure to Blame in Terror Attempt," CNN, 30 December 2009, http://edition.cnn.com/2009/POLITICS/12/29/airline.terror.obama/index.html; "Obama on Intel System: 'This Was a Screw-Up,'" CNN, 6 January 2010, http://edition.cnn.com/2010/POLITICS/01/05/obama.terror.meeting/index.html.

29. "'This Was a Screw-Up,'" CNN.

30. Priest and Arkin, "Top-Secret America."

31. Noah Feldman, "How Different Is Obama from Bush on Terrorism," *Foreign Policy,* 3 September 2010.

32. *Washington Post,* 14 February. 2010; *New York Times,* 17 March 2010; David Cole, "License to Kill," *The Nation,* 16 April 2010.

33. Adam Entous, "Special Report: How the White House Learned to Love the Drone," Reuters, 18 May 2010; Feldman, "How Different Is Obama from Bush on Terrorism."

34. Adam Entous, Julian E. Barnes, and Siobhan Gorman, "CIA Escalates in Pakistan," *Wall Street Journal,* 2 October 2010; Mark Mazetti and Eric Schmitt, "C.I.A. Steps Up Drone Attacks on Taliban in Pakistan," *New York Times,* 27 September 2010; Peter Bergen and Katherine Tiedemann, "The Year of the Drone: An Analysis of U.S. Drone Strikes in Pakistan, 2004-2010," 24 February 2010, Counterterrorism Strategy Initiative Policy Paper, New America Foundation, http://www.newamerica.net/publications/policy/the_year_of_the_drone.

35. "U.S. Believes It Can Now Destroy al Qaeda," Reuters, 3 May 2011.

36. Kimberly Dozier, "U.S. Counterterror Chief: Al-Qaeda Now on the Ropes," Associated Press, 1 September 2011.

37. Ibid.

38. Peter Bergen and Katherine Tiedemann reached a similar conclusion in their policy paper, "The Year of the Drone," which analyzed drone attacks from 2004 to 2010. They found that since Obama entered office, the use of drone attacks had risen considerably. Using US military sources and media reports, they observed that the civilian casualty rate of drone attacks is 32 percent, and that these attacks had hit their target the majority of the time. While the accuracy of the drone attacks is convincing, Bergen and Tiedemann called into question their efficacy. First, they have stopped neither the rise of terrorist attacks in Afghanistan and Pakistan nor the placement of new operatives and the launching of new operations. Second, the drone attacks are questionable under international law. Third, the employment of drones is a tactic, not a strategy; they do not provide a solution to winning the war against the Taliban. Finally, they have been received very negatively by the Pakistani public and serve as a recruitment tool for the Taliban and Al Qaeda. However, the accuracy of these attacks has been greatly underestimated in this study. Employing Pakistani and human rights organization sources to calculate the casualty rate, this number is found to be significantly higher. Thus, the accuracy and the efficacy of drone attacks indicate that the costs of these attacks far outweigh the benefits.

39. Addicott quote in Entous, "Special Report." See also Bergen and Tiedemann, "The Year of the Drone." In *Dying to Win: The Strategic Logic of Suicide Terrorism* (New York: Random House, 2005), Robert Pape sheds light on the reasons for suicide terrorism and the link between drone attacks and the occurrence of suicide terrorism plots against the United States. He examined over 400 terrorist attacks between 1980 and 2003 and concluded that instead of ideological motivations or economic reasons,

suicide terrorism's logic is driven by strategic means to end the foreign occupation of Muslim lands. Individuals who carry out suicide attacks are often used by groups to achieve their strategic objectives, and on the personal level, their actions are supported by their community and motivated by the perceived altruism of their actions.

40. Fawaz A. Gerges, "The Truth about Drones: They Are Inspiring Homegrown Terror," *Newsweek*, 7 June 2010.
41. Tom Hays, "Guilty Plea in Failed N.Y. Car Bombing: Faisal Shahzad Called the Times Square Plot a Response to 'the U.S. Terrorizing . . . Muslim People,'" Associated Press, 22 June 2010.
42. "Faisal Shahzad, Times Square Car Bomber, Details His Chilling Plot," *Christian Science Monitor*, 22 June 2010.
43. "Interview: John Brennan," The Dark Side, *Frontline*, http://www.pbs.org/wgbh/pages/frontline/darkside/interviews/brennan.html.
44. Bob Woodward, *Obama's Wars* (New York: Simon & Schuster, 2010), 121.
45. Ibid.
46. Glenn Somerville, "U.S. Says Pakistan Taliban behind Bomb Attempt," Reuters, 9 May 2010.
47. Ibid.
48. Josh Gerstein, "'As Long as Is Necessary' Terror Bill," *Politico*, 30 July 2010, http://www.politico.com/news/stories/0710/40491.html.
49. Evan Perez, "Rights Are Curtailed for Terror Suspects," *The Wall Street Journal*, 24 March 2011, http://online.wsj.com/article/SB10001424052748704050204576218970652119898.html; Feldman, "How Different Is Obama from Bush on Terrorism."
50. Warren Richey, "Eric Holder: US Does Not Expect to Capture Osama bin Laden Alive," *Christian Science Monitor*, 16 March 2010.
51. Ibid.
52. Ibid.
53. Ibid.
54. "Clinton Takes Heat for Drone Attacks," CBS News, 30 October 2009, http://www.cbsnews.com/stories/2009/10/30/world/main5458871.shtml.
55. Zach Zagger, "State Department Legal Adviser Defends Unmanned Drone Strikes," *Jurist Legal News and Research*, University of Pittsburgh Law School, 26 March 2010, http://jurist.law.pitt.edu/paperchase/2010/03/state-department-legal-adviser-defends.php.
56. Cited in "Latest Drone Strikes in Northwest Pakistan Kill 15," CNN, 16 September 2010.
57. Jennifer Loven, "Obama Praises Troops in Surprise Afghan Visit," *Thestar.com*, 29 March 2010, http://www.thestar.com/.
58. Ibid.
59. Peter Bergen, "The FP Survey: Terrorism," Foreign Policy, January/February 2011.
60. Charlie Savage, "In G.O.P Field, Broad View of Presidential Power Prevails," *New York Times*, 29 December 2011.
61. John Mueller, *Overblown: How Politicians and the Terrorism Industry Inflate National Security Threats, and Why We Believe Them* (New York: Free Press, 2006).
62. Warner R. Schilling, "Surprise Attack, Death, and War," *Journal of Conflict Resolution* 9, no. 3 (September 1965): 285-90.
63. Robert Jervis, *Perception and Misperception in International Politics* (Princeton, N.J.: Princeton University Press, 1976), 275.
64. Mueller, *Overblown*, 8-10.
65. For a similar argument, see William Pfaff, *The Irony of Manifest Destiny: The Tragedy of American Foreign Policy* (New York: Walker, 2010).
66. Peter Beinart, *The Icarus Syndrome: A History of American Hubris* (New York: Harper, 2010), 7-9.
67. Ibid., 7-9.
68. Sandra Silberstein, *War of Words: Language, Politics and 9/11* (London: Routledge, 2002), xi-39.
69. Ibid., xi.
70. Kimberly Dozier, "Mullen Says Al-Qaeda Threat from Yemen Is Serious," Associated Press, 21 November 2010; "Qaeda Thousand Cuts Threat 'Very Serious,' Says Mullen," Agence France-Presse, 21 November 2010.
71. "Qaeda Thousand Cuts Threat 'Very Serious,' says Mullen."

72. David E. Sanger and Mark Mazzetti, "New Estimate of Strength of Al Qaeda Is Offered," *New York Times,* 30 June 2010.

73. "U.S. Counterterror Chief."

74. Mark Mazzetti and Scott Shane, "Data Show Bin Laden Plots," Associated Press, 3 May 2011; Mark Mazeetti and Scott Shane, "Phone Call by Kuwaiti Courier Led to bin Laden," Associated Press, 3 May 2011.

75. See the Pew research polls or Shibley Telhami's 2010 poll of Arab opinion available here: http://www .brookings.edu/reports/2010/0805_arab_opinion_poll_telhami.aspx. Also see John L. Esposito and Dalia Mogahed, *Who Speaks for Islam? What Do a Billion Muslims Really Think* (New York: Gallup Press, 2007).

76. Ibid.

77. David D. Kirkpatrick, "Egyptian Vote Forces Islamists to Confront Their Divide Over Rule by Religion," *New York Times,* 3 December 2011.

78. Fawaz A. Gerges, "The Irresistible Rise of the Muslim Brothers," *New Statesman,* 28 November 2011.

79. In his press conference after Egyptian President Mubarak was forced to resign, Obama echoed a similar sentiment: "Egyptians have inspired us, and they've done so by putting the lie to the idea that justice is best gained through violence. For Egypt, it was the moral force of non-violence—not terrorism, not mindless killing—but non-violence, moral force that bent the arch of history toward justice once more." Robert Mackey, "Updates on Day 18 of Egypt Protests," The Lede, *New York Times,* 11 February 2011.

80. Juan R. Cole, *Engaging the Muslim World* (New York: Palgrave Macmillan, 2009); Rashid Khalidi, *Resurrecting Empire: Western Footprints and America's Perilous Path in the Middle East* (Boston: Beacon Press, 2005); Robert Jervis, *American Foreign Policy in a New Era* (New York: Routledge, 2005); Francis Fukuyama, *America at the Crossroads: Democracy, Power, and the Neoconservative Legacy* (New Haven, Conn.: Yale University Press, 2006); "Iraq/Middle East," Project for the New American Century, http://www.newamericancentury.org/iraqmiddleeast2000-1997.htm.

81. Loretta Napoleoni, *Insurgent Iraq: Al Zarqawi and the New Generation* (New York: Seven Stories Press, 2005); Jean-Charles Brisard, *Zarqawi: The New Face of Al-Qaeda* (Cambridge: Polity Press, 2005).

82. Priest and Arkin, "Top-Secret America: A Hidden World."

83. John Barry and Evan Thomas, "A War Within," *Newsweek,* 12 September 2010.

84. Benjamin H. Friedman, Jim Harper, and Christopher A. Preble, *Terrorizing Ourselves: Why U.S. Counterterrorism Policy Is Failing and How to Fix It* (Washington, D.C.: Cato Institute, 2010).

85. Daniel Luban, "The New Anti-Semitism," *Tablet,* 19 August 2010, http://www.tabletmag.com/news -and-politics/43069/the-new-anti-semitism-2/; Emran Qureshi and Michael Sells, eds., *The New Crusades: Constructing the Muslim Enemy* (New York: Columbia University Press, 2003); Matti Bunzl, *Anti-Semitism and Islamophobia: Hatreds Old and New in Europe* (Chicago: Prickly Paradigm Press, 2007); Peter Gottschalk and Gabriel Greenberg, *Islamophobia: Making Muslims the Enemy* (Lanham, Md.: Rowman and Littlefield, 2008); Bobby Ghosh, "Does America Have a Muslim Problem," *Time,* 30 August 2010. For a deeper historical account, see Thierry Hentsch, *Imagining the Middle East* (Montreal: Black Rose Books, 1992), and Norman Daniel, *Islam and the West: The Making of an Image* (Oxford: Oneworld, 2009).

86. James Shanahan and Erik C. Nisbet (Media & Society Research Group of Cornell University), "Restrictions on Civil Liberties, Views of Islam, & Muslim Americans," 17 December 2004, Institute for Social Policy and Understanding, http://www.ispu.org/reports/articledetailpb-64.html.

87. Luban, "The New Anti-Semitism."

88. Shibley Telhami and Steven Kull, "The American Public on the 9/11 Decade: A Study of American Public Opinion," Anwar Sadat Chair, University of Maryland, Program on International Policy Attitudes (PIPA), 8 September 2011, 11. Report can be accessed at: http://www.brookings.edu/~/media /Files/rc/reports/2011/0908_opinion_poll_telhami/0908_opinion_poll_telhami.pdf.

89. Martin Peretz, "The New York Times Laments 'A Sadly Wary Misunderstanding of Muslim-Americans.' But Really Is It 'Sadly Wary' or A 'Misunderstanding' At All?," The Spine, *The New Republic,* 4 September 2010, http://www.tnr.com/blog/77475/the-new-york-times-laments-sadly-wary-misun derstanding-muslim-americans-really-it-sadly-w; Nicholas D. Kristof, "Is This America?" *New York Times,* 11 September 2010.

90. Martin Peretz, "An Apology," The Spine, *The New Republic,* 13 September 2010, http://www.tnr.com/blog/the-spine/77607/martin-peretz-apology.

91. Matthew Duss, "Some Zionist Groups Stoke Fear of Islam for Political Profit," *Jewish Daily Forward,* 1 October 2010.

92. Sheila A. Marikar, "Bill O'Reilly Was 'Condescending,' 'Disrespectful,'" *The View,* ABC, 18 October 2010.

93. "Egypt Mufti Says Swiss Minaret Ban Insults Muslims," *Agence France-Presse,* 29 November 2009, http://www.google.com/hostednews/afp/article/ALeqM5geRfhlTwImkMsEipD-A2sZYSO7og.

94. "French Burqa Ban Clears Last Legal Obstacle," CNN, 7 October 2010.

95. Laurie Goodstein, "Across Nation, Mosque Projects Meets Opposition," *New York Times,* 7 August 2010; Ron Scherer, "Ground Zero and Beyond: Four Mosque Battles Brew across US," *Christian Science Monitor,* 19 August 2010; Anne Barnard, "Developers of Islamic Center Try a New Strategy," *New York Times,* 1 August 2011, http://www.nytimes.com/2011/08/02/nyregion/new-quiet-effort-for-big-islamic-center-near-ground-zero.html?_r=1.

96. "Address by Newt Gingrich, America at Risk: Camus, National Security and Afghanistan," 29 July 2010, American Enterprise Institute for Public Policy Research, http://www.aei.org/docLib/Address%20by%20Newt%20Gingrich07292010.pdf.

97. Andy Barr, "Newt Gingrich Compares Mosque to Nazis," *Politico,* 16 August 2010, http://www.politico.com/news/stories/0810/41112.html; Maureen Dowd, "Our Mosque Madness," *New York Times,* 17 August 2010.

98. "Address by Newt Gingrich, America at Risk: Camus, National Security and Afghanistan." See also Robert Dreyfuss, "Newt's Well of Hate," *Metro Times,* 4 August 2010.

99. "Address by Newt Gingrich, America at Risk: Camus, National Security and Afghanistan."

100. Ibid.

101. Ibid.

102. See Jay Bookman, "Newt Gingrich Has Become, Frankly, a Hate-Mongering Bigot," *Atlanta Journal Constitution* Blog, 28 July 2010, http://blogs.ajc.com/jay-bookman-blog/2010/07/28/newt-gingrich-has-become-frankly-a-hate-mongering-bigot/?cxntfid=blogs_jay_bookman_blog.

103. Jillian Rayfield, "Oklahoma State Rep. Aims To Stop 'Liberal Judges' from Imposing Sharia Law," *Talking Points Memo,* 11 June 2010, http://tpmlivewire.talkingpointsmemo.com/2010/06/oklahoma-state-senator-aims-to-stop-liberal-judges-from-imposing-sharia-law.php; Nathan Koppel, "Oklahoma Faces Appellate Showdown over Anti-Sharia Law," Law Blog, *The Wall Street Journal,* 8 September 2011, http://blogs.wsj.com/law/2011/09/08/oklahoma-faces-appellate-showdown-over-anti-sharia-law/.

104. "Oklahoma's Muslims: Peace Be on You," *The Economist,* 8 July 2010.

105. Stephan Salisbury, "Mosque Mania," *Asia Times,* 12 August 2010, http://www.atimes.com/atimes/Front_Page/LH12Aa01.html.

106. Gallup and the Co-Exist Foundation, "Religious Perceptions in America," Muslim West Facts Project, 3 February 2010, http://www.abudhabigallupcenter.com/143762/religious-perceptions-america.aspx; Shibley Telhami and Steven Kull, "The American Public on the 9/11 Decade: A Study of American Public Opinion," Anwar Sadat Chair, University of Maryland, Program on International Policy Attitudes (PIPA), 8 September 2011, 11. Report can be accessed at: http://www.brookings.edu/~/media/Files/rc/reports/2011/0908_opinion_poll_telhami/0908_opinion_poll_telhami.pdf.

107. Gallup and the Co-Exist Foundation, "Religious Perceptions in America"; James Carroll, "How to Spot an Islamophobe," *The Daily Beast,* 30 January 2010, http://thedailybeast.com/blogs-and-stories/2010-01-30/how-to-spot-an-islamph.

108. Carroll, "How to Spot an Islamophobe."

109. "The 'M-word'": Is 'Muslim' Political Code for 'I Don't Like You!,'" *USA Today,* 19 August 2010.

110. "Religion, Politics, and the President: Growing Number of Americans Say Obama Is a Muslim," 2010 Annual Religion and Public Life Survey, 19 August 2010, http://pewforum.org/uploadedFiles/Topics/Issues/Politics_and_Elections/growingnumber-full-report.pdf.

111. "Newsweek Poll: Obama/Muslims," 27 August 2010, Princeton Survey Research Associates International, http://nw-assets.s3.amazonaws.com/pdf/1004-ftop.pdf; Nicholas D. Kristof, "Is This America?," *New York Times,* 11 September 2010.

112. "The 'M-word': Is 'Muslim' Political Code for 'I Don't Like You!'"

113. Maureen Dowd, "Our Mosque Madness," *New York Times,* 17 August 2010.

CONCLUSION

1. Fareed Zakaria, "The Strategist," *Time,* 30 January 2012.
2. Jordan Michael Smith, "Zbig: Israelis 'Bought Influence' and Outmaneuvered Obama," *Salon,* 20 January 2012, http://www.salon.com/2012/01/20/zbig_israelis_bought_influence_and_outmaneuvered _obama/singleton
3. Sarah El Deeb, "US Raises Outreach to Egypt's Muslim Brotherhood," Associated Press, 11 January 2012.
4. Abdullah Gul, "The Revolution's Missing Peace," *New York Times,* 20 April 2011.
5. Brent Scowcroft, "Obama Must Not Delay in Brokering a New Mideast Peace," Atlantic Council, 13 April 2011, http://www.acus.org/trackback/37222.
6. Greg Miller, "CIA Digs In as Americans Withdraw from Iraq, Afghanistan," *The Washington Post,* 8 February 2012; Kimberly Dozier, "Special Ops Teams First In, Last Out in Afghan War," Associated Press, 8 February 2012; Missy Ryan and Warren Strobe, "U.S. Aims for Afghan Talks Breakthrough at May Summit," Reuters, 8 February 2012.
7. Michael Inbar, "Obama: Diplomacy 'Preferred Solution' with Iran," Today.com (MSNBC), 5 February 2012.
8. Gary Sick, "Iran, U.S. Need a Crisis Exit Ramp," CNN, 12 January 2012, http://www.cnn.com /2012/01/12/opinion/sick-iran-us-relations/index.html
9. Ibid.
10. Adam Entous and Julian E. Barnes, "Pentagon Seeks Mightier Bomb vs. Iran," *Wall Street Journal,* 28 January 2012.
11. Trita Parsi, "How Obama Should Talk to Iran," *The Washington Post,* 13 January 2012.
12. Trita Parsi, *A Single Roll of the Dice: Obama's Diplomacy with Iran* (New Haven, Conn.: Yale University Press, 2012).
13. Scott Peterson, "Iran's Top Ayatollah: We're Trumping the West, but Beware Infighting at Home," *Christian Science Monitor,* 3 February 2012.
14. Trita Parsi, "How Obama Became Vulnerable on Iran," Salon, 31 January 2012, http://www.salon .com/2012/01/31/how_obama_became_vulnerable_on_iran/.
15. Parsi, *A Single Roll of the Dice.*
16. Ibid.
17. Aaron David Miller, "Arab Spring, American Winter," *Los Angeles Times,* 13 November 2011.

INDEX